•••

Protecting Indigenous Knowledge and Heritage

Purich's Aboriginal Issues Series

Protecting Indigenous Knowledge and Heritage

•••

A Global Challenge

Marie Battiste
and
James [Sa'ke'j] Youngblood Henderson

Purich Publishing Ltd.
Saskatoon, Saskatchewan
Canada

Canadian Cataloguing in Publication Data

Battiste, Marie, 1949-

Protecting indigenous knowledge and heritage : a global challenge (Purich's aboriginal issues series)

Includes bibliographical references and index.

ISBN 1-895830-15-X

1. Indigenous peoples--Legal status, laws, etc.
2. Ethnoscience. 3. Eurocentrism. I. Henderson, James Youngblood. II. Title. III. Series.

GN380.B38 2000 306'.08 C00-920064-9

(ISBN 978-1895830-156)

Editing and design by Page Wood Publishing Services
Index by Geri Rowlatt
Cover redesign by Jamie Olson
Printed in Canada by Houghton Boston, Saskatoon

We acknowledge the financial assistance of the Government of Canada through the Canada Book Fund, and the Creative Industry Growth and Sustainability program made possible through funding provided to the Saskatchewan Arts Board by the Saskatchewan Ministry of Parks, Culture and Sport.

Purich Publishing Ltd., Saskatoon, Canada
www.purichpublishing.com; purich@sasktel.net

Fifth printing 2012 on 100% recycled paper

Erratum: portions of paragraph 2 on page 12 are from Greaves, Thomas. 1996 Tribal Rights, in *Valuing Local Knowledge: Indigenous People and Intellectual Property Rights*, Island Press, Washington, DC. eds, Stephan Brush and Doreen Stabinsky.

Contents

Part V
Conclusion

Acknowledgments

The authors gratefully acknowledge all those who have made this book possible. We are especially grateful to Russell Barsh, Leroy Little Bear, Shelley Wright, and Erica-Irene Daes, lawyers, scholars, and friends who provided research, analysis, and written texts in earlier studies and discussions on these issues. We thank Elizabeth Maier for her reference checks and work on the bibliography.

Special thanks are extended to Professor Len Findlay of the English Department at the University of Saskatchewan and Dr. Isobel Findlay of Commerce Communications for their astute appraisals and editing of an early draft of this book, for their valued suggestions, and for their continuous support in the many stages of this project; to Jane Billinghurst of Page Wood Publishing Services for her copious editing of the manuscript; to our extended community who shared their support, advice, and laughter during many needed times; and to our children, Jaime Youngmedicine, Mariah Sunday Lace, and Annie Wintersong, whose understanding and support for our collective Indigenous community have made it possible for us to do the much-needed work.

• • •

Preface

Empire has located its existence not in the smooth recurrent spinning time of cycles of the seasons but in the jagged time of rise and fall, of beginning and ends, of catastrophe. Empire dooms itself to live in history and plot against history. One thought alone preoccupies the submerged mind of Empire: how not to end, how not to die, how to prolong its era. — J.M. Coetzee, *Waiting for the Barbarians* (1980, 133)

A brief history of the struggle for Indigenous rights through the mechanism of the United Nations shows how urgent the need is for a better understanding of the relationship between Indigenous knowledge and Eurocentric thought, and illustrates some of the dilemmas in which we find ourselves as we seek to build some measure of understanding between these two very different ways of viewing the world. It also explains the perspectives of the authors as they embark on writing this book.

The UN Universal Declaration of Human Rights in 1948 was viewed by Indigenous peoples as a tool for decolonizing our oppressed lives. For the first time in history, the "equal and inalienable rights of all members of the human family" were asserted and recognized as the "foundation of freedom, justice and peace in the world." The statement of principles in the Universal Declaration was transformed into two legally binding agreements: the International Covenant on Economic, Social and Cultural Rights and the International Covenant on Civil and Political Rights. Those member-states who signed and ratified these agreements agreed to uphold the rights and freedoms defined by the covenants in their own states. The first article in both covenants asserts that "[a]ll peoples have the right of self determination." By virtue of that right, all peoples have the right to "freely determine their political status and freely pursue their economic, social and cultural development." In answering the question of where universal rights begin, the chair of the UN Human Rights Commission, Eleanor Roosevelt, stated that universal rights begin in "the places where every man, woman, and child seeks equal justice, equal opportunity, equal dignity without discrimination. Unless these rights have meaning there, they have little meaning anywhere. Without concerned citizen action to uphold them close to home, we shall look in vain for process in the larger world" (Lennox & Wildeboer 1998, 7).

In the 1950s and 1960s, practically every colony in Asia, Africa, and Oceania availed itself of the right of self-determination and opted for political independence. A few colonies chose incorporation or free association with member-states. These decisions were the colonizers' choices, since most of the colonized Indigenous peoples were not given the right to self-determination or other human rights (Anaya 1996). Despite the move by previously colonized countries toward self-determination, it was clear that governments were not extending human rights to Indigenous peoples. By the middle of 1970, Indigenous lawyers and leaders around the world attempted to have the international and national régimes respond to the growing crisis in human rights. One result was the international Indigenous network.

The network began as a talking circle in which Indigenous peoples discussed their failure to persuade governments to extend human rights to Indigenous peoples. The network was botanical in structure and operation. Liberation was defined, to the extent it ever was defined, as cultural and physical survival. The network was a manifestation of continued resistance to colonization, and it combined efforts that had been going on in isolation for many generations. The idea slowly arrived that Indigenous peoples needed a safe and peaceful place to meet, to talk, and to grow. We needed to extend our kinship and relationships.

We were the unofficially colonized peoples of the world, the tragic victims of modernization and progress. In every state and educational system, we were underrepresented or, more often, ignored. We were the forgotten peoples. Our daily wretchedness, violent deaths among our peoples, and our powerlessness to remedy our situations drove us to the United Nations, which had a long list of international treaties and convenants that could assist our survival. We sought to understand why the UN human rights covenants or the provisions of UNESCO (the United Nations Educational, Scientific and Cultural Organization) had never been used to protect us. Eventually, the United Nations responded to our questions and created the Working Group on Indigenous Populations in Geneva.

The Working Group on Indigenous Populations is a subgroup of the UN Commission on Human Rights Sub-Commission on Prevention of Discrimination and Protection of Minorities. Five human rights experts from Africa, Asia, Central and South America, Eastern Europe, and the West lead the group, and Dr. Erica-Irene Daes of Greece is the chair. The members of the group are selected from the twenty-eight representatives of the sub-commission, who are elected based on their non-partisan expertise in the field of human rights. The purpose of the group is to review developments promoting and protecting the human rights and fundamental freedoms of Indigenous peoples, giving special attention to the development of new international agreements.

Geneva became a strange journey to the heart of our darkness: we had to travel into Europe to articulate our problems with Eurocentric colonization. We had no wealth to fund our travels from the margin to Geneva; we had no wealth to live in the exorbitant style of Geneva. Yet, we could not continue to live and die in utter hopelessness and despair. We traveled and lived thanks to random acts of kindness and occasional support from organizations. Most participants in the international initiative were forced to live solitary, nomadic lives.

Our first talks at the working group in the summer of 1982 were as fragile as clay pots. We had to learn to trust each other, but our experience did not allow such trust. It was a time of listening. It was a time of understanding our teachings and experiences. In all the languages of the earth, we discussed our suffering and our dreams. Across countless generations, we were comforted by the safety of Indigenous languages, elders, and storytellers as they revealed Indigenous teachings. In different languages, at greater length and with more details than we can ever hope to grasp, these teachings gave form to an ecologically based vision of humanity.

As the discussion in Geneva progressed, the Indigenous people gathered there became people of a shared persuasion. We shared our experiences and ideas of humanity and justice, and we used these ideas to persuade others of the good and just road. These paths called on us to face others and ourselves on pivotal issues. We faced the unresolved and the unknown with awareness, courage, kindness, and honesty. We faced Eurocentric thought from the perspective of our own experience and our visions. From the small meeting rooms where we began to the cavernous, curved meeting rooms of the United Nations where we ended up, our dialogues were formalized.

The working group became the first international ceremony for Indigenous peoples. Each Indigenous group shared different parts of the new ritual as we struggled to eliminate colonialism and to learn the UN legal system. Through the long, hot days in the UN meeting rooms and restive obsidian nights in Geneva, we pursued an elusive consensus. As the summers slid by, our loneliness receded as we extended our friendships and sympathy to the Indigenous peoples around our mother, the earth. Our extended discussions were an effort to crystallize our vision of a postcolonial order into ink words. As the Lakota holy man Black Elk revealed in an ancient teaching: "A human being who has a vision is not able to use the power of it until after they have realized this vision on earth for people to see." In the alien and expensive meeting places of Geneva, which none of us could call home, we pondered the meaning of our humanity and our vision of a fair and good society. According to our teachings of our oral traditions, we explored the unknown territory of relationships with each other. In many languages and styles, we sought to initiate a creative, transformative vision of human rights to a complaisant world order. We probed for agreement on how the existing human rights convenants of the United Nations should be applied to Indigenous peoples.

It was not sufficient for the working group to have visions and talks. If we wanted a better life in an improving world, we had to have the courage to envision the impossible and translate it into text. We also had the obligation of explaining our dreams to the human rights experts and baffled government representatives. We had the task of reconciling our visions within the six languages of the UN law. Each year the discussion and drafting of our declaration grew. From all four directions, Indigenous delegates arrived each summer to renew and criticize the drafts prepared by the five human right experts and their drafting teams. The working group began with a few dozen delegates and after a few years soared to more than eight hundred. Our loneliness was replaced by our deep doubts on how to compromise between all the deep and beautiful visions. Who could choose the "best" among these visions to create a fair and just order? Who could choose which visions could heal our peoples? We talked, we listened, and we learned. We networked and cared our visions into draft text.

As we worked, state representatives challenged our visions and our aspirations, practicing their old superior privileges. Many degrading ceremonies and embarrassing discussions arose. These representatives rejected our understanding of humanity and our aspirations. They insulted our efforts to change the way the "world" thought about us. They questioned our motives—were we socialists or communists?—never imagining that we rejected all these categories. When our delegates were killed, persecuted, and imprisoned when they returned home, the representatives mocked our efforts to bring the terrorists to justice. Often the representatives became complicit with our terrorizing: when we could get no visible results because of lack of agreement, governments spread rumors about our lifestyles and about the sources of funding among our people.

The arguments and strategies of the nation-states were neither new nor creative; they were familiar to our lives under oppressive régimes. What was new was that these governments had to hear our responses. Within the nation-states we were silenced and ignored; in the working group, these same governments had to live with our visions and voices. We forced a debate on the philosophy of total denial of our humanity. We were not anti-Eurocentric humanists; we merely questioned our exclusion from the category of human rights. We forced a debate on whether we were entitled to have the dignity of our humanity and personhood recognized by law. Specifically, we clashed with the nation-states over whether Indigenous populations were a "people" or "peoples" in the existing UN human rights covenants, in the famous struggle over the final "s." Through the debate, the state representatives implemented their juridical traditions of humiliation and terror. They urged us not to hold fast to our highest visions, labeling them impossible. They urged us to reach a consensus on the lowest common denominator. Because the nature of the multilateral forum is a maze of competing and conflicting interests, the lowest common denominator strategy created fears and doubts among the Indigenous participants. In the process, we left many ink trails or cognitive droppings in the fragmentary processes of the United Nations.

Based on our consensuses, we created new standards in UN law, the most comprehensive being the 1989 International Labour Organization Convention on Indigenous and Tribal Peoples. This convention defined Indigenous self-government in national contexts. Through this convention, we created the foundation of an ecological order. We also lobbied for a special chapter for Indigenous peoples' programs in Agenda 21, which was adopted by the UN Conference on the Environment in 1992. We lobbied for the inclusion of the traditional ecological knowledge of Indigenous peoples in the UN Convention on Biological Diversity that same year. In addition, we lobbied the UN General Assembly to have the International Year of the World's Indigenous Peoples in 1993. We lobbied for a permanent forum for Indigenous peoples, and for an International Decade of the World's Indigenous Peoples to be held from 1995 to 2004. And we lobbied for a special UN study on how to protect the heritage of Indigenous peoples, their treaties, their lands, and their natural resources. Combined, these UN documents manifested an Indigenous vision of our humanity for all people to read, and unleashed the power of the vision of an ecological theory of good order and human rights (Anaya 1996; Barsh 1994).

The final unfolding of the Indigenous vision was the Draft Declaration on the Rights of Indigenous Peoples. After twelve years, the working group reached a consensus on the declaration. The declaration articulated forty-five articles, which are minimum standards of Indigenous human rights. It was a first step in a slow journey to justice and respect. This remedial task witnessed a new style of collaboration between technical experts and oppressed people. The resulting text is an interpretive tool for applying the UN human rights covenants to the Indigenous peoples of the earth. The declaration is an enterprise of translating hope into insight, and experience into enactment. Our emerging compromises were fragile and tenderly spoke of honor, caring, and healing; still they had to be placed in the context of the drafting protocol of UN conventions on human rights and their normative categories. Translating our aspirations into human rights protocols was difficult. It was an aloof and sterile experience; the linguistic protocol contains the bitterness of our experience.

"Affirming that indigenous peoples are equal in dignity and rights to all other peoples, while recognizing the right of all peoples to be different, to consider themselves different, and to be respected as such" was the deep agreement with which the intricate declaration began. Article 3 provides: "Indigenous peoples have the right of self determination. By virtue of that right they freely determine their political status and freely pursue their economic, social and cultural development." Our humanitarian and linguistic rights are articulated in part III of the declaration. Article 14 reads: "States shall take effective measures, especially whenever they may affect any right of indigenous peoples, to ensure this right and also to ensure that they can understand and be understood in political, legal and administrative proceedings, where necessary through the provision of interpretation or by other appropriate means." In addition, article 15 on the education of children provides: "All indigenous peoples . . . have the right to establish and control their educational systems and institutions providing education in their own languages, in a manner appropriate to their cultural methods of teaching and learning. Indigenous children living outside their communities have the right to be provided access to education in their own culture and language. States shall take effective measures to provide appropriate resources for these purposes." Article 17 provides that "Indigenous peoples have the right to establish their own media in their own languages."

The declaration is a statement of principles for postcolonial self-determination and human rights, and as such it is not legally binding on the nation-states. However, if the declaration is passed by the UN General Assembly, it will have a certain intellectual force and political weight, and it will create certain troubling inconveniences for member-states. If the declaration is then enacted as a convention, it will be a legal treaty among ratifying states. We view the agreement as the first international postcolonial treaty among Indigenous peoples. The working group has taken the position that it will accept no changes to or censorship of the declaration. The states have no authority to appropriate Indigenous visions or consensus for their purposes. Human rights are universal and not relative. We feel it would be pointless and unavailing to accept human rights' standards less than those accorded to other peoples of the United Nations.

The Sub-Commission on Prevention of Discrimination and Protection of Minorities passed the declaration, but the Human Rights Committee found it to be too threatening. The review committee found the declaration consistent with existing UN human rights. Then the states lobbied the Human Rights Committee not to adopt the declaration. Yielding to the pressure, in 1995 the Human Rights Committee created a working group of fifty-three representatives from the nation-states to review the Indigenous declaration. It is called the Working Group on the Draft Declaration of Indigenous Rights; the ambassador of Peru was elected chair and rapporteur. Thus, Indigenous peoples were exposed to yet another degrading ceremony manufactured by the resisting states.

The necessity of striking the Working Group on the Draft Declaration of Indigenous Rights makes it clear that to a majority of nation-states, Indigenous humanity remains problematic. Despite many calls for the universalization of human rights, the nation-states fail to understand the necessity of the equal application of existing human rights to Indigenous peoples. In particular, the nation-states reject the right of Indigenous peoples to self-determination, since this might lead to unacceptable freedoms for them. They interpret the right of self-determination as being reserved to those who are already privileged to exercise it—the colonizers. Such rights cannot be tolerated for those peoples who do not already exercise this privilege—the colonized (see Eide 1993; Hannum 1990). The resistance of the nation-states is based on their interpretation of state legitimacy and territorial integrity. They ignore the requirement laid out in the Principles on Friendly Relations Among States in Accordance with the Charter (1970) that they grant such ideas only to those states that conduct themselves in conformity with the principles of equality and self-determination of all peoples.

The daily existence of Indigenous peoples in the nation-states also reflects the debates and intellectual violence of the working group. In Eurocentric thought, the legal system is where the ideal of colonization has taken on a detailed institutional form. Eurocentric legal doctrine makes it possible to represent and discuss civilization and its institutions, and thus to sustain and develop the privileges of the colonists. We must grasp the negative role assigned to Indigenous peoples before we can effect positive change.

The governments of the day, often our legal guardians and fiduciaries, do not want to discuss ways of transforming legal or political institutions to include Indigenous peoples in nation-states. They do not want to end their national fantasies and myths about their nations. They do not want to expose the injustices that have informed the construction of state institutions and practices. They do not want to create postcolonial states. They do not want to sustain efforts at institutional reform. They reject the idea of hybridized states that include Indigenous peoples in the political and adjudicative realms. They want Indigenous peoples to vanish into separate replicative or imitative institutions or into organizations without equalized funds or capacities or shared rule. All these efforts are attempts to conceal the constitutive contradiction or unwanted side effects of the artificial, imaginative settler state and law, whose search for innate order has failed. Most of the nation-states of the Working Group on the Draft Declaration want to rewrite the entire text of the declaration to conform to their colonial orthodoxies and views of Indigenous peoples as minorities. They have no remedies for colonization. They are preoccupied with a different idea: how not to end colonization, and how to prolong their gross privileges.

In this new, mean-spirited venue, Indigenous peoples continue a creative and chaotic dialogue about the wording of the declaration with the nation-states. In this dialogue, impenetrable ideas derived from colonialism and the failures of liberalism, socialism, and communism confront the ecological consciousness and order of Indigenous peoples. The ecological–human rights movement of the Indigenous representatives challenges the Eurocentric idea of the modern nation-state. An innovative and transformative dialogue is emerging. In an awkward way, this dialogue is forging the future of the environment and of the peoples of the world.

In the working group, the nation-states' ramshackle compromises and makeshift apologies drawn from Eurocentric colonial ideology, humanities, philosophy, and legal traditions dominate daily discussions. It is a complicated discourse. Most of these efforts affirm that the UN human rights covenants protect only the colonizers, while they deny the colonized the same rights. In the context of human rights—the antidote for colonization—the nation-states seek the daring and implausible sanctification of colonization in the draft declaration. Only Canada has stated that Indigenous peoples have a right to self-determination. Nevertheless, even the Canadian state needs a more comfortable wording to limit the Indigenous peoples' right to unilateral succession. In many ways, the resisting state representatives resemble a "priesthood" that has lost its faith in the idea of human rights, but still keeps the instructions. Intransigent hope among the betrayed Indigenous peoples continues in the delight that the peoples can occasionally confront and render incoherent the priests of secular nationalism in the United Nations. Often, we find the mind's opportunity in the journey of the heart.

The chair of the Working Group on Indigenous Populations, Dr. Erica-Irene Daes, for the Sub-Commission on Prevention of Discrimination and Protection of Minorities, described our position accurately when she stated to the United Nations that the declaration is "belated state-building." Indigenous peoples know that the nation-states are strong and that we are vulnerable and poor. The discussion over Indigenous rights confirms this power imbalance. Compromising is difficult when Indigenous people know they are right. The states worry about the implications of the Indigenous rights. They refuse to return their stolen privileges and rights.

We continue to stress that our articulated vision is not subject to censorship by the states. We want our black-ink version passed without paternalistic amendments. We root our support of these minimal standards in a sense of injustice, our felt indignation, and our abhorrence of the wrong we have experienced. It is our expression of our humanity and our human rights.

As Indigenous peoples enter the twenty-first century, the need is great for the world's people to embrace a consciousness that enables all peoples to enrich their character and dignity. This consciousness should allow the once-powerless voices of Indigenous peoples to emerge from their roots and cultural experiences, and should welcome these voices as positive contributions to diversity rather than as sources of prejudice. To be heard in this way is one of the fundamental rights Indigenous peoples seek, but it is a right that is countered with state forms of structural marginalization and contested sites of struggle. For Indigenous peoples to emerge from these contested sites with harmony and dignity requires a consideration of the worldviews from which these sites have evolved.

Introduction

We come from the land, the sky, from love and the body. From matter and creation. We are, life is, an equation we cannot form or shape, a mystery we can't trace in spite of our attempts to follow it back to its origin, to find out where life began, even in all our stories of when the universe came into being, how the first people emerged. — Linda Hogan, *Dwellings* (1995, 95–96)

From the beginning, the forces of the ecologies in which we live have taught Indigenous peoples a proper kinship order and have taught us how to have nourishing relationships with our ecosystems. The ecologies in which we live are more to us than settings or places; they are more than homelands or promised homelands. These ecologies do not surround Indigenous peoples; we are an integral part of them and we inherently belong to them. The ecologies are alive with the enduring processes of creation itself. As Indigenous peoples, we invest the ecologies with deep respect, and from them we unfold our structure of Indigenous life and thought.

Ecological insight creates our vision of the animate "natural" world. It informs our communion with the land, our wisdom, and the various dimensions of our faith and our hopes. Indigenous order, consciousness, and heritage are shaped and sustained by ecological forces and by the interrelationship of their changing forms. Ecologies are not static or gentle; they are places of eternal and often violent change. Indigenous orders are not singular modes of existence, but are manifested in diverse ways. We carry the mysteries of our ecologies and their diversity in our oral traditions, in our ceremonies, and in our art; we unite these mysteries in the structure of our languages and our ways of knowing. The forces and aspects of our ecologies are manifest in our stories, which are to us what water is to plants (Hogan 1998, 227).

Ecological teachings have defined for Indigenous peoples the meaning of life, our responsibilities, and our duties. They have also developed our consciousnesses, our languages, and what others have categorized as our "cultures." These teachings have allowed us to flourish. They have always been mysterious and sacred processes, emanations of our responsibilities to and solidarity with the particular environments in which we participate. They create our multilevels of connection with the land.

These teachings have been passed on through our oral traditions in symbolic literacies to each generation (Battiste 1984). They offer succeeding generations the path of knowledge that informs their heritage. An example of these traditions is the understanding the Mi'kmaq of Atlantic Canada have of their beginnings.

> In the beginning when the Mi'kmaq people awoke naked and lost, we asked our Creator how we should live. Our creator taught us how to hunt and fish and how to cure what we took, how to make clothes from the skins, to cure ourselves from the plants of the earth. Our Creator taught us about the constellations and the stars, how to make our way in the darkest of nights, and about the Milky Way which was the path of our spirits into the other world. Our Creator taught us how to pray, to sleep, and to dream and told us to listen to the animals that would speak to us in our dreams bringing us guidance and support. Our Creator taught us all that was wise and good and then gave us a language, a language in which we might be able to pass on this knowledge to our children so that they could survive and flourish. Our Creator also taught us about the two worlds that were divided by a cloudlike substance that opened and fell at various intervals and the firm and believing of heart would be able to move between those worlds unscathed but the weak and unbelieving would be crushed to atoms. (Battiste 1984, 45–46)

These teachings reveal to the Mi'kmaq how to live and how to communicate with and respect other life forms. They reveal to the people how to hunt and fish, how to take medicines from the earth, and how to respect what they harvest (Henderson 1995, 225–36). They teach succeeding generations how to acquire new teachings and deeper understandings through prayers, ceremonies, and dreams, all of which offer replenishment of the body and soul. These teachings emphasize that through dreams and visions people will find additional lessons and guidance. The teachings also make the Mi'kmaq aware that all that is wise and good in the ecology is related to them, and give them a language to share this knowledge with others so that they too may survive and flourish.

The excerpt above is a brief outline of a longer story of how the ecological forces are the teachers of the Mi'kmaq. Many similar versions exist among other Indigenous peoples. Every force is interrelated throughout the stories and in ceremonies in a complex system of ecological kinship. The interaction of these forces is necessary to achieve a constantly shifting balance and harmony. Through language, ritual, prayer, and an intimate knowing of their ecologies, Indigenous peoples assist the forces in maintaining these fragile harmonies. Only by respectful activities and sharing can Indigenous peoples sustain creation's forces. Our Indigenous order, our shared and personal responsibilities, and our caring for the ecology animate our ancestors' legacies and heritages to the present generation. These shared legacies inform our vision of a sustainable future. It is a form of belonging for the present generation, a manifestation of caring that extends for at least seven generations. These heritages create a choice of lifestyles for each generation. These choices and the responsibilities that follow from them are the defining characteristics of our collective order and wisdom.

Protecting Indigenous peoples' relationships to their ecologies has never been easy. We believe that no part of the earth is expendable or can be considered as "waste." We respect and appreciate the inherent value of every life force and place in the ecological order. The creators have taught us this consciousness and created this awareness. Yet, we know by experience that not all peoples share our worldview. Indigenous peoples have experienced the migratory predators of the world in the process of European colonization and have been forced to change. We have experienced the colonization of our creation, our ecologies, our minds, and our spirits. Yet, even with horrendous losses, we have resisted and endured. Tragically, the struggle has left Indigenous peoples' order, knowledge, and languages vulnerable and endangered. Indigenous knowledge disappears when Indigenous peoples are stripped of their lands, their languages, and their lives. Although many of the processes of old-style colonization have waned in the new millennium, a new threatening transformation has emerged. "Globalization" with its cognitive and linguistic imperialism is the modern force that is taking our heritages, knowledge, and creativity.

As the twenty-first century dawns, industrialized societies are demanding that Indigenous peoples share their knowledge, their hearts, bodies, and souls so that Eurocentric society can solve the various problems that its worldview has created. In view of the history of relations between the colonizers and the colonized, this is an extraordinarily bold request. The colonizing peoples have done nothing to create trust or to build relationships with our ecologies or with our knowledge. They have contaminated the land, and they have refused to have respectful relations with the forces of the ecologies. Indeed, they have competed with these forces. Now they are beginning to suffer the consequences implicit in their actions, and they look toward Indigenous peoples for help.

The erosion of Indigenous knowledge concerns both the Indigenous people to whom this knowledge belongs and the non-Indigenous people who seek to know more about it. In its summer 1991 edition, *Cultural Survival Quarterly* described the need of the industrialized world for Indigenous knowledge as the latest "great resource rush." Over the past decade, scientists, industries, and governments have expressed an astonishing interest in the knowledge of Indigenous peoples. This interest has reinstalled the predatory mentality of Eurocentric thought, raising questions about the ethics of the new global enterprise and about Indigenous peoples' ability to survive it. The parallels between the dispossession of Indigenous land and the dispossession of their intellectual knowledge are riveting. Without effective protection of the special interests that Indigenous peoples have in their ways of knowing and heritage, Indigenous cultures are threatened and endangered. Our heritage and teachings are open to pillage in the same way and by the same peoples who have been taking our lands and resources for more than five hundred years.

Survival for Indigenous peoples is more than a question of physical existence; it is an issue of preserving Indigenous knowledge systems in the face of cognitive imperialism. It is a global issue of maintaining Indigenous worldviews, languages, and environments. It is a matter of sustaining spiritual links with the land. As Indigenous knowledge and heritage become more intensely attractive commercially, the cognitive heritage that gives Indigenous peoples their identity is under assault from those who would gather it up, strip away its honored meanings, convert it to a product, and sell it. Each time that happens, the heritage and knowledge die a little, and with them, the people.

The rush on Indigenous knowledge systems, teachings, and heritage by outsiders is an effort to access, to know, and to assert control over these resources. The need to conserve disappearing biological resources raises the issues of development ideology and the lack of economic benefits flowing to Indigenous peoples for the use of their knowledge and their resources. At the intersection of these trends is the issue of the legal status of Indigenous groups and their control over specific and widely useful knowledge.

Currently in many different disciplines, communities of researchers and advocates are calling attention to the effects of rapid global change on Indigenous peoples, their knowledge, their languages, and their understanding of their environments. Indigenous scholars trained in the Eurocentric tradition are challenging the assumptions and methodology of their professions and are beginning the dialogue about the new forms of cognitive imperialism and systemic discrimination (Kawagley 1993; G. Smith 1997; L. Smith 1999; Battiste 2000; Cajete 1995; 1999; 2000). The subtle effects of the cognitive and linguistic frameworks created and legitimized by imperialism have displaced the systemic discrimination against Indigenous peoples during colonial times, and pose the most crucial cultural challenge facing humanity today. Meeting the responsibility of challenging these frameworks is not just a task for the colonized and the oppressed; it is the defining challenge and the path to a shared and sustainable future for all peoples.

The decolonization of existing thought and law is already under way in the works of many scholars. However, the experiences of Indigenous peoples engage decolonization in a distinct manner. Maori educator and scholar Linda Tuhiwai Smith is one of the leading Indigenous theorists of the decolonization of the Maori in New Zealand. Dr. Smith clarifies the nature of the task when she writes: "Decolonization is about centering our concerns and world views and then coming to know and understand theory and research from our own perspectives and for our own purposes" (1999, 39). These interrelated strands intersect to weave solutions not only to decolonize cognitive imperialism, but also to sustain the Indigenous renaissance and empower intercultural diplomacy.

Indigenous peoples have been robbed of their humanity and called less than human. Savages, slaves, commodities, half-castes, and half-breeds are just some of the names that have been used to describe them. Indigenous scholars are now struggling to define Indigenous humanity for the benefit of their people and for the education of others. First they need to understand the systems of thought that gave rise to this alienation, and then they need to create a shared language both sides can use to discuss education, science, social sciences, the humanities, and politics, which together have created "an epic story telling of huge devastation, painful struggle and persistent survival" (L. Smith 1999, 19).

Within this long and abusive history, Indigenous peoples have attempted to break free from their worldwide subjugation. Colonization brought disorder to Indigenous peoples' lives, to their languages, to their social relations, and to their ways of thinking about, feeling, and interacting with the world. Their ways of being have been systematically fragmented and devalued in Western knowledge, sciences, and other dominant modes of knowing. Cognitive imperialism is the hierarchical and patrimonial monologue that has been created by Eurocentrism (hooks 1988; Minnick 1990). This is often referred to as "the Eurocentric monologue" or as "the voice of truth," as "progress," and as "historical accountability." Indigenous people are now contesting the Eurocentric monologue and its predictable distribution of "poison and prosperity" (Findlay in press).

The challenge for Indigenous peoples is one of restoring their spirit and bringing back into existence, health, and dignity the world of the fragmented and dying. Some postcolonial Indigenous writers call for Indigenous intellectuals and artists to create new literatures or to construct new national cultures based on Indigenous thought and heritages. Many Indigenous writers have attempted to take up the cause. Their writings and their intellectual practices have sought to determine the breaks between the past and the present, and to offer theory from their distinctive knowledge and heritage and their response to their conditions. Other Indigenous scholars have begun to reclaim their own perspectives, their own designs, their own strategies, and their own visions. Reclaiming and revitalizing Indigenous heritage and knowledge is a vital part of any process of decolonization, as is reclaiming land, language, and nationhood.

Indigenous elders and scholars are creating an Indigenous renaissance that can be likened to the European renaissance after the Dark Ages. The Indigenous renaissance is based on Indigenous peoples' precolonial civilizations, heritage, and knowledge. It involves stabilizing and restoring Indigenous languages, and honoring Indigenous worldviews, cognitive categories, and communicable powers. It also involves interrogating Eurocentric concepts of civilization and knowledge. In articulating and sustaining the Indigenous renaissance, Indigenous peoples assert that the existing concepts of "culture" need to be demystified and decolonized. As comparative literalist Edward Said has stated, it is necessary to approach European perspectives on culture with an awareness of the "all-pervasive, unavoidable imperial setting" (1993). It is also necessary to see Indigenous resistance to the imperial culture. Abundant Eurocentric perspectives on culture, cultural analysis of differences, cultural policies, and cultural industries speak to ethical pluralism; however, these perspectives often weaken pluralism rather than empower diversity.

Indigenous peoples are investigating fair methodologies for exploring their own ways of life and for understanding and respecting other peoples' ways of life. Many Indigenous people view "culture" as a fluid concept of an interactive and negotiated consciousness. They live in an "intercultural" environment created by colonialism, but they value and celebrate all manifestations of their cognitive heritage. While Indigenous people agree that their heritage is "a complete knowledge system with its own concepts of epistemology, philosophy, and scientific and logical validity" (Daes 1994, para. 8), they do not view their complicated consciousness and way of life as an exotic, independent, closed, or internally uniform realm.

Indigenous peoples' forced and voluntary interactions with other peoples and their views of life have created an Indigenous consciousness that is a web of intertwining heritages and thoughts. Indigenous consciousness is dynamic. It tolerates diversity as it seeks to create opportunities to secure and enhance the qualities of Indigenous living. The ways Indigenous peoples relate to their ecologies and to others honors their heritage and their knowledge, especially as embodied in their languages. Yet, most Indigenous peoples also want to belong with dignity to humanity and to be at home in the global community. They want to participate in the future on an equal basis with others and to have their worldviews and heritage respected.

Protecting and enhancing Indigenous languages are the prime challenges of the Indigenous decade. The diverse Indigenous ways of life "can only be fully learned or understood by means of the pedagogy traditionally employed by these peoples themselves, including apprenticeship, ceremonies and practices" (Daes 1994, para. 8). The recovery of our histories, our contested stories, our knowledge, and our experience is inextricably linked to the recovery of our languages. It is all about reconciling what is important about the past with what is important about the present. Today, scholars are investigating the cognitive and social correlates of multilingualism and orality versus literacy.

Another challenge is revising educational policies. As Indigenous peoples reclaim the oral traditions stored in the minds and hearts of their people, these traditions must be respected by modern curricula and thought. Curricula are the organized portion of education that has been the silencing tool of Western education of all "others." They are the compacts that represent the consensus of teaching, and these compacts are politically charged, not neutral (Minnick 1990). An education that does not critique the connections or lack of connections in knowledge is not education but indoctrination. Indigenous peoples must participate in educational decision making; they must be allowed to design and create the tools they need to transform the existing crises (L. Smith 1999).

There is a growing body of literature on vanishing cultures, language endangerment, and environmental destruction. Ethnobiologists, human ecologists, and other social as well as biological scientists are recording Indigenous use of ecosystems, Indigenous ecological concepts, and Indigenous strategies for resource management. They are also documenting the causes and consequences of local cultural and environmental disruption. Cognitive anthropologists and psychologists are studying Indigenous peoples' perceptions and categorizations of the natural world, their biological learning and reasoning, their environmental beliefs, and their environmentally relevant decision making. Political scientists and ecological economists are looking at Indigenous institutions and economic models from the point of view of Indigenous ecological sustainability.

As ethnolinguist Luisa Maffi (1996) has pointed out, these efforts attest to the perceived gravity and urgency of protecting Indigenous peoples, their knowledge, and their languages from extinction. They also attest to a keen shared interest in the future of humanity and of life on earth. Accompanying this literature are specialized meetings and international conventions. Delegates at these meetings are drawing up principles and guidelines for protecting Indigenous heritage; creating ethical standards for large-scale research; and developing professional societies, training programs, international research centers, and advocacy groups for the benefit of Indigenous peoples. Much of their work has taken the form of international declarations. There are also innumerable Indigenous movements, grassroots movements, and local organizations working in the area of Indigenous rights. However, there has been little intercommunication across this remarkable convergence of interests. There is also little understanding of how existing legal frameworks help or hinder Indigenous peoples in their quest to secure knowledge and languages.

The scope of the challenge is vast. In 1994 Rural Advancement Foundation International reported to the United Nations that 80 percent of the world's people depend on Indigenous knowledge for health and security, and half rely on Indigenous knowledge and crops for food. Trade and tourism that rely on Indigenous knowledge translate into tens of billions of dollars a year. Indigenous cultural artifacts and art that manifest Indigenous peoples' spiritual images or dreamings and their relationships with sacred environments now turn many millions of dollars a year. Regrettably, existing legal régimes, both internationally and nationally, provide little protection from unauthorized takings or reproductions of intellectually, culturally, and spiritually sensitive knowledge, and often actively discriminate against this knowledge. Neither international nor national law has kept pace with these commercial developments, and understanding this controversy and the deficiencies in existing law requires one to contemplate disturbing issues about the rule of law and the idea of knowledge.

When decolonizing Eurocentrism, it is easy to offer analyses that have little explanatory power. In this book, we seek to offer practical explanations that we hope will lead to concrete solutions. The overall rhythm of the text is synthetic and conceptual—we attempt to move forward from the experiences and shared lessons of the past. Our discussion occasionally spirals back on itself as we seek to integrate fragmented dimensions into a complex whole. We base our understanding on our experiences as Eurocentric-trained scholars, one trained in education and the other in law, and on linguistic, cultural, and ecological awarenesses drawn from our Mi'kmaw and Chickasaw heritages. Throughout the book, we will be manifesting the teachings of both worlds through our Indigenous consciousness.

We begin by discussing Eurocentrism, its assumptions, and its biases toward Indigenous knowledge and heritage. Then we examine the contexts of Indigenous knowledge and heritage, focusing our attention on the vast contemporary issues. We will attempt to outline the various international, constitutional, and national legal régimes that currently seek to protect Indigenous knowledge and heritage. By offering a coherent view of the wide legal tapestry of cultural and intellectual property régimes and their increasingly important nexus within the global economy, we seek to clarify the extent to which these régimes can enable or limit Indigenous knowledge. Our intellectual journey is as difficult as it is urgent. It is an intercultural and interdisciplinary journey into the conflicted heart of Eurocentric and Indigenous thought. It is a challenging journey through unquestioned acquiescence to Eurocentric thought and law, a journey into humanity, and a journey into the uncharted options of a postcolonial world.

Indigenous peoples have devoted remarkable energy to establishing intercultural protocols for eliminating the systemic discrimination introduced through colonization. We have asserted that all interactions between cultures and among development processes must be understood from an intercultural perspective that tolerates constructive diversity, rather than from any particular cultural perspective. Intercultural diplomacy must empower a fair and just space between cultures that must be respected and honored. If progress is to be made toward building more peaceful, cooperative, and just societies where human security is valued as paramount, Indigenous peoples and communities must be involved. Such efforts must respect the unique approaches to peace building and ways of living together that Indigenous peoples can offer. The return to the teachings of Indigenous ecologies and lands is a rebirthing of Indigenous connections with the spirit of their teachings. This rebirthing must be nourished and reconciled in the collective responsibilities to the challenges of Indigenous peoples in this new millennium.

To exclude Indigenous peoples from the dialogue of culture, equity, and fairness is to further cognitive imperialism and systemic and direct discrimination—thus enlarging the pool of development's victims. New attempts must be made to create intercultural venues for dialogue and cooperation, to empower intercultural diplomacy, and to prevent ethnic warfare, separatism, and apartheid. Our shared future can be a proud one. Together the international and national communities, institutions, and legal systems can open the greatest era of cooperation, understanding, and respect among diverse peoples of the earth and forge a true renaissance. Only a global effort can ensure that respecting Indigenous heritages and perspectives is an integral part of all that we do. In this process, everyone has a powerful and indispensable role. And when we meet these challenges, the judgment of history will be that each intellectual tradition met and respected the others' heritage and knowledge. Together this honor and respect will lift our cultures and heritage into a fair global order and into a new and higher level of civilization the world needs. We cannot afford not to do it.

Part I

The Lodge of Indigenous Knowledge in Modern Thought

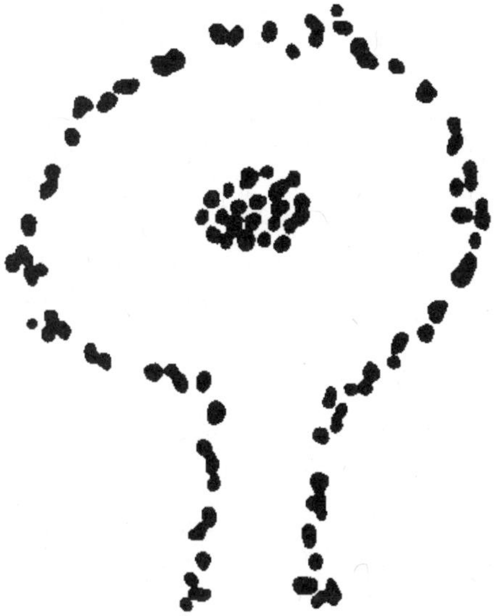

[T]he heritage of an indigenous people is not merely a collection of objects, stories and ceremonies, but a complete knowledge system with its own concepts of epistemology, philosophy, and scientific and logical validity. The diverse elements of an indigenous people's heritage can only be fully learned or understood by means of the pedagogy traditionally employed by these peoples themselves, including apprenticeship, ceremonies and practice. Simply recording words or images fails to capture the whole context and meaning of songs, rituals, arts or scientific and medical wisdom. This also underscores the central role of indigenous peoples' own languages, through which each people's heritage has traditionally been recorded and transmitted from generation to generation. — Dr. Erica-Irene Daes, *Preliminary Report of the Special Rapporteur: Protection of the Heritage of Indigenous Peoples* (1994, para. 8)

Chapter 1

•••

Eurocentrism and the European Ethnographic Tradition

The future cannot be a continuation of the past and there are signs . . . that we have reached a point of historic crisis. . . . We do not know where we are going. We only know that history has brought us to this point. — Eric Hobsbawm, *The Age of Extremes* (1996, 585)

To understand Indigenous knowledge, it is necessary to explain the orthodox context of knowledge, which is now called Eurocentrism (Amin 1988; Blaut 1993). Eurocentrism is the imaginative and institutional context that informs contemporary scholarship, opinion, and law. As a theory, it postulates the superiority of Europeans over non-Europeans. It is built on a set of assumptions and beliefs that educated and usually unprejudiced Europeans and North Americans habitually accept as true, as supported by "the facts," or as "reality."

A central concept behind Eurocentrism is the idea of diffusionism. Diffusionism is based on two assumptions: (1) most human communities are uninventive, and (2) a few human communities (or places, or cultures) are inventive and are thus the permanent centers of cultural change or "progress." On a global scale, this results in a world with a single center—Europe—and a surrounding periphery. Europe, at the center (Inside), is historical, invents, and progresses, and non-Europe, at the periphery (Outside), is ahistorical, stagnant, and unchanging. From this framework, diffusionism asserts that European peoples are superior to Indigenous peoples. This superiority is based on some inherent characteristic of the European mind or spirit and because non-European peoples lack this characteristic, they are empty, or partly so, of ideas and proper spiritual values. The theory argues that because Europeans are superior, Indigenous peoples need the diffusion of creativity, imagination, invention, innovation, rationality, and sense of honor or ethics from Europe in order to progress.

Classical Eurocentric diffusionism exists as many variations of this proposition. First, for much of the non-European world, diffusionist literature asserts an emptiness of basic cultural institutions and people and equates an absence of established settlements with a lack of law. This idea has a particular connection to settler colonialism and to the physical movement of Europeans into non-European regions, such as North America, Africa, Australia, and New Zealand, displacing or eliminating the Indigenous inhabitants (Blaut 1993). This proposition of emptiness supports a series of claims about an Indigenous emptiness of intellectual creativity and spiritual values, sometimes described by Europeans (as, for instance, by sociologist Max Weber) as an absence of "rationality." Classical diffusionism allows that some non-European regions were "rational" in some ways and to some degree at different times. Thus, for instance, the Middle East during biblical times was rational. China was somewhat rational for a certain period in its history. Other regions, such as North America and Africa, were unqualifiedly lacking in rationality.

Diffusion explains any progress made by non-Europeans as resulting from the spread of European ideas, which flow into the non-European world like air flows into a vacuum. This diffusion may also be achieved by the spread of products through which European values are distributed. The diffusion of great civilizing ideas from Europe to non-Europe was thought to be compensation enough for the European confiscation of material wealth from non-Europeans. The diffusion of superiority had its drawbacks, however. There was always the possibility that non-Europeans' traits could counterdiffuse back into Eurocentric society, corrupting the civilized core. These ancient traits were evil things like black magic, vampires, plagues, and " bogeymen." Since Europe was believed to be advanced and non-Europe backward, any ideas that diffused into Europe from elsewhere were perceived to be inevitably uncivilized (Blaut 1993).

The core of Eurocentric thought is its claim to be universal. There were two inspirations that forbade Europeans to rest content with developing their own part of the world. The first inspiration was curiosity. The quest for knowledge was an outgrowth of the "wonder" that Aristotle found at the beginning of all European thought and of the dialogue in which Socrates sought to engage each person capable of listening and willing to listen. Life was to be tested by questioning its universal good. These early philosophers examined every discovery for what it was and for its universality. This quest for truth and value informed the concept of universal purpose and explains why Europeans left their lands and went to such efforts to discover the world. The second inspiration was the messianic prophecy contained in monotheistic religions. Eurocentric thought has a belief in, and commitment to, a messianic dream of a millennium: a new heaven, a new earth, and a transformed people. This belief was expressed in the Judaic vision of linear time moving toward a predetermined end and in the Christian vision of the spiritual transformation of the old into the new. What is particular to both Socrates and the prophets of the Bible is the notion of a universal mission that invites the attention of all humans. Had Socrates stopped conversing or Isaiah stopped volunteering or Peter stopped preaching, the idea of a universal civilization might have disappeared.

At the beginning of a new millennium, this idea of a universal mission has created a global crisis. Although Eurocentrism has created unheard-of material wealth for the European minority, it has also created a techno-scientific realm that is threatening the foundations of human life, especially among the Indigenous majority. It is a dismaying legacy. Violence, war, and oppression have taken a heavy toll on Indigenous peoples' ecologies, lives, and knowledge. The global nature of the crisis lies in the interconnected, transboundary, and widespread problems faced by peoples in all parts of the world (Peccei 1979); in the contradictory forces of economic globalization and ethnic fragmentation; and in the awareness that the crisis can be dealt with only by concerted action across the borders of nation-states.

Eurocentrism and its belief in its superiority, in its explanation of the developmental patterns of progress, and in its synthesis of individualism, rationalism, and scientism has made modern scholarship unable to grasp the crisis or to resolve it. The Eurocentric synthesis has had such preeminence in the minds and affairs of nations, education systems, and societies that for many centuries it has been unanimously accepted as the only means of ensuring a viable future under the banner of modernization. Eurocentric intellectuals have abandoned ancient truths, values, and ways of life, and have accepted Eurocentrism as their measure of progress. Today the Eurocentric synthesis of ideas and values seems no longer able to offer a sure guide to human survival. The global state of affairs casts doubt on the once-dominant and persuasive Eurocentric model and its beliefs about the natural world and human nature. These beliefs have to be reevaluated.

Assumptions About the Natural World

In Eurocentric thought the natural world is usually thought of as a single, wholly determinable realm. The world is a background against which the mind operates, and knowledge is regarded as information that originates outside humanity. Eurocentric thought can be justified only if several assumptions about the nature of the world and anyone's knowledge of it are accepted. These assumptions can be reduced to four fundamental statements: (1) the natural world exists independent of any beliefs about it; (2) perceptions may provide an accurate impression of the natural world; (3) linguistic concepts may describe the natural world; and (4) certain rules of inference are reliable means for arriving at new truths about the natural world. Upon these four delicate assumptions rest most Eurocentric beliefs about reality. To reject any one of them requires the rejection of a large number of other beliefs that depend upon it and introduces a massive dislocation in the Eurocentric system of beliefs about the world.

These four assumptions about the relation of Eurocentric thought to the natural world are empiricist in character—that is to say they rely on practical experience. The problem is that these assumptions are impossible to prove. Within modern Eurocentric thought, humans can have no access to a world independent of their beliefs and experiences of it, so they cannot check, in a God-like manner, upon the truth of their assumptions. The elusive justification for holding these assumptions in Eurocentric thought is that it has been useful to do so.

(1) The Natural World Exists Independent of Any Beliefs About It

Most Eurocentric and Indigenous thinkers agree that an animate natural world exists, and that we are born into it. The difference between Eurocentric and Indigenous thought lies in the perceived relationship between people and the natural world. Eurocentric thought wants humanity to be at one with the natural order, but believes people are denied this unity because of their terrifying exclusion from the Garden of Eden. Because people do not have a predetermined place in the natural world, their knowledge of the natural world is necessarily incomplete, and they must overcome the separation between self and the natural world using subjective, artificial structures. As Eurocentric consciousness artificially constructs a place for its existence, it treats the natural world as a practical source of the means to achieve its own objectives. In contrast to the Eurocentric view, Indigenous peoples do not view humanity as separate from the natural world; thus they do not have to face the Eurocentric terror of separation from nature, nor do they have to construct artificial organizations—or human "culture"—to overcome this separation.

(2) Perceptions May Provide an Accurate Impression of the Natural World

In attempting to bridge the gap between humanity and the natural world, European philosophers have asserted that something in the Eurocentric mind can "see" facts in the raw data of the natural world and can order those facts in ways that produce other facts. The Eurocentric consciousness perceives events in the natural world as sensations, and these sensations are the basis for Eurocentric knowledge. In an indefinite number of ways, the Eurocentric mind can combine and recombine sensations, but these mental processes do not change the events themselves, since the natural world is oblivious to the working of the Eurocentric consciousness.

In the Eurocentric view, perceptions always act as a filter between human consciousness and the natural world so people can never experience reality directly. For example, humans describe objects as having a certain smell and some events as noisy, implying that these are properties of the objects and events themselves. According to modern thinkers, these properties do not lie in the objects themselves but in individuals as they perceive these objects. In this view all reality is contextual and depends on the way sensations are categorized. Contexts can be modified, but they can never be transcended.

Indigenous thought is closer to the ancient Greek idea of "intelligible essences." This theory argues that everything in the world contains within itself characteristics that can be known directly to the human mind; hence categories exist independently of the mind, and the mind can understand what the world is really like.

(3) Linguistic Concepts May Describe the Natural World

Eurocentric philosophers have consistently attempted to demonstrate that human beings are significantly different from all other forms of life, and they have stressed that this uniqueness lies in language. To the ancient Greeks, language depended on the comprehension of intelligible essences in the natural world. Since the European Renaissance, modern thinkers have rejected the idea of intelligible essences and have asserted instead that creating categories is an arbitrary procedure. Because of the modern denial of intelligible essences, most sensory qualities are rejected as forming the categories of language. Instead it is thought that every person has the power to create rules of inference and to apply these rules to conceptualize and describe the natural world. The modern view of linguistics considers any language to be an arbitrary but conventionally agreed upon code. Language is a way of representing the perceived natural world, without any objective connection to the world.

If language is about categorizing sensations and creating rules of inference, then what language names is not the natural world but the ideological realm. What the speakers of European languages know and talk about are ideas. The ideas come first, the words follow. No intrinsic bond exists between a particular sound or written word and what it stands for. This raises the issue of translatability. If the meaning of a word depends on the idea behind it, can it be translated into another language built upon a different set of ideas? One is left with the question of the extent to which language describes the natural order. Reflecting the belief of monotheistic religions that one God created the world in His image, Eurocentric universal grammar theorists teach that only one linguistic tradition—the Indo-European tradition—and its rules of inference can reveal the operation of the world. In contrast, the relative grammar theorists argue that since all languages describe the world, and many different languages exist, no single linguistic tradition or set of rules of inference can describe the natural world, and hence language is readily separable from the world.

In the Indigenous worldview, humans perceive the sensuous order of the natural world through their eyes, noses, ears, mouths, and skins (Abram 1996). Perceptions of the sensory world unfold as affective sounds and rhythm. As these sounds become words, humans participate in "singing the world"

(Merleau-Ponty 1962). Since people enter into language through their sensory relationships with the natural world, languages cannot be understood in isolation from the ecologies that give rise to them.

(4) Certain Rules of Inference Are Reliable Means for Arriving at New Truths About the Natural World

In Eurocentric thought, the idea that languages are conventional codes is reflected in the rules of inference used for arriving at truths about the natural world. The Eurocentric mind is understood to be a machine that analyzes sensations and combines them into categories. This process of analysis and combination produces ideas, but it does not affect the natural world, which is oblivious to the workings of the human intellect. As categories are not fixed in anything that exists independently of the human mind, these ideas can be broken down again into their elementary sensations and recombined into new categories.

Eurocentric thought asserts there is an artificial kind of knowledge, exemplified by mathematics and logic, that does not originate in the analysis and combination of sensations, but rather in the relationships among categories that exist outside the world of facts. Perfect certainty can only be achieved in the study of these artificially constructed categories because they do not rely on any interpretation of sensations. Because mathematical physics carries furthest the comparison of the order of events to the order of ideas, it is viewed as the most accomplished of the modern sciences.

The problem with Eurocentric theoretical analysis is that it is a way of looking at the world; it is not knowledge of how the world is, and Eurocentric theories of how the world operates change over time. Historian and philosopher of science Thomas Kuhn studied the process of intellectual transformations in the Eurocentric sciences. In his book *The Structure of Scientific Revolutions* (1970), Kuhn argued that there are long periods of "normal science" in which fundamental assumptions and concepts are accepted and not seriously questioned. The unreflective era then gives way to a "scientific revolution," in which new assumptions, theories, and ideas change the conceptual foundations of science. Kuhn called these competing conceptual foundations "paradigms." Paradigms include not only fundamental assumptions but also theories, principles, and doctrines. A paradigm shift occurs when scientists cannot explain certain data or natural phenomena by reference to established scientific theories. The unexplainable events are often called anomalies. Periodically, scientists discover that these anomalies have a unity that leads to a new theory, and a new scientific paradigm and rules of inference are created. The paradigm shifts in the history of Eurocentric science, from the Copernican to the Newtonian, and from the Newtonian to the Einsteinian, demonstrate how scientists change their views about how the world works.

Kuhn showed that science progresses by sharp ruptures rather than by steady incremental evolutions and that scientific knowledge is formulated in terms of a particular shared paradigm in effect at any given time, rather than in terms of knowledge of the natural world or the "truth" or "reality" in some Platonic sense.

Modern thinkers have shown that the standards of inference, logical entailment, and causality, once thought reliable for arriving at truths about natural world, are no longer judged to be reliable. Modern Eurocentric theorists have asserted that they need to find an alternative to logical and causal explanation. This insight was behind the development of such structural explanations of causality as Karl Marx's dialectical method, Max Weber's ideal-type, Noam Chomsky's deep structure in linguistic analysis, Claude Lévi-Strauss's anthropology, and Gestalt psychology. Yet modern thought has not been able to develop a precise and detailed definition of a non-logical, non-causal method of inference that is both generalized in its method and rich in its historical references. The persistent inability of Eurocentric theories to resolve these issues illustrates how unreliable they are as means for arriving at truth about natural world. In the Indigenous worldview, the world operates according to a dynamic, circular flux in which human beings participate directly. Life is to be lived not according to universal, abstract theories about the way things work but as an interactive relationship in a particular time and place.

Assumptions About Human Nature

The rules of inference used to arrive at truths about the natural world are reflected in the Eurocentric view of human nature. Given certain assumptions about the natural world, the human mind uses reason to discover that some things are "by nature" right for human beings and that others are created by artificial convention. As the categories imposed by reason are arbitrary, the question is, What impels the mind to analyze the world in one way rather than in another? The generally accepted answer is desire. In the seventeenth century, the British philosopher Thomas Hobbes in *Leviathan; or the Matter, Form, and Power of a Commonwealth, Ecclesiastical and Civil* explained:

> [F]or the Thoughts are to the Desires, as Scouts, and Spies, to range abroad, and find the way to the things desired: All Stediness of the mind's motion, and all quickness of the same, proceeding from thence. (1651, 57)

This relationship of desire to reason establishes the modern context of Eurocentric philosophy, liberal psychology, humanities, and social sciences. It creates the categories of a human will that desires, and a mind that understands and knows. These ideas create the Eurocentric notions of self, morality, society, and law. People are subject to arbitrary desires and accept certain assumptions about the natural world. Based on their desires and assumptions, they use reason to explain and structure the world around them.

Scientific paradigms, therefore, have their counterparts in the rules of inference used in the social sciences and in law. In Eurocentric disciplines, such explanatory paradigms are called "contexts." Just as a paradigm reflects current scientific thought about the natural world, so a context reflects current social, political, and legal thought about the human social order. Brazilian legal scholar Roberto Unger has asserted that if a context allows people to move within it to discover everything about the natural world they can discover, it is a "natural" context. If the context does not allow such natural movement, it is an "artificial" context derived from selected assumptions (1984, 5–15; 1987, 18–25).

Unger asserts that three theses define artificial contexts. The first thesis is the principle of contextuality. It is the belief that assumptions or desires that humans take as given shape their mental and social lives. These assumptions form a picture of what the world is really like, and even a set of premises about how thoughts and languages are or can be structured. They also provide a framework for explaining and verifying worldviews. These worldviews are artificial because they are dependent on assumptions made about human nature or society and not on what the world is really like independent of people's beliefs about it (1984, 18–19).

The second thesis is that these artificial worldviews are conditional and can be changed, but such changes are exceptional and transitory. Any context can be supplemented or revised by other empowering ideas about features that make one explanatory or society-making practice better than another (1984, 9). Thus, small-scale, routine adjustments in a context can turn into a more unconfined transformation. If the conditionality of any context is overcome, people do not simply remain outside all context, but rather they create new assumptions and contexts (1987, 19).

The third thesis is that, just as in Kuhn's "normal science," the conditionality of any artificial context is rarely recognized. Changes to artificial contexts are exceptional and transitory because the contexts are relatively immune to theories or activities. The distinction between routine and transformation maintains the immunity of the artificial context and prevents its conditionality from being questioned or opened up to revision (1984, 10). Against the background of change, the context is viewed as "normal" or "natural." As Unger explains, however, the more people become aware of the conditionality of a context, the more likely they are to be able to effect meaningful change to that context (1984, 10–11).

Assumptive Quandaries

Because of the artificial nature of Eurocentric thought, all that has been said so far is unavoidably abstract. Whether or not these assumptions about the natural world and human nature are well founded, they have profoundly influenced Eurocentric thought, and colonization has carried them around the earth. Although these assumptions have been challenged by both Eurocentric and Indigenous thinkers, they remain the foundations of orthodox educational and political thought.

If these assumptions about the natural world and human nature cannot be proven, can people abandon their quest for the truth about the natural world? Can they be content with the coherence of their beliefs about "reality"? If they can, there is no reason to insist on empirical evidence to support ideas. If any group can view the world and human nature through its own theoretical insights without reference to an independent natural world, however, this immediately raises the specter of domination, propaganda, and false realities.

If modern Eurocentric thought, in seeking to understand the natural world and human nature, employs linguistic concepts that do not correspond to an independent natural order and that are justified by questionable standards of inference, is it unreasonable to think that even those ideas that are well supported do not accurately describe the natural world and human nature? If this is the case, what are the implications of imposing Eurocentric models on Indigenous peoples? Why should we be forced to assimilate to an artificial reality?

What options remain in this disturbing predicament? The easy way out, the traditional solution of some Eurocentric thinkers, is to deny the primary assumption: that the natural world exists independent of any beliefs about it. Instead, they assert their beliefs and concepts constitute reality. The only authoritative reality, in this contradictory worldview, is the one of Eurocentric paradigms, theories, and contexts. However, because of the endless diversity of these constructs, Eurocentric thinkers quarrel among themselves if they have to learn more than one version of an artificial reality. Often the quarrel is about interpretative monopolies or power.

Another option is to retain faith in the four basic assumptions despite clear evidence of the falsity of all but the first. Faith or practical grounds usually justify this approach. This option asserts that as a framework of belief, those assumptions have enabled Eurocentric thinkers to relate successfully to the physical environment and there is no better framework of beliefs that modern thinkers could adopt. Both apologies assert a bold mystical metamorphosis: if it works then it must be *true;* and if it is *true,* then it alone must be *true.* This position is based on Eurocentric artificial ways of thinking represented by logic and causality. But this practical option is a partial view—a censored view. It ignores the tragic consequences of this thinking, consequences that have brought the world to the brink of ecological disaster. A key issue today is whether these Eurocentric assumptions contain the latencies of ecological ruin. To our mind there is also the critical question of whether it matters that biological creatures are attempting to inhabit a non-biological, ideological environment. As Indigenous peoples, we find the Eurocentric assumptions could more accurately be described as *imaginality* than *reality*. The fundamental issue to us is this: does reality matter or is desire enough?

In our view, a fundamental adjustment of the Eurocentric assumptions about the natural world and human nature is necessary. The adjustment should accommodate unlimited human desires and needs to a limited planetary ecosystem. A sustainable relationship between humans and the natural world must enable us to manage our livelihoods by controlling humans while sustaining and nourishing the complexity and stability of diverse ecologies. This relationship requires a revision of the Eurocentric view of humans being separate from the natural world. It also requires a revision of ideas about language and about causal-positivistic modes of inference. The new context must view Europeans and colonialists as one species among others embedded in the intricate web of natural processes that contain and sustain all forms of life.

Revision of the Eurocentric view of the relationship of humans to the natural world leads naturally to the concept of what constitutes humanity and what constitutes the meaning of life or human fulfillment. Both of these reconceptualizations are important if we are to respect Indigenous peoples and their knowledge and heritage.

The Ethnographic Tradition

For Eurocentric thought to adjust its assessments of non-European peoples and their attributes requires an interrogation of the Eurocentric ethnographic tradition. The study of Indigenous peoples has been a staple of the Eurocentric discipline of anthropology. To avoid the perils of subjective analysis, anthropology and the related discipline of ethnography seek to describe human societies as manifest through their cultures in scientific terms. The idea of "culture" is derived from the idea of tillage—the cultivation of the soil in English, *cultura* in Latin. In Eurocentric thought, culture represents the totality of human achievement and awareness: the transmitted behaviors, arts, beliefs, institutions, and styles of human works and thoughts characteristic of a people, community, society, or class. The disciplines of anthropology and ethnography impose rational patterns on human behavior in the same way that science imposes general paradigms on observed events.

Eurocentric anthropologists have traditionally organized the descriptive details of the Indigenous cultures they studied into ethnographies. In these ethnographies they recorded the languages, child-rearing practices, totems, taboos, signifying codes, work and leisure interests, standards of behavior and deviance, social classification systems, and jural procedures shared by members of the studied people. From these descriptive data, they inferred patterns that knit the societies they were studying into integrated wholes with all-embracing and largely taken-for-granted ways of life. They then inferred the pattern or patterns that differentiated these societies from other societies that had been studied.

By defining culture as a set of shared meanings, the classic norms of anthropological analysis made it difficult to study zones of difference within and between cultures. Indigenous cultures became homogenous rather than diverse. Yet, Indigenous consciousness has always required particular responses to particular ecologies built on flux. European ethnographers understood these cultural borderlands as annoying exceptions rather than as central areas for inquiry. Actual Indigenous knowledge, heritage, and consciousness came to be seen as too messy, even too downright chaotic, to be studied. The Eurocentric emphasis on coherent wholes at the expense of unique processes of change and internal inconsistencies, conflicts, and contradictions was and remains a serious limitation to Eurocentric understanding of Indigenous knowledge and heritage. In this sense, Eurocentric thinkers have taken culture as their abstract possession and Indigenous knowledge as merely symbolic and ideational. This search for stable, systematic régimes has reduced the knowledge that Eurocentric scholars claim to value "on its own terms."

Eurocentric anthropologists and ethnographers were inescapably complicit with the imperial domination of their epochs. For example, anthropology has always focused on the powerless, yet few anthropologists have attempted any evaluation of the effects of colonialism on these cultures. Behind their analyses of Indigenous people lay an assumptive realm continually betrayed in their writings. Their mask of innocence (or, as they put it, their "detached impartiality") barely concealed their role in perpetuating the colonial control of "distant" places and peoples. The contents of their writings represent the human objects of the civilizing mission's global enterprise as if Indigenous people were the ideal recipients of the White man's burden. Most often, they depicted Indigenous people as members of harmonious, internally homogeneous, unchanging cultures. From such a perspective, Indigenous knowledge and heritage appeared to "need" progress, and economic and moral uplifting.

Moreover, the Eurocentric concept of static traditional Indigenous knowledge and heritage served as a self-congratulatory reference point against which Eurocentric society could measure its own progressive evolution. Europeans conceived the civilizing journey as more of a rise than a fall, as a process more of perfection than of degradation—a long and arduous journey upward, culminating in being "them." Often they called this process "assimilation." Eurocentric values not only had to be accepted, they also had to be absorbed.

As a result, some colonized peoples immersed themselves in the imported Eurocentric culture; many even denied their origins in an attempt to become "more English than the English."

The contexts of colonial rule shaped the works of the classic ethnographers. By assuming the answers to questions that they should have asked, Eurocentric scholars confidently asserted that Indigenous knowledge and heritage do not change, only European society progresses. The monumentalism of timeless accounts of homogeneous Indigenous cultures and the objectivism of strict divisions of labor between the detached ethnographers and their Indigenous subjects are symptoms of imperial value contagion. As anthropologist Renate Rosaldo argued in *Culture and Truth: The Remaking of Social Analysis* (1989), these strict divisions of labor were basic to the initiation into the mysteries of anthropological knowledge; that is, the general rubric of fieldwork. The ethnographers were literate, the Indigenous peoples were not. The ethnographers recorded the "utterances" their Indigenous peoples spoke and then returned to their university communities to write "definitive works" on culture based on raw data provided by Indigenous people in the field.

The ethnographers portrayed cultures sufficiently frozen to be objects of scientific knowledge. Drawing on models of natural history, ethnographies usually moved upward from environment through family to spiritual life. Produced by and for specialists, these ethnographies portrayed different forms of life as totalities. These books were storehouses of purportedly incontrovertible information to be mined by armchair theorists engaged in comparative studies. The genre was supposed to be a mirror that reflected other cultures as they really were. These books served as models for aspiring ethnographers, and were regarded as exemplary cultural descriptions. The norms of distanced descriptions created an illusion of objectivity. Their authority was so self-evident that the ethnographies became the only legitimate form for telling the "literal" truth about Indigenous knowledge and heritage. They recreated the Indigenous realm in their own likeness and confidently taught it to society as the actual Indigenous truth.

Because the classic descriptions do not present fair interpretations of Indigenous worldviews, Indigenous people have had to suggest a total revision of anthropological analyses. Around the globe, Indigenous thinkers have had to prove that European scholars were mistaken in their notion of Indigenous culture as unchanging and homogeneous. We have had to prove that Indigenous societies are not timeless events in nature, that the so-called classic works confuse local cultures with universal human nature. We have had to demonstrate how ideology often makes cultural facts appear natural. We have had to use social analysis to attempt to reverse the process: to dismantle the ideological to reveal the cultural (a peculiar blend of objective arbitrariness and subjective taken-for-grantedness). The interplay between making the familiar strange and the strange familiar is part of the ongoing transformation of knowledge.

Still, the classic notion that the stability, orderliness, and equilibrium that the Eurocentric scholars described actually characterizes Indigenous society prevails in modern thought. The rhetoric of ethnography derives part of its resiliency from the Eurocentric concept of time and the illusion of a timeless Indigenous culture that it created. The classical understanding of Indigenous life, of how Indigenous people should look and act, and even what lies ahead of them, are now seen as being a part of Eurocentric time and thought. So strong are these written views that one can often predict from them what modern society demands of Indigenous people. Much too often these classic notions organize Indigenous lives and limit Indigenous futures.

The alleged timelessness of Indigenous culture creates another demon: the total demise of this culture, wherein any change in material reality is equated with the demise of Indigenous consciousness. The pioneering ethnographers achieved some insights into Indigenous consciousness, but more often they made interpretative mistakes. Central to their cultural confusion is the myth of a "primitive culture," untouched by Eurocentric influences. Following in the footsteps of their predecessors, later ethnographers made their own mistakes, as well as duplicating or replicating those of others: the cumulative snarl is difficult to untangle. What is more important is that this timelessness is a Eurocentric attempt at limiting the future—another way of forcing Indigenous culture to accept the inevitability of imitating Eurocentric modes of thought and dress.

It is important to note that many scholars, both Indigenous and non-Indigenous, have been examining similar phenomena from various perspectives. In attempting to understand Indigenous knowledge and its processes of knowing, we recognize that the existing knowledge system used in educational systems must be interrogated. This means challenging Eurocentric researchers, their methodologies, and their investigators' skill. Often this interrogation causes discomfort. Grasping the holistic structure and processes of Indigenous knowledge requires an investigator's assumptions and perspective to stretch and develop. The researcher will have to explore uncharted territory without a conventional map.

A strong critique of Eurocentrism is under way in all fields of social thought. These critiques, such as postcolonial, poststructural, and postmodern thought, reveal that the assumptions that constructed Eurocentrism are not universal: they are derived from local and artificial knowledge. Under such thought, many assumptions of Eurocentrism are being exposed as false (e.g. Rosaldo 1989; Coombe 1991; Said 1992; Blaut 1993; Noël 1994; RCAP 1996b). Moreover, critical scholars have exposed the empirical beliefs of Eurocentric history, geography, and social science, which have often gained acceptance not because they relate to existing structures but rather because Eurocentric thought only recognizes confirming evidence as valid. These critiques raise anguished discourses about knowledge and truth; discussions about respecting diversity quickly slip into paradigm maintenance. Thus, as long as Eurocentrism retains its persuasive intellectual power in academic and political realms, it will be resistant to change.

The limited awareness of Indigenous knowledge and heritage in academia indicates the biases and weakness of Eurocentric thought. Contemporary anthropologists have focused on developing a critique of ethnocentrism in both academic theory and popular culture, and have sought to develop participatory and collaborative research methodologies based on the assumption that anthropological texts are the product of dialogues between researchers and research subjects, rather than the authoritative, objective accounts of individual experts (Clifford 1983; Clifford & Marcus 1986; Marcus & Fisher 1986). Others have created a critical anthropological perspective concerned with the situated, constructed, and political processes of knowledge production, distribution, and consumption. They attempt to contribute to the development of a critical anthropology of colonial and postcolonial relations (Coombe 1991; Rosaldo 1989; Said 1992). What has emerged is an anthropology of anthropology and a recognition of the historicity of the discipline (Fox 1991; Rosaldo 1989). Critical theorists argue that the traditional liberal critique of ethnocentrism does not address the relationship of colonialism or racism (Coombe 1991; Morre 1988; Ulin 1991). They argue that the anthropologist's "canon" is not a realist's description of Indigenous peoples or their knowledge, but a history of European colonial thought (Said 1992). One of the tasks of this book is to attempt to replace the anthropologists' canon with a more realistic assessment of Indigenous knowledge.

Chapter 2

•••

What Is Indigenous Knowledge?

[P]recise universal definition, while of philosophical interest, would be nearly impossible to attain in the current state of global realities, and would in any event not contribute perceptibly to the practical aspects of defending groups from abuse. — Mr. Capotorti, Special Rapporteur, *Study on the Rights of Persons Belonging to Ethnic, Religious and Linguistic Minorities* (1991, paras. 561–62)

Indigenous knowledge is different from the internal view of the ethnographic tradition in Eurocentric thought. This difference is illustrated simply by asking the question "What is Indigenous knowledge?" No short answer exists, since this is a question about comparative knowledge and no legitimate methodology exists to answer it. In the past few centuries, the context of this question has been "What can savages know or how do they think?" It is a question loaded with Eurocentric arrogance. It continues to be a difficult question for non-Europeans to answer because Eurocentric thought has created a mysticism around Indigenous knowledge that distances the outsider from Indigenous peoples and what they know.

The first problem in understanding Indigenous knowledge from a Eurocentric point of view is that Indigenous knowledge does not fit into the Eurocentric concept of "culture." In contrast to the colonial tradition, most Indigenous scholars choose to view every way of life from two different but complementary perspectives: first as a manifestation of human knowledge, heritage, and consciousness, and second as a mode of ecological order. We can find no notion similar to "culture" in Algonquian thought. There are several sounds in Mi'kmaq that could refer to this notion. How we maintain contact with our traditions is said as *telilnuisimk*. How we maintain our consciousness is said as *telilnuo'lti'k*. How we maintain our language is said as *tlinuita'sim*. Based on our experience, we reject the concept of culture for Indigenous knowledge, heritage, and consciousness, and instead connect each Indigenous manifestation as part of a particular ecological order.

The second problem is that Indigenous knowledge is not a uniform concept across all Indigenous peoples; it is a diverse knowledge that is spread throughout different peoples in many layers. Those who are the possessors of this knowledge often cannot categorize it in Eurocentric thought, partly because the processes of categorization are not part of Indigenous thought.

The third problem is that Indigenous knowledge is so much a part of the clan, band, or community, or even the individual, that it cannot be separated from the bearer to be codified into a definition. Those who have the knowledge use it routinely, perhaps every day, and because of this, it becomes something that is a part of them and unidentifiable except in a personal context. These personal cognitive maps are created by humor, humility, tolerance, observation, experience, social interaction, and listening to the conversations and interrogations of the natural and spiritual worlds (Kawagley 1993, 18). This practical, personal, and contextual aspect of Indigenous knowledge makes it a sensitive subject of study, and discussing it out of context may be viewed as intrusive or insensitive.

Decolonizing the Eurocentric Need for Definitions

Eurocentric thought demands universal definitions of Indigenous knowledge, even though Indigenous scholars have established no common usage of the term. The quest for precision and certainty is a typical Eurocentric strategy. Eurocentric scholars impose a definition, attempt to make it apply universally, then, when it fails to comply with any universal standard by deductive logic, quibble over its meaning. This is the strategy of a language system that is not attached to an ecology or to its intelligible essences. It is a strategy explicit with the appropriating narcissism of Eurocentric thought (Livinas 1961). Using their artificial tools of classification, the colonizers attempt to Europeanize all knowledge and heritage, even when they are extending beyond their knowledge into the unknown.

Since most modern Eurocentric contexts reject the idea of intelligible essences in an ecology, they rely on arbitrary definitions that have no relationship with the life forces that Indigenous peoples use to understand life. Eurocentrism rejects the idea that the human mind can understand an ecology through these life forces. Instead, modern Eurocentric thinkers believe there are numberless ways in which they can classify ideas, objects, and events in an ecology. The system of classification and the definitions used within it are based on the desires or purposes of those who created the system. The definitions are judged to be valid if they advance the desires or purposes of the people who fabricated them, allowing them to measure, predict, or control events. Since the validity of the system rests on its ability to contribute to particular ends, no basis exists for saying that one classification system portrays the "real" world more accurately than another does. Given the principles of diffusionism and universality, however, Eurocentric thinkers automatically assume the superiority of their worldview and attempt to impose it on others, extending their definitions to encompass the whole world. Typically, this quest for universal definitions ignores the diversity of the people of the earth and their views of themselves. This destructive process has been described as "ontological imperialism" (Livinas 1961) and "cognitive imperialism" (Battiste 1986).

From the Indigenous vantage point, the process of understanding is more important than the process of classification. Tewa Pueblo educator Dr. Gregory Cajete argues that the Eurocentric system of classification limits objective knowledge of the universe. Generally speaking, Indigenous thought classifies ecological phenomena based on characteristics observed through experience; such classifications rely on a high degree of intuitive thought. Eurocentric science, in contrast, "relies more on properties that are inferred from necessary relations in the structure of the objects classified" (Cajete 1986, 124).

The Eurocentric quest for universal definitions has raised suspicion among Indigenous peoples, who do not want to be assimilated into Eurocentric categories. Indigenous people do not understand the purpose of manifesting their knowledge and heritage to Eurocentric researchers. Cajete's writings illustrate this problem. He asserts that Eurocentric anthropology cannot say that any cultural paradigm is based upon a completely rational and objective perception of reality; however, general agreement exists on three points. First, the way in which a people perceives and understands the world is directly dependent on the unique configurations of its belief system. Second, the meanings attached to natural phenomena are directly dependent on the conceptual structure of which they are a part, and this conceptual structure is highly conditioned by the people's culture and system of thought. Third, what constitutes a fact depends on the consensus of the community or group that evaluates what is real and what is not, and such consensuses are based on mutually held belief systems, rather than on rationality (Cajete 1986, 123).

Unless Eurocentric thought is willing to qualify the principle that categories are constructed by human minds for human purposes, it cannot sustain any confidence in the possibility of comparing Indigenous worldviews and languages with Eurocentric worldviews and languages. Comparison of worldviews relies on the idea that a realm of things and events exists in nature, independent of the human mind, and that the human mind is capable at some point of perceiving nature as it truly is. However, this idea is grounded in the doctrine of intelligible essences, which has been rejected by modern Eurocentric thought and replaced with the concept of human purposes. This creates a contextual incoherence in Eurocentric thought. When Eurocentric thought is faced with a choice between two different paradigms, each paradigm's ability to measure, predict, or control mediates its validity. This solution does not resolve the dilemma. Eurocentric scientists must still interpret the results of every experiment they perform and justify the methods of proof they have chosen. Since such purposes are arbitrary in conception, there are limited ways to prove better results.

Similar challenges emerge in social thought. Cajete (1986; 2000) has described this challenge. He examined how the ethnoscience movement in Eurocentric thought has generated substantial research concerning Indigenous cultures in such areas as ethnobotany, ethnopharacology, ethnozoology, ethnomedicine, ethnopsychiatry, ethnoentomology, and ethnoastronomy. All these cultural sciences have attempted to present the "native perspective," which refers to its "emic" (inside view) features. Yet, each of these sciences uses Eurocentric categories as both the framework and a point of reference. None of them respect Indigenous knowledge or the different ways in which Indigenous peoples develop their knowledge from their ecologies. Epistemologist Magorah Maruyama has argued that Native American epistemologies are in general highly "mutualistic" and oriented toward holistic and contextual processes. This orientation involves a kind of logic that is symbiotic, relational, qualitative, and interactionist, and that reflects the notion of many possible directions in the relationship between cause and effect (1978, 455–58).

The Eurocentric strategy of universal definitions and absolute knowledge has made its scholarship unable to know and respect Indigenous knowledge and heritage. To attempt to evaluate Indigenous worldviews in absolute and universal terms is irrational. Using Eurocentric analysis, one cannot make rational choices among conflicting worldviews, especially those held by others. No worldview describes an ecology more accurately than others do. All worldviews describe some parts of the ecology completely, though in their own way. No worldview has the power to describe the entire universe. Eurocentric thought must allow Indigenous knowledge to remain outside itself, outside its representation, and outside its disciplines. It cannot attempt to capture an incommensurable knowledge system in its web of purposes. Eurocentric contexts cannot do justice to the exteriority of Indigenous knowledge.

Entering Uncharted Territory

Many partial definitions of Indigenous knowledge have been offered in the literature, most given by non-Indigenous scholars. Some Eurocentric-trained Indigenous scholars have provided better insights into the relationship between Indigenous knowledge and Eurocentric knowledge. Each of these definitions has its limitations. Philosopher Douglas West clearly stated the issue:

> Any discussion of indigenous knowledge begins with a statement of qualifications and a qualification of statements. In order to appreciate the depths and meanings of indigenous knowledge, the reader should avoid the revered

> social science position of an objective "veil of ignorance." We are confused, perplexed and in awe when considering the plurality of differences inherent among indigenous knowledge. We carry the biases of centuries of interpretations and categorizations that fill the pages of academic and popular literature. (O'Meara & West 1996, 1)

Writer Martin Bell (1979) asserts that existing descriptions of Indigenous knowledge are largely defined in terms of socio-economic and spatial locations of particular groups. The director general of UNESCO (Mayor 1994, cited in Emery 1997, 4) has attempted to define Indigenous knowledge:

> The indigenous peoples of the world possess an immense knowledge of their environments, based on centuries of living close to nature. Living in and from the richness and variety of complex ecosystems, they have an understanding of the properties of plants and animals, the functions of ecosystems and the techniques for using and managing them that is particular and often detailed. In rural communities in developing countries, locally occurring species are relied on for many—sometimes all—foods, medicines, fuel, building materials and other products. Equally, people's knowledge and perceptions of the environment, and their relationship with it, are often important elements of cultural identity.

Typically, rather than attempting to understand Indigenous knowledge as a distinct knowledge system, researchers have tried to make Indigenous knowledge match the existing academic categories of Eurocentric knowledge. They have relied on these categories for comfort and security, instead of embarking on an intellectual adventure to connect more deeply with Indigenous ecologies. The viewing of Indigenous knowledge and heritage through Eurocentric categories is the result of the researchers' formal training and of their belief that these categories are universal standards. These processes cause the researchers to miss the real adventure on this journey and distract them from developing deeper insights that might lead them into a vast, unforeseen realm of knowing. For knowledge to flourish, scholars need to see Indigenous knowledge as a new *sui generis* (self-generating) path, as a new opportunity to develop greater awareness and to discover deeper truths about ecologies and their forces.

Most Eurocentric scholars begin the search for Indigenous knowledge by seeking to define its parameters. The path to Indigenous knowledge, however, does not start with race or racial knowledge, which is the most common Eurocentric false perspective. This perspective seeks to incorporate Indigenous knowledge within Eurocentric thought as a racial subset. It does this because to acknowledge Indigenous knowledge as an alternative to Eurocentric thought would limit the universal validity of the Eurocentric worldview. This bias distracts researchers from the real issue: discovering the processes of Indigenous knowledge, not what is already known.

Eurocentric structures and methods of logical entailment and causality cannot unravel Indigenous knowledge or its processes of knowing. These methodologies derive from a noun-centered language system, and they are ineffective in verb-centered Indigenous language systems. The best way to understand Indigenous knowledge is to be open to accepting different realities (however one uses this term). Indigenous peoples' worldviews are cognitive maps of particular ecosystems. As Dr. Angaayuqaq Oscar Kawagley, a Yupiaq scholar, explains in his book *A Yupiaq World View*, to have power is to be aware of your surroundings. Yupiaq cultural life is a certain way of caring for the ecological cycle (1993, 8).

In his doctoral dissertation, *Science: A Native American Perspective* (1986), and his book, *Native Science: Natural Law of Interdependence* (2000), Cajete reaches a similar conclusion. He asserts that the ethnoscience of each Indigenous people is unique in that it reflects adaptation to a certain place. Cajete defines ethnoscience as "the methods, thought processes, mindsets, values, concepts and experiences by which Native American groups understand, reflect and obtain empirical knowledge about the natural world" (1986, 123). Ethnoscience is a cognitive process by which Indigenous peoples develop strategies to make nature accessible to inquiry. Indigenous peoples differ in the methods, concepts, experiences, and values used in gaining knowledge of their ecologies, and different interpretations exist among Indigenous peoples in the application and exploitation of knowledge gained through these inquiries (1986, 124).

Strands of connectedness do exist, however, among Indigenous thought. Cajete sees these strands stretching all the way from the polar regions of North America to the tip of South America. He illustrates his point by showing how the various Indigenous teachings of the Trickster, the Sacred Twins, the Earth Mother, the Corn Mothers, the Thunderbirds, the Great Serpents, the Culture Hero, Grandmother Spider-Women, and the Tree of Life reflect similar ecological understandings. Cajete finds all these teachings reflect a cultural interpretation based on observation of processes inherent in nature. He views them as representing an Indigenous understanding of the ecology (1986, 17–18). He further asserts that the Eurocentric approach to studying human cultural systems has fragmented the unity of Indigenous worldviews into the distorted perspectives of arts, science, and culture.

Unlike others who have explored this issue of Indigenous knowledge and heritage, we are not concerned with a lack of a comprehensive definition of Indigenous knowledge. We are not creating a grand theory or a universal conceptualization of Indigenous knowledge or heritage. We are intimately aware that each Indigenous régime is characteristic of the creative adaptation of a people to an ecological order. Given the existing ecological diversity, a corresponding diversity of Indigenous languages, knowledge, and heritages exists. For any research to seek to give a comprehensive definition of Indigenous knowledge and heritage in any language system would be a massive undertaking, which would probably be misleading. Other scholars have also reached the conclusion that comprehensive definitions cannot contain the diversity of Indigenous peoples or their knowledge. As the working paper *On the Concept of "Indigenous People"* (1996a), by the chairperson-rapporteur of the UN Working Group on Indigenous Populations, Dr. Erica-Irene Daes, has concluded, the best practice is to allow Indigenous people to define themselves.

Dr. Daes, in her report on the protection of the heritage of Indigenous peoples, points out that Indigenous knowledge is "a complete knowledge system with its own concepts of epistemology, philosophy, and scientific and logical validity" (1994, para. 8). She further concludes that diverse elements of any Indigenous knowledge system "can only be fully learned or understood by means of the pedagogy traditionally employed by these peoples themselves, including apprenticeship, ceremonies and practice" (1994, para. 8). Moreover, she stresses the role of land or ecology as the Indigenous knowledge system's "central and indispensable classroom," in which the heritage of each Indigenous peoples has traditionally been taught (1994, para. 9).

Indigenous perspectives of Indigenous knowledge are not found in the literature. To learn about Indigenous perspectives requires a different method of research. For instance, Indigenous thinkers in Canada know that to acquire an Indigenous perspective on knowledge requires extended conversations with the elders of each language group. To sustain Indigenous knowledge, one must be willing to take on responsibilities associated with that knowing, especially putting the knowledge into daily practice. When an Indigenous elder says, "I know," it is a temporary reference point. If such knowledge is to be contained or if the relationship is to be sustained over time, then the elder must not just know the relationship, he or she must respectfully live it and know how to renew it.

Locating Indigenous Knowledge

Indigenous peoples regard all products of the human mind and heart as interrelated within Indigenous knowledge. They assert that all knowledge flows from the same source: the relationships between a global flux that needs to be renewed, the people's kinship with the other living creatures that share the land, and the people's kinship with the spirit world. Since the ultimate source of knowledge is the changing ecosystem itself, the art and science of a specific people manifest these relationships and can be considered as manifestations of the people's knowledge as a whole. Perhaps the closest one can get to describing unity in Indigenous knowledge is that knowledge is the expression of the vibrant relationships between the people, their ecosystems, and the other living beings and spirits that share their lands. These multilayered relationships are the basis for maintaining social, economic, and diplomatic relationships—through sharing—with other peoples. All aspects of this knowledge are interrelated and cannot be separated from the traditional territories of the people concerned. Similarly, there is no need to separate reality into categories of living and nonliving, or of renewable and nonrenewable. What tangibles and intangibles constitute the knowledge of a particular Indigenous people must be decided by the people themselves.

In Indigenous ways of knowing, the self exists within a world that is subject to flux. The purpose of these ways of knowing is to reunify the world or at least to reconcile the world to itself. Uniting these ways of knowing is necessary, as each can contribute to human development and each requires its own appropriate expression. Indigenous ways of knowing hold as the source of all teachings caring and feeling that survive the tensions of listening for the truth and that allow the truth to touch our lives. Indigenous knowledge is the way of living within contexts of flux, paradox, and tension, respecting the pull of dualism and reconciling opposing forces. In the realms of flux and paradox, "truthing" is a practice that enables a person to know the spirit in every relationship. Developing these ways of knowing leads to freedom of consciousness and to solidarity with the natural world.

Indigenous ways of knowing share the following structure: (1) knowledge of and belief in unseen powers in the ecosystem; (2) knowledge that all things in the ecosystem are dependent on each other; (3) knowledge that reality is structured according to most of the linguistic concepts by which Indigenous describe it; (4) knowledge that personal relationships reinforce the bond between persons, communities, and ecosystems; (5) knowledge that sacred traditions and persons who know these traditions are responsible for teaching "morals" and "ethics" to practitioners who are then given responsibility for this specialized knowledge and its dissemination; and (6) knowledge that an extended kinship passes on teachings and social practices from generation to generation.

In addition, many definitions of Indigenous knowledge stress that it is the principle of totality or holism. The Royal Commission on Aboriginal Peoples views Indigenous knowledge "as a cumulative body of knowledge and beliefs, handed down through generations by cultural transmission, about the relationship of living beings (including humans) with one another and their environment" (RCAP 1996b, 4:454). Cajete shows that mutualistic logic and its orientation to reciprocal causality is evidenced in most Indigenous knowledge systems. Mutual relationships exist among all forces and forms in the natural world: animals, plants, humans, celestial bodies, spirits, and natural forces. Indigenous peoples can manipulate natural phenomena through the application of appropriate practical and ritualistic knowledge. In turn, natural phenomena, forces, and other living things can affect humans. Everything affects everything else.

Cajete elaborates on the holistic aspect of Indigenous knowledge. He explains how Indigenous peoples view harmony as a dynamic and multidimensional balancing of interrelationships in their ecologies. Disturbing these interrelationships creates disharmony; balance is restored by applying appropriate actions and knowledge. Thus, knowing the complex natures of natural forces and their interrelationships is an important context for Indigenous knowledge and heritage. No separation of science, art, religion, philosophy, or aesthetics exists in Indigenous thought; such categories do not exist. Thus, Eurocentric researchers may know the name of a herbal cure and understand how it is used, but without the ceremony and ritual songs, chants, prayers, and relationships, they cannot achieve the same effect.

The Inuit illustrate the principle of the totality of knowledge. In English translations, the Inuit define their traditional knowledge as practical teaching and experience passed on from generation to generation. Their knowledge is a total way of life that comprises a system of respect, sharing, and rules governing the use of resources. It is derived from knowing the country they live in, including knowledge of the environment and the relationship between things. Inuit knowledge is rooted in the spiritual life, health, culture, and language of the people. It comes from the spirit in order to survive, and it gives credibility to the Inuit. They assert it is a holistic worldview that cannot be compartmentalized or separated from the people who hold it. It is using the heart and head together in a good way. It is dynamic, cumulative, and stable. It is the truth and reality (Environmental Assessment Workshop 1995, cited in Emery 1997).

Traditional Ecological Knowledge

As a foundation for commenting on Indigenous knowledge, we believe it will be useful to review some general aspects of Indigenous knowledge called traditional ecological knowledge. This review is based upon our own cultural experiences and on contemporary community-level research in North America—in particular, in Canada's Atlantic and Pacific coastal regions, which include boreal and temperate forests, including temperate rainforests; and in the prairie, plateau, and mountain regions of western Canada and the United States, which include scrub, savanna, and alpine forests. We believe, from discussions with scholars and leaders from other Indigenous communities in

North America and other regions, that the following observations can be generalized.

In English translation, the director of the Dene Cultural Institute in the Northwest Territories of Canada writes:

> Traditional environmental [ecological] knowledge [TEK] is a body of knowledge and beliefs transmitted through oral tradition and first-hand observation. It includes a system of classification, a set of empirical observations about the local environment, and a system of self-management that governs resource use. Ecological aspects are closely tied to social and spiritual aspects of the knowledge system. The quantity and quality of TEK varies among community members, depending on gender, age, social status, intellectual capability, and profession (hunter, spiritual leader, healer, etc.). With its roots firmly in the past, TEK is both cumulative and dynamic, building upon the experience of earlier generations and adapting to the new technological and socioeconomic changes of the present. (Emery 1997, 5–6)

The traditional ecological knowledge of Indigenous peoples is scientific, in the sense that it is empirical, experimental, and systematic. It differs in two important respects from Western science, however: traditional ecological knowledge is highly localized and it is social. Its focus is the web of relationships between humans, animals, plants, natural forces, spirits, and land forms in a particular locality, as opposed to the discovery of universal "laws." It is the original knowledge of Indigenous peoples. Indigenous peoples have accumulated extraordinarily complex models of species interactions over centuries within very small geographical areas, and they are reluctant to generalize beyond their direct fields of experience. Western scientists, by contrast, concentrate on speculating about and then testing global generalizations, with the result that they know relatively little about the complexities of specific, local ecosystems. As a consequence of these different levels of analysis, the Indigenous people who have traditionally lived within particular ecosystems can make better predictions about the consequences of any physical changes or stresses that they have previously experienced than scientists who base their forecasts on generalized models and data or indicators from relatively short-term field observations.

The localization of traditional ecological knowledge has several important spiritual, social, and legal corollaries. Ecological knowledge is conceptualized as a way of understanding the web of social relationships between a specific group of people (whether a family, clan, or tribe) and a place where they have lived since their beginning. Many Indigenous peoples speak of their knowledge in terms of the "operating instructions" for the land, given to them from time to time by the Creator and the spirit world, not just through revelations or dreams but also through frequent contacts with the minds and spirits of animals and plants. They further describe the ecosystem itself in terms of historical marriages or alliances between humans and non-humans, and among different non-human species. Hence, the present structure of the local ecosystem is the cumulative result of a large number of historical contracts, which create reciprocal obligations of kinship and solidarity among all the species and forces which co-exist in that place. The ecosystem is seen as a product of historical choices with an inherent legal structure. It is a moral and legal space characterized by negotiated order, rather than by mere chance. Interactions of species are regarded as competitive and strategic, but in a social and political sense. The need to continually renegotiate order tends to be explained as a result of the random elements in the universe, often personified as "tricksters," as well as of choices made by individual humans and non-humans. This explanation of knowledge should not be mystified. Long periods of contact with and observation of animals result in empathy and insights that are impossible to reduce to words—as most field naturalists would surely attest.

It is important to realize that there is more to traditional knowledge than the repetition, from generation to generation, of a relatively fixed body of data—or the gradual, unsystematic accumulation of new data over generations. In each generation, individuals make observations, compare their experiences with what they have been told by their teachers, conduct experiments to test the reliability of their knowledge, and exchange their findings with others. Everything that pertains to tradition, including cosmology and oral literature, is continually being revised at the individual and community levels. Indeed, we suggest that the knowledge systems of Indigenous peoples are more self-consciously empirical than those of Western scientific thought—especially at the individual level. Everyone must be a scientist to subsist by direct personal efforts as a hunter, fisher, forager, or farmer with minimal mechanical technology. Since every individual is engaged in a lifelong personal search for ecological understanding, the standard of truth in Indigenous knowledge systems is personal experience. Indigenous peoples may be suspicious of secondhand claims (which form the bulk of Eurocentric scholars' knowledge), but they are reluctant to challenge the validity of anyone's own observations.

Some examples may be useful here. A young apprentice hunter travels the land with an experienced older hunter. Learning by observation (rather than by words) what cues to use in forecasting the seasonal and daily movements of wildlife, the hunter ensures success in the hunt when animals can be intercepted reliably and with a minimum of effort. Many factors, such as time of day, temperature, humidity, the distribution of forage plants, and the movements of other species are experienced directly under varying conditions until the pupil begins to think, unconsciously, like the prey. At the same time, stories are told that explain in symbolic terms, such as kinship and alliances, the ecological relationships between the prey and other species. Eventually, the young hunter travels alone and begins to notice new connections, either because they were not observed by prior generations or because they are the result of changes in the ecosystem. Indigenous cosmologies generally describe the universe as chaotic, in the strict mathematical sense of a system defined by random as well as non-random forces. Everything is expected to change, in both predictable and unpredictable ways, thus requiring human vigilance and adaptation. The usefulness of new knowledge will be tested in practice, for instance, by trying to intercept the prey at a location where older hunters would not have looked. Success has tangible rewards, leading to prestige and opportunities to teach others.

The speed by which new knowledge can be tested and taught is suggested by a recent development in Blackfoot traditional medicine. Diabetes first appeared among Blackfoot people only seventy-five years ago, and it has now reached epidemic proportions. Within the past generation, Blackfoot traditional healers have begun to use a herbal tea that is effective in controlling the metabolic symptoms of the disease. The same plant had unrelated medicinal uses at least a century ago, so it appears that healers have been experimenting with the applications of their existing pharmacopoeia to diabetes and other new and introduced diseases. It is important to recognize that Blackfoot healers generally agree today on a single herbal remedy as the most effective; hence they have not only been experimenting, they have also been sharing their results with each other.

Thus what is traditional about traditional ecological knowledge is not its antiquity, but the way it is acquired and used. In other words, the social process of learning and sharing knowledge, which is unique to each Indigenous knowledge and heritage, lies at the heart of its traditionality. Much of this knowledge is relatively recent, but it has a social meaning and legal character entirely unlike the knowledge Indigenous peoples have acquired from settlers and industrialized societies.

Historically, Indigenous peoples not only utilized the naturally occurring biodiversity of North America for food, medicine, materials, and ceremonial and cultural life, but routinely took steps to increase the biodiversity of their territories. Indigenous peoples continue to harvest a variety of wildlife and plants for food and for materials such as cedar and ash for basketry. The role of harvesting is important in maintaining adequate nutrition (Barsh 1994; RCAP 1996a, 219ff). Indigenous peoples generally cannot afford adequate store-bought diets and are healthier in places where they have access to traditional foods. Traditional foods are also important in community feasts, in religious ceremonies, and in exchanges of gifts used to reinforce kinship ties (Robertson 1990). In the Pacific Northwest, business cannot be conducted without salmon and other traditional feast foods. In western Ontario and Manitoba, there is an essential link between Anishnabe identity and the annual harvest of *mahnomen* (wild rice). Among the Newfoundland Mi'kmaq and the Innu of Labrador, seasonal moose and caribou hunts are as central to social relations and personal identity as they are to human health. The role of marine-mammal hunting in Inuit health and culture, and the profound adverse impacts of declining harvests in the 1980s, have been reported in depth (Wenzel 1991).

Harvesting obviously involves access to places where wildlife and plants can be collected efficiently and at appropriate seasons of the year. Land ownership, fences, use-permits, and roads are major factors in determining the extent to which harvesting can be maintained. The quantity or quota that can be taken within sustainable limits is also obviously an issue, especially in the case of scarce or threatened species that are valued by non-Indigenous people for recreational uses (for example, moose and Atlantic salmon) or for aesthetic reasons (for example, harp seals). Indigenous peoples contend that they should take priority in harvesting any surplus, while others argue that Indigenous harvesting should be "equal" or else limited in its purposes (for example, for food but not for trade).

Another issue is freedom to use particular methods of capture, such as dip-nets and spears for salmon in the falls of Northwest river systems, which can have great social and cultural significance. People must also be free to use more efficient, less wasteful technologies if they choose. For example, although traditional weirs are the most efficient method of intercepting migrating salmon (Barsh 1982), there is little disagreement about the usefulness of high-powered rifles for land-mammal hunting. Freedom to trade harvested wildlife for other foods or for cash to purchase and maintain hunting outfits is another issue (Freeman 1993).

There is also the issue of quality. Indigenous peoples are concerned about avoiding health hazards from the chemical contamination of forage plants and water; for example, organochlorines bioaccumulating in marine-mammal fats. Animals' diets also affect the palatability and nutritional value of the flesh. After switching to different forage, otherwise healthy herbivores may taste different—a phenomenon surely understood by careful shoppers and chefs the world over. Hence, the integrity of the ecosystem as a whole determines the safety, nutritive content, and palatability of harvested foods.

Harvesting cannot be completely removed from the problem of human settlements. Indigenous peoples must live reasonably close to routine harvesting places. Distance involves expense as it leads to dependence on planes and motor vehicles (automobiles, snowmobiles, and power boats) and purchased fossil fuels. Even if the activity is maintained, it requires larger amounts of cash. People either need wage employment to meet this cost, reducing the time they can devote to harvesting, or they must engage in additional harvesting for sale. This was the dilemma for Inuit in the 1980s, when they were facing growing distances between hunting areas and jobs in centralized towns, as well as a declining world market for sealskins and furs.

There are additional concerns when it comes to collecting medicines. Medicinal plants and other natural material, including insects, vertebrate animals, and inorganic minerals, are frequently found in small, highly sensitive niches such as stream margins, marshes, and isolated stands of ancient trees. The medicinal potency of these materials can be affected by the nature of the growth substrate, associations with other plant species, and the time and season of harvesting. The issue is not simply one of continued access to those places where medicinal species flourish, but access to high-potency gathering sites at the proper seasons—and the protection of these sites from chemical contamination or disturbances. Water quality—a cross-cutting issue for all the concerns raised by Indigenous peoples—is particularly relevant to medicine.

There have been few thorough studies of medicinal ecology in North America. Experience elsewhere suggests that medicines are dispersed in patches throughout Indigenous peoples' territories, so that injury to any associated ecosystem or domain is likely to destroy part of the pharmacopoeia and adversely affect peoples' health (Anyinam 1995). In the case of the Warao of Venezuela, for instance, 292 drugs are prepared from 100 species (Wilbert & Haiek 1991).

Indigenous knowledge is based on awareness, familiarity, conceptualization, and beliefs acquired about an ecosystem. Its relationships with an ecosystem are maintained by accumulating experiences, conducting non-formal experiments, and developing intimate understandings of the given consciousness and language, at a specific location and during a specific period of time. Also, Indigenous knowledge is not static but, like the shifting dynamics of particular ecologies, changes over time. It is a learned way of looking at the world that may have different forms of acquisition, transmission, and manifestation for different Indigenous peoples.

The Transmission of Indigenous Knowledge

Where Indigenous knowledge survives, it is transmitted primarily through symbolic and oral traditions. Indigenous languages are the means for communicating the full range of human experience and are critical to the survival of any Indigenous people. These languages provide direct and powerful ways of understanding Indigenous knowledge. They are the critical links between sacred knowledge and the skills required for survival.

Since languages house the lessons and knowledge that constitute the cognitive-spiritual powers of groups of people in specific places, Indigenous peoples view their languages as forms of spiritual identity. Indigenous languages are thus sacred to Indigenous peoples. They provide the deep cognitive bonds that affect all aspects of Indigenous life. Through their shared language, Indigenous people create a shared belief in how the world works and what constitutes proper action. Sharing these common ideals creates the collective cognitive experience of Indigenous societies, which is understood as Indigenous knowledge. Without Indigenous languages, the lessons and the knowledge are lost.

Anguished by the historical record of residential schools, by missionary invasion in communities, and by cognitive-imperialistic public schooling, Indigenous peoples have testified repeatedly about the importance of their languages and to the need to arrest their erosion (AFN 1988, 1990, 1992; Standing Committee on Aboriginal Affairs 1990; RCAP 1996b). Eli Taylor, an elder from the Sioux Valley First Nations in Manitoba, eloquently explains the importance of maintaining Indigenous languages:

> Our Native language embodies a value system about how we ought to live and relate to each other. . . . [I]t gives a name to relations among kin, to roles and responsibilities among family members, to ties with the broader clan group. . . . [T]here are no English words for these relationships. . . . Now, if you destroy our languages you not only break down these relationships, but you also destroy other aspects of our Indian way of life and culture, especially those that describe man's connection with nature, the Great Spirit, and the order of things. Without our languages, we will cease to exist as a separate people. (AFN 1992, 14)

Indigenous languages are not only vital links to Indigenous knowledge, they are also descriptive of Indigenous peoples' relationships with their ecosystems. Knowing an ecosystem is not a knowing derived from curiosity or the need to control, but rather a knowing derived from caring about other people and about the world. Fundamental to Indigenous knowledge is the awareness that beyond the immediate sensible world of perception, memory, imagination, and feelings lies another world from which knowledge, ability, or medicine is derived and on which Indigenous peoples depend to survive and flourish. The complementary modes of knowing and caring about the sensory and the spiritual realms inform the essence of Indigenous knowledge. This way of knowing has been continually transmitted in the oral tradition from the spirits to the elders and from the elders to the youth through spiritual teachings (Battiste 1986).

The process of cognitive transmission reveals another important aspect of Indigenous knowledge: its transmission is intimate and oral; it is not distant or literate. Indigenous peoples view their languages as forms of spiritual identity. In them are the lessons and knowledge that are the cognitive-spiritual power of a certain group of people in a specific place, passed on through the elders for their survival. Any attempt to change Indigenous language is an attempt to modify or destroy Indigenous knowledge and the people to whom this knowledge belongs.

For example, the Mi'kmaw language is more than just a knowledge base, it is essential for the survival of the Mi'kmaq. It reflects the Mi'kmaw philosophy of how we shall live with one another, how we shall treat each other, and how the world fits together. We all live in a circle of life and within the circle we are all dependent on each other and are in a constant relationship with each other. These processes are illustrated by the teachings, as translated into English, quoted in the introduction to this book. This story begins to explain ecological relations and how the Creator wanted the Mi'kmaq to learn.

A linguistic analysis of the Mi'kmaw language offers a first look at the critical elements of Mi'kmaw thought. Mi'kmaq is a verb-based language that focuses on the processes, cycles, and interrelationships of all things (Ingles in process). Unlike English and its related languages, which are noun-based, Mi'kmaq identifies objects and concepts in terms of their use or their relationship to other things in an active process. This is similar to the Lakota concept of *nigila* of "that which dwells in everything" and the concept of *mitakuye oyasin* or "I am related to all that is" (Dooling 1989, 171). The Mi'kmaw language resonates with relations and relationships, for these are important to our total survival. The Mi'kmaq hold that all things are connected. Therefore, all of us must depend on each other and help each other as a way of life, for that is what it means to be in balance and harmony with the earth. If we do not care about each other and about the animals, about the plants and their survival, about the trees and their survival, then we will not survive ourselves for very long. Thus a strong element of the socialization of children is built around family and extended family relationships, and around sharing and respect.

The extended family is the base of Mi'kmaw knowledge. It is related to Maori concept of *whakapapa,* which can be translated as "kinship" (Roberts & Wills 1998, 45). In a Mi'kmaw community, a family is not just a mother and a father and siblings, it is a larger set of relationships that includes grandparents, godparents, aunts and uncles, and cousins. In fact, a whole community becomes one's relations. Each child is special and each child will receive the protection of many significant others, who will nurture the child through the child's growing years.

Godparents are especially important. A godmother is equal to a mother in Mi'kmaw culture, just as a godfather is equal to a father. It is believed that one cannot be saved nor can one survive without a godmother or godfather

(Gould, personal communication, July 1992). A godparent or *kekunit* is a person to whom the parent turns to seek traditional teachings, advice, and help with the raising of the child. The relationships are fostered with love, attention, gifts, and sharing of time together. At each milestone in a child's life, he or she has parents and his or her own special set of godparents to share birthdays, holidays, and the child's spiritual growth. A godparent will be there always, even when there is a breakdown in the family, or when at adolescence a youth seeks his or her independence.

The family helps the child to form his or her Mi'kmaw consciousness and identity. From the moment of conception, a child is called *mijuaji'j* or "child," for there is no word in the Mi'kmaw language for "fetus." The oral traditions transmit the Mi'kmaw worldview. These teachings offer essential support and good advice for the mother and her child. Elders continue to offer much advice and information about the responsibilities of the new mother to herself and to her child. She is reminded gently how to behave appropriately because the health of her child will be determined by how she behaves during her pregnancy and how she copes with change. These events may help or hurt her, and thus her child. When the child comes into the world, the extended family offers support and facilitates the transition of the child into the community and the transmission of heritage to the child. The most important early knowledge passed on to the child is the value of relationships. Children soon come to know all the people around them and look to them for love and guidance.

Mi'kmaw society is an extended community of relations in which dialogue and togetherness are valued and respected. Children grow in an adult-centered world in which they are objects of everyone's attention. At all gatherings, at all events of the Mi'kmaw people, one will find our elders and our children. They are ever-present, talking, listening, and participating in their community in the context of the Mi'kmaw culture.

The language-acquisition process of a Mi'kmaw child begins in a rich language environment of gregarious people. The mother at home with her child will usually have an unlimited number of face-to-face encounters with other people during the day. They will visit or be visited. Since all adult women are referred to as *Sukwis* or "Auntie," a child may not know until much later who are the direct descendants of his or her own family. If a mother finds employment, then an auntie will come in, and with unemployment so high on our reserves, fathers will assuredly be there, as well as uncles, brothers, and sisters. In this environment of Mi'kmaw speakers, the child will have many language models, some of whom may speak English as well as Mi'kmaq, although in many families the Mi'kmaw language is preferred and wholly encouraged. Children's patterns of visiting will reinforce relationships and bonding, and expose them to bilingual environments.

Language acquisition is the traditional way of transmitting knowledge. The Mi'kmaw language is rich in prefixes and suffixes that enable a verb to assume multiple meanings. Since the language is so descriptive, it encourages a tremendous scale of perceptual observations, which are reflected in words that can be made into verbs or adjectives to describe seemingly everything. The Mi'kmaq combine a multiplicity of perceptual details with their wonderful sense of humor to create lively dialogues full of laughter and insight. The descriptive nature of the language makes teasing and storytelling especially vivid.

The Mi'kmaw perception of and attention to the environment and to the people, animals, and things in that environment are important to the survival of the Mi'kmaq. The people have enriched their perceptions of their environment and each other so that the slightest variation is noticed. Patterns of season, of nature, of animals, birds, and fish are acknowledged and any variations noted, as are the individual traits and gifts of each person. These perceptions are important to the survival of the people and to their connectedness with one another.

In the traditional theory of the transmission of the language and the heritage of the Mi'kmaq, Mi'kmaw families seek to understand their children's gifts and to enhance those gifts. From the time a child is conceived, there is an acceptance that the child's spirit has also been conceived. There is no notion of a *tabula rasa* or blank slate from which that spirit will grow. Rather, each person has a unique spirit that is predetermined before his or her body grows into it. The full acceptance that babies have feelings and attitudes that are vibrant and rich toward life is evident in the banter Mi'kmaw adults engage in with newborns. Even though the child may not have the vocabulary or the control of the language to express his or her attitudes and feelings, Mi'kmaq provide the child with an awareness of his or her feelings and attitudes when talking to the child.

For example, an aunt or uncle will approach a newborn with tenderness and love, and will offer an inferred child's point of view. Using multiple facial expressions and vocal tones that capture the baby's attention, the adult will relate the child's view. The baby's body movements affirm that the baby is thinking, responding, and agreeing. The adult in the interaction will interpret these movements and sounds, and the conversation will continue with the baby. The baby's attitudes and values will be confirmed and reinforced, while the community of onlookers will smile and laugh at the notions expressed in the monologue. As adults interpret the baby's attitudes and values as expressed in the baby's body language, they are reinforcing their own cultural worldview in the language context of the Mi'kmaw community. Thus, the process of language acquisition evolves from a ready store of feelings, attitudes, and beliefs shared in the intimate circle of family, friends, and babies.

In the Mi'kmaw transmission model, children establish who they are and what values they embrace through the core of adults and families with whom they share face-to-face encounters. It is important that adults make regular visits to people because this is at the core of community culture. Every person is a teacher. This reinforces and confirms relationships. A child will grow up in this adult population with laughing, teasing, sharing, enjoying, gossiping, and all the while the child is learning about his or her heritage, community, and language by listening, hearing, and being constantly engaged in conversation. The child will be protected, looked after, and given attention, hugged or simply sniffed on the head, which is a Mi'kmaw sign of affection.

Most children have nicknames or endearment terms, as that is the Mi'kmaw way of showing affection for children, and these names will follow the children throughout their lives. These names are also unique to each child and demonstrate the child's individuality, which is fostered in the community culture. It is in this affectionate, loving, and caring family that the child begins his or her journey into the world.

As children approach toddlerhood and begin to explore their environment, adults begin to offer them some flexibility beyond this core group of adults. But their exploration is guided carefully by older siblings, by both girls and boys. Children are given some freedom to explore, and a wide array of experiences and nurtured independence help them to learn. Mi'kmaw adults recognize that guided discovery helps children to learn that there are dangers and how to cope with them. Children come to know about the complexities of their environment as they are allowed to explore in the company of older children, who help them come to know these things.

About the time children are five or six years old, they begin to move outside the adult- and sibling-centered group. Always, they are surrounded by a group of older children. Within these new groups, they move in clearly delineated spaces in the neighborhood. Adults will have warned the children about vehicles, ponds, and other areas that are not child-proofed.

Within that core group of children who play together, there is at least one child who will intuitively understand that as the oldest in that group, he or she has special teaching responsibilities toward the others, especially toward the younger children. Oldest or older children develop a keen sense of being responsible for the younger members of their playgroup. If something happens to a young child while in the group, the mother or father, aunt or godparent will ask: "Who was in charge here? Who was there when this happened? How was it that that person didn't correct this before it has to come to me? Somebody else out there should have been correcting this." And if they say, "Oh, there was someone who told them not to do it, but they didn't listen!" then the parent will remind the children that they have to listen to the oldest in the group.

Mi'kmaq constantly remind children the oldest in the group is the teacher or "boss." So when children begin to explore beyond the bounds of the immediate family home, they begin to realize there is always someone in charge and those in charge are given the right to chastise the children for their behavior. So in the large network of the Mi'kmaw community, adults are responsible for other children who are in their view. When someone sees something happening, that person cannot walk away with the thought, "They aren't my children," but rather that person has the responsibility to intervene.

Around the ages of five to fourteen, Mi'kmaw children socialize with each other in small groups that move from peer house to peer house. In every household there will be a group of children carrying on diverse activities. They cross ages and sexes, until the girls turn eleven or twelve, when they start having their own groups of friends. Boys seem to have fewer age separations in their groups, although by the time they are thirteen or fourteen, they spend much more time in age-specific activities. But in Mi'kmaw communities they all learn early the importance of responsibility and cooperation within a group. The children are thus well socialized in group behaviors and group-conformed norms.

Children are taught early that mothers and grandmothers are to be especially honored and respected. Children are taught never to talk back to their parents, and to respect their advice and suggestions. In addition, children learn early that there are certain teachings or customs that must be obeyed. One such custom is that one should never cross the path or walk over the feet of an elder. At any costs, children must find another route around the elder or stay put until the situation changes.

As our children begin to turn into adolescents, new teachings begin. The teachings focus on dignity and integrity. These discussions revolve around how to live in a good way, what Mi'kmaq consider is right and wrong, and what are considered appropriate and valued community norms and behaviors. Mi'kmaq assume that children will have socialized these ideas well before adolescence, which is a time when our children begin to exercise personal choice. When a Mi'kmaw adolescent does something he or she should not do, the uncles, aunts, and godparents intervene to clarify values with the adolescent. It is acknowledged that by the time children are thirteen or fourteen, they have mostly solidified the values that will influence their choices; however, through teasing, the family shares their values and expectations and attempts to bring the young person in line with their expectations.

The Mi'kmaq are deeply spiritual people who throughout their daily lives demonstrate their spiritual consciousness. Spirituality is a strong part of a child's development and is evident in all aspects of Mi'kmaw life. The formal and ceremonial rituals of spirituality have been imbedded in Christian traditions, although there have been changes occurring as Mi'kmaq search for their identity through pan-Indian spirituality.

Mi'kmaw people share an alternative vision of society. While it is compatible with universally recognized human rights, its stress is on wholeness and relationships, in particular, on the responsibilities among families, clans, communities, and nations. At the minimal level, Mi'kmaw thought teaches that everyone and everything are part of a whole in which the parts are interdependent on each other. Each person has a right to a personal identity as a member of a community but also has responsibilities to other life forms and to the ecology of the whole. Thus Mi'kmaw thought values the group over the individual and the extended family over the immediate or biological family. It is inconceivable to a Mi'kmaw that a human being could exist without a family or a kinship regulation. There are no strangers in Mi'kmaw thought. "Guests" within their territory were typically assigned to a local family or clan for education and responsibilities. Such kinship is a necessary part of Indigenous peace and good order. Within the vast fabric of families, clans, and confederacies, every person stands in a specific, personal relationship to the other.

The Indigenous order of kinship implies a distinct form of rights. Everyone has the right to give and receive according to his or her choices. Those who give the most freely and generously enjoy the strongest claims to sharing, and these claims are directed to their relations, not to an outside community, state, or nation. Instead of a state, the Mi'kmaq recognize a web of reciprocal relationships among individuals.

In the Mi'kmaw Indigenous order, rights are the freedom to be what each person was created to be. Because no person knows what that path is for another, each person has the independence and security to discover that path without interference. From infancy, children are born into a family and surrounded by relatives and friends. Children are constantly reminded to respect and to respond to the feelings of all of their kin. They are praised for showing sensitivity and generosity to others; they are teased for being self-centered, rude, or acquisitive; but they are rarely punished. Childhood experiences of intense collective support and attention combine with self-discipline and responsibilities to create a personality that is cooperative and independent, self-restrained yet individualistic, attuned to the feelings of other people but non-intrusive. At the same time, the Mi'kmaq are left free to discover their gifts and talents and choose their courses of action by their personal choices and integrity. This kind of personality is compatible with the kind of social order that strives for consensus but tolerates a great deal of diversity and nonconformity (Little Bear 2000).

The Mi'kmaw worldview is a consensual paradigm in which the ideals of self-discipline and tribal self-determination can be manifested. Because of shared philosophies about the animacy of all things that are interrelated and interdependent, citizenship in a tribal community is governed by a collective consciousness of what is good. In this way, each person is connected in a multitude of reciprocal relationships—some derived by birth and others by socialization—to a holistic worldview or consciousness.

Imbued within this consciousness, the Mi'kmaw individual is seen as vital to the collective, and the consciousness of that collective is seen as vital to the sustenance of the whole. Culture then is the collective agreement of the members of the society about what is accepted, valued, and sanctioned—both positively and negatively—and about what will be the society's protocol and beliefs. The informal agreement says: "This is how we are going to run our society." Philosophies and worldviews are the theoretical aspects of cultures, while customs and ways of doing things are the practical and functional applications of philosophies and worldviews (Little Bear 2000). Language is vital to the whole collective as it is the repository of the collective knowledge and awareness of society.

In this collective, each person has both rights and advantages from being part of the whole but also has obligations and responsibilities that define membership and citizenship. Further responsibilities build from one's relationships to oneself and to others embraced in the whole. To oneself, one is responsible for recognizing and developing one's talents and gifts, and for cultivating and mastering these gifts in order to build a secure foundation to attain self-realization. As one understands oneself—spiritually, mentally, physically, and emotionally—one becomes centered and focused, and thus becomes a vital force in enabling others to do the same. Wholeness speaks to the totality of creation in which the welfare of the group is the locus of the consciousness as opposed to the welfare of the individual. Non-interference is respect for the wholeness, totality, and knowledge of others, and therefore, each person must be allowed independence to find his or her own path and purpose.

To others, each person has responsibilities and obligations. These responsibilities support the social values of sharing. They contribute to the good feelings of the group through humor and support for the sustenance and maintenance of the interconnected and interdependent whole. This whole necessarily contains many concentric circles, among which are those that embrace the cycles of nature and the life that it supports. Since everything is more or less animate, everything has spirit and knowledge. The social value of sharing manifests itself in the relationships of the whole. These relationships result from interactions with the group and with all of creation. Since all things in nature are interrelated and interdependent, it is vital that each person views his or her relationships not just with other humans but with all of nature. Each person has an individual responsibility to sustain the renewable resources that enable the whole to survive.

Part II

•••

Towards an Understanding of the Rights of Indigenous Peoples to Their Knowledge and Heritage

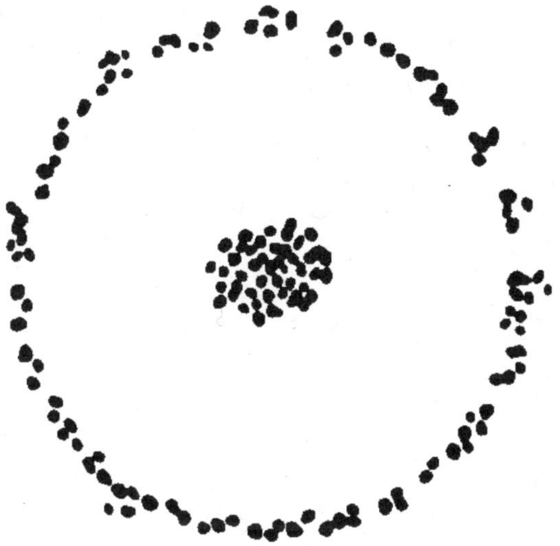

One of the characteristics of our contemporary world is the domination of men [and women] by strong centralized nation States which have the power to increase cultural uniformity and homogeneity within their borders and outside. While such cultural uniformity and homogeneity is understandable from the point of view of the political and economic interest of the ruling groups of such societies, means have to be found to mobilize those cultural traditions, the richness of which can provide people with a sense of belonging to coherent groups and which can contribute to the development of a sense of personal identity in the face of forces which often tend to alienate or estrange men [and women] from the organized centres of power. . . . The rights to culture include the possibility for each man [or woman] to obtain the means of developing his [or her] personality, through his [or her] direct participation in creation of human values, and of becoming, in this way, responsible for his [or her] situation, whether local or on a world scale. — UNESCO, *Cultural Rights as Human Rights* (1970, 106–7)

Chapter 3

•••

The Concept of Indigenous Heritage Rights

> *The effective protection of the heritage of the indigenous peoples of the world benefits all humanity. Cultural diversity is essential to the adaptability and creativity of the human species as a whole.*
>
> *To be effective, the protection of indigenous peoples' heritage should be based broadly on the principle of self-determination, which includes the right and the duty of indigenous peoples to develop their own cultures and knowledge systems, and forms of social organization.* — Principles and Guidelines for the Protection of the Heritage of Indigenous Peoples (1995, arts. 1 and 2)

Human societies and artificial states are slowly beginning to understand the global damage wrought by colonization. Beginning in the fifteenth century, colonization led to the rapid appropriation by European empires of Indigenous peoples' lands and natural resources, as well as to the subjugation of Indigenous nations. But the dominance and oppression did not end here. European empires also acquired Indigenous knowledge of plants for medicines and food. The discovery of maize and potato, for example, made it possible to feed the growing urban concentrations of laborers needed to launch Europe's industrial revolution (Weatherford 1988; 1992). As industrialization continued, European tastes turned to the acquisition of tribal art and the study of exotic cultures, despoiling Indigenous peoples of their sciences, ideas, and arts. Indigenous peoples did not benefit from this systematic confiscation of their knowledge; rather they were dominated and oppressed and became the poorest peoples in the colonized areas.

Many previously colonized societies are seeking to end the reign of Eurocentric singularity by building postcolonial diversity and equality. Yet Indigenous scholars, peoples, and institutions are struggling to displace the systemic discrimination that dominates modern worldviews. Despite the implementation of constitutional reforms to correct the legacies of colonialism, systemic discrimination persists. It is manifested in all institutions, policies, and law; its assumptions, practices, and singular viewpoints are so common that they appear to be natural, neutral, and justified. Because of these discriminatory worldviews, modern nation-states are unable to comply with international treaties and calls for national constitutional reform. This has serious consequences for Indigenous peoples.

By denying dignity, equality, and respect to Indigenous peoples, colonialism has created a violent world (UNESCO 1945, 93). World War II was the boldest manifestation of this legacy. When this war was over, the peoples of the world created the United Nations to remedy this toxic worldview. The UN Charter was a victims' rights document. It asserted the equality of all humans without distinction of any kind—race, color, sex, language; religion, political affiliation, or other opinion; natural or social origins, property, birth, or other status. It established a new standard for challenging government policy and led to the creation of multilateral international human rights treaties and related conventions.

Despite these efforts discrimination remains prevalent in most societies, and it takes many cognitive and pragmatic forms. Few definitions of discrimination exist and the definitions that do exist are often inconsistent. The International Convention on the Elimination of All Forms of Racial Discrimination (1965), ratified by Canada in 1970, states that discrimination is "a distinction, exclusion, restriction or preference which is 'based on' one of a number of specified grounds, and which has the purpose or the effect of nullifying or impairing the right of every person to full and equal recognition and exercise of . . . human rights and freedoms" (Tarnopolsky & Pentney 1985, 4-3E).

One of Eurocentrism's discriminations involved representing Indigenous peoples as savages who lived in a state of primal anarchy without any culture, society, or laws (Hobbes 1651, 87–88). The question of Indigenous humanity has been a subject of discussion since Greek and Roman times. One of the legacies of imperial Rome—with its idea of *civitas,* barbarians, and conquest—was the enslavement of Indigenous peoples. In the great Christian debates of the conquistador élite in Spain at the beginning of colonization (1530–50), the Vitorian–De Las Casasian idea of the Indians as human was to confront Aristotle's theory of natural slavery. In 1651, the philosopher Thomas Hobbes's discussion of "the state of nature" became the foundation upon which Eurocentric discussions of government and laws were built. Eurocentric colonialism embellished the Indigenous savage as a terrifying repository of negative values to justify its ancient wrongs and vast privileges, and those who were attempting to construct a rational theory of the state began from the dichotomy between Indigenous peoples in a uncivilized state of nature and an antithetical civilized society. This false dichotomy allowed the colonizers to rationalize their disregard of Indigenous human rights. When the missionary and educational efforts at assimilation failed, the colonizers saw Indigenous peoples as degenerates stuck in an irreversibly primitive condition. This rationalization projected Indigenous peoples into the past, created the vanishing-race theory, and allowed colonial legal systems to ignore Indigenous human and treaty rights.

The processes of colonization are continuing in all parts of the world at new levels. States and corporations are expanding their activities into regions previously considered remote, inaccessible, or worthless, such as deserts, Arctic tundra, mountain peaks, and rainforests. The victimization of Indigenous peoples in these newly exploited areas has renewed Europeans' interest in acquiring Indigenous peoples' arts, cultures, and sciences. Tourism in Indigenous areas is growing, along with the commercialization of Indigenous arts and the looting of archeological sites and shrines. At the same time, the Green Revolution, biotechnology, and the demand for new medicines to combat cancer and AIDS are resulting in an intensified interest in collecting the medical, botanical, and ecological knowledge of Indigenous peoples.

The fact that many of these peoples are in jeopardy has been advanced as a justification for acquiring their knowledge even more rapidly. There is an urgent need, then, for measures to enable Indigenous peoples to retain or assert control over their remaining cultural and intellectual, as well as natural, wealth so that they have the possibility of survival and self-development. These issues have created reforms in international law, in Eurocentric intellectual, religious, and cultural property régimes, and in research methods surrounding Indigenous knowledge and heritage. By defining who are Indigenous and articulating their rights to their heritage, the United Nations and Indigenous peoples are seeking to eliminate the vast discrimination against them and their inherent human and legal rights.

International Definition of Indigenous

All the world's six thousand to ten thousand original cultures were Indigenous, but most of them were absorbed during the growth of nation-states. Some survive as minorities that are identifiable or that self-identify as culturally distinct groups, but many no longer maintain distinct communities within distinct territories. It is not always clear whether a particular group is a minority or an Indigenous people, and the difference is largely a matter of perspective and degree.

There is no simple or precise definition of Indigenousness that applies equally well to all countries. Studies by two UN legal experts, José Martínez Cobo (1986/7) and Dr. Erica-Irene Daes (1996a), both focused on aboriginality (being the first on the land), cultural distinctiveness, and self-identification. The chair of the Working Group on Indigenous Populations, Dr. Erica-Irene Daes, has stated that the concept of "Indigenous" is not capable of a precise, inclusive definition that can be applied in the same manner to all regions of the world. She explained:

> [T]he international discussion of the concept of "indigenous" evolved, from the late nineteenth century until the establishment of the Working Group in 1982, within the framework of European languages, notably English, Spanish, and German. English and Spanish share a common root in the Latin term indigenae, which was used to distinguish between persons who were born in a particular place and those who arrived from elsewhere (*advenae*). The French term *"autochthone"* has, by comparison, Greek roots and, like the German term *"Ursprung"*, suggests that the group to which it refers was the first to exist in the particular location. Hence, the semantic roots of the terms historically used in modern international law share a single conceptual element: priority in time. (1996a, para. 10)

Within the linguistic framework of European colonization, Daes noted that the term "Indigenous" acquired an implicit element of race (1996a, para. 11).

International law has recognized Indigenous populations. For example, article 22 of the Covenant of the League of Nations required each member of the league to accept a "sacred trust of civilization." This trust was the duty of promoting the well-being and development of the "Indigenous population" of those "colonies and territories" that remained under their control. Hence, the covenant used the term "Indigenous" to distinguish between colonial powers and peoples who were living under colonial domination. The covenant also used colonial domination and institutional capacity as integral factors in determining the degree of supervision that was appropriate to particular territories and peoples.

Article 73 of the Charter of the United Nations (1945) refers to "territories whose peoples have not yet attained a full measure of self-government" rather than to "Indigenous populations." The use of the category of "peoples" evidences a shift from a geographical concept to a legal category. The change infers the application of the principle of self-determination to include non-dominant groups within the boundaries of independent states.

In 1949, the General Assembly of the United Nations began studying the condition of these peoples. In its resolution 275(III), the United Nations recommended a study of the conditions of the "Indigenous population and other underdeveloped social groups" of the Americas to promote their integration and development. In Mr. J. Martínez Cobo's *Study of the Problem of Discrimination Against Indigenous Populations,* the special rapporteur of the UN Sub-Commission on Prevention of Discrimination and Protection of Minorities offered a cautious, preliminary analysis:

> Indigenous communities, peoples and nations are those which, having a historical continuity with pre-invasion and pre-colonial societies that developed on their territories, consider themselves distinct from other sectors of the

> societies now prevailing in those territories, or parts of them. They form at present non-dominant sectors of society and are determined to preserve, develop and transmit to future generations their ancestral territories, and their ethnic identity, as the basis of their continued existence as peoples, in accordance with their own cultural patterns, social institutions and legal systems. (1986/7, para. 379)

This definition combines the element of cultural distinctiveness; the experience of colonialism, discrimination, or marginalization; and the desire of Indigenous peoples to continue their cultural integrity into the future.

The International Labour Organization, in its Convention on Indigenous and Tribal Peoples in Independent Countries (1989), defines both "Indigenous" and "tribal peoples." "Indigenous peoples" are defined in terms of their distinctiveness, as well as their descent from the inhabitants of their territory "at the time of conquest or colonization or the establishment of present state boundaries." "Tribal peoples" are defined as those people "whose social, cultural and economic conditions distinguish them from other sections of the national community, and whose status is regulated wholly or partially by their own customs or traditions or by special laws or regulations." However, article 1.2 of the convention provides that "self-identification" shall be a fundamental criterion when determining the status of particular groups.

The inseparability of cultural distinctiveness and territory from the concept of "Indigenous" was noted by the 1992 UN Conference on Environment and Development in Rio de Janeiro, Brazil, in paragraph 26.1 of Agenda 21, which was adopted by a consensus of member-states:

> Indigenous people and their communities have a historical relationship with their lands and are generally descendants of the original inhabitants of those lands.
>
> The centrality of land tenure systems and ecological knowledge to the knowledge and heritages of indigenous peoples was reaffirmed, again by consensus, at the International Conference on Population and Development at Cairo. (1992)

The chairperson-rapporteur of the Working Group on Indigenous Populations, Dr. Erica-Irene Daes, was compelled to conclude that

> any inconsistency or imprecision in previous efforts to clarify the concept of "indigenous" was not a result of a lack of adequate scientific or legal analysis, but due to the efforts of some Governments to limit its globality, and of other Governments to build a high conceptual wall between Indigenous and "peoples" and/or "Non-Self-Governing Territories". No one has succeeded

> in devising a definition of "indigenous" which is precise and internally valid as a philosophical matter, yet satisfies demands to limit its regional application and legal implications. All past attempts to achieve both clarity and restrictiveness in the same definition have in fact resulted in greater ambiguity. (1996a, para. 73)

The chairperson-rapporteur, with the assistance of Indigenous legal experts, members of the academic family, legal experts, and modern international organizations and legal experts, established four relevant factors that inform the concept of "Indigenous peoples":

> (a) Priority in time, with respect to the occupation and use of a specific territory;
> (b) The voluntary perpetuation of cultural distinctiveness, which may include the aspects of language, social organization, religion and spiritual values, modes of production, laws and institutions;
> (c) Self-identification, as well as recognition by other groups, or by State authorities, as a distinct collectivity; and
> (d) An experience of subjugation, marginalization, dispossession, exclusion or discrimination, whether or not these conditions persist. (Daes 1996a, para. 69)

The chairperson-rapporteur cautioned that these foregoing factors may be present, to a greater or lesser degree, in different regions and in different national and local contexts. Any definition must be applied in the context of national history and local peoples' own aspirations. As such, they may provide some general guidance to reasonable decision making in practice (Daes 1996a, paras. 69–70).

Few countries keep detailed or reliable statistics on Indigenous peoples, and those statistics that do exist are not based on the same definition of "indigenous." At best we can make a conservative estimate of the global number and distribution of Indigenous peoples as a starting point for discussion. Indigenous people worldwide number at least 200 million, of whom about 15 percent live in the Americas, and 75 percent in southern and southeast Asia. A larger figure, perhaps as high as 500 million, would be possible if tribal peoples in China, former Soviet central Asia, and western Asia were included.

North and South American Indians, Aboriginal Australians, and the Maori of New Zealand clearly satisfy the criteria of aboriginality, cultural distinctiveness, and self-identification. In southern and southeast Asia and China, many groups that regard themselves as Indigenous are less clear-cut, and their status is disputed by the countries in which they live. By contrast, India includes all members of particular "scheduled" ethnic and linguistic groups as "tribal" regardless of where or how they live. By this standard, one-fifth of India's total population is tribal or Indigenous. Africa poses problems of definition, because most Africans consider themselves Indigenous people who have achieved decolonization and self-determination. Yet many relatively small nomadic herding and hunter-gatherer societies such as the Tuareg (in Niger), Maasai (in Kenya), Mbuti (in the Congo), and San (in southern Africa's Kalahari) have been displaced and oppressed ("internally colonized") by ethnically unrelated African peoples who have been their neighbors for a thousand years and longer. The Ogoni of Nigeria claimed to be an Indigenous people during their land struggle with Shell Oil. Ogoni poet and dramatist Ken Saro Wiwa was executed by the Nigerian authorities for treason after he went to the United Nations to promote the rights of the Ogoni as an Indigenous people (Barsh 1999).

Indigenous Knowledge and Heritage

The failure of Eurocentric philosophy to study Indigenous knowledge has led some researchers to the conclusion that it is both simpler and more appropriate to refer to Indigenous knowledge as the collective heritage of Indigenous peoples. Heritage is broadly defined as everything that belongs to the distinct identity of a people and which is theirs to share, if they wish, with other peoples. This broad definition includes all those things that international law regards as the creative production of human thought and craftsmanship, such as songs, stories, scientific knowledge, and artworks. However, the definition also includes inheritances from the past and from nature, such as human remains, natural features of the landscape, and naturally occurring species of plants and animals with which a people has long been connected.

With the assistance of many Indigenous organizations and peoples, UN Special Rapporteur Dr. Erica-Irene Daes has presented an operational definition of Indigenous knowledge and heritage. The Principles and Guidelines for the Protection of the Heritage of Indigenous Peoples (1995) merge the concepts of Indigenous knowledge and heritage into a definition of the heritage of Indigenous peoples:

11. The heritage of indigenous peoples is comprised of all objects, sites and knowledge the nature or use of which has been transmitted from generation to generation, and which is regarded as pertaining to a particular people or its territory. The heritage of an indigenous people also includes objects, knowledge and literary or artistic works which may be created in the future based upon its heritage.
12. The heritage of indigenous peoples includes all moveable cultural property as defined by the relevant conventions of UNESCO; all kinds

of literary and artistic works such as music, dance, song, ceremonies, symbols and designs, narratives and poetry; all kinds of scientific, agricultural, technical and ecological knowledge, including cultigens, medicines and the rational use of flora and fauna; human remains; immoveable cultural property such as sacred sites, sites of historical significance, and burials; and documentation of indigenous peoples' heritage on film, photographs, videotape, or audiotape.

13. Every element of an indigenous peoples' heritage has traditional owners, which may be the whole people, a particular family or clan, an association or society, or individuals who have been specially taught or initiated to be its custodians. The traditional owners of heritage must be determined in accordance with indigenous peoples' own customs, laws and practices.

It should be pointed out that these principles and guidelines are drafted in the nature of a declaration, rather than as a binding convention. In UN practice, a declaration is aspirational. It ordinarily goes further than the existing practices of states, with the aim of encouraging all states to adopt more effective legislation. This declaration of principles and guidelines, should it be approved by the General Assembly, would constitute an invitation to states to consider taking additional steps.

The definition provides a guideline for protecting the interrelated manifestations of Indigenous knowledge and heritage. The heritage definition means not only the ability to possess a distinct heritage, but the ability to share some aspects of this heritage from time to time with others. As long as this heritage remains within the control of a people, it can continue to be shared at appropriate times and in appropriate ways. For example, the Indigenous peoples of the North American Pacific Northwest are harvesters of the sea. Each clan or community has been associated, for centuries, with the subspecies (or "runs") of salmon that return annually to its territory and that are viewed as its kinfolk. The dignity and honor of each community depends on the ability to hold feasts and share these fish with others, which in turn depends on wise management of the ecosystem. Salmon are a major part of these peoples' heritages—not just the eating or trading of salmon, but the sharing, which would come to an end if a particular subspecies were to disappear. The songs, stories, designs, artworks, and ecological wisdom connected with salmon are all interrelated elements of this heritage. In the cases of *R. v. Sparrow* (1990) and *Delgamuukw v. British Columbia* (1997), the Supreme Court of Canada affirmed this worldview as part of its analysis of Indigenous tenure and rights.

Sacred Ecologies and Legal Corollaries

Indigenous peoples construct their teachings around the belief that at certain places there is a sacred ambiance that can and does empower human consciousness and spirituality. Indigenous conceptions of "sacred ecology" have five major legal corollaries, which must be respected in any framework for the protection of Indigenous peoples' intellectual and cultural rights.

The first corollary is that every individual human and non-human in the ecosystem bears reciprocal personal responsibilities for the maintenance of their relationships. Knowledge of the ecosystem is, to this extent, essentially legal knowledge, and the people who acquire this information bear especially heavy burdens of responsibility for teaching others and for mediating conflicts between humans and other species.

Second, since knowledge bears heavy personal responsibilities, as well as the power to interfere with relationships between humans and non-humans, it must ordinarily be transmitted personally to an apprentice who has been spiritually prepared to accept those burdens and to bear the power with humility. Much attention is given to the preparation of the pupil, both ritually and through tests of courage, maturity, and sincerity.

Third, knowledge is ordinarily transmitted among kin, because it has to do with the responsibilities of a particular lineage or clan to its territory. In a large society composed of many families and clans, some knowledge may attach to the lineage level, some to the clan level, and some to the entire tribe or nation. This "nesting" of different layers of knowledge is unique to each people. It has nothing to do with other families or peoples; it may indeed be dangerous for outsiders to obtain information that could be used to meddle with what is conceived as an internal affair of the local human and non-human "family." Furthermore, because Indigenous knowledge is localized to an environment and its peoples, it is not conceived as having general application to other ecosystems.

Fourth, knowledge may sometimes be shared with visitors to the territory, so that they can travel safely and subsist from local resources, but it cannot be alienated permanently outside the territory to which it refers. In effect, knowledge can be lent, for a specific time and purpose, usually in exchange for reciprocal forms of knowledge possessed by the borrowers. The lenders retain the right to conclude the arrangement if the knowledge lent is misused or if the responsibilities that attach to its possession are not fulfilled.

Fifth, misuse of knowledge can be catastrophic, not only for the individual abuser, but for the people, the territory, and (potentially) the world. Misuse of knowledge is tantamount to an act of war on other species, breaking their covenants and returning the land to a pre-moral and pre-legal vacuum. This concept explains why the overall approach of Indigenous peoples to the ecosystem is precautionary in the extreme. Any human activity that goes beyond the bounds of known relationships and interaction among species is, again, tantamount to war and invites chaos.

Within these general principles, Indigenous peoples possess their own locally specific systems of jurisprudence with respect to the classification of different types of knowledge, proper procedures for acquiring and sharing knowledge, and the rights and responsibilities that attach to possessing knowledge, all of which are embedded uniquely in each culture and its language. Any attempt to devise uniform guidelines for the recognition and protection of Indigenous peoples' knowledge runs the risk of collapsing this rich jurisprudential diversity into a single model that will not fit the values, conceptions, or laws of any Indigenous society. A better approach, we believe, would be for the national and international community to agree that traditional knowledge must be acquired and used in conformity with the customary laws of the peoples concerned.

Interconnected Rights

Most Algonquian federations, including the Mi'kmaw Nation in the Atlantic region and the Blackfoot Confederacy in the Western plains and Canadian Rockies, are composed of several allied nations, each of which is divided into several territorially localized clans. Each nation also has its own unique system of "societies," which are voluntary associations of women or men with special skills, knowledge, and responsibilities. Although one language is spoken throughout the confederacy, ecological knowledge is divided among the clans, "societies," and individual specialists. The natural history of particular places is generally clan-level knowledge. Relationships with the animal and spirit worlds are knowledge for this purpose. The possession of different kinds of hunting or foraging knowledge, by comparison, varies by species: clans for berries and small animals, "societies" for some large animals such as bison, and individual specialists for the most powerful animals such as bears. In addition, different clans are associated with different species, and through these relationships, they maintain special knowledge of them. The clan system is thus a kind of mirror of the ecosystem. A complete model of the Mi'kmaw or Blackfoot ecosystem, therefore, can only be reconstructed through the cooperation of all segments of the population; no one individual or group possesses or has rights to share all the relevant knowledge. There is also a gender dimension. Women tend to be the bearers of knowledge of medicinal and food plants in Blackfoot culture, while men possess most knowledge of animals.

This complex distribution of knowledge has an important political significance. Decisions can only be made cooperatively (ordinarily by consensus) because no one family, allied nation, or skilled élite possesses all the relevant knowledge. Every individual, clan, "society," and nation is knowledgeable about, and primarily responsible for, a different component of the regional ecosystem. As a result, management decision making involves the sharing of specialized knowledge and the balancing of all interests and concerns—including the concerns of non-humans. One clan might speak for its kinfolk, the otters; another "society" might speak in defense of the foxes, from whom they originally gained their power.

Obviously, this Indigenous way of organizing the control of knowledge is incompatible with the "commoditization" of scientific discoveries in contemporary international intellectual property law. The objective of intellectual property law is twofold: to encourage innovation by providing the innovator with monopoly control of commercial applications and to encourage the diffusion of technology by limiting the duration of the innovator's monopoly. Among Indigenous peoples, innovation and diffusion are regulated through the social relationships among kinship groups and voluntary associations, not through markets. Moreover, the main focus is the proper use and sharing of knowledge rather than maximizing its quantity.

Indigenous Knowledge as Intellectual Property

One important area of research has been to demonstrate the structural similarity between Indigenous knowledge and Eurocentric scientific knowledge (Atran 1987). This similarity is the foundation for the syllogism at the heart of the intellectual property debate. If Indigenous and Eurocentric knowledge share structural similarities, then specific knowledge from Indigenous peoples should be entitled to the same legal status as specific scientific knowledge.

Indigenous peoples throughout the world regard their traditional knowledge as proprietary and confidential (UNDP 1994; Daes 1993). Ethnobiologist Darrell Posey's 1990 report to the United Nations lists several types of traditional scientific knowledge that exist within Indigenous knowledge. These include ethnoecology (the understanding and cultivation of distinct ecosystems or ecological zones), ethnopedology (the understanding of soil composition and its uses), ethnozoology (the knowledge and use of animal phenomena, especially in pest control), ethnopharmacology and ethnomedicine (the use of plants and animals in Indigenous medicine), ethnobotany (the uses of plants and animals by Indigenous peoples), and ethnoagriculture and agroforestry (the knowledge of forest management techniques, natural pest-repellent techniques, and other cultivation methods). Rituals, magic, and shamans or medicine peoples also play important roles in Indigenous knowledge. Traditions for the transmission and use of traditional Indigenous knowledge are highly localized and resist generalizations.

In *Beyond Intellectual Property: Toward Traditional Resource Rights for Indigenous Peoples and Local Communities,* Posey and Dutfield (1996) propose a new covenant as an experimental model for the protection of Indigenous intellectual property. The model states that the first concern of Indigenous peoples is their right not to sell, commoditize, or have expropriated from them certain domains of knowledge and certain sacred places, plants, animals, and objects. The protected Indigenous knowledge is described as

> knowledge of current use, previous use, and/or potential use of plant and animal species, as well as soil and minerals; knowledge of preparation, processing, or storage of useful species; knowledge of formulations involving more than one ingredient; knowledge of individual species (planting methods, care for, selection criteria, etc.); knowledge of ecosystem conservation (methods of protecting or preserving a resource that may be found to have commercial value, although not specifically used for that purpose or other practical purposes by the local community or the culture); biogenetic resources that originate (or originated) on indigenous lands and territories; cultural property (images, sounds, crafts, arts and performances); and classificatory systems of knowledge, such as traditional plant taxonomies. (1996, 176–77)

Louise Grenier in *Working with Indigenous Knowledge: A Guide for Researchers* (1998) has stated that Indigenous knowledge is an integrated body of knowledge. Her definition of Indigenous knowledge includes learning systems; local organization, controls, and enforcement; local classification and quantification; human health; animal behavior and animal diseases; water management and conservation systems; soil conservation practices; agriculture, agroforesty, and swidden agriculture; textiles and crafts; building materials; energy conversion; tools; and changes to the local ecosystem over time (2–3).

The protection and wider application of Indigenous knowledge involve three related issues: identification of the traditional owners of this knowledge under Indigenous peoples' own systems of laws; respect for customary procedures required for learning and borrowing Indigenous knowledge; and compensation for the right to learn and use this knowledge. Two points can validly be made about these diverse legal systems. The traditional owners may be individuals, societies, family groups (clans or lineages), or whole nations, depending on the kind of knowledge involved and the culture of the peoples concerned. Assuming that "bands" as defined in the Canadian federal *Indian Act* (1995) are the true owners of knowledge, for example, is a gross oversimplification that would do injustice to the beliefs and feelings of most Indigenous peoples. The second point is that few Indigenous legal systems accept the possibility of ever alienating their traditional knowledge completely. Like the land itself, the people's knowledge of the land is connected with them forever. It can be shared under certain circumstances, but borrowers must observe the continuing supervisory authority of the original owners.

Indigenous peoples do not view their knowledge in terms of property at all—that is, something that has an owner and is used for the purpose of extracting economic benefits—but in terms of community and individual responsibilities. Their knowledge is incompatible with European property law, which is based on the separation of state and society, the disintegration of community, and the division of labor and social hierarchy (Unger 1976). Modern property law refers to a set of legal rules defining the rights of ownership of something having value. There is one set of rights that relates to tangible property and another set of rights that relates to intangible or intellectual property. Both sets of rights include the exclusive rights of ownership to use and dispose of the property.

Among Indigenous peoples, possessing a song, story, or medicinal knowledge carries with it certain responsibilities to show respect for, and to maintain a reciprocal relationship with, the human beings, animals, plants, and places with which the song, story, or medicine is connected. Cajete (1986) and Maruyama (1978) have discussed this as mutualistic logic and reciprocal causality. For Indigenous peoples, heritage is a bundle of relationships, rather than a bundle of economic rights or policy considerations. The "object" has no meaning outside the relationship, whether it is a physical object such as a sacred site or a ceremonial tool, or an intangible such as a song or a story. To sell it is necessarily to bring the relationship to an end.

Indigenous Legal Systems

Indigenous peoples have always had their own laws and procedures for protecting their heritage and for determining when and with whom their heritage can be shared. The rules can be complex and they vary greatly among different Indigenous peoples. A thorough description of these rules would be almost impossible; in any case, each Indigenous people must remain free to interpret its own system of laws as it understands them. There are similarities in the structure of Indigenous peoples' legal systems, however, which will be summarized here.

Indigenous knowledge is ordinarily a communal right and is associated with a family, clan, tribe, or other kinship group. Only the group as a whole can consent to the sharing of Indigenous knowledge and its consent must be given through specific decision-making procedures, which may differ depending on whether songs, stories, medicines, or some other aspect of heritage are involved. In whatever way consent is given, it is always temporary and revocable; heritage can never be alienated, surrendered, or sold, except for conditional use. Sharing, therefore, creates a relationship between the givers and receivers of knowledge. The givers retain the authority to ensure that knowledge is used properly, and the receivers continue to recognize and repay the gift.

Although Indigenous knowledge is a *sui generis* communal right, there is usually an individual who can best be described as the custodian or caretaker of each song, story, name, medicine, sacred place, and other aspect of a people's heritage. Such individual responsibilities should not be confused with Eurocentric concepts of ownership or property rights, however. Traditional custodians serve as trustees for the interests of the community as a whole, and they enjoy their privileges and status in this respect for only so long as they continue to act in the best interests of the community.

Both the United States and Australia have developed legal models based on the heritage principle. In the United States, the *Native American Graves Protection and Repatriation Act* (NAGPRA 1990), which applies to human remains and culturally important objects, and the *National Museum of the American Indian Act* (1991), by which a majority of relevant collections in the national museum are placed in a new museum, are managed by a committee of Indigenous people appointed by the president. In Australia, the *Aboriginal and Torres Strait Islander Heritage Act 1984* provides that the minister for Aboriginal affairs, on request by Aboriginal people, may declare that a particular site or object is protected as part of Australia's Aboriginal heritage. In 1987, a much stronger measure was adopted with respect to the State of Victoria in southeastern Australia, under which Aboriginal communities in Victoria may request the minister to protect any "Aboriginal cultural property" and, if the minister declines, the matter is submitted to arbitration. This covers not only sites and objects, but also "folklore," which is defined as including songs, rituals, ceremonies, dances, art, customs, and spiritual beliefs.

In summary, each Indigenous community must retain permanent control over all elements of its own knowledge. It may share the right to enjoy and use certain elements of its knowledge, under its own laws and procedures, but it always reserves a perpetual right to determine how shared knowledge is used. This continuing, collective right to manage its knowledge is critical to the identity, survival, and development of each Indigenous society.

Chapter 4

•••

The Importance of Language for Indigenous Knowledge

To protect their heritage, indigenous peoples must control their own means of cultural transmission and education. This includes their right to the continued use and, wherever necessary, the restoration of their own languages and orthographies. — Principles and Guidelines for the Protection of the Heritage of Indigenous Peoples (1995, art. 7)

In human consciousness, language is a manifestation of the finite contained in an infinite mystery. Everywhere we are born to a language, everywhere it binds our consciousness (Hutchinson 1984). It is a unique manifestation of instinct or telepathic knowing, the silent police of the mind (Hutchinson 1984, 236). The development of language reflects the inherent paradoxes of the mind and the world. A great syncretic Eurocentric thinker of the twentieth century, Benjamin Whorf (1956), who unraveled part of the mystery, suggests that languages with radically different structures create radically different worldviews. Whorf argues that worldviews grow out of the structures of language, and that long and deeply held ideas are frozen into ways of thinking and speaking. One resonant implication of his thought is that no "universal logic" exists as part of our common humanity: what is *logical, rational,* and *reasonable* to one group of speakers may just as easily be *illogical, irrational,* and *unreasonable* to another.

Another part to this mystery is that Indo-European languages and worldviews are based on nouns and most Aboriginal languages are not (Whorf 1956, 59). A noun-based system that is not based on the sensory natural world but on artificially created ideas proceeds from mastery to enslavement. As the German philosopher G.W.F. Hegel showed with great brilliance, the closed-circle history of European thought is an ever-changing pattern of great liberating ideas that eventually turn into suffocating constraints (Hegel [1806] 1910). Like all attempts to make people aware of the categories in which they think, the attempt to make people aware of how the language they speak affects the way they view the world is a difficult and sometimes agonizing activity.

Philosopher Owen Barfield, in his theory of the origin of languages, calls the verb-centered process the "original participation." He states that people's preconscious stance is that language *evokes* and *pulls forth* from the manifesting realms into the manifest realm, rather than merely *refers*. Such action is a way of being watchful in a processual world of verbs. When people speak from within this view of "participation between perceiver and perceived, between [hu]man and nature," their oratory and writings sound like poetry rather than prose. A noun-based system, in contrast, takes the "it-ness" of things for granted and causes people to be careful when they speak.

Barfield uses the term "original participation" to distinguish this way of speaking from a similar participation in which we engage occasionally with poetry and art. To speak is to create, and to repeat is to re-create. But to speak in "original participation" is a sacred, mindful act of speaking the manifesting into the manifest. One develops a healthy respect for silence, an acknowledgment of the presence of the manifesting, as well as an acute previewing (or presaying) process concerning things one is about to say. This original participation can also be called, from an Indigenous perspective, a sacred or medicine way of language. What is for Indigenous people a natural embeddedness, however, must be for modern thinkers a conscious attitude chosen instead of our normal cultural attitudes toward speaking.

In contrast, the modernist Eurocentric worldview insists that there are numberless ways in which objects and events in the world might be classified. It is the convention of naming that determines the classification rather than any perceived qualities in the objects or events themselves. Separated from any biological reality, not surprisingly modern thought is obsessed with language. Still, there is no basis for saying that one language in modern theory portrays reality more accurately than another, for the only measure of the "truth" of a language is its power to advance the ends of the communities who speak it. Thus the implicit sovereigns in modern thought are the interests that lead humans to choose a language. The people who have the power to decide what a thing will be called have the power to decide reality.

The underlying incoherence of the Eurocentric view of language is that since Eurocentric thought mediates the entire world through its theories, then there is little possibility for an independent comparison of Eurocentric and Indigenous theories about physical reality. How can Indigenous people sustain any confidence in Eurocentric languages or worldviews if any comparisons between Eurocentric and Indigenous worldviews must be qualified by the principle that the Eurocentric worldview is the "right" one?

To insist on analyzing Indigenous thought from a Eurocentric point of view is cultural racism and cognitive imperialism. Under modern thought, at least in theory, every language describes the world completely, though each in its own way. Indigenous languages and worldviews must be strengthened and developed within their own contexts. Any interference is domination, both cognitively and culturally. Thus, every Indigenous language has a right to exist without conforming to Eurocentric languages or worldviews. Equally as important as strengthening Indigenous languages and worldviews is being honest about Eurocentric languages and worldviews. The failure to admit the differences in worldviews is also domination. The absence of an objective theory of reality, in particular, contains gross inequalities for Indigenous peoples' attempts to understand their realities and to give their people choices in their lives. Do Indigenous people want to be forever confined by Eurocentric purposes and imagination, or do we want to continue to seek the truth about our relations to the biological world? These issues are questions about truth versus vanity, ecological knowledge versus artificial knowledge, and the daily experience of Indigenous peoples. According to modern Eurocentric theories of subjective realities, there is a crucial question about the value of learning their particular words.

Indigenous Languages and the Natural World

In looking at the relationship between Indigenous languages and the natural world, we want to explore an Algonquian language and worldview. We will examine this realm because we have experienced it, but also because this Indigenous language group spans most of North America, from the Atlantic coast to the Rocky Mountains (and even in small pockets on the northwestern coast of California), thus forming the dominant Indigenous consciousness of the continent.

Our example of Algonquian reality is the Mi'kmaw (allied people) language of the North Atlantic coast. The Mi'kmaq were among the first to meet the Europeans and have fought to retain their language the longest. Understanding the differences between Indigenous languages and worldviews and Eurocentric languages and worldviews is directly tied to restoring Indigenous dignity and linguistic integrity. Understanding the difference makes the illogical, irrational, and unreasonable understandable, and creates new policy environments. This awareness is the missing link between wholeness and fragmentation, between wellness and doubt.

Most Indigenous people view the world as independent of their beliefs about it. It is an external reality that is in a continuous state of transformation. The entire universe is seen as creative local space, as sacred realms of change. Together the realms create a flowing, transforming existence. Each realm is related to the movement and is described only in order to understand the process of change. The energy of the realms comes with transformations. These transformations do not always cause physical changes; they often cause changes in the manifestations or behaviors only of those who are aware of the subtle changes. If there is no change, the energies waste away. The realms are not outside each other, but are interactional. It is the interaction of all these parts that is important, rather than the different parts per se. Thus, the sacred space is considered as a transforming flux that constitutes an indivisible web of meanings. The web can be perceived, and occasionally reflections of the realms can be experienced. The total order, described as an indivisible world, can be best understood in English as the "implicate order." Traditionally, this order has been understood in English by the words the "most" or the "great mystery" or the "great silence." Our concept of the implicate order and its relations to Indigenous thought has been enriched by our conversations with physicist David Bohm and Blood philosopher Leroy Little Bear (see especially, Bohm 1980).

In the Algonquian worldview, perceptions, under certain conditions, do provide an accurate impression of reality. These perceptions are not directed at external forms of life, however, but to understanding the invisible forces beneath the external forms. Algonquian languages describe these forces as *mntu, manidoo, manito, manitu,* or *manitou. Mntu* could better be called a verb than a noun; but over the years, missionaries, ethnologists, and even some linguists have twisted the concept into a pejorative noun. Even better is to think about *mntu* as an essential part of the ever-transforming flux. The Algonquians are not unique in this understanding: the South American Guarani call this concept *namandu*, the Melanese say *mana*, the Iroquois say *orenda*, the Lakota say *nigila* or "that which dwells in everything" and *wakan.* Most Indigenous peoples believe *something* gives rise to the living organism that contains it and survives this organism when it perishes.

The Mi'kmaw language has always been made up of forces (*mntu'k*) that underlie the perceived world—these forces give rise to the perceived world; they transcend it, they energize it, and they transform it. All these forces can change their shape and content. This view is consistent with the modern scientific view that all matter can be seen as energy, shaping itself into particular patterns.

The Mi'kmaw language builds on verb phrases that contain the motion of the flux, with hundreds of prefixes and suffixes to choose from to express a panorama of energy. The reliance on verbs rather than on nouns is important: it means that there are few fixed, separate objects in the Mi'kmaw worldview. What the people see is the great flux, eternal transformation, and interconnected space. With this fluidity of phoneme, every speaker can create new vocabulary "on the fly," tailored to meet the experience of the moment, to express the finest nuances of meaning.

Experiences are the Mi'kmaw rules of inference for arriving at new truths about reality. Experiencing the realms takes the form of an intimate, personal relationship. The process is more than a matter of defining phoneme or phone or words and phrases. Such experiences are focused on helping one understand the nature and structure of particular realms: how they interchange yet remain related, how language creates an elegant way of explicating an implicate order composed of complex systems of relationship.

The Mi'kmaw relationships to the forces of the Earth Lodge realm (*maqmikewo'ko'm*) are direct and visceral. This is often simply called "nature" in English, but it is a difficult concept to express in Mi'kmaq. Perhaps it can best be expressed as *kisu'lk mlkikno'tim* (creation place). The Mi'kmaq understand how limited their knowledge is about this realm of the transforming flux. It makes little sense to create any fixed worldview in this realm; the known truth is about unending change that requires both cognitive and physical flexibility. Mi'kmaw knowledge does not describe reality; it describes ever-changing insights about patterns or styles of the flux. Concepts about "what is" define human awareness of the changes, but add little to the actual processes. To see things as permanent is to be confused about everything: the alternative to understanding is the need to create temporary harmonies through alliances and relationships with all forms and forces. This process is a never-ending source of wonder to the Indigenous mind and to other forces that contribute to the harmony.

Understanding the flux involves learning the existing oral legacy, which involves an intimate and endless listening to stories and dialogue with elders and parents. This process takes time and patience, and requires learning the languages, the distortions, and the diverse realms and forces contained within and beyond the languages. Indigenous languages share this knowledge about the overlapping processes within chosen societies and extended families. The sounds are transformational and relative; they create a realm formed out of spiritual dignity, which they comprehend and act out.

Stories are enfolding lessons. Not only do they transmit validated experience; they also renew, awaken, and honor spiritual forces. Hence, almost every ancient story does not explain; instead it focuses on processes of knowing. Stories discuss how to acquire these relationships on every level, how to properly use them, how to lose them. They also discuss the consequences attendant on the relationships. One is said to be lost without allies, and stories about allies are guides to the unseen as well as to the seen. Only in the last century of contact with modern consciousness have these stories become explanations. As represented by the structure of the language, in a connected world, the whole is no longer the whole when it is a part of an explanation. A holistic process cannot be explained by shattering it into its component parts and assigning local explanations to the segments. If such a process occurs in Indigenous thought, new forces are unleashed. These forces have always existed, and are said to be held in check, contained, by the structure of language.

While the flux and forces are objective, the rules of inference and perception are viewed as personal. Some people are born with the ability to create relationships with the essential forces in nature; others have to acquire this ability through experience. The vision quest is one way to make alliances with the *mntu'k*. These alliances with certain forces give dignity to both parties. As well as contributing to ecological harmony, these alliances are usually intensely private matters. Such connections can also occur by bonds, adoption, or marriages among animals, plants, or families.

Mi'kmaw consciousness and order converge in the Mi'kmaw people's view of the world and their ways of perceiving it, containing it in language, and interpreting it. The resulting view is a sacred realm. The Mi'kmaw order, like Mi'kmaw consciousness, language, and worldview, is founded on two sources. First, although it views the world as eternal, it views it as subject to endless renewal and realignments. Second, it asserts that each part enfolds or encapsulates the whole. These understandings focus the Mi'kmaw consciousness on humans' dependence on the forces of nature outside and within themselves, as well as on the need for respectful behavior to all parts of the sacred spaces. The forces express nature instead of creating it. The various forces of nature are perceived as strands in a larger pattern that enfolds an uncreated, timeless, and experienced reality. Thus, order is said to be *ta'n tela'sik koqoey* or *tela'skl wistqamoe'l*. The root verb is *tela'sikl,* which means "the process which is meant to be."

To inform stability in a transforming universe, Mi'kmaw speakers believe humans have to create consensual relationships with these forces. Any part enfolds or encapsulates the entire force, and that principle signifies the meaning of alliance: alliance enfolds the forces in harmony. The ability to establish these enabling or protective relationships is embodied in the concept of *mntu*. An English approximation to this concept is available among the words "dignity," "power," and "force." Working in combination, these English words approximate a unified Algonquian thought.

The Mi'kmaw concept of dignities thus becomes a tacit model of proper conduct toward nature and humans; these models are transmitted as part of the experience of learning to participate in the great flux. The models were originally formulated as anecdotes, rather than as a catalogue of explicit rules. In most of these systems the trickster stories symbolically represent the great flux and possible sources of transformations. Explicit rules are useless in a spontaneous world: no system of rules can do justice to nature's subtle refinements and complex forces.

Instead of established rules, principles, or laws, a highly integrated communion of values and understandings informs a concept of acknowledged dignities, respect, and solidarity sustaining the relationship between nature and the Mi'kmaq. This solidarity is conceived of as being acknowledged and understood instead of being manmade. Individual behavior faithfully accommodates the collective flux. The Mi'kmaw belief is a firm consensus of proper respect toward inherent dignities. Deference to the forces of nature and alliances are processes by which individual passions are contained. Proper behavior is also a mixture of dignity and protection, requiring exemplary conduct. It is an interesting emotional mixture. Improper behavior violates dignity and usually leads to a loss of protection from spiritual forces.

In Mi'kmaw society, "reason" is the awareness of implicit forces in a changing reality, an understanding of solidarity, love, and caring. This linguistic awareness knows no distinction between "is" and "ought" or between theory and practice. The Mi'kmaw pursuit is to be with the flux, to experience its changing form, and to develop a relationship with the forces, thus creating harmony. The Mi'kmaw language is an attempt to learn from being part of the view, to create a complementary and harmonious relationship with nature, to experience the beauty of the moment, and to release such inspirations back to where they came from without fear of loss. The Mi'kmaw language has not developed a method to explain the forces or to change them, merely to contain them. This is the vital and vitalizing context of the Mi'kmaw worldview.

As the Mi'kmaq contemplate the implicate order, they have a processual faith in the beauty of quiet consciousness and in the sacred space between thoughts. They have a faith in experiencing parts of the vast world and inner space, and in performing rituals for renewing the world's beauty. This contemplation is a way of operating in the unknown, with humble respect for its vastness. Too often, it has been dismissed as "the state of ignorance." The resulting form of life for the Mi'kmaq is an active relationship with the elements of a particular environment. The Mi'kmaw worldview is one of common meaning (appositeness) or aptness. In this unity of meaning, each form of awareness represents a way of being with others and with the self.

The Eurocentric Illusion of Benign Translatability

Eurocentric legal and political thought has not confronted the problem of differing languages and worldviews. In *Mahe et al. v. The Queen in Right of Alberta* (1990), the Supreme Court of Canada understands: "Language is more than a mere means of communication, it is part and parcel of the identity and culture of the people speaking it. It is the means by which individuals understand themselves and the world around them" (82). The intercultural conflict between worldviews extends beyond questions of linguistic relativity and cultural pluralism, however, to the question of translatability. The traditional Eurocentric response is that worldviews can be translated. Yet, there are indications that this may not be true. Consider the problems within a single language family—the Indo-European family—of translating common law into French and civil law into English. Consider the problems between different academic disciplines that write in English. Consider the fact that some ideas do not exist in all languages of a linguistic family. Add to this Eurocentric predicament, the feminist awareness of the existing gender bias in the modern construction of reality (Spender 1980). Faced with these acknowledged tensions and biases within the Eurocentric worldviews, how can governments and scholars assume that differently constructed worldviews, such as those available within Indigenous languages, are not only translatable into English and French, but translatable without substantial damage or distortion? This assumption is habitually minimized or left unexamined.

The illusion of benign translatability, of course, has a practical purpose: it maintains the legitimacy of the Eurocentric wordview and the illegitimacy of Indigenous worldviews. Many dictionaries between these languages implicitly assert translatability. It is well known that European spiritual leaders tried to destroy all collections of Indigenous knowledge. That was the explicit plan, which still continues in government agendas today. It is a plan that sustains the ideal of a universal consciousness. There is, however, a much more subtle process at work to destroy Indigenous knowledge—more effective but less mean-spirited. This process works through language and is often called cognitive imperialism, cognitive terrorism, or simply, assimilation.

This subtle process began with the immigrants who attempted to learn Indigenous languages for their own purposes. Since 1492, much has been written about this topic in North America, first and most frequently by missionaries and later by academics. Neither group of observers attempted to bridge the gap between Eurocentric and Indigenous worldviews: both clerics and academics unquestioningly assumed a universal human nature based on the noun-God consciousness inherent in their society—an assumption that is incompatible with Indigenous consciousness. Thus, neither the English nor the French grasped the nature of Indigenous knowledge, consciousness, or order. Imposing foreign categories on other people's lives is sheer folly, primarily because the categories probably do not apply, at least not without serious revision. Just as the European mind could not possibly have dreamed up, much less described impartially, the different realms of Indigenous thought, Indigenous people could never have dreamed up European consciousness and order.

The missionaries, for example, attempted to match Indigenous spiritual concepts to those of the Christian religion: they sought to exchange one set of verbal symbols for another, based on an assumption that there was a universal God who created the world and a mercantilist version of exchange. The Indigenous people of America never envisioned this view. Among the Algonquians, instead of a noun-God, a written bible, or God's Talk, we had the ecology with the wind, the rain, the waters, and all their lessons. The missionaries' purpose, consciously or unconsciously, was to use the sounds of Indigenous languages to explain the belief forms of Christianity. The translators' unannounced beliefs determined the relevance of the Indigenous sounds.

In most situations, the Europeans terminated Indigenous languages and beliefs—but they never destroyed the human need for harmony that tied language and belief together. Some Indigenous nations have survived the five-hundred-year nightmare of destruction; others remain little more than memories—collections of vulnerable, abused, and disadvantaged peoples. After the imposed dark ages, all Indigenous peoples struggle with memory and forgetting. Still we passionately and intuitively seek the sacred realms, cultural restoration, and integrity. It is part of our humanness as Indigenous people, and a part of our consciousness and identity that most Eurocentric governments ignore when establishing language policies.

The limited lexicons and dictionaries have deluded Indigenous peoples into thinking that Eurocentric languages and worldviews are a shared heritage and are complementary to their languages. They begin to think there is no difference. This may be true of daily conversations. Yet, the more an Indigenous person learns and tries to express Eurocentric ideas in his or her Indigenous language, the more that person realizes that Eurocentric languages constitute an imposed context that Indigenous people have neither authored nor experienced. Indigenous peoples are asked to reproduce and confirm Eurocentric languages and worldviews, even if to do so prevents their own self-actualization, linguistic integrity, and empowerment. The illusion of benign translatability shields Eurocentric worldviews from comparison with or contamination by Indigenous worldviews; it urges Indigenous thinkers to translate in such a way as to assimilate Eurocentric worldviews; and it maintains the explanatory power of Eurocentric thought in modern life.

The illusion affirms the idea of a universal language and worldview, while it conceals the inequalities encoded in the dominant language and worldview. The illusion is a tool of assimilation and power: it thrives on ignorance and dependence, and it perpetuates certain languages and worldviews over others. Most people do not recognize the purposes encoded into their language or worldview. This is the power of "newspeak" of George Orwell's *Nineteen Eighty-Four*, the idea that if people have only one language available to them, then their range of thought will be accordingly contained. As Dale Spender states, "The group that has the power to ordain the structure of language, thought, and reality has the potential to create a world in which they are the central figures" (1980).

More importantly, the illusion of benign translatability prevents the linguistic development and mobilization of Indigenous communities. It prevents them from being persuaded that their languages are both beneficial and necessary for their growth as human beings. It allows colonial myths about languages to continue: for example, the idea that Indigenous children will learn English better if they learn only English and not their own languages in school.

For any revitalization of Indigenous languages to succeed, the parents and relatives of Indigenous children must be persuaded that their languages are valuable and relevant. Typically language loss occurs because parents and relatives no longer teach their languages to their children, because they think of them as being of little value. This attitude is directly connected with the daily operations of the illusion of benign translatability. The illusion of translatability between Indigenous languages and English or French devalues the uniqueness of Indigenous languages and worldviews. It prevents Indigenous speakers from understanding how to correct the interactions of Eurocentric languages with Indigenous languages, so that the former will not contradict or overpower Indigenous languages or worldviews. The illusion also hides Eurocentric fragmentation from the wholeness of Indigenous languages until it is too late to correct the problems associated with this fragmentation. Additionally, the illusion is often used to excuse inaction on the problems affecting Indigenous peoples.

Consequences of the Eurocentric Illusion

Recent studies make it clear that Indigenous languages and worldviews are critically endangered. Linguist Ken Hale has estimated that half of the world's 6000 Indigenous languages are doomed because no children speak them. Other researchers estimate that Africa has lost 1800 Indigenous languages, New Guinea has lost 800, and Indonesia at least 642 (Linden 1991). Europeans estimate that Indigenous peoples at the beginning of the American holocaust spoke more than 2000 separate languages. Five hundred years later, only 500 Indigenous languages are spoken in the Americas, and only 200 are phonemically written. In the United States and Canada, the immigrants extinguished and replaced about 67 percent of Indigenous consciousness with Eurocentric consciousness (Champagne 1994, 427).

Recent studies in Canada show that all fifty-three Indigenous languages are critically endangered (AFN 1988, 1990, 1992; House of Commons Standing Committee on Aboriginal Affairs 1990). Only three Indigenous languages in Canada—Cree, Ojibway, and Inuktitut—have a chance of surviving this century with a sufficient number of proficient speakers to sustain them unless governments and churches take immediate measures. In their 1990 survey of 151 First Nations' communities, the Assembly of First Nations found

> only slightly over one-third of the communities have languages classified as *flourishing* (over 80 per cent of all age groups are fluent in their native language) or *enduring* (over 60 per cent of all age groups are fluent); one-quarter have *declining* languages (the number of speakers declined in each age group); thirty per cent have *endangered* languages (only the older adult

> population are fluent with few or no speakers in younger age groups), and just over 10 per cent were in *critical* condition (less than 10 speakers remain in the community); over three-quarters of the older age groups are fluent in their Indigenous language, although this proportion rapidly drops to less than 10 per cent among the young children. (AFN 1992, 3)

These statistics reflect the Canadian policies of cultural genocide, cognitive and cultural imperialism, isolation, and forced assimilation, which have greatly eroded Indigenous languages and in some cases destroyed Indigenous cultures. For example, federal residential school policies removed children from their homes; placed them in unloving environments; forced them to surrender their identities, their languages, their relationships, and their religions; and fostered a breakdown of family and cultural institutions (Jaine 1993; Knockwood 1992; Millon 1999). The resulting cultural discontinuity, dislocation, and disintegration have been critical factors in the loss of Indigenous knowledge.

Although considerable research has documented the losses to Indigenous languages in Canada (AFN 1990, 1992; Fredeen 1988; RCAP 1996b; Saskatchewan Aboriginal Languages Committee 1991; Standing Committee on Indian Affairs 1990), none of this research has yielded a successful national or regional approach to curbing Indigenous language loss and to maintaining Indigenous knowledge and heritage. Outside federal territories, Canadian governments have overlooked the right of Indigenous knowledge, heritage, and languages to exist. They have overlooked the right of Indigenous languages to exist as a medium of instruction in the schools, they have failed to recognize the official status of Indigenous languages for conducting Indigenous business, and they have failed to encourage educational institutions to allow the same academic credit for proficiency in Indigenous languages as they allow for proficiency in foreign languages.

There is convincing evidence that student achievement, community pride, and educational opportunity is directly tied to respect for the students' Indigenous languages. Yet, although it is clearly in the interest of the educational system to encourage the full academic and human achievements of Indigenous students, at present the federal and provincial governments in Canada have not responded with a remedy to this educational problem. Too little has been done to preserve, protect, or promote the rights and freedoms of Indigenous people to use, practice, and develop Indigenous languages in Canada. In contrast, other governments have firmly recognized the importance of restoring Indigenous knowledge and languages through legislation. The U.S. *Native American Language Act* (1990), the Maori language nest experience in New Zealand and their language legislation, the UN human rights covenants, and the International Labour Organization Convention on Indigenous and Tribal Peoples in Independent Countries (1989, arts. 26–28) are the most significant documents for recognizing the right of Indigenous peoples to use their traditional languages.

With the introduction of Indigenous language and cultural education in the First Nations schools in Canada, Indigenous people are attempting to sustain their Indigenous knowledge and heritage through the assistance of elders and a few curriculum development programs. However, Indigenous knowledge and heritage and elders, though accessible to public schooling, have not been included in the curriculum of the public school at any significant level. Texts and public schools provide only Eurocentric knowledge bases, thus denying Indigenous children their cultural inheritance and perpetuating the Eurocentric belief that different cultures have nothing to offer but exotic food and dances or a shallow first chapter in the history books.

Most Eurocentric governments and academics encourage the continued destruction of Indigenous languages. Canadian governmental officials and academics offer excuses that the Indigenous language problems are too complex, when in fact they do not perceive the value of Indigenous languages and thus do not care about their revitalization. They think all languages are merely communicative tools and that nothing significant is being lost with their non-use. They do not want to know about the consequences of destroying Indigenous languages, instead they seek to immunize themselves from blame. These thoughts are part of a bigger problem: the implicit state theory of European cultural and linguistic superiority.

The existing colonial bilingual language policy in Canada is not based on helping or persuading Canadians and Indigenous people to understand the value of Indigenous languages and worldviews. Instead it is aimed at assimilating Indigenous thought into English or French thought. It thus represents an unacceptable continuation of the Eurocentric interpretive monopoly over reality and, as such, it represents neither a short-term nor a long-term solution to maintaining linguistic vitality or integrity. Although many Indigenous scholars have developed strategies for linguistic renewal (Battiste 1986, 1996; SIIT 1992; Ayoungman & Brandt 1989; Ahenakew & Fredeen 1987), no governmental plan exists to promote the linguistic development of Indigenous communities or to integrate Indigenous worldviews into a more effective and harmonious structure of self-government.

Confronting linguistic and cultural racism in Canada involves understanding Indigenous languages and worldviews as protected Indigenous rights. They are constitutionally protected zones of linguistic and philosophical integrity (Turpel 1989–90). Indigenous languages and worldviews are protected by sections 2(b), 21, 22, 25, 27 of the Canadian *Charter of Rights and Freedoms* and section 35 of the *Constitution Act, 1982*. In these constitutional vehicles, they are understood as existing Aboriginal rights independent of the liberal ideology of personal rights. Even within the liberal ideology of personal rights, Indigenous worldviews exist as the fundamental freedoms of conscience, religion, thought, belief, opinion, and expression. As such, they are not to be withheld or obstructed except in accordance with the principles of fundamental justice outlined in section 15 of the *Charter* and the reasonable limits prescribed by law in section 1 of the *Charter*.

Some Canadian government programs assist Indigenous people in the federal territories to communicate in and preserve their Indigenous languages. Much more limited assistance is provided for Indigenous peoples elsewhere in Canada. The Northwest Territories government is the leader in this field, affording a wide range of government services in Indigenous languages; the other provincial and territorial governments generally do not make much effort in this regard. Although there is no constitutional reason for the omission, Indigenous languages are seldom mentioned in statutes or regulations in any jurisdiction. The provincial and territorial legislatures are free to permit and promote the official use of Indigenous languages whenever it would be helpful or appropriate. One of the few examples of regulations that require the use of an Indigenous language are the Narwhal Protection Regulations (1978), which provide that the tags issued to an Inuit to permit the hunting of narwhals shall be printed in English, French, and Inuit syllabic.

Chapter 5

•••

Decolonizing Cognitive Imperialism in Education

Indigenous people have the right to revitalize, use, develop and transmit to future generations, their histories, languages, oral traditions, philosophies, writing systems and literatures, and to designate and retain their own names for communities, places and persons. — Draft Declaration on the Rights of Indigenous Peoples (UN 1994, art. 14)

The military, political, and economic subjugation of Indigenous peoples has been well documented, as have social, cultural, and linguistic pressures and the ensuing damage to Indigenous communities, but no force has been more effective in oppressing Indigenous knowledge and heritage than the educational system. Under the subtle influence of cognitive imperialism, modern educational theory and practice has, in large part, destroyed or distorted Indigenous knowledge and heritage.

Eurocentric societies have long accepted some of the fundamental assumptions underlying modern education. They assume that education is a kind and necessary form of mind liberation that opens to the individual options and possibilities that ultimately have value for society as a whole. On the face of it, education appears beneficial to all people and intrinsic to the progress and development of modern technological society.

However, Eurocentric public schooling for Indigenous peoples has not been benign (Memmi 1963; Freire 1973; G. Smith 1997; Milloy 1999). It has been used as a means to perpetuate damaging myths about Indigenous knowledge and heritage, languages, beliefs, and ways of life. It has also established Eurocentric science as the dominant mode of thought, a mode of thought that distrusts diversity and jeopardizes us all as we move into the next century. After nearly a century of public schooling for Indigenous peoples in Canada, for example, the most serious problem with the current system of education lies not in its failure to liberate the human potential among Indigenous peoples, but rather in its quest to limit their thought to cognitive imperialistic practices. This quest denies Indigenous people access to and participation in the formulation of educational policy, constrains the use and development of Indigenous knowledge and heritage in schools, and confines education to a narrow positivistic scientific view of the world that threatens the global future.

There are two different points at issue here. The first is the right of Indigenous peoples to exercise and transmit their own knowledge and heritage as they see fit. The second is the benefit the Western world can derive from this knowledge and heritage. Some European and Canadian scholars are beginning to realize how important Indigenous knowledge may be to the survival of our world. Not only is it important that Indigenous knowledge and heritage are preserved and enhanced; it is also important that they are recognized as the domain of Indigenous peoples and not subverted by the dominant culture.

Two international conferences since the mid-1970s have drawn attention to the right of Indigenous peoples to preserve their knowledge and heritage in the face of cognitive imperialism. The World Conference on Indigenous People in 1978 "endorse[d] the right of Indigenous Peoples to maintain their traditional structure of economy and culture, including their own language" (Barsh 1989). In 1989, a UN seminar on the effects of racism and racial discrimination on the social and economic relations between Indigenous peoples and states concluded that global racism was taking on the new form of state theories of cultural, rather than biological, superiority, resulting in rejection of the legitimacy or viability of the values and institutions of Indigenous people (Barsh 1989).

Ironically, although cognitive imperialism devalues Indigenous knowledge and heritage, the dominant society has a tendency to take elements of Indigenous knowledge out of context and claim them for itself. In 1993, the chair of the Working Group on Indigenous Populations, Dr. Erica-Irene Daes, prepared a report condemning the widespread and continued exploitation of Indigenous knowledge and heritage by Eurocentric institutions and scholars. She described this activity as the final stage of colonialism, following the exhaustion of Indigenous peoples' tangible assets.

The School System

School curricula teach Eurocentric thought. The focus of Eurocentric thought is outward toward the world as object, an arena in which humans do not interact but which they can change. Eurocentric thought ignores the inner consciousness of humans, and students learning from curricula based on the Eurocentric way of viewing the world are never given a chance to explore this domain. Elizabeth Minnick writes of the critical importance of curricula to society's objectives: "It is in and through education that a culture, and polity, not only tries to perpetuate but enacts the kinds of thinking it welcomes, and discards and/or discredits the kind it fears" (1990, 5). Eurocentric curricula isolate the known self; instead of creating communities, they reinforce specialized interests among students. These curricula teach that knowers are manipulators who have no reciprocal responsibilities to the things that they manipulate. Thus students may know a body of transmitted knowledge or set of skills but they do not know how to learn or how to live in freedom. Often, these students have no inner sense of truth or justice.

International and national recognition of and respect for Indigenous peoples' own customs, rules, and practices for the transmission of their heritage to future generations are essential to Indigenous peoples' enjoyment of human rights and dignity. Indigenous students must see themselves and their heritage as part of the educational system. In most existing educational systems, Indigenous heritage and the transmission of that heritage are missing. Even if part of the heritage is present, it is presented from a Eurocentric perspective. Often, this presentation is inaccurate and not very nourishing.

Minnick argues that the modern Eurocentric curricula are built on the roots of four errors: faulty generalizations, circular reasoning, mystified concepts, and partial knowledge (Minnick 1990). Faulty generalizations arise from universalism, the concept that there is one ideal, norm, or standard that holds voice, power, and privilege. Universalism is viewed as the highest, most significant, and most valuable of categories. Circular reasoning arises when a standard is derived from particular studies of particular groups or limited samples and then applied as if the standard were universal. Mystified concepts are those categories or ideas that are so familiar they are accepted as natural, but their meanings reflect and perpetuate old exclusivities masquerading as universals. Partial knowledge comes from posing and resolving questions within a tradition in which thinking is persistently shaped and expressed by the other three errors.

For most Indigenous students in Eurocentric education, realizing their invisibility is like looking into a still lake and not seeing their reflections. They become alien in their own eyes, unable to recognize themselves in the reflections and shadows of the world. In the same way that Eurocentric thought stripped their grandparents and parents of their wealth and dignity, this realization strips modern Indigenous students of their heritage and identity. It gives them an awareness of their annihilation. Often when Indigenous students recognize and reject the colonizers' vision of them, they experience what scholar W.E.B. Du Bois, in *The Souls of Black Folk*, called "double consciousness" (1903, 45). Double consciousness refers to the sense of always looking through the eyes of others, of measuring one's soul by the tape of a world that looks on in amused contempt. Double consciousness occurs when the dominators reject the assertions of the colonized that they are human and insist on imposing the standards of the colonizers as universal and normal (Noël 1994, 149).

At best, Canadian universities and educational systems teach this double consciousness to Indigenous students. Canadian educational systems view

Indigenous heritage, identity, and thought as inferior to Eurocentric heritage, identity, and thought. However, the Eurocentric theory of knowledge does not validate such a conclusion. No foundation exists for saying that Indigenous worldviews are inferior ways of knowing. According to Eurocentric reasoning, Indigenous worldviews can only be evaluated according to their ability to meet Indigenous ends. Indigenous worldviews cannot be evaluated with reference to Eurocentric purposes or desires, even if Eurocentric thinkers believe their purposes and desires to be universal.

Early literature in Indigenous education has focused on assimilation (Johnston 1988; Knockwood 1992; Grant 1996; Milloy 1999). A few commentators have addressed the transmission of knowledge within Indigenous traditions (Lipka 1990; Kawagley 1993; Cajete 1995; 2000). In the existing literature, the focus has been on adjusting Eurocentric teaching styles to accommodate Indigenous students; discussing jurisdiction, responsibilities, and inclusivity in curriculum content; and recommending Indigenous teacher training programs (Cleary & Peacock 1998). Some early psychological studies have identified particular behaviors (shyness, eye contact, timing) of Indigenous students of which educators should be aware when they are developing motivational and education strategies (Phillips 1972; Wax et al. 1964). Despite this literature, educators still know very little about how Indigenous students are raised and socialized in their homes and communities, and even less about how Indigenous heritage is traditionally transmitted. If they knew more about either of these areas, they could better understand students' behavior in school and how education could be shaped to create environments more conducive to learning for Indigenous students.

Cognitive Clashes

Because of the diversity of Indigenous languages, it is difficult to generalize about the transmission of knowledge and heritage in Indigenous communities. Any examination of how knowledge and heritage are transmitted must rely on oral traditions because how knowledge is transmitted depends on the language in which it is expressed. The extended family is the place where the transmission of the teachings takes place. To give a limited example of the transmission of knowledge, we will return to Mi'kmaw traditions.

The Mi'kmaw language embodies relationships. How we are kin to each other is far more important than how much material wealth we have accumulated. How we treat one another and how our lives unfold within a community are more important than the amount of education or the kinds of jobs we have. So within the philosophy of the Mi'kmaw language are the notions of how we should relate to one another and how we can retain those relationships. Our verb-based language provides the consciousness of what it is to be

Mi'kmaq and the interdependence of all things. The word *Mi'kmaq* thus refers to our kinship as allied people.

This verb consciousness has implications, especially for the transmission of Mi'kmaw heritage. It is a consciousness that has not yet been developed in most schools—even those run by the Mi'kmaq themselves. Mi'kmaw students are usually taught English noun-based concepts in the primary grades, starting with concrete nouns, numbers, and colors. The unreflective theory behind these teachings is that students need lots of concrete nouns to help them make connections with their prior knowledge. However, providing many things to name and categorize does not match the previous experience of children whose first language is Mi'kmaq. Children who are raised with the Mi'kmaw language are used to focusing on verbs and relationships, rather than on nouns and things. Moreover, the categories into which they place noun-objects will not be the same as the categories they encounter in schools that use Eurocentric models, because how a noun is categorized differs across cultures based on the context of its use. Early childhood teachers of Mi'kmaw students would find the use of events as relational concepts from which experience is derived a more useful tool than the use of nouns and categories.

Another methodological barrier to understanding Mi'kmaw knowledge and heritage is the mediation of Mi'kmaw thought by Eurocentric thought. For example, the Mi'kmaw language is based on animacy, yet Mi'kmaw living relationships are translated in Eurocentric thought through the relative relationships of animacy and inanimacy and inclusion and exclusion. The English language holds that only things that are animate are alive; the Mi'kmaw language holds that all things have a spirit and a relationship. Sometimes an object develops a special and close relationship to the people and thus develops animacy status. Thus, the Mi'kmaw language expresses the closeness of relationships rather categorizing things as either living or non-living. The process is difficult to explain, but each Mi'kmaw speaker understands how to create the appropriate usage and how to internalize it.

To teach a view that the earth is either living or not living distorts the Mi'kmaw concept of the earth. This affects how Mi'kmaw students view their environment. This Eurocentric teaching method instills the modern idea that the environment can and should be manipulated. Eurocentric thought envisions water, earth, sun, moon as inanimate—without life. But in the Mi'kmaw language, some things are close to us because we build alliances with their spirits. In time, such things reflect animate relationships with us. Many of these animate things in our language are things we need for our survival, such as our tools and our food. Our bows and arrows, nets, thread, spoons, soup, berries, kettles, pails, dolls, baby's bottles, cucumbers, pumpkins, all have animate relationships with us. It is not the "thing-ness" that is important when referring to these objects in language, it is the way or manner in which these things are used.

Another methodological problem with the Eurocentric teaching of Mi'kmaw children is that the Mi'kmaw language is not gender consciousness. Most Mi'kmaw speakers initially have trouble with the "he/she" forms of European languages and interchange them repeatedly. Over time, with adequate models and frequent usage, this usage will be sorted out. However, children need to be made aware that the languages are different and that the Mi'kmaw language does not recognize this category. With the appropriate transmission of Mi'kmaq and a metacognitive awareness of English, this problem would not arise.

Although exposure to other cultures is valuable, it is critically important for Mi'kmaw children to be taught their knowledge and heritage through Mi'kmaw transmission processes. Some Mi'kmaw communities have their own First Nations schools, which foster the values of the Mi'kmaw people and try to provide a Mi'kmaw curriculum; however, the mandated provincial curriculum continues to mirror a center that is not Mi'kmaq. It is a colonial curriculum with outcomes aimed to serve the needs of colonial governments; it is not a nourishing milieu for Indigenous students. New legislation holds some hope for revisions to the educational system, but Mi'kmaw communities need a decolonizing agenda if they are to successfully deconstruct and then reconstruct the curriculum for their students. The transformed educational curriculum will have to reflect a cultural and historical balance. It will need to be developed by educators who understand the traditional transmission models of Mi'kmaw knowledge and heritage, and the learning styles and behaviors of Mi'kmaw students. While most Mi'kmaw communities have their own Indigenous educators, the transformation of education is not yet fully achieved as schools still represent the hegemony of dominant Eurocentric knowledge, values, and expectations.

The Canadian history of cultural genocide, segregation, isolation, and coercive assimilation has greatly eroded, if not destroyed, much of the cultural and linguistic base of Indigenous peoples in Canada, but the traditional transmission of Indigenous knowledge and heritage still exists in most communities. Mi'kmaw communities are being left alone to solve the immense problem of how to restore and revitalize their teachings, their cultures, their languages, and their economies. Probably the most difficult challenge has been to free our people from the self-doubt, inferiority complexes, and confusion created by public and federal schooling. Now we need to develop the self-confidence and tools necessary to reclaim and restore our knowledge through curriculum development and implementation. The challenge is great for "Old knots and tangles that are in all our minds and practices must be located and untied if there are to be threads available with which to weave the new into anything like a whole cloth, a coherent but by no means homogeneous pattern" (Minnick 1990, 36).

Decolonizing the System

Cognitive imperialism must be dismantled in all aspects of public education; and in Indigenous communities, separate Indigenous schools must be created. In both public and community schools, the educational experience must be designed to enhance Indigenous knowledge and the transmission of that knowledge must be effected holistically. Although the notion of "one best educational system" has been largely discredited in Eurocentric thought, the notion that there is "one best remedy" for the educational ills of Indigenous peoples has not. Modern society is still looking for and frequently offers one-ingredient prescriptions that claim to be panaceas, but there is no cure-all, no educational antibiotic, that can be injected into the state from the outside to cure the modern ills.

Enhancement is a prominent concept in Indigenous knowledge. It is concerned with accruing rather than replacing knowledge and with developing the full potential of students. It differs from teaching or training, which is concerned with transmitting knowledge, to ask if the person has the right knowledge and if the person knows how to use that knowledge well. Indigenous student enhancement seeks to include the person's vitality or spirit. Whereas teaching and training offer students new data and methods, enhancement offers them help in discerning their identities and integrity.

The relationship between Indigenous knowledge and Eurocentric knowledge in the educational system must be sensitive to both ways of knowing. It cannot be a singular method of giving information and developing calculative skills. An enhanced curriculum would teach Indigenous students in a holistic manner, offering them a way of living and learning in a changing ecology. It would teach them to believe that knowing requires a personal relationship between the knower and the knowledge. It would offer them an integral, interactive relationship based on trust in the face of unknowable risks in a realm where they are vulnerable. The task of adequate Indigenous education is to enhance students' awareness of their human capacities and of the dignities of Indigenous knowledge and heritage. Such education should develop, at a minimum, the following capacities in Indigenous youth: (1) the ability to care and be responsible for the ecology, for others, and for oneself; (2) the ability to discern new and flexible images of meaning and patterns in these relationships; (3) the ability to hope and to have courage in an ecological realm filled with vitality and insight; and (4) the ability to develop a sense of "truthing" in all relationships.

All these human capacities, and others, are interrelated. All are related directly to Indigenous ways of learning and knowing. They also are involved in the development of our capacity for knowing the qualities of an ecological reality and a Eurocentric construct. It is the qualities of reality and the possibility of our knowing them that lead to the freedom of Indigenous consciousness.

Educational Contexts

Many ways of teaching will have to be modified in an enhanced educational curriculum for Indigenous students. In every educational circumstance, much of what is learned depends on the context in which it is learned. In Canada, for instance, one can identify a few basic preconceptions about reality that exercise an overwhelming influence over the educational system. The modern Eurocentric educational structure has its theoretical ambitions pinned to the development of a supposed science of history and society; however, this supposed science is based on false concepts of race and evolutionary thought.

The false assumptions of Eurocentric thought present humans as the products of evolutionary or cultural logic on the one hand, and of deep-seated, unalterable economic, organizational, and psychological constraints on the other. Educational institutions insist that abandoning this way of viewing the world would lead to theoretical nihilism and destroy the established social order. Educational theory does not argue that society can be remade or reimagined, instead it postulates that if people do not recognize this evolutionary logic and these practical constraints, they will lose intellectual guidance. As a result, education must affirm Eurocentric social order and its theory of control. Other forms of culture or social life are recognized as expressions of a different way of being human within this evolutionary logic and these practical constraints.

In Eurocentric education, it is important to learn to think and act within the colonizer's strategy of differences (Memmi 1963). The strategy of differences is about unpacking events so that the opposites will come out pretty much the same regardless of who is doing the unpacking. Examples of these opposites are the distinctions between savage and civilized, colonizer and colonized, and public and private. In Eurocentric thought, "objectivism" is the name given to this strategy of differences, and it is the dominant method in Eurocentric educational transmission. It is knowing through fragmentation and it is evident in the ways knowledge is broken down into grade levels and disciplines. It is a commitment to the idea that we cannot know *anything* truly and well unless we know it from such a distance that the "object" of knowledge remains uncontaminated by our own subjectivity or personal beliefs (whether that "object" is a piece of literature, nature, history, or human nature). Despite its claims to objectivity, the strategy of differences is a subjective commitment to a way of knowing. It works if everyone buys into the system, but if there is no agreement between knowledge systems on how to categorize differences (or if one concludes it no longer matters), then the distinctions between opposites collapse—an outcome that is fatal to modern thought. The strategy of differences is inconsistent with Indigenous thought and interrelationships, and its dualisms have to yield to more holistic thought if there is to be a relationship between Indigenous and Eurocentric knowledge.

The arm's-length approach to truth manifest in the strategy of differences has been presented with such confidence, even arrogance, that it is hard to see the subjective fears that drive its agenda. Nevertheless, objectivism is full of fears: the fear of subjectivity, the fear of relationships, and the fear of being challenged and changed by what we know. It is the alien-observer perspective. Good reasons exist to fear unfettered subjectivity, of course. We have no desire to return to an age when a subjective whim reigned supreme in colonial thought. Yet, when the cultural pendulum swings to unreflective belief in objectivism, the results are no better.

Eurocentric thought has always been necessary and proper for those who wish to divide things up and separate them from themselves. This fragmentation of human problems into manageable components created special fields of inquiry. The ability to put distance between humans and their environment allowed people to come up with convenient solutions to their problems and to engage in practical activities. What happened next, though, is that objectivism took its creative thoughts for a description of the world as it is. Attempts to live according to the fragmented worldview created endless conflict and confusion, which led directly to the growing crises that are confronting everyone today.

Indigenous educators need to transform this way of knowing. They need to balance traditional Indigenous ways of knowing with the Eurocentric tradition. They must respect and understand the other ways of knowing. They must embrace the paradox of subjective and objective ways of knowing that do not collapse into either inward or outward illusions, but bring us all into a living dialogical relationship with the world that our knowledge gives us.

Indigenous educators need to understand that Eurocentric thought—which uses the lens of objectivism to hold humans at arm's length from the environment—gives the illusion of human power over things. The need for such power is directly related to the Eurocentric fear of living in an environment. We need to balance this false premise with Indigenous ways of knowing that acknowledge humans not as masters of but as partners in sustaining ecologies. We need to restore a way of knowing that gives Indigenous peoples and their communities the ability to survive by transforming their lives. We need a way of knowing that brings us into a living relationship with all we know so that our knowledge will be a source of community rather than of control. This way of knowing emerges only as we address the fear that lies behind our commitment to Eurocentric objectivism.

We do not mean that Eurocentric techniques for teaching have no legitimate place in Indigenous classrooms. We do suggest that the question of method needs to place a distant second to understanding Indigenous methods for the transmission of knowledge. The central issue in a postcolonial educational system is to help Indigenous students explore the primary questions of who they are, where they live, and how they are to be enriched by learning.

There is so much to be done and there are so many questions to be answered. For example, how can we maintain learning spaces where Indigenous students can know their natural identities, feel connected with Indigenous teachings, and become fully aware of a shared environment? How can we create spaces where they can experiment with different kinds of human encounters, and with the roles of their languages, knowledge, and heritage? Why have Eurocentric educational systems not moved closer to Indigenous methods of transmitting knowledge, and why have they not embraced a vision of essential human dignity and freedom? Why do these systems not aim to develop the full potential of Indigenous peoples? Why is this vision viewed as a utopian dream instead of as a change that is attainable in our generation? To answer these questions and improve conditions for Indigenous students, educators must attempt to understand the tensions that obscure cooperative efforts in educational reform.

This can be said more precisely. The educational system and Indigenous teachers do not need to invent a new way of transmitting Indigenous knowledge and heritage. All they need to do is to develop concepts that more faithfully reflect our traditional educational transmission processes. Educators need to understand the traditional methods. This requires creating and supporting training centers that are controlled by Indigenous elders and educators. These centers must strengthen educators' capacity to document, protect, teach, and apply the traditional transmission of heritage and must be operated in the language of the people.

Students trained in Eurocentric educational institutions do not understand the relationship between human capacities and freedom of consciousness, for the fragmented constructs of Eurocentric thought are primarily concerned with limiting experience. Using partial contexts, Eurocentric awareness categorizes the world into separate religious, political, economic, and racial groups, and the Eurocentric educational community divides human capacities into the separate categories of art, science, and technology. Dissatisfied with this fragmented vision, some Eurocentric scholars have set up interdisciplinary studies. Although these disciplines seek to unite these parts, they often create further fragmentation. Eurocentric thought even fragments human beings into their desires, aims, ambitions, loyalties, and psychological characteristics. With so many separate and conflicting compartments in each individual, some degree of neurosis seems inevitable. These partial contexts are illusionary. They are observer-created categories, reflections of an abused human consciousness. They expose an era of great poverty of spirit.

Eurocentric objectivism, with its emphasis on cold facts and logic, reflects how a minority of the world's population knows the world, and it gives a very skewed picture of this world. Indigenous people need to know that the vast majority of the world's population view the world from their point of view, and that their knowledge and heritage can exist as complementary to the Eurocentric construct. One way to let them know this is to teach them how their knowledge and heritage is transmitted. They also need to be exposed to an honest assessment of the Eurocentric self-serving vision of the world that is now dissolving around us.

Chapter 6

•••

Religious Paradoxes

What does God look like? These fish, this water, this land. — Linda Hogan, *Dwellings* (1995, 98)

In colonial times, Eurocentric religions were exported to Indigenous people as superior commodities that it was deadly to refuse (Rahner 1979, 717). Christian leaders transformed the divine order into a fierce religious export firmly controlled by serial killers. Eurocentric academic disciplines and educational systems were complicit with Christian domination and religious oppression. All of them contributed to the American holocaust and to cognitive imperialism; none have accepted responsibility or attempted to compensate for all the wrongs to Indigenous peoples—indeed, the export of Eurocentric religious thought continues.

As the historian Lewis Hanke noted, in *Aristotle and the American Indians* (1959), the personal God of the Europeans omitted to mention Indigenous peoples and their lands in His teachings. Because of the Bible's failure to mention the American continent and its people, church authorities argued that Indigenous peoples were infidels, natural slaves, children, or backward savages. Although Pope Paul III declared on June 9, 1537, that "Indians are truly men. . . . [T]hey may and should, freely and legitimately, enjoy their liberty and the possession of their property" (MacNutt 1909, 430–31), these teachings did nothing to prevent the brutal genocide of Indigenous peoples and the ecological destruction of their land. Many complex beliefs created the need to destroy Indigenous spiritual teachings: Indigenous peoples were uncivilized (*R. v. Syliboy* 1929), they had the wrong religion (*Jack and Charlie v. The Queen* 1986), and for their salvation they needed to convert to Christianity, the only true religion. In the Christian tradition, the Pauline "natural man" has to become a "new creature" in order to be saved (I Corinthians 2:14; II Corinthians 5:17). In short, Eurocentric thought rejected Indigenous spirituality.

Divine Order and Secular Law

Under their belief in a universal, singular, personal God, Eurocentric religions strove to convert Indigenous people. Religious coercion left deep scars in the minds and hearts of Indigenous people. Such oppression marked European society as well. The first half of the seventeenth century was a time of religious wars between the Catholics and Protestants. After the Treaty of Westphalia in 1648, the nation-states emerged as a remedy to these religious wars. Each nation-state was to decide for itself the issue of religion, and religion was no longer a valid cause for international warfare. In the eighteenth century, to maintain peace in the nation-states, the aristocracy developed the political principle that asserts that religion could be separated from the state, and that one could be a full member of civil society without having to belong to a particular religion. This principle attempted to maintain religious peace by forbidding government constraints on the private choice of beliefs, thus affirming an inherent freedom for everyone to act upon their religious beliefs. Yet, in colonialization, the secular state and the church recombined to create a new era of religious wars—this time against Indigenous peoples around the world.

The core belief of the Eurocentric church is that a personal God created the world. Because the personal God made the world, these religions believe that the world cannot fully share the divine nature of its Creator. Yet, most of these religions also believe that the functioning of the world reveals the cosmic order of the divine lawgiver. For instance, Eurocentric religions see these regularities of the cosmic order as God's Talk, which describes what happens and establishes what ought to be (Wolfson 1968, 439–60). Unfortunately, because the personal God is considered divine, Eurocentric thinkers see His commands as universal and believe they hold equally for all peoples. They believe that the divine order transcends human society, just as the personal God transcends the world. The divine order is the reference point for evaluating all people, and it is superior to the laws of human sovereigns and to the customs of different peoples. To accept the cosmology of the transcendent religion and the related idea of higher law, humans must commit themselves to universal, objective standards rather than to their own beliefs and desires (Neumann 1957, 69–91). The belief in the existence of standards of conduct given by a personal God has sustained the ideas of universality in religion, generality in the rule of law, and equality under the positive law (Fitzpatrick 1991, 167).

Semitic monotheism (represented by Judaism, Christianity, and Islam) asserts that all humans have an immortal soul made in the image of the personal God. This immortal soul is distinct but not necessarily separate from the earthly body. For example, the fundamental assumption of the French political philosopher Montesquieu is that there is a single spirit of law that can be found in the soul of the people. The soul of the people is inherent and immanent in the law (Lyotard 1987, 37–38, 177–78). Monotheism affirms the dichotomy between humans and the world.

Monotheistic religions also believe that the personal God allows some members of the human race to live in His presence forever. This forges a theory of salvation (Weber 1972, 319–21); it also creates a binary distinction between the elect and the damned. This distinction brings us once again to the colonialist strategy of differences between the civilized and the savage, the colonizer and the colonized, the Occidental and the Oriental, the scientific and the superstitious (Blaut 1993, 1–50). In monotheistic religions, the priesthood or learned men systematized the divine commandments, which became the sacred laws of the personal God's salvation: for example, the Jewish *halakhad*, Roman canon law, and the Islamic *sharï'a.* These beliefs are unexplored in Indigenous thought, which focuses on what is rather than on what ought to be.

Invariably, divine law became an ally of and a limitation on secular authority. As a system of beliefs and practices, divine law presides over democratic forms of society. It expresses the true and right order, and provides a framework of legitimacy for Eurocentric political and legal order. The divine order is partially articulated and sanctioned by elected legislators in the name of the rule of law; however, it sets boundaries to majoritarian choice and establishes the principles and values that justify and criticize the positive law of the state. The religious orthodoxies operate by supporting the idea that there are entitlements that no secular law or political decision can disregard. The rule of law requires impartial judges to apply the legislation. Lacking legislation, impartial judges apply the system of beliefs and practices. Consequently, the secular laws governing human relations are drawn from the religious orthodoxies, their universal discourse, and their values. French poststructuralist and postmodern thinkers (Derrida, Foucault, Baudrillard, and Lyotard) argue that the European Enlightenment did not secularize thought or render law or society or humankind independent of the divine order. Instead, law incorporated religious assumptions into its own categories as "white mythology" (Young 1990, 90).

Correcting False Translations

Most Indigenous spiritual teachings and practices flow from ecological understandings rather than from cosmology. The relationship between ecologies and Indigenous consciousness has long been noted in Eurocentric classification (Vecsey & Venables 1980; Hughes 1983). Indigenous thought does not view ecology as a mass noun, but rather as a synthesis or vector of processes. Most believe these processes sustain a sacred living order, self-subsisting if not self-generating and independent of human will (Levy-Bruhl 1966; for a Eurocentric analogy, see Otto 1957). N. Scott Momaday, a Kiowa-Navajo writer, summarized this understanding:

> Sacred ground is ground that is invested with belief. Belief, at its root, exists independent of meaning. That is, expression and object may escape what we can perceive as definable meaning. The intrinsic power of sacred ground is

> often ineffable and abstract. I behold a particular sacred space, and I understand that it is in some way earned. It is consecrated, made holy with offerings—song and ceremony, joy and sorrow, the dedication of the mind and heart, offerings of life and death. The words "sacred" and "sacrifice" are related. And acts of sacrifice make sacred the earth. The indigenous people of the world know this as they know the sunrise and sunset. (1993, 1)

Indigenous spiritual teachings are found in the ability to apprehend the hidden harmony of changing ecologies and to create alliances with these transforming forces. These understandings inform Indigenous consciousness and languages (Brown 1964). A typical experience in attempting to understand Indigenous religions is described by writer Joseph Brown:

> In my first contacts with Black Elk, almost all he said was phrased in terms involving animals and natural phenomena. I naively would begin to talk about religious matters, until I finally realized that he was, in fact, explaining his religion. (1964, 16)

Eurocentric religious leaders have difficulty understanding Indigenous teachings because most of them do not appear to have any holy books, any priesthoods, any churches, any philosophy, or any history. The reason for this is that Indigenous peoples encased all these elements in their ecological contexts and languages. Where there were written texts, priests, and temples, the Christians destroyed them.

In the modern secular order, religions are complex phenomena that defy definition. Nevertheless, Indigenous spiritual practices are not viewed as legitimate religions. The report of the UN Seminar on the Effects of Racism and Racial Discrimination on the Social and Economic Relations Between Indigenous Peoples and States (1989) concludes that colonial prejudices have been transformed into religious and state theories of spiritual and cultural superiority, which reject the legitimacy of Indigenous peoples' values and institutions.

In Indigenous thought, ecologies are considered sacred realms, and they contain the keepers that taught Indigenous ancestors the core of Indigenous spiritual practices (Deloria 1973; Snow 1977). The core belief of Indigenous spirituality is that everything is alive, and Indigenous peoples seek spirituality through intimate communion with ecological biodiversity (USFATF 1979, 52). Such beliefs deny the distinction between the sacred and the profane, since all life processes are sacred.

The relationships between the people and the land, and the kinship of the people with the other living creatures that share the land and with the spirit world create the context of the sacred. Experiencing an ecology in which one lives is a personal necessity and an integral part of spiritual practice. This sacred order is not considered either a paradise or natural; it has to be renewed and sustained by humans. Human creativity is a great responsibility, for human creativity is needed to see the patterns of change and to adjust to the flux, and creativity manifests the spiritual nature of all life.

Spirituality in Indigenous thought revolves around forces that are called "creativity" in English. Since Indigenous peoples connect everything with a continuous state of transformation, creativity or spirituality is the matrix that holds everything together. The Indigenous vision of creativity is distinct from Eurocentric thought. It is encased in and manifested through Indigenous linguistic structures. Learning Indigenous spiritual teachings involves intimate and endless talks with elders and relatives, and is a process that takes patience and prudence. Indigenous sounds enfold an elegant way of explicating an ecological order. Spiritual teachings comprise complex systems of relationship enfolded in stories, songs, prayers, rituals, and talks. These sounds inform a remarkable connection to the livingness within a spiral of life and to the power to renew livingness.

Indeed, the sounds of songs and prayers created certain ecologies. For example, the Dene-Navajo ceremonial *hózhóójí* (blessingway) demonstrates how the Navajo envision the thought and the sounds of a *yattíii* (speaker) creating the world and sustaining life. Other examples are the "songlines" of the Australian Aborigines. Songs give Indigenous peoples a great human responsibility in maintaining an ecosystem rather than a divine order. These sounds are creative acts of caring. Thus, Indigenous languages are indispensable and irreplaceable in Indigenous consciousnesses, spiritual teachings, and ceremonies. With the loss of these languages, Indigenous worldviews and spiritual teachings about an ecosystem vanish.

Indigenous spirituality exists for immigrants as distorted translations that must be corrected. Few Europeans have ever mastered any Indigenous languages, in part because of their difficult sounds and unfamiliar grammar systems. Most Eurocentric writings fragment Indigenous consciousness and teachings into separate, artificial categories of Eurocentric thought such as "religious," "spiritual," "supernatural," "cultural," "artistic," "intellectual," or "legal." This is misleading and inappropriate, but unavoidable to Eurocentric thinkers. It is an act of appropriating Indigenous spirituality for Christian purposes.

Eurocentric thought about Algonquian consciousness, for example, is derived from missionaries, explorers, anthropologists, and linguistic researchers. These immigrants have little understanding of the original meaning of the Algonquian consciousness or of the original composition of this linguistic group. They usually derive the name from Champlain's interpretation of *Algounequins,* as meaning "the people of the place" (Biggar 1922–36, I:105).

The original meaning of the sound, it is said by some Mi'kmaw elders, was derived from a depression in the land caused by a comet landing in the area of Quebec. Other speakers refer to distinct rock formations around the Great Lakes, where an ancient ideographic script and rock drawings were carved. Some Eurocentric linguists assert that the word is derived from the Mi'kmaw term *alkoome,* which refers to people who stand in the canoe and spear fish in the water, or *állegonkin,* which refers to dancers, or *el legom'kwin,* which refers to friends or allies (Vessel 1987, 11–14).

Many Indigenous peoples in Canada have been placed in this linguistic category (Dickason 1992, 63–67). There are few consistencies between Canada and the United States for names given to the speakers or how the speakers identify themselves. In Eurocentric linguistic traditions, this consciousness is called the Macro-Algonkian Phylum. Typically it is subdivided into two branches: the Algic and the Gulf (Voegelin 1977). In one classification system, this would be a part of a single macrophylum called Amerindian (Greenberg 1987).

Eurocentric translations of Algonquian teachings have misinterpreted them. The core of the problem is that missionaries, anthropologists, and linguists have tried to understand Indigenous languages from the perspective of Eurocentric linguistic conventions. Their methodology was to impose foreign categories on Indigenous knowledge, languages, and teachings. Eurocentric thought teaches one to be an impartial observer of nature to gain objective knowledge of an external realm of thing-objects. This creates a reality of two items only: the observer and the observed, which are, respectively, the knower and the known, or the subject and the object (Von Maltzahn 1994, 3–6). English habitually categorizes the world into nouns, to the dismay of Algonquian people, who believe that everything moves in an interdependent process. The sounds of Indigenous languages put great emphasis on prefixes and suffixes and syntax around verb structures. Whereas in English verbs *require* nouns to make complete thoughts or sentences, in Algonquian there is no concept of a sentence, each sound serving that purpose. Our cognitive orientation is toward relationships, processes, and flux rather than toward things.

The missionaries attempted to match Algonquian spiritual teachings to Christian ideas. Their purpose was to use Algonquian sounds to affirm Christian beliefs. The translators' beliefs determined the relevance of Algonquian beliefs. To affirm the belief in a universal noun-God who created the world, the translators manipulated Eurocentric words for Algonquian sounds. One of the toughest tasks Indigenous people had was explaining to Europeans who their noun-God was. Since the Europeans insisted one God created all humans and that all humans just had different nouns, different names, which referred to the same person, eventually they discovered their God among

Algonquian beliefs in the powers that reside in the ecology and in "cultural heroes." In a Eurocentric examination of the process, anthropologist Åke Hultkrantz argues that the concept of a Supreme Being did not exist in Northern Algonquian thought before the arrival of the Europeans (1981, 187–211).

Usually the attempts to impose the existence of a transcendent God and the principles of God's Talk on Algonquian thought provided false analogies. This process of imposition was not benign: it was part of a Christian plan to initiate the hostile processes of theological indoctrination. At best the Christian efforts have been acts of faith; at worst they have been part of an attempt to destroy the belief systems and languages of entire groups of peoples through spiritual and cultural appropriation.

Let us briefly review the appropriation process. Indigenous peoples often talk about forces of creativity rather than about a personal Creator. The creative processes can be expressed using verbs of being and becoming. Using these sounds, the missionary-linguists imposed the idea of a personal God. Thus, such terms as *Knij'kaminau* or *Niskam* (Mi'kmaq), *Gichi-manidoo* (Ojibwewin-Ikidowinan), *Ma'ura* (Winnebago), or *Ma?heo ?e* (Tsistsistas or *Tsetsehestahase*) were manipulated to create God. Other Indigenous languages also express the vastness of the realms. The Hopis call the creative forces *a'ne himu* (really process or mighty something) said to be the realm of soft, unmanifested essence as opposed to hard, manifested forms. Missionaries and ethnologists have often described the Lakota phrase *wakan anka* (the Great Spirit) as their person God. In Lakota thought, *wakan* means "sacred" and *tanka* means "vast" or "great"; thus *wankantanka* symbolizes all sacred processes in the universe. If the sound must be translated, one should discuss it as "the most sacred" or "vast creative forces" (Powers 1987, 23). Similarly, in Cherokee thought and linguistic structure, *unehleanvhi* represents the spiritual nature of the universe, but it has been reduced to "the creator" by Eurocentric theology.

These phases are not analogous to the noun-God, Supreme-God, or Son-of-God concept of Eurocentric theology. They are more than simply divergent—they exist in an altogether different realm. For example, the process of maintaining Mi'kmaw consciousness is called *tlilnuo'lti'k* and is distinguished from the process of maintaining thought, sounds, or language, which is signified by the sound *tlinuita'sim*. These differences provide different foundations for ethics, personal decision making, and purposes. Among those who still think and speak in Indigenous languages, the distinct and coherent worldview remains operative. Sometimes, perhaps surprisingly, it also remains operative in many who do not speak Indigenous languages but who can understand them. Instead of disintegrating, the implicit order has transformed into different sentiments of obligations and accepted practices common to Indigenous societies.

In most situations, the Europeans' interpretations continue to be destructive to the cognitive solidarity of Algonquian teachings and practices. In some cases, European attempts to appropriate Indigenous peoples' symbols and languages for European religious purposes have distorted tribal teachings and understandings or have forced them underground (Duran & Duran 1995). Still, the destructive approach of the Europeans has never ended the inherent Indigenous need for harmony. Intuitively and passionately, we continue to seek to be in harmony with the sacred processes and to live with ecological integrity in dignity.

In the modern reformation of Algonquian spirituality, Indigenous peoples often have to rely on European writings about their languages and beliefs. Young Algonquian people cannot assume that these writings translate Algonquian realms faithfully (Reddy 1993, iii). Similarly, they cannot understand Algonquian spiritual ideas by attempting to match them up with Christian ideas, since the alien learning method and the alien language create paradoxes and confusion. Yet such translation was, and is, the general goal of cognitive imperialism (Battiste 1986). It is important that we look beyond the available translations to the original ideas to see the multiple layers of meaning and subtle channels of communication. In the restoration, we have to be aware of the value contagion inflicted on Algonquian languages and spiritual ideas. The dilemma is that Indigenous peoples cannot achieve and act in accordance with such awareness if they speak only European languages.

Freedom from Missionaries

The Indigenous survivors of the missionary efforts in North America and elsewhere cling to vestiges of their beliefs and teachings. We are a vulnerable, marginalized, abused, and disadvantaged people. Eurocentric thought has deprived us of any firm sense of how we fit into the environment and society around us, and we suffer a consciousness of aversion. All too often, we feel homeless in nature and at a loss to judge or justify the conduct of our lives. We seem powerless to create a secular society that is nourishing or sustainable. All too often we exist as cultural blanks (Little Bear 1994, 69–78), fragmented by our search for spirituality among squabbling teachings and promises by the churches and the state. Guided by Eurocentric evaluations, and living with the effects of poverty and racism, we often blame ourselves or our ancestors for our terrible abuse, and doubt our capacity to rebuild our lives according to our traditional beliefs. Terrible ecological damage denies us the relationship with the environment we need to reconstruct our spiritual lives.

The constitutional protection of Aboriginal teachings and practices in

Canada raises hard questions about continued evangelization. To those Indigenous families who are committed to living traditional lives, this is a recurring theme. Relentless Eurocentric evangelization among Indigenous peoples is a huge obstacle to their healing. This issue has never been adequately addressed by Eurocentric religions or their complicitous governments. These institutions see evangelization as an issue of a universal divine right, rather than as an issue of freedom of religion or exploitation. But divine or not, evangelization has been forced on Indigenous peoples and it has harmed them. Because religious leaders have not confronted this issue, it continues to hinder the Indigenous struggle to heal the scars of oppression, to renew our self-confidence, and to recover our dignity. This is a complex issue that needs an authentic solution. We suggest that other religions suspend their missionary activities until they negotiate evangelization protocols or covenants with Indigenous spiritual teachers and peoples.

Indigenous people have long been aware of the limitations of Eurocentric religions. As early as 1777, Old Tasse, a Cherokee, commented about Eurocentric thought:

> Much has been said of the want of what you term "Civilization" among the Indians. Many proposals have been made to us to adopt your law, your religion, your manners and your customs. We do not see the propriety of such a reformation. We should be better pleased with beholding the good effects of these doctrines in your own practices than with hearing you talk about them or of reading your newspapers on such subjects. (Hill 1994, 36)

Indigenous peoples are still waiting to see the "good effect" of religious doctrines in daily practice. We should not be expected to fulfill the spiritual needs of strangers.

Indigenous spiritual teachings and Christian faiths can be complementary. Indigenous teachings allow each person his or her harmony without forcing absolute conformity on experiences or values; Indigenous communities accept more diversity than most linguistic communities (Champagne 1994, 658–83). Despite the Eurocentric compulsion to drive Indigenous thought to formalize its spiritual teachings into a theology, Indigenous teachers have rejected the ideas of canonized, authoritative codifications and universal principles. There are secret societies among Indigenous people, but there is no public coercion. Indigenous consciousnesses and languages honor creativity and spiritual growth, and tolerate their members being both traditional and Christian (Vecsey 1991, 12–15). Once Eurocentric thought accepts its teachings as local ideals instead of universal principles and respects the ecology as sacred, there will be few substantial differences between most religious teachings. From a Mi'kmaw perspective, the teachings of Moses, Jesus Christ, and

Mohammed are part of the teachings of *npuoinaq* or medicine people—nothing more, nothing less.

Some Indigenous peoples have created complementary relationships between Indigenous and Eurocentric spiritual teachings. For example, the Mi'kmaw rites under the 1610 concordat with the Holy See exempt them from Roman canon law (Henderson 1997). Many Indigenous spiritual teachers are seeking new covenants with other religions on many issues. They are especially interested in partnerships to protect and enhance the environment and to restore Indigenous consciousness and languages. The development of concerted strategies to protect Indigenous teachings and practices is long overdue. Each religion must establish new relationships with Indigenous spiritual teachers so that they can grasp Indigenous teachings and practices in the context of sacred geographies and Indigenous thought.

Indigenous people are asking for genuine respect for their spiritual teachings and practices. Other religions must recognize the legitimate needs of Indigenous peoples to preserve and enhance their spiritual integrity. Indigenous spiritual teachers and practitioners are asking for space and time to practice their freedom of belief. They are asking for the opportunity to nourish and to spiritually heal their people, in privacy and with solidarity.

In Canada, because of the Aboriginal shield in section 25 of the *Charter of Rights and Freedoms*, no Eurocentric or other religion can coerce any Aboriginal person to affirm a specific religious belief or to manifest a specific religious practice for sectarian purposes. If necessary, Aboriginal people in Canada will raise their constitutional shield to create a "wall of separation" between Eurocentric religions and Aboriginal teachings and practices to ensure the exercise of their spirituality. Their only other choice is cognitive extinction. Such a course would mark the failure of the world's religions to find dignity.

Sacred Healing Sites

Most religions have noted the unique relationships that exist between the land and Indigenous peoples. In his discussion of the rights of minorities, Pope John Paul II was the first pope to recognize this unrivaled unity among Indigenous peoples. He stated:

> Certain people, especially those identified as native or indigenous, have always maintained a special relationship to their lands, a relationship connected with the group's very identity as a people having their own tribal, cultural, and religious traditions. When such indigenous peoples are deprived of their land they lose a vital element of their way of life and actually run the risk of disappearing as a people. (as cited in Stogre 1992, 182)

The pope inferred that Indigenous peoples' right of life embraces an adequate land base to practice their religious freedoms. He also stated that minorities have a fundamental right to "exist," to "preserve and develop their own culture," and to exercise "religious freedom."

After legally required consultation with traditional Indigenous religious leaders to decide appropriate religious rights and practices, the U.S. Federal Agencies Task Force Report acknowledged that

> the Native people of this continent believe that certain areas of land are holy. These lands may be sacred, for example, because of religious events which occurred there, because they contain specific natural products, because they are the dwelling place or embodiment of spiritual beings, because they surround and contain burial grounds, or because they are sites conducive to communicating with spiritual beings. (USFATF 1979, 52)

Indigenous peoples construct spiritual teachings around the belief that at certain places there is a sacred ambiance that empowers human consciousness and spirituality. These locations range from burial grounds to mythic, legendary, or petroglyphic places; from places of purification, healing, and fertility to sacred plant, rock, and animal places; from medicine wheels and sun temples to vision and dreaming places.

Protecting these ecologies and their biodiversity is an integral part of protecting Indigenous spirituality. Properly understood, protecting ecologies gives birth to a new proprietary category—that of sacred lands. The Supreme Court of Canada has held that Aboriginal tenure, title, and interests in the land are *sui generis*, that is, they are structured as a legal system distinct from Eurocentric concepts of property and tenure (*R. v. Guerin* 1984; *Delgamuukw v. British Columbia* 1997). The nature of Aboriginal tenure "cannot be totally captured by a lexicon derived from European legal systems" (*Mitchell v. Peguis Indian Band* 1990, 82).

Indigenous people need protection of the environment so they can end their grieving and generate a balance that can heal a dominated and oppressed spirituality and, eventually, heal countries. Protecting the ecology is protecting Indigenous worldviews, languages, identities, spiritual teachings, and practices. Enhancing the biodiversity of the ecologies is essential to self-preservation and also to the preservation of a sacred way of life. New policies must be based on respectful dialogue and cooperation between spiritual healers.

Canadians recognize the existence of Indigenous "sacred sites" and other places of particular historical and cultural significance. The full complexity of sacred geography in Canada is still poorly understood, however. Although Bruce Chatwin's popular personal narrative *Songlines* (1993) drew attention to the linkages between songs, sites, larger landscapes, and peoples' periodic travels through the countryside in Australia, this concept of the ecosystem as a sacred whole has not been applied in a Canadian context. Indeed, Hugh Brody's *Maps and Dreams* (1981) described the Northern spiritscape almost as if it did not relate intelligibly to the physical landscape.

The report of the Canadian Royal Commission on Aboriginal Peoples (RCAP 1996b) recommended that sites of sacred or historical significance should be considered in the reallocation of lands in Canada. For lands under the primary control of Aboriginal nations, those nations will make decisions about protection and use. For lands under the joint jurisdiction of the Crown and Aboriginal nations, protection and access can form part of co-management agreements. Where sacred or heritage sites are part of lands under primary jurisdiction of the Crown or subject to fee-simple interests or ownership rights, then Aboriginal access to and involvement in management will be negotiated (vol. 2, chap. 4). The commission also saw that a necessary first step is for Aboriginal people and communities to identify and assess the condition of sites that are historically and culturally important to them. The legislation on historic sites must be reviewed to ensure recognition and protection of Aboriginal interests, interim measures must be taken to protect significant sites that are endangered, and consideration must be given to heritage and sacred sites for Aboriginal people living in urban areas (vol. 4, chaps. 6 and 7).

For Indigenous peoples, the sanctity of species and landforms in ecosystems is a matter of degree (Vecsey & Venables 1980; Daes 1993). All species are regarded as kinfolk, and, like human kin, stand in varying individual and historical relationships to one another. Those with unusually close and important relationships are the most sacred, but no element of the environment lacks some form of potentially significant and useful power. Similarly, certain features of the landscape may be regarded as critical nodes in ecosystems. These are places where relationships between species converge and where their power is felt. Sacred sites often do, in fact, contain important habitats such as nurseries, nesting areas, or groves of trees that act as central points for the dispersal of seeds and as migration landmarks. The ancient stands of red cedars in the Pacific Northwest temperate rainforest are an example.

Sacred sites are not limited to ceremonial places or places that are periodically used for purification or healing. Many are simply known, respected, and left relatively undisturbed. They may, therefore, function as refugia and help maintain the populations of many species over a wider area. For Indigenous peoples, major issues include unrestricted access to sacred sites for ceremonial and healing purposes; the protection of sites from any disturbance, contamination, or inappropriate human activity; privacy when visiting or using sites; and the continuing integrity of the larger ecosystems with which sites are connected. Sites tend not to be publicly identified until threatened by some project, because of fears that public knowledge, demarcation, and government supervision—for example, by Parks Canada—will lead to restrictions on Indigenous peoples' activities and an increase in non-Indigenous traffic.

The *American Indian Religious Freedom Act* (1981) in the United States and the *Native Title Act* (1993) in Australia are appreciated legislation, since control of the land and sacred sites is essential to the protection of cultural and intellectual heritage. However, land alone is not enough; further specific measures dealing with the rights of Indigenous peoples to control their cultural heritage are also required.

Most countries have adopted procedures for the identification and protection of historically and culturally important places. For example, protection can be given to buildings, groups of buildings, landscapes, and landforms (1) that are associated with important historical events or historically significant persons, (2) that have the potential of yielding important historical information, or (3) that represent a characteristic type of historical human activity or environment.

Such laws are not always applied consistently to sites of interest to Indigenous peoples, and often do not prevent governments from disposing of sites or developing them for other purposes. Culturally important places may include locations where Indigenous peoples gathered foods or medicines, and landforms associated with Indigenous cultural traditions and religious practices. In determining whether a site is important, government agencies are advised to consult directly with Indigenous peoples. They are also advised to respect Indigenous peoples' desire for confidentiality, for example, where a site has been associated with traditional spiritual teachings.

Little has been done in Canada to identify and protect spiritual practices or sacred sites. In *R. v. Sioui* (1990)—a case concerning the use of park land within a treaty area for religious and customary purposes—the treaty rights of Huron Indians pursuant to the Treaty of 1760, which guaranteed "the free exercise of their religion, their customs," were upheld by the Supreme Court of Canada and the Quebec Court of Appeal. In this case, the accused had cut trees and lit fires to carry out certain customary and religious activities, all of which were contrary to the *National Parks Act* (1985). The court held that the activities constituted customary practices guaranteed by the treaty.

Tourism, Vandalism, and Problems of Privacy

There continue to be some instances of the involuntary display of Indigenous peoples and their communities as tourist attractions. The public display of Indigenous peoples at Eurocentric zoos and international expositions was commonplace a century ago. Like the reported display of tribal peoples to tourists in some Southeast Asian countries today, these activities may involve covert forms of coercion and are likely to continue as long as Indigenous peoples lack complete freedom under law and access to their own means of subsistence and development.

In response to a request by Congress, the United States National Parks Service conducted a study, in cooperation with American Indian organizations, of measures needed to protect and develop Indian historical sites. The report of this study, *Keepers of the Treasures* (1990), noted that while some Indian tribes were strongly opposed to research, others had begun to establish their own archeological programs and museums. Once they are assured of control of the disposition and interpretation of their cultural heritage, Indigenous peoples are willing to collaborate with government agencies and academic institutions.

In the U.S. case of *Fools Crow v. Gullet* (1982), Lakota (Sioux) elders complained that the development of their most sacred mountain, Bear Butte in South Dakota, as a public park would desecrate the site and lead to the exploitation of their religious practices. Tourists had already begun to interrupt some ceremonies and to disturb the privacy of individual Lakota who were seeking visions in remote parts of the mountain. A federal court rejected these claims, stating that interference from tourists would not be an insurmountable obstacle to the continued ceremonial use of Bear Butte. Lakota continue to use the mountain within sight of trails and parking lots built for tourists.

The Bear Butte dispute was only one of several cases, since 1980, in which American courts refused to protect Indigenous peoples' ceremonial sites on government-owned land. *Sequoyah v. Tennessee Valley Authority* (1980) involved the flooding of the ancient capital city of the Cherokee Nation by a hydroelectric power project. In *Badoni v. Higginson* (1980), Navajo elders tried to prevent Rainbow Bridge, a unique natural feature long used as a ceremonial site, from being opened to tourism. In *Wilson v. Block* (1983), Hopi elders tried unsuccessfully to block the construction of a ski resort on a sacred mountain, and finally, in *Lyng v. Northwest Indian Cemetery Protective Association* (1988), the Supreme Court allowed the disturbance of Hoopa ceremonial sites in California by the construction of logging roads. The Supreme Court, in *Lyng,* reasoned that the government has a right to do whatever it wishes with public property, even when this appears to conflict with the guarantee of the "free exercise of religion" in the U.S. Constitution.

Right to Harvest and Use Ceremonial Materials in Religious Practices

A related issue has been the right to harvest and use ceremonial materials, such as medicinal plants and feathers. Canada has not focused on this issue. In the United States, there has been considerable litigation over the right of Indians to obtain feathers from bald eagles, which are a protected species, or to use *peyote*, which U.S. laws classify as a dangerous narcotic. In both of these cases, the solution thus far has been to make a special, legislated exception in favor of Indigenous cultural practices. U.S. courts have generally agreed, however, that these exceptions are not required by the constitutional guarantee of "free exercise of religion." Similar problems will arise in the Andean countries—for example, with respect to Indigenous peoples' traditional medicinal and social use of *coca*—and in Amazonia with respect to ceremonial uses of feathers from increasingly scarce species of birds. Indigenous peoples insist that their enjoyment of religious and cultural integrity take priority over commercial and recreational uses of wildlife by others.

Indigenous Burial Grounds

Certain parts of ecological territories hold special significance for Indigenous peoples. Ancestral burial grounds or sites for spiritual ceremonies are considered sacred land, and the spirit of such sites are of central importance. Threats to the integrity of sacred and historical sites come not only from development projects and legislation but also from archeological endeavors. The search for culturally significant objects often leads archeologists to burial grounds. Indigenous peoples have asked that these objects be left in the ground and that graves not be disturbed out of respect for the dead and in recognition that the burial grounds remain the collective property of Indigenous peoples.

Indigenous peoples must be involved in designating archeological sites, in designing interpretive materials, and in managing resources. However, control over excavation is outside their jurisdiction. In some Canadian jurisdictions, Aboriginal groups are consulted as a matter of courtesy before excavation permits are issued, and in the newly created territory of Nunavut any excavation permits will require Inuit approval. Generally, however, no consistent policies or laws are in place to ensure that Indigenous peoples control this central element of their heritage.

In a series of applications and motions, the Poplar Point Ojibway Nation has attempted to protect its sacred sites and burial grounds. In *McCrady v. Ontario* (1991), the nation applied for an injunction to stop construction of a dam at High Falls on the Namewaminikan River on the basis that the hydroelectric project would irreparably damage their Indigenous rights, including their right to prevent damage to their burial grounds. The court rejected their claim because they had entered into a contract with the minister of natural resources under which they permitted the hydroelectric project to proceed.

Following the court's ruling, workers on the construction site discovered human skeletal remains on a slope overlooking High Falls. After investigation it was concluded that the remains were those of an Amerindian person of unknown origin and antiquity, buried in accordance with the religious customs of the cultural group. It was also concluded that the burial site had special spiritual and spatial significance. The nation brought a notice of motion for an order compelling the registrar of cemeteries to declare a portion of the watershed of the Namewaminikan River an "unapproved Indigenous Peoples Cemetery" under section 71 of the Ontario *Cemeteries Act* (1990). The nation also moved for an injunction against further construction or activities related to the hydroelectric project pending the registrar's decision. In *McCrady v. Ontario* (1992), the court dismissed the motion for an order compelling the registrar to make a declaration, but granted an injunction restraining work on the hydroelectric project until the registrar had made a declaration under the act. In applying the traditional test for injunctions, the court noted that respect for the dead, which is a fundamental tenet of Indigenous culture and White society, cannot be measured or regulated in monetary terms.

On November 3, 1992, the registrar declared that the upper slopes of a knoll overlooking High Falls were an unapproved Indigenous peoples' cemetery. However, the registrar excluded the High Falls area from the "burial site." The nation considered this area to be an integral part of the cemetery and raised a number of *Charter* arguments in *McCrady v. Ontario* (1993). Specifically, the nation argued that the completion of the hydroelectric project would negatively affect their freedom of conscience, freedom of worship, and freedom of religion, thereby infringing their rights under section 2 of the *Charter.* They also argued that the exclusion of High Falls from the "burial site" was contrary to section 15 of the *Charter,* in that it discriminated against them as Indigenous people as they considered the falls to be part of the cemetery. With respect to section 2 of the *Charter,* the court held that the *Charter* did not oblige the state to support any religion or religious belief. The *Cemeteries Act* and regulations placed a spatial limitation upon a "burial site," which was based upon the site of human remains and not upon religion, religious beliefs, or the contravention of anyone's freedom of religion or conscience. The court also rejected the nation's argument under section 15 of the *Charter,* stating that the nation's complaint was not that they were denied equal protection and equal benefit of the law without discrimination, but that they were not receiving preferential treatment. The court held that no such right existed.

Another Canadian case, *Nanoose Indian Band et al. v. The Queen and Intrawest Corporation et al.* (1995), involved the discovery of several hundred Indigenous skeletons and a village site on land that was being developed as a sewage pump station near Craig Bay on Vancouver Island. Archeologists obtained a permit under the British Columbia *Heritage Conservation Act*

(1979) to investigate the site. The court found that the permits had not been issued properly and were void. New permits were issued. In a second proceeding, the Nanoose Band's request for injunctive relief against further development on the land was denied, since the B.C. government agreed to buy the land from the developer. The court did not think that the amended *Heritage Conservation Act* infringed upon Indigenous religious freedoms but was protecting the burial remains. It rejected any constitutional basis to prevent the provincial permits, but agreed that the action raised a fair question to be tried.

Return and Reburial of Ancestors' Remains and Artifacts

The historical alliance between Eurocentric religions and law makers has forced Indigenous peoples to seek secular legal protection from the taking of their ancestors' remains. Protection of sacred sites, recovery of human remains so that proper burial can be arranged, repatriation of artifacts that are the private property or sacred inheritance of particular families and communities—these are all essential to the spiritual health of Indigenous communities. Because of Indigenous peoples' deep relationship with the land, the control of sacred sites, burial grounds, and archeological sites is important to them. Their concerns about the appropriation of cultural property and uses that violate Indigenous laws and traditions extend beyond material objects to stories, songs, and representations in masks and crests.

As a general rule, national legal systems treat anything found in the soil as belonging either to the government or to the owner of the land. This permitted archeologists and other individuals in the United States to acquire ownership of skeletons and other materials found in graves of Indigenous people, which were typically not legally designated and protected as "cemeteries." In 1986, however, a court in the State of Louisiana decided that the contents of several graves of Tunica-Biloxi Indians belonged to the surviving members of that tribe (*Charrier v. Bell* 1986). The court reasoned that burial does not amount to an intention to abandon rights to the body and the objects buried with it. Whether the community retains rights to the grave after burial must be determined by the cultures and customs of the people. The Tunica-Biloxi showed that they had maintained a cultural and religious attachment to their gravesites long after any external markings had disappeared. Several other U.S. states have now adopted laws protecting Indigenous graves, and the national government has enacted the *Native American Graves Protection and Repatriation Act* (NAGPRA 1990).

Under NAGPRA, all museums and other institutions owned or funded by the federal government must conduct inventories of the Indigenous human remains in their collections and notify the relevant Indigenous peoples. Human remains must be returned upon demand to any modern-day group that is "culturally affiliated" with them. Any human remains, grave objects, "sacred objects," or objects having ongoing cultural or historical importance, which may be discovered on government lands in the future, are declared to belong to the modern-day Indigenous group that is "culturally affiliated" with them. The meaning of "cultural affiliation" is still under discussion between Indigenous leaders and government officials. A definition proposed by governmental officials in October 1992 would require proof of kinship and cultural "identity" and, in the event of competing claims by two present-day groups, would award custody of objects to the group with the "closest" cultural ties to them. Since U.S. policies aggressively relocated and consolidated tribes up to the 1880s, tracing these connections between nineteenth- and twentieth-century groups will undoubtedly be complicated.

According to reports prepared by the U.S. Congress, the remains of thousands of Indigenous people have been stored in the collections of museums and scientific institutions. About 18,500 individuals were found in the collection of the Smithsonian Institution alone. The Indigenous Alutiiq people of Larsen Bay, Alaska, discovered the remains of 756 individuals from their area at the Smithsonian, and with the assistance of the Native American Rights Fund, an Indigenous-controlled legal services organization, waged a two-year struggle with museum officials for their return. The Larsen Bay skeletons were excavated in the 1920s and 1930s by Ales Hrdlicka, who was famous for his publications on American Indian physiology. According to village elders, some of the graves he opened were only ten to twenty years old. Museum officials resisted returning the remains, arguing that they were much too old to be traced reliably to present-day Alutiiq. Even after they agreed to return the remains, museum officials argued that they should be preserved in a museum in Alaska, rather than reburied. The Alutiiq eventually prevailed and reburied the remains in 1991. The estimated cost of proving their claims was over US$100,000.

Collecting Indigenous peoples' human remains was popular for many years in North America, and large numbers of human skulls and other materials remain in private hands. For example, in British Columbia between 1875 and 1900, grave-robbing and confiscation were so generalized that by the early 1900s New York City housed more Indigenous skulls, skeletons, poles, canoes, baskets, feast bowls, and masks than British Columbia (Hume 1989). One notable case was the confiscation of the Whaler's Washing Shrine of the Nootka. The shrine was a plank-and-beam structure filled with ninety-five carved Indigenous images and human skulls. It was confiscated from Friendly Cove, Vancouver Island, while the Indigenous people were away sealing. It has been in storage at the American Museum of Natural History in New York since 1904, although negotiations are under way for its return (Hume 1989).

Similar thefts continue today. For example, the Farewell Canyon stone, a carved basalt monolith belonging to the Setl people in British Columbia, was removed from its site in 1989. The Royal Canadian Mounted Police were called in to investigate (Glavin 1989). Additionally, a large number of Indigenous burial sites have been looted by academic archeological digs: the Canadian Museum of Civilization has about three thousand partial or complete skeletons, and at least seventy-one of the Smithsonian collections are from British Columbia and Ontario (G&M 1989). Occasionally, ceremonial items are sold by Indigenous people, although these individuals usually lack the authority to enter into these transactions.

Similar patterns occurred in the United States. In 1908 a gold miner removed two "mummies" from Inupiat territory in Alaska and displayed them for many years as part of a traveling curiosity show. In 1993, the family of this man contacted Inupiat community leaders through the Cincinnati Museum of Natural History and returned the two bodies for reburial at Barrow, Alaska, in accordance with the beliefs of Inupiat people. A Pawnee burial area near Salina, Kansas, was excavated in the 1930s. The skeletons were displayed as a local tourist attraction until 1989, when Pawnee leaders succeeded in having the graves closed. Hundreds of other Pawnee skeletons were recovered from the Nebraska State Historical Society. In such cases, NAGPRA can provide little assistance. It also has proven ineffective in cases of removal of human remains to other countries.

Eurocentric religious and political leaders have carried out a plan to extinguish Indigenous teachings and practices, Convinced of Eurocentric superiority (Blaut 1993; Amin 1988), religious and political institutions destroyed many Indigenous consciousnesses, languages, and spiritual practices with their rampant intolerance. Philosopher E. Dussel in "Was America Discovered or Invaded?" labels this process the "original sin" of the Americas (1988, 130). Few Indigenous peoples survived the five-hundred-year nightmare of genocide, ethnocide, and ecological destruction, or the various shaming ceremonies in which Indigenous peoples had to prove that they were human and entitled to be accorded human rights (Stogre 1992). Where Indigenous consciousnesses and teachings have survived, Indigenous people have learned of their inferiority and live with restless doubts about their traditions.

Indigenous peoples rely on their traditions to give them spiritual sustenance and to keep them safe. Their traditions are intimately linked to the lands where they live. Their spirituality is represented in ceremonial objects that have taken on sacred significance. The histories of territories, family lineages, and entitlements are recorded in stories and songs, and represented in masks and crests. As Indigenous people gradually lost control of their lands and other elements of their environment, they became separated from many of these sacred symbols. The protection of sacred sites, the recovery of human remains so that proper burial can be arranged, the repatriation of artifacts that are the sacred inheritance of particular families and communities—these are all essential to the spiritual health of Indigenous communities. Recovering this health requires rethinking religion and state and their united interpretive monopolies, and understanding how to protect Indigenous ecologies, cognitive spaces, and ways of life.

The appropriation of Indigenous cultural properties has been persistent; it has been conducted in multiple sites with overlapping and intersecting dimensions. Some laws, legislation, and courts have intervened both to the loss and sometimes to the benefit of Indigenous peoples; however, there has been little consistency in the application of legislation and a stronger hegemonic relationship is needed. The fact remains that Indigenous peoples have little power and control in matters concerning their cultural and spiritual knowledge and property.

Chapter 7

•••

Paradigmatic Thought in Eurocentric Science

Governmental and non-governmental organizations should sustain traditional knowledge systems through active support of the societies that are keepers and developers of this knowledge, their ways of life, their languages, their social organization and the environments in which they live, and fully recognize the contribution of women as repositories of a large part of traditional knowledge. — UNESCO, *Modern Science and Other Systems of Knowledge* (1999, sec. 3.4, para. 86)

In the late Middle Ages, mysticism and scientific reason began to unite to establish the foundation for Eurocentric thought. Both mysticism and scientific reason were empowered by experience, senses, and thought. The knowledge obtained and the conclusions drawn were descriptions of the spiritual and material worlds, as well as an exercise of freedom. Originally, *theoria* meant seeing for yourself. The first European theorists were "tourists"—like the Greeks Solon and Herodotus, who traveled to inspect the visual world. Modern Eurocentric scientific reason establishes that facts can be perceived solely through the categories the Eurocentric mind uses to order experience. Thus modern scientific reason rejects the ancient Greek idea of intelligible essences and asserts that there is no predetermined classification of the earth or even the entire universe (whatever that means).

Without an objective system of classification, modern Eurocentric scientists can distinguish among facts only by reference to theoretical standards. Thus it is the theory or paradigm behind scientific thought that determines what is to count as a fact and how those things that are identified as facts are to be distinguished from one another. In other words, a fact becomes what it is for scientists because of the way they categorize it. And how they classify it depends on the categories available to them in the languages they speak and on their ability to replenish the fund of categories at their disposal. The important implication is that regardless of how they view the place of tradition and conscious purpose in the manipulation of their categories, they have no direct appeal to "reality." For their reality is put together by their individual minds and shared languages. As Richard Goodwin, a legal and policy tactician, wrote:

> Neither the mystic nor man of scientific reason can permit any institution, any collective and historical authority to mediate between him and the truth. God or the world is the revelation of his own experiences and what is revealed may stand in contradiction to beliefs and perception of the entire race. . . . If logic or observation lead the man of scientific reason to contradict all received knowledge, he has found nonetheless, the truth, not for himself alone, but for all men. (1974, 31)

Eurocentric scientific method is a way of knowing that draws on principles of empirical inquiry that certain individuals have deemed to be valued, valid, and reliable processes for acquiring knowledge. Eurocentric knowledge draws from a full array of experiences, ways of collecting, adopting, and sustaining old knowledge (books) and gaining new knowledge (experimentation), but ultimately it is socially constructed.

The two strands—scientific thought and mysticism—helped to liberate human consciousness from the restraints of the medieval order, yet they also contained within them the possibilities for new tyranny and new enslavement. Mysticism was more threatening than scientific reason, as we can see from one of its more virulent manifestations—racism. The conclusions of scientific reason were at least subject to analysis, criticism, and correction. What could not be challenged, however, was the process of reason itself, which pumped riches from the earth, illuminated the night, and carried humans up into the skies and onto the moon.

The mystic and the man of science both devised truths not just for themselves but for all peoples, as if such beliefs could be enforced on all thought. Although the idea of universal truth, of validity, came to be defined as the product of scientific reason, it is an idea that is empowered by the mystical assumptions that surround the Eurocentric belief in the scientific method—the logical process of inferring conclusions from facts, observations, or assumptions. Scientific reason is not the same as the general Eurocentric idea of reason, which means to come to terms with the world through the use of the intellect (Goodwin 1974, 31–62).

Eurocentric science is based on observations and interpretations that take place within a context of assumptions, ideas, and beliefs. Within this context, strong personal and social motivations influence what a person does and sees. Sociology tells us that when new phenomena fall within the current scientific paradigm, it is relatively easy for them to be considered objectively. When they fall outside this paradigm, they are much less likely to be taken seriously. As a result, the validity of a particular observation often becomes less important than how well it meets with the beliefs, aspirations, and worldview of the influential majority of scientists (Peat 1994).

Since the fifteenth century, aspects of Eurocentric knowledge have been put into forms of writing and later into technical and mathematical languages that mask the ambiguities behind and the contradictions within scientific thought. Scientific knowledge has become structured according to certain writing and mathematical styles and is passed on in schools in organized curricula, lectures, and programmed courses. Textbooks that embrace parts of that knowledge signify through their content and form particular constructions of reality, organizing the vast universe of possible knowledge into a selective Eurocentric tradition (Apple & Christian-Smith 1991). As Goodwin notes:

> The conclusions, the "truths," of scientific reason and mysticism originate with individuals, but they pretend to universal validity. Both have powerful inclinations toward system, toward a total order, a structure of belief or fact which contains and defines all of reality. Once this structure is established, opposition can only be perceived as ignorance, superstition or malevolence. If these thoughts are linked to power under the right historical circumstances, such opposition must logically be re-educated or suppressed—in the name of truth, on behalf of freedom, to the everlasting benefit of mankind. (1974, 46)

The content of Eurocentric scientific knowledge is thus a selective accumulation of measurements, facts, and information. However, such measurements have no existence independent of the one who knows them or independent of the purposes surrounding their use. Without a record noted in a book or on a computer, captured in chemical and electrical signals in a human brain, or encoded as muscular skills in the human body, knowledge cannot exist, for it would be lost forever if these physical systems were destroyed (Peat 1994). Yet, many scientists spend much of their time trying to establish universal truths that lie beyond human perception.

Learning precisely what another experiences with a minimal loss caused by cultural or subjective experience is thought to be achieved through measurable observation. This way of thinking leads one to conclude not only that experience can be accurately measured, but that these measurements are reliable and valid processes for describing reality. Objectivity in the Eurocentric mind is contradictory. It is given a higher value than subjectivity, promising in its measured mathematical model to enable one to experience a universal truth that is independent of subjective experience, which is a tainted perception grounded in particular social, cultural, and religious contexts. This trust in objectivity is based on a supposed value-free framework, which to the Eurocentric mind is essential to the search for eternal truths (Peat 1994). At the same time, objectivity can only be achieved by a competitive, subjective, and desiring individual.

As a result of its faith in objectivity, Eurocentric science carries an aura of authority about measurement that has made the majority of its users believe that they can know, understand, control, and manage their surroundings. As Eurocentric science is the selected official knowledge base, it operates from a position of strength and power, a position that also claims the highest orders of wealth and prestige. Those who are recipients of this knowledge believe in their own personal strength and power, as well as in the tradition that creates that power.

Many criticisms have been offered on the inadequacies of Eurocentric science and its faith in objectivity, including the following elaboration of race, gender, and class (Poovery 1988; 1995):

- The application of scientific principles is derived from studying an inadequate, limited, non-inclusive sample. Women, Indigenous peoples, cultural minorities, and others have been virtually excluded from the canons of knowledge (Minnick 1990).
- In Eurocentric science, one can know the whole (the universal) only by fragmenting and examining the parts (Suzuki 1997; Peat 1994; Bohm 1980).
- Eurocentric science poses questions and resolves them within a tradition that is shaped and expressed by partial, fragmented knowledge. It suggests a worldview in which only one ideal, norm, or standard exists, and it thus empowers that one norm with voice and privilege (Minnick 1990; Banell 1992).
- Eurocentric science seeks principles that are universal and replaceable anywhere and anytime. Born of empirical observations, made sense of by hypotheses, which can in turn be empirically tested, Eurocentric science contradicts the faith it acknowledges. In effect, it suggests that all information is open to be disproved, thus severing that information from temporal and geographic specificity. Facts have their meaning in context. Eurocentric science is "[a] story that has lost its meaning, its purpose and its abilities to touch and inform" (Suzuki 1997, 19).

Eurocentric science stresses the use of quantitative measures to calculate the status of the object of inquiry, and to predict and control changes in the future. The absolute makes its first appearance in a commitment to process—logical analysis and mystical communion are the only ways to construct realities. The absolute then makes its journey from process to result, from method to system, to endow the more persuasive and appealing conclusions of thought and revelation with the quality of being absolute.

Goodwin notes that mysticism and scientific reason are forced to share their dominion, "not only because they originate in individualism and tend toward the absolute, but because scientific reason opened a gap in the scheme of thought which could only be filled by mysticism" (1974, 47). Scientific or logical reason was used to prove that certain mystical assumptions about race, religion, and civilization required certain colonial policies and action. However, the rational pursuit of a mystical idea is not a rational process, and if carried far enough, it loses whatever reason it once contained.

Eurocentric scientific thought rejects the ancient doctrine of intelligible essences. The authoritative statement of the doctrine of intelligible essence is Aristotle's revision of Plato's theory of ideas in *Metaphysics*. The essence is the form in matter that lends each being its distinctive identity. The supporters of the doctrine of intelligible essences held that the standards of right and wrong must also have "essences" that thought can comprehend. Plato's ethics and St. Thomas Aquinas's theory of natural law exemplify this line of argument. Their worldviews are "similar" to the Algonquian worldviews of *manitou* or forces in nature. Modern Eurocentric scientific thought, however, denies the existence of essences that allow thinkers either to infer from particular things in the world or to perceive facts in their abstract form. The ideological leader in Europe's rejection of the doctrine of intelligible essences was the British philosopher Thomas Hobbes, and the modern liberal tradition is summed up in the writings of the British utilitarian John Stuart Mill. If there are no intelligible essences, the validity of scientific theory must rest upon its ability to contribute to particular ends, such as the prediction or control of events, rather than on its fidelity to a true world, since no way of dividing the world describes what the world is really like.

Without resolving this contradiction, scientific knowledge posits itself as *the* knowledge not *a* knowledge. Modern scientific knowledge rejects intelligible essences or *mntu,* and ignores the majority of the knowledge and linguistic categories of more than half the earth. It cannot explain what creates desires or whether desires are a proxy for essences. It has also not been able to explain why it has ignored women and kept knowledge lodged within the continuity of male tradition (Minnick 1990). When the "other's" knowledge is acknowledged, it is acknowledged as located in its difference from the privileged normative traditions and described as "Black" literature or "Native" studies. Thus Eurocentric knowledge is not inclusive, and the principles and problem solving derived from it cannot be universally applied to other groups' experiences, ways of knowing, or voices. Modern Eurocentric knowledge is a limited knowledge that erodes the value and authority of any other knowledge base but its own, creating among other things a permanent self-doubt that renders the knowledge of others extinct. It also imposes silence upon all others whose knowledge is not privileged.

Since Eurocentric scientific knowledge deems itself to be the only knowledge base, it has diminished its capacity to see beyond its own measurements and perceptions or to solve problems beyond those Eurocentric researchers desire to study. These limitations have caused Eurocentric scientific thought to continue along its path of destruction. Unless modern Eurocentric scientists are willing to qualify the principle that the world of fact is constructed by the mind according to a particular purpose, they cannot sustain any confidence in the possibility of comparing Indigenous science with Eurocentric science. Scientific comparison relies on the idea that there is a realm of things in nature, independent of the mind, and capable at some point of being perceived as it truly is. Yet, this idea relies on the doctrine of intelligible essence or spiritual forces, which is inconsistent with the modern idea of science. Because all fact is mediated through Eurocentric purposive paradigms, no independent comparison of Indigenous spiritual forces and Eurocentric scientific theories is possible. The systems are contradictory and any comparison would require a drastic revision of their respective views of natural world.

There is a fundamental contradiction in the relationship of the particular and the universal in Eurocentric thought. Scientific facts (which are particular) exist only through the purposive analysis of the Eurocentric theory or paradigm (which is viewed as universal), but the context of Eurocentric scientific knowledge requires the facts and the theory to be separate and distinguishable entities. The scientific relationship, however, denies any separation of theory as form and the fact as substance. Theories and facts are independent of one another, as well as independent of the researcher's purposes. Since theories and facts are not separate from one another, facts become integral parts of the purposive theory, which leads to the conclusion that there is no world independent from what we think it ought to be. If one accepts the idea of intelligible essences, however, the unification of fact and theory leads to a different theory of nature. It leads to an Indigenous knowledge view of nature, which sanctifies the actuality and operates under an ethic of caring for a particular ecology and its forces.

This appears to be a paradigmatic incoherence in Eurocentric science, indeed in Eurocentric knowledge in general. Eurocentric science is not a description of the natural world; it describes a paradigmatic world. Consequently, it always seems possible to stand apart from the particular theory one is considering. We forget that when we stand apart from a particular paradigm in Eurocentric thought, we are actually stepping into another paradigm, rather than into the realm of plain facts. This is the conflict of hypotheses or assumptions.

When faced with a choice between two radically different theoretical systems—for example, between Newtonian and quantum mechanics—scientists hold on to standards of instrumental justification such as the ability to predict or control objects and events. However, if there are no intelligible essences or *mntu*, the facts of the experiments may mean different things to different theoretical languages. And the methods of proof will have to be defended by their relations to purposes available to the scientists, whether they be an interest in the power over nature, in the simplicity of explanation, or in the corroboration of beliefs or assumptions. In the absence of intelligible essences or spiritual forces, such purposes are necessarily arbitrary.

Eurocentric scientists tend to replace the idea of intelligible essences with artificial measurements. This objectified interest takes the care and concern out of their knowledge, including their ethics, which then must be externally legislated or controlled. It creates a detachment from that which is known, so that knowledge does not inform or create meaning. Canadian geneticist and broadcaster David Suzuki astutely notes: "A world that is raw material, resources, dead matter, to be made into things, has nothing sacred in it. So we cut down the sacred grove, lay it waste and declare it does not matter, because it is only matter" (1997, 204).

Steven Augustine, Mi'kmaw historian and keptin in the Grand Council, (1997) talks about this lack of feeling as a lack of connection with the earth, which explains the lack of respect Eurocentric science has shown toward other living creatures. As animals are injected with multiple diseases for science, the earth is exhausted by overproduction and subjected to chemical baths, the air is polluted with chemicals, and the biosphere is altered by scientific experimentation, no part of earth or its living creatures has escaped the heavy hand of Eurocentric science.

Excluding intelligible essences from natural sciences continues the riddle about the relationship between paradigms and facts. The exclusion of experience takes the conflict to a higher level of abstraction. Even though scientific knowledge is reductionistic, it asserts that it progresses by becoming steadily more abstract and universal. It achieves perfection only at the cost of partiality. Its purposive paradigms reject the substance of things in nature, the rich and particular appearances with which they strike our senses. Science relegates these sensations to other theories, such as Indigenous knowledge, art, common sense, or passions.

By purposive exclusions, empirical science may be able to better explain why we have the particular impression of the world that we do, and it may be able to explain this precisely because science has become more formal. But it can never fully describe what the senses see and feel. Formal measurement cannot replace sensory knowledge, expressive intelligibility, and topistic awareness. On the contrary, science must constantly go from substance to form, and from the particular to the universal. It achieves this task by accepting a plurality of paradigms and theories at different levels of abstraction. Thus, at any given moment, what one scientist considers significant in a phenomenon may be dismissed by another as accidental, and theory is removed to the level of irrelevant substance. For example, physics may have little to say about the anatomy of moose, but even zoology will be incapable of accounting for everything that is peculiar to an individual moose. The ineffability of the individual or the particular is the necessary consequence of the modern view of Eurocentric science.

To attribute the limitation simply to a stage or developmental sequence in scientific knowledge is to misunderstand the way science develops. The rejection of intelligible essences creates the separation of the universal from the particular. The scientific view that it is necessary to attain universality through abstraction from particularity rather than through the direct elucidation of the particular, as in Indigenous knowledge, is the core weakness of the Eurocentric purposive view of facts and negates the possibility of an independent comparison of theory and fact.

These contradictions of the relations between theory and fact can be rephrased and summarized in a more familiar way. Thinking and language depend on the use of categories. Humans must classify to think and speak. But we have no assurance that anything in the world corresponds to the linguistic categories we use. The ideas of Eurocentric science about nature seem to imply that our classifications can be both true and false. These ideas also seem to imply that the question of their truth and falsehood is unanswerable or illusory. They also seem to imply that human purposes are the measurement of the world.

Eurocentric science has made many mistakes in its quest to understand the world. The quest has moved from the views of Copernicus, Galileo, and Descartes to the views of Darwin and Einstein. Since Einstein, however, the world of knowledge has been observed through a new lens, which sees all things as being connected and related. Context, and relationships within that context, has taken on new meaning. In quantum theory, Einstein reduced the link between the observer and the observed. The physicist David Bohm (Bohm 1980; Bohm & Peat 1987) extended the scientific proof of interconnectedness. Bohm has aptly defined this phenomenon of holism in a concept of implicate order in which the whole is enfolded within each part. This is a far deeper physical reality than explicate order or than the order that is derived from our perceptions. In modern physics, then, the essential truths of the universe and ultimately of humanity cannot be derived from atoms, but exist as relationships and fluctuations at the boundary of what we call matter and energy (Peat 1994).

The latest trends in theoretical physics and biology are moving toward Indigenous thought. Scientific reflection is moving away from analysis, which splits and fragments experience, toward wholeness and holistic thinking. According to Bohm, "science itself is demanding a new non-fragmentary worldview, in the sense that the present approach of analysis of the world into independent existent parts does not work very well in modern physics." The new scientific movement carries wide implications, for, as Bohm says:

> the proper order of operation of the mind requires an overall grasp of what is generally known, not only in formal, logical, mathematical terms, but also intuitively, in images, feelings, poetic usages of language, etc. (Perhaps we could say that this is what is involved in harmony between the "left brain" and the "right brain.") This kind of overall way of thinking is not only a fertile source of new theoretical ideas: it is needed for the human mind to function in a generally harmonious way, which could in turn help to make possible an orderly and stable society. (1980, xiv)

Indigenous knowledge emerged from the processes of Indigenous peoples' collective experience with ecologies, including the products of their human minds and hearts. Indigenous peoples embody their knowledge in dynamic languages that reflect the sounds of the specific ecosystems where they live and maintain continuous relationships. All Indigenous knowledge flows from the same source: relationships within the global flux, kinship with other living creatures and the life energies embodied in their environment, and kinship with the spirit forces of the earth. Around the surface of the earth, Indigenous peoples are striving to protect their sacred ecologies by acquiring, developing, using, and sustaining relationships with their environments and their forces. Each generation passes this knowledge, these experiences, and these teachings to succeeding generations through language, thereby sustaining Indigenous knowledge and heritage. Today many Eurocentric scientists are spending much time, money, and energy rediscovering "scientific" Indigenous knowledge for a variety of purposes.

Medical Research and "Biopiracy"

Medical research and bioprospecting are hugely lucrative endeavors and getting to be more so. In 1993, the special rapporteur for the UN Sub-Commission on Prevention of Discrimination and Protection of Minorities, Dr. Erica-Irene Daes, stated that the annual market value of pharmaceutical products derived from medicinal plants discovered by Indigenous peoples exceeds US$43 billion, but the profits are rarely shared with Indigenous peoples. Most of the 7000 natural compounds used in modern medicine have been employed by traditional healers for centuries, and 25 percent of American prescription drugs contain active ingredients derived from Indigenous knowledge of plants (Daes 1993, 1).

Where naturally occurring plants or animals are manipulated and redesigned using processes that isolate strands of DNA in severed genes and alter and/or splice them into quite different DNA, the very nature of reproduction is being altered. It becomes the object of manipulation, appropriation, and control. Life itself is being reshaped to the requirements of proprietary interests, regulated by the laws of intellectual property.

Although many important medicines have been discovered in the field, finding medicines in nature is extremely difficult and unpredictable, according to biochemist Georg Albers-Schonberg (1984). Hundreds of thousands of species remain unstudied, so the selection of species for study is critical. Random screening of species can be extremely time-consuming and costly. These costs can be minimized by focusing on species that are used in traditional medicine. Michael Balick (1990) found that using traditional knowledge increased the efficiency of screening plants for medical properties by more than 400 percent.

Developing countries with relatively undisturbed ecosystems are "gene-rich" compared with industrialized countries, but typically Indigenous peoples have not received any economic benefits from discoveries made within their territories. For example, the drugs Vincristine and Vinblastine have been used for forty years in treating some forms of cancer. Both drugs were originally discovered in the rosy periwinkle, *Vinca rosea*, a flowering plant that is native to Madagascar and that has long been used by traditional healers in that country. Current sales of these drugs are about US$100 million, but neither Madagascar nor its traditional healers have received any share of this money (Findeisen & Laird 1991). Estimates of the total world sales of other products derived from traditional medicines run as high as US$43 billion. Among the major U.S. pharmaceutical companies now screening plant species are Merck & Co., SmithKline Beecham, Monsanto, Sterling, and Bristol Meyers.

In 1960, the U.S. National Cancer Institute (NCI) began a global program to collect and study naturally occurring substances. By 1981, it had tested 35,000 plant species, and even larger numbers of micro-organisms. This effort has been intensified since 1986, with an added emphasis on discovering drugs to combat AIDS. Three U.S. institutions have been employed by NCI since 1986, at a cost of US$6.5 million, to collect plant species in twenty-eight countries. Most of this work is performed through subcontracts with twenty-two national organizations and institutions in the countries concerned, only one of which (in Zimbabwe) represents traditional healers. Although NCI requires subcontractors to obtain the consent of "native healers" who participate in this research, it does not specify that Indigenous peoples be compensated for their medicinal knowledge or that they be included in any resulting patents (NCI 1992).

In June 1992, the U.S. National Institutes of Health (NIH) launched a new program in cooperation with USAID (a US agency for international development) to finance "drug discovery" projects in developing countries, making use of "the wealth of knowledge held by traditional cultures where medicinal potential can most likely be realized" (NIH 1992). Approximately US$1.5 million was committed for three projects in 1994. Grants were made to large institutions, which in turn employed smaller organizations in developing countries to conduct the actual field research. Recipients of these grants were responsible for making arrangements to share any profits arising from their research "equitably" with all participating organizations in the countries concerned; however, there was no mention in the documentation for this new program of the rights of the Indigenous peoples whose knowledge was to be sought and exploited.

At an August 1992 workshop convened by the NIH to discuss this program, NIH officials acknowledged the value of studying Indigenous peoples' traditional knowledge. There was some doubt as to whether researchers needed to obtain the informed consent of Indigenous peoples or whether Indigenous peoples providing useful medical and botanical information would be entitled to compensation as co-owners of any resulting patents. NIH officials maintained that the rights of Indigenous peoples would depend entirely on the terms of any contracts made with them, or with the government of the host country. In the past, however, bioprospectors have generally not made contracts with Indigenous peoples, but rather with academic institutions in the host countries, which have coordinated field researchers and collectors.

The number of pharmaceutical companies engaged in bioprospecting is growing, but most contractual arrangements follow the same pattern. A transnational company, which has the laboratory facilities necessary for testing the chemical properties of specimens, contracts with local universities and non-governmental organizations, which collect specimens in the field. Collectors generally receive a flat fee per specimen or per kilogram of specimens. Their contracts may also entitle them to royalties from the sale of products that may be derived from their specimens. These royalties may be between 1 and 10 percent of sales. Collectors do not ordinarily have any formal contractual arrangements, however, with the Indigenous peoples upon whose knowledge of ecology they may rely.

Merck & Co., one of the world's largest pharmaceutical companies, with headquarters in the United States, made an agreement in 1991 with the Instituto Nacional de Biodiversidad (INBio) in Costa Rica, for the collection of plant and insect samples (Caporale 1992). Merck had the exclusive right to study the potential commercial value of the species collected by INBio for two years, and the right to obtain patents for any useful chemical compounds that might be discovered. In exchange, Merck agreed to provide INBio with laboratory facilities and to pay royalties to INBio on any profits derived from patents. The agreement did not specify how INBio would identify potentially valuable species, and did not indicate whether Indigenous peoples would be compensated for information they provided to INBio. However, INBio reportedly planned to educate rural people in the collection of samples, hoping to win support for conservation efforts. The actual extent of this local involvement is unclear.

A somewhat different approach was taken by Shaman Pharmaceuticals, also based in the United States. Shaman adopted what it called an "ethnobotany-based discovery process," which focused on understanding traditional medicine rather than on attempting to screen large numbers of previously unstudied species. About half of the four hundred species collected by this means have shown some medicinal potential, including two anti-viral drugs, which are currently undergoing clinical trials. The cost to Shaman of discovering and developing these new drugs was only one-tenth the cost of laboratory synthesis and screening methods. Shaman has entered into cooperative agreements with Indigenous organizations for plant collection, such as its December 1992 contract with the Consejo Aguaruna y Huambisa in Peru. It also organized a special foundation, The Healing Forest Conservancy, to support grassroots initiatives by Indigenous peoples. Dr. Stephen R. King, vice-president of Shaman Pharmaceuticals says, "We are committing ourselves to returning a portion of sales to all the peoples we work with," whether or not they provided the information that led to valuable products. "If we visit 55 villages in the course of two or three years we would be very happy to have one or two products come out of those visits" (Shaman 1992).

Some research organizations in developing countries are trying to win more benefits for Indigenous peoples. The Fundacao Brasiliera de Plantas Medicinais (FBPM) has convinced some pharmaceutical companies to purchase plant materials from Indigenous communities in processed form, such as extracts, which increases local employment, and to share profits equally with communities that provide useful information. In its arrangements with foreign companies, FBPM also tries to obtain the right to distribute any medicines produced from Brazilian species, so that Indigenous peoples and other Brazilians can share in the medical as well as the economic benefits of research. It is not yet known whether major biotechnology companies will find such terms acceptable. It should also be noted that Eurocentric pharmaceutical firms are chiefly seeking treatments for problems of particular concern to Eurocentric populations, such as cardio-vascular disease and cancer, while most people in developing countries have different priorities.

In principle, the industrial-property laws of most countries only protect "new" knowledge. "Old" knowledge, such as the herbal remedies used by traditional healers for centuries, has generally been regarded as not patentable. However, biotechnology companies have been able to obtain patents for laboratory-synthesized replicas of molecules found in naturally occurring and widely used species of plants. For example, two companies recently obtained U.S. patents for synthetic derivatives of *azadirachtim*, the active substance in the seeds of neem trees, which have been used by people in rural India for centuries as a pesticide.

It is important to recognize that the knowledge has greater long-term value than the plant itself. Once studies of a plant have led to the identification and chemical analysis of the active molecule, it is only a matter of time before a process is developed to synthesize this molecule in the laboratory. For example, Mexican wild yams (*Dioscorea* spp.) were once the main source for the manufacture of steroids, but a sharp increase in the price of the Mexican product in the 1970s led to the development of several methods of synthesizing the active molecule, diosgenin. Mexico accordingly lost this market.

In terms of compensation or benefits, two approaches have emerged thus far in industry practice. One approach is to pay individuals for information; the other, pioneered by Shaman Pharmaceuticals, relies on intermediary organizations to distribute economic benefits more widely among all participating communities. Thus far, the existing political leadership of Indigenous peoples has largely been bypassed. Concerns have been expressed, however, about the social impacts of paying large sums of money directly to Indigenous community leaders. Royalty payments might increase traditional leaders' power and reduce their accountability to their own people. They might also provoke conflicts between different clans and communities regarding the ownership of traditional knowledge—for example, if several tribes have traditionally used a medicinal plant, but only one of them sells its knowledge to a pharmaceutical company. Distributing funds through intermediary non-governmental organizations does not resolve these problems; the intermediaries cannot avoid choosing which communities and which individual leaders they will support. In either case, Indigenous peoples themselves will need to develop new institutions for dealing effectively with outsiders and external financing. This, rather than the development of intermediary institutions, should be encouraged.

Genetic Diversity in Agricultural Biotechnology

Although attention is currently focused upon the screening of naturally occurring plant and insect species for their potential medical applications, there may eventually be an even larger market for genetically modified plants and animals. For example, unusual traits either in naturally occurring species or in cultivars (such as the hundreds of local varieties of rice, maize, and potatoes found in Indigenous and tribal communities) could be isolated. These could then be used to alter the genetic structures of commercial food and fiber crops—for example, to increase their resistance to extreme temperatures, drought, or disease. Alternatively, plants that are cultivated today only by Indigenous peoples could be genetically modified for commercial development. This is illustrated by recent scientific interest in the peach palm, a tree long cultivated by Indigenous peoples in Amazonia for its fruit. In yields per hectare, the protein content of the peach palm is superior to maize (Balick 1984). With financing from USAID, agronomists have been collecting different genetic strains of peach palm with the goal of developing a variety with commercial potential. The Indigenous peoples who first cultivated the species will receive no direct benefits.

It should be noted that UN agencies contribute to the financing and technical support of a number of projects involving the hybridization of commercial plant species with varieties developed by Indigenous peoples. The United Nations Development Programme (UNDP) recently approved a global project with the Centro Internacional de la Papa in Peru, at a cost of US$4.7 million, using biotechnology to transfer the insect-resistant characteristics of potato varieties grown by Indigenous peoples into commercially grown potato varieties (DP/PROJECTS/REC/48). A similar effort, at the same cost level, is being pursued for bananas (DP/PROJECTS/REC/49). Project documents do not indicate an awareness of the intellectual-property rights of Indigenous peoples.

Researcher Barbara Laine Kagedan reports that since 1990 international agricultural research centers (IARCs) have taken the position that they are not the owners of the germplasms in their collections, but that they hold them in trust on behalf of the beneficiaries, who have been variously identified as "humanity, developing nations, the farming communities and research workers" (1996, viii). The Canadian Institute on Environmental Law and Policy (Bjorkquist 1999) reported that no legislation and almost no formal policy exists in Canada regarding owning, controlling access to, or sharing the benefits of *in situ* genetic resources, as contemplated by the 1992 UN Convention on Biological Diversity. It reports that while there are literally hundreds of pieces of federal and provincial legislation that regulate plants and animals (forestry acts, fisheries acts, livestock acts, bees acts, wild rice acts, Irish moss acts, and so on), these acts do not regulate genetic resources. There is no provision in any Canadian act that provides for the legal status of genetic resources or for the rights of owners of genetic resources. The institute reports that Canada's Biodiversity Strategy is mostly silent on questions of ownership and access, and provides only that sharing benefits is an area for "exploring mechanisms" to "facilitate access to samples of Canada's genetic resources' with Aboriginal peoples on specific mutually-agreed terms (Attridge 1996, 65).

A more defined policy regime exists regarding Canada's substantial holdings in its *ex situ* gene banks. Agriculture Canada's policy has been to accord free access to samples of genetic resources preserved in Agriculture Canada gene banks to any bona fide scientist or breeder anywhere in the world for purposes of research and breeding. The question of who actually owns the genes has not been definitively answered, but many Indigenous peoples have asserted claims.

Canadian governments do not view their genetic resources as valuable, rare, or exceptionally diverse in comparison with genetic resources in the Southern Hemisphere. Most of the resources stored in Canadian gene banks have been there since before the Convention on Biological Diversity came into force and are therefore not subject to it. The status of *ex situ* holdings in botanical gardens around the world is becoming controversial, and most holdings are not subject to the convention.

Canada perceives its role in the genetic resources' "market" as that of a banker and a consumer, not as a source. Most of the holdings in Agriculture Canada gene banks are not species indigenous to Canada. The federal government has already determined that one of the growth industries in Canada is biotechnology, particularly in the area of agricultural plants. Canadian policy positions Canada as a leader in technology, not as a leader in supplying the raw material for the technology.

These manifestations of the emerging biogenetic paradigm shift reveal the precariousness of the future. Scientists are able to transform genetic resources without being able to understand them in their natural contexts or in their nexus with Indigenous peoples. This paradigm shift creates a devastating potential in human history, a potential rooted in mysticism united with scientific technology and in the avoidance of Indigenous sciences.

Chapter 8

•••

Ethical Issues in Research

The term "research" is inextricably linked to European imperialism and colonialism. The word itself, "research", is probably one of the dirtiest words in the indigenous world's vocabulary. — Linda Smith, *Decolonizing Methodologies* (1999, 1)

Ethical research systems and practices should enable Indigenous nations, peoples, and communities to exercise control over information relating to their knowledge and heritage and to themselves. These projects should be managed jointly with Indigenous peoples, and the communities being studied should benefit from training and employment opportunities generated by the research. Above all, it is vital that Indigenous peoples have direct input into developing and defining research practices and projects related to them. To act otherwise is to repeat that familiar pattern of decisions being made for Indigenous people by those who presume to know what is best for them.

Some Indigenous communities want to share what they know and create. Others do not. But both want their communities and their knowledge and heritage to be respected and accorded the same rights, in their own terms and cultural contexts, accorded others in the area of intellectual and cultural property. They want a relationship that is beneficial to all. Indigenous peoples should be supported in developing their knowledge for commercial purposes when it is appropriate and they choose to do so. When this knowledge creates benefits for others, policy and legislation should ensure that Indigenous people share those benefits.

The commoditization of knowledge has been in practice for five hundred years. At their core, Eurocentric research methods and ethics are issues of intellectual and cultural property rights. The issues vary from whether life forms and their DNA should be patented to make them private property, to whether knowledge that is freely given in one culture should be commoditized for private profit in another, to confidentiality and trade secrets. Indigenous knowledge can become protected intellectual property in modern society, thus raising new ethical issues.

Eliminating the Eurocentric Bias in Research

Most existing research on Indigenous peoples is contaminated by Eurocentric prejudice. Ethical research must begin by replacing Eurocentric prejudice with new premises that value diversity over universality. Researchers must seek methodologies that build synthesis without relying on negative exclusions or on a strategy of differences. At the core of this quest is the issue of how to create ethical behavior in a knowledge system contaminated by colonialism and racism. Nowhere is this work more needed than in the universities that pride themselves in their discipline-specific research. These academic disciplines have been drawn from a Eurocentric canon, an ultra theory that supports production-driven research while exploiting Indigenous peoples, their languages, and their heritage.

Few academic contexts exist within which to talk about Indigenous knowledge and heritage in a unprejudiced way. Most researchers do not reflect on the difference between Eurocentric knowledge and Indigenous knowledge. Most literature dealing with Indigenous knowledge is written and developed in English or in other European languages. Very few studies have been done in Indigenous languages. This creates a huge problem of translatability.

Linguistic competence is a requisite for research in Indigenous issues. Researchers cannot rely on colonial languages to define Indigenous reality. If Indigenous people continue to define their reality in terms and constructs drawn from Eurocentric diffusionism, they continue the pillage of their own selves. The reconstruction of knowledge builds from within the spirit of the lands and within Indigenous languages. Indigenous languages offer not just a communication tool for unlocking knowledge, they also offer a theory for understanding that knowledge and an unfolding paradigmatic process for restoration and healing. Indigenous languages reflect a reality of transformation in their holistic representations of processes that stress interaction, reciprocity, respect, and non-interference. For Indigenous researchers, there is much to be gained by seeking the soul of their peoples in their languages. Non-Indigenous researchers must learn Indigenous languages to understand Indigenous worldviews. As outsiders, non-Indigenous researchers may be useful in helping Indigenous peoples articulate their concerns, but to speak for them is to deny them the self-determination so essential to human justice and progress.

Indigenous peoples who have lost their languages due to government genocidal and assimilationist policies are presented with a great challenge. Second-language research, however, has confirmed that language is more than just sound. Language includes ways of knowing, ways of socializing, and non-verbal communication. Some aspects of culture, in fact, are thought to be distinct from language (Harvey-Morgan as cited in Cleary & Peacock 1998). In some communities, the recovery of Indigenous languages, especially among the Maori of New Zealand, suggests that the spirits of languages are remarkably persistent and are still embedded in many Indigenous communities. Indigenous languages have spirits that can be known through the people who understand them, and renewing and rebuilding from within the peoples is itself the process of coming to know.

Universality is another ethical research issue. Eurocentric thought would like to categorize Indigenous knowledge and heritage as being peculiarly local, merely a subset of Eurocentric universal categories. These negative innuendoes are the result of European ethnocentrism. The search for universality is really just another aspect of diffusionism, and claiming universality often means aspiring to domination. Mainstreaming is another term that raises concerns. It suggests one main stream and diversity as a mere tributary. The goal is to try to achieve some normalcy (Minnick 1990). Together mainstreaming and universality create cognitive imperialism, which establishes a dominant group's knowledge, experience, culture, and language as the universal norm. Colonizers reinforce their culture by making the colonized conform to their expectations. Because Eurocentric colonizers consider themselves to be the ideal model for humanity and carriers of a superior culture, they believe they can assess the competencies of others. They do this using intelligence and normative educational achievement tests and psychological assessments. They define deviancies from the norm as sins, offenses, and mental illness. Eurocentric thinkers also believe they have the authority to impose their tutelage over Indigenous peoples and to remove from those peoples the right to speak for themselves.

In his analysis of colonial racism, writer Albert Memmi identifies four related strategies used to maintain colonial power over Indigenous peoples: (1) stressing real or imaginary differences between the racist and the victim; (2) assigning values to these differences, to the advantage of the racist and the detriment of the victim; (3) trying to make these values absolutes by generalizing from them and claiming that they are final; and (4) using these values to justify any present or possible aggression or privileges (1969, 186). All these strategies have been the staple of Eurocentric research, which has created and maintained the physical and cultural inferiority of Indigenous peoples.

In assessing the current state of research on Indigenous knowledge, researchers must understand both Eurocentric and Indigenous contexts. A body of knowledge differs when it is viewed from different perspectives. Interpretations of Indigenous knowledge depend on researchers' attitudes, capabilities, and experiences, and on their understanding of Indigenous consciousness, language, and order. Indigenous knowledge may be utilitarian or non-utilitarian or both; it may be segmented or partial depending on Eurocentric reductionistic analysis. Indigenous knowledge needs to be learned and understood and interpreted based on form and manifestation as understood by Indigenous peoples. Indigenous knowledge must be understood from an Indigenous perspective using Indigenous language; it cannot be understood from the perspective of Eurocentric knowledge and discourse.

The fact that the modern ethical dilemma is Eurocentric consciousness itself has profound implications for how to conduct ethical research using Eurocentric paradigms. The failure of Eurocentric paradigms to understand other people's beliefs and values was part of the reason that one of the most massive social science projects of the century, the U.S. Central Intelligence Agency's study on communism, failed to predict the demise of the Soviet Union, even though it was using the best methodologies available in Eurocentric thought. It is part of the reason that the most massive economic development projects in Africa and the developing countries have failed.

In terms of research ethics, where are Indigenous people to find experts who can rise above the value contamination of their consciousness? Where are these experts being trained? By what faculty are they being taught? Because of the pervasiveness of Eurocentric knowledge, Indigenous peoples today have at their disposal few, if any, valid or balanced methods to search for truth. Every academic discipline has a political and institutional stake in Eurocentric knowledge. Every university has been contrived to interpret the world in a manner that reinforces the Eurocentric interpretation of the world and is thus opposed to Indigenous knowledge. The faculties of contemporary universities are the gatekeepers of Eurocentric knowledge in the name of universal truth; they represent little more than the philosophy of Western Europe to serve a particular interest. Most academic research is methodologically flawed with multiple forms of cognitive imperialism when it approaches Indigenous issues.

The persistent current quest for Indigenous knowledge has inspired many Indigenous writers, scholars, and researchers to pursue institutional protection for Indigenous knowledge. At least one university, University of Alaska Fairbanks, has developed a cross-cultural master's level program that centers Indigenous knowledge and develops students' awareness of Indigenous peoples' cultural and intellectual property rights and the distinctive protocols and practices for investigating Indigenous knowledge. The Royal Commission of Aboriginal Peoples in Canada (RCAP 1994) and some institutions of higher learning, particularly in Australia and New Zealand, have established policies and programs to protect Indigenous peoples and their knowledge. Some of these programs involve committees, such as university ethics committees or the newly organized Indigenous ethics committees at the University of Auckland and University of South Australia, who vet all research activity dealing solely with Indigenous communities. The universities must respect the committees' identification of what comprises Indigenous cultural and intellectual property and must respect the gatekeepers of knowledge within Indigenous communities. This respect includes drawing up appropriate protocols for entering into reciprocal relationships following traditional laws and rights of ownership. The reciprocal relationships embody both recognition of the custodians of knowledge and awareness of the associated responsibilities of the custodians and the receivers of knowledge. Further, the universities must accept that Indigenous peoples are living entities and that their heritage includes objects, knowledge, literacy, and artistic works that may be created in the future (Janke 1998).

As discussions develop regarding the ethics governing Indigenous research, issues of control and decision making reverberate as the most important principle. Indigenous peoples must control their own knowledge and retain a custodial ownership that prescribes from the customs, rules, and practices of each group. This control can only be realized if the groups that hold these custodial relationships are involved in the research. Often these groups are not elected community leaders, but others whose responsibilities are directly related to the knowledge and the teachings of the clan, family, or nation.

This raises the problem of how a group that vets any research in the community can be controlled by the right owners. Local groups must be informed of threats to their cultures, communities, and knowledge by virtue of the research being done on them. Local people must also be trained in the holistic understanding of the issues, practices, and protocols of doing research. This will enable Indigenous peoples to utilize research for their benefit, using it to strengthen and revitalize their communities, places, and people, while warding off threats to their cultures from those who seek to take their knowledge from them for benefits defined outside their communities.

RCAP Ethical Guidelines for Research in Canada

In 1993, the Royal Commission on Aboriginal Peoples, with the advice of Aboriginal and non-Aboriginal researchers, formulated a set of ethical guidelines to guide its research (RCAP 1996b, vol. 5, app. C). These guidelines emphasized that Aboriginal peoples have distinctive perspectives and understandings, which are derived from their knowledge, culture, and history, and which are embodied in Aboriginal languages. Those researching Aboriginal experiences must respect these perspectives and understandings. They must also observe appropriate protocol when communicating with Aboriginal communities. The oral traditions and teachings of Aboriginal peoples must be viewed by researchers as valuable research resources, along with documentary and other sources. Proficiency in Aboriginal languages should always be an issue in Aboriginal research projects.

In setting research priorities and objectives for community-based research, the Royal Commission and its researchers were required to give serious and due consideration to the benefit of the communities concerned. Researchers were to consider the widest possible range of community interests and the impact of the research at the local, regional, and national levels. They were to identify potential conflicts of interest within the communities, and they were to employ problem-solving strategies before commencing their research and while their research was in progress. Whenever possible, the guidelines provided that the commission's research was to support the transfer of skills to individuals and to increase the capacity of the community to manage its own research.

The commission required informed and written or recorded consent to be obtained from all individuals and groups participating in the research, with parents or guardians signing for children. Individuals and groups participating in the research were to be provided with information about the purpose and nature of the research activities, including expected benefits and risk. The degree of confidentiality maintained in the study was to be stated. No pressure was to be applied to induce participation, and participants were to be informed that they were free to withdraw from the research at any time.

In studies located principally in Aboriginal communities, researchers were to establish collaborative procedures to enable community representatives to participate in the planning, execution, and evaluation of research results. If the research might affect particular Aboriginal communities, similar consultations with appropriate leaders were to be sought. In research portraying community life or community-based studies, the multiplicity of viewpoints or cross-section of interests present within Aboriginal communities was to be represented fairly, including viewpoints specific to age and gender groups. Advisory groups convened to provide guidance on the conduct of research were not allowed to preempt the commission's guidelines. Above all, researchers were to accord fair treatment to all persons involved in the research activities.

The commission's researchers had an obligation to observe ethical and professional practices relevant to their respective disciplines; however, because of the ethnocentric and racist interpretations of past researchers, the existing body of research, which normally would provide a reference point for new research, was open to reassessment. Researchers had to disclose if Aboriginal knowledge or heritage or perspectives in any way challenged the Eurocentric assumptions brought to the subject by previous research or the design of the commission's research. They also had to disclose how they would resolve any conflicts and how they would portray conflicting Aboriginal knowledge, heritage, or perspectives.

The commission's ethical guidelines stated that reviews of research results were to be solicited both in the Aboriginal community and in the scholarly community prior to any publication. The guidelines provided that the commission was to maintain a policy of open public access to the final reports of the research activities. In cases where scholarly and Aboriginal community responses were deemed useful, these reports were to be circulated in draft form. Research reports or parts of the reports were not to be published if there was reasonable grounds for thinking that publication would violate the privacy of individuals or cause significant harm to participating Aboriginal communities or organizations. The results of community research were to be distributed as widely as possible within participating communities, and reasonable efforts were to be made to present results in Aboriginal languages or non-technical English where appropriate.

Canadian Research Councils Policy Statement of Ethical Conduct on Research on Human Subjects

In 1998, when Canada's three research councils—the National Science and Engineering Research Council, the Social Sciences and Humanities Research Council, and the Medical Research Council—were drafting their policy statement on ethical conduct in research on human subjects, suggestions were made to create a section dealing with research involving Aboriginal peoples. The councils, however, had not had much discussions with representatives of Aboriginal groups or with the various organizations or researchers involved. Thus, they decided that it was not appropriate to establish policies in this area. However, they did carry out a literature review on research involving Aboriginal peoples that was intended to serve as a starting point for such discussions.

The councils affirm that Aboriginal peoples have rights and interests that deserve to be recognized and respected by the research community. Guidance on ethical conduct comes from at least two sources. The first source is the ethical principles, standards, and procedures articulated in *Ethics: Guidelines for Research with Human Subjects* (SSHRC 1977). The second source is the specific additional provisions developed in Canada and other countries for research involving Indigenous peoples. These international and national guidelines suggest additional requirements to the ethical standards for the conduct of research on individuals to ensure that the rights and interests of Indigenous communities are respected. The councils found the high degree of consensus among these guidelines remarkable, perhaps reflecting commonalties in the experience of these communities and the sharing of existing guidelines among communities. The councils' policy statement (SSHRC 1998) recognizes the international consensus that Indigenous peoples have a unique interest in ensuring accurate and informed research concerning their heritage, customs, and community.

The councils noted three documents that are especially relevant to research on Aboriginal peoples in Canada. They were prepared by the Association of Canadian Universities for Northern Studies (ACUNS 1982), the Inuit Circumpolar Conference (1991), and the Royal Commission on Aboriginal

Peoples (1994). Institutions and persons considering research involving Aboriginal communities in Canada should be familiar with these documents. They affirm the general principle that a researcher is obligated to respect human dignity in research involving Aboriginal groups. Such respect gives rise to special considerations and to basic ethical duties regarding ethics review, informed consent, confidentiality, conflict of interest, and inclusivity. The tri-council's policy statement provides:

> [R]esearch that is premised on respect for human dignity entails high obligations to individuals and groups. Indeed, there are historical reasons why indigenous or aboriginal peoples may legitimately feel apprehensive about the activities of researchers. In many cases, research has been conducted in respectful ways and has contributed to the well-being of aboriginal communities. In others, aboriginal peoples have not been treated with a high degree of respect by researchers. Inaccurate or insensitive research has caused stigmatization. On occasion, the cultural property and human remains of indigenous peoples have been expropriated by researchers for permanent exhibition or storage in institutes, or offered for sale. Researchers have sometimes treated groups merely as sources of data, and have occasionally endangered dissident indigenous peoples by unwittingly acting as information-gatherers for repressive regimes. Such conduct has harmed the participant communities and spoiled future research opportunities. (1998, sec. 6(A))

Many aspects of research involving Aboriginal peoples present ethical challenges. For example, since researchers may belong to different cultures debates may arise because of different definitions of public and private life. Notions of property will sometimes differ between the researcher, the sponsors of the research, and the community being researched. Language differences may impede the clear communication and understanding that is necessary to the informed consent process. A researcher may also be confronted with ethical dilemmas because of competing interests among different sections of the community.

A central issue for discussion is when it is legitimate for researchers to interview members of Aboriginal communities in their own right as individuals, without regard to the interests of the group as a whole and without seeking permission from any group authority or spokesperson, and when the approval of the community as a whole is required. When research involves Aboriginal individuals, or when properties or private information belonging to the group as a whole are studied (for example, cultural property or human tissues), the policy statement suggests that researchers should consider the competing interests of the Aboriginal group. They cannot rely on individual consent or on the consent of leaders. Similarly the interest of Aboriginal communities must be considered even when leaders of the group are involved in the identification of potential participants or are required to give official approval and permission for access to their lands or cultural property. In any research designed to analyze or describe characteristics of the group or in research in which individuals are selected to speak on behalf of, or otherwise represent, the group, then the researchers must consider the collective interests of the group.

The councils also provide a list of "good practices" drawn from the existing documents to guide decisions on research in Aboriginal communities. The councils considered it a good practice for researchers to respect the culture, traditions, and knowledge of the Aboriginal group; to conceptualize and conduct research in partnership with the Aboriginal group; to consult members of the group who have relevant expertise; to involve the group in the design of the project; to examine how the research may be shaped to address the needs and concerns of the group; and to make best efforts to ensure that the emphasis of the research, and the ways chosen to conduct it, respect the many viewpoints of different segments of the group in question.

The councils also recommend that it is good practice to provide the Aboriginal group being researched with information respecting the following: how the Aboriginal group's cultural estate and other property will be protected; when a preliminary report will be available for comment; and whether there is potential for appropriate employment without prejudice of members of the community. It is also good practice to underscore the researchers' willingness to cooperate with community institutions and their willingness to deposit data, working papers, and related materials in an agreed-upon repository.

Since Aboriginal peoples may wish to react to research findings, it is inappropriate for researchers to dismiss matters of disagreement with the group without giving such matters due consideration. If disagreement persists, researchers should afford the group an opportunity to make its views known, or they should accurately report any disagreement about the interpretation of the data in their reports. The councils consider it a good practice to acknowledge in the publication of the research results the various viewpoints of the community on the topics researched; and to afford the community an opportunity to react and respond to the research findings before the completion of the final report, in the final report, or even in all relevant publications.

Breaches of Confidentiality of Sacred Knowledge

Access to sacred knowledge is ordinarily restricted to particular individuals and organizations within Indigenous communities, such as initiated men or women, or to the members of special religious societies. This can pose two kinds of problems for researchers. No single individual can ever be aware of all the cultural concerns that may exist in the community; a broad process of consultation with different groups and elders may be needed before determining whether a site, object, or design is important. In addition, the necessary information may be confidential, such that it cannot be revealed completely to outsiders, or even to the rest of the community.

The Zuni, a Pueblo people in New Mexico, have struggled with these problems. Spiritual knowledge among the Zuni is divided among six *kivas*, fourteen medicine societies, and a number of clans, priesthoods, and individual specialists. In order to be capable of responding promptly and accurately to government development plans affecting their territory, the Zuni held a meeting of their religious leaders and agreed to form a committee of six key leaders to serve as an advisory group and intermediary. This group ensures that all appropriate elders are contacted before a decision is made. Unfortunately, there are still instances in which the Zuni are consulted about the possible adverse impact of a government project and decide that it is more culturally appropriate to say nothing, and risk the destruction of the site, than to reveal its religious nature and location.

An interesting Australian court decision in this regard is *Foster v. Mountford* (1976), which barred the sale of a book containing sacred knowledge that had been shared by elders, in confidence, with a well-known anthropologist. It was argued that the anthropologist was aware of the restricted nature of the information when he received it, since he had studied the people concerned for many years. In other cases, it might be difficult to establish the restricted nature of information without the evidence of some kind of written agreement.

Community Control of Research

In the United States, where Indigenous peoples already exercise a large degree of local autonomy, a number of Indian tribes have enacted laws to regulate archeological and cultural research. The Colville Confederated Tribes, in the State of Washington, established their own Archeological and Historical Resources Board, which determines whether sites are culturally important, issues permits for research, and makes recommendations for protecting and restoring sites. In addition, the Colville tribal authorities have adopted rules forbidding any kind of socio-cultural research in the community without first applying for a permit and agreeing to respect the privacy of individuals. Similar rules have been adopted by many other American Indian tribes and have the force of laws under the U.S. legal system. The Navajo Nation, the largest Indigenous people in the United States with a territory extending over more than 25,000 square kilometers, has adopted laws to punish Navajos and physically remove non-Navajos who engage in unauthorized research or trade in cultural property.

Similarly, the Kuna people in Panama, who enjoy a degree of local autonomy under national laws, require scientists visiting their 60,000-hectare Kuna Yala Forest Reserve to pay an entry fee, hire Kuna people as guides and assistants, train Kuna scientists, provide copies of research reports to the Kuna authorities, and share the products of research such as photographs and plant specimens. The Kuna have published a twenty-six-page handbook entitled "Scientific Monitoring and Cooperation" to serve as a guide for visiting scholars (Chapin 1991).

The establishment of community-based institutions for supervising research, promoting education and training, and conserving collections of important objects and documents, is clearly essential. However, in most countries, this process is only beginning. In the United States, national financial support for Indigenous cultural and educational institutions became available in the 1970s. At present, 123 museums and cultural institutions are located in, and operated by, Indigenous communities in the United States, offering a large pool of expertise for the launching of such programs in other countries.

In February 1992, representatives of twenty-nine Indigenous peoples living in tropical forests met at Penang, Malaysia, where they agreed, *inter alia*, that "[a]ll investigations in our territories should be carried out with our consent and under joint control and guidance according to mutual agreement, including the provision for training, publication and support for Indigenous institutions necessary to achieve such control" (Posey & Dutfield 1996, 203). The threshold issue is guaranteeing community control of research activities. Only if Indigenous peoples can impose conditions on entry into their territories can they insist on negotiating for a share of any future benefits of research.

Professional Organizations and Ethics

There is a growing tension between the interest of Eurocentric scholars in Indigenous peoples' knowledge and protecting the right of Indigenous peoples to control the dissemination and use of their knowledge. Newly established academic periodicals, such as the *Journal of Ethnobiology,* the *Journal of Ethnopharmacology,* and the *Indigenous Knowledge and Development Monitor*, are devoted to studies of Indigenous peoples' knowledge. Information disclosed in these journals can be exploited before Indigenous peoples have the opportunity to assert their rights. Similarly, the recently established Fonds Mondials pour le sauvegarde des Cultures Autochthones (FMCA), based in France, has as its goal the collection and dissemination of Indigenous peoples' knowledge. While FMCA promises to restrict access to its archives, it can be asked whether it would not be preferable to strengthen the capacity of communities to have their own research and documentation facilities. Accelerating the rate of Eurocentric research on Indigenous knowledge and heritage is, at this time, more of a threat than a benefit to Indigenous peoples.

In 1988, the International Society for Ethnobiology, at its first international congress held in Belem, Brazil, adopted a declaration of ethics governing research with Indigenous peoples. It calls upon scientists to return the products of their research in useful forms to the peoples they study, and to pay "just compensation" for the acquisition and commercial use of traditional knowledge.

The Society for Economic Botany, to which a large proportion of molecular prospectors belong, is currently considering the adoption of a professional code of ethics (SEB 1991). The current draft encourages researchers to respect the privacy of individual informants, to preserve the confidentiality of information when asked to do so, and to ensure that individuals who provide useful data are compensated.

Other relevant professional associations, such as the Society for Applied Anthropology, are also in the process of developing standards of conduct (SAA 1991). Many anthropologists now argue that researchers can best repay Indigenous communities by playing the role of "brokers" between these communities and corporations. One such study in Canada is the Belcher Islands Reindeer Management Project (Johnson 1992). Anthropologists also advocate creating non-governmental organizations, like The Healing Conservancy, to repay communities indirectly through small grants and training programs. Many Indigenous organizations, particularly in Amazonia, have criticized these proposals as creating a kind of neo-colonialism, with Eurocentric academics and non-governmental organizations controlling the financial resources flowing to Indigenous communities.

The Code of Professional Ethics of the International Council of Museums (ICOM 1971) encourages museum officials to consult with the cultural authorities of the country of origin before acquiring any doubtful objects. When a museum acquires a culturally important object without first contacting the country of origin, it should not be deemed an "innocent" purchaser in any subsequent dispute over ownership. ICOM applies this to objects "which are of major importance for the cultural identity and history of countries." There can, of course, be a wide difference of opinion as to whether a particular object is "important." In addition, it would be important to involve Indigenous peoples directly in the work of the national ministries and agencies responsible for cultural matters in each country, so that they can give complete and accurate information when contacted by foreign museums.

Indigenous peoples' own languages, knowledge systems, and laws are deeply interconnected with ethical issues. Over the past centuries, Eurocentric researchers have examined and dissected Indigenous peoples. Every facet of their existence has been examined, their dead have been dug up by the thousands for medical research, and their ceremonies have been described in the literature. Almost all these efforts have been filtered by Eurocentrism, its professional organizations, and their views of ethics rather than by Indigenous laws and ethics. As this chapter demonstrates, an essential and defining element of ethical issues in research on Indigenous peoples is respect for Indigenous peoples' laws and institutions. The starting point for any ethical research of Indigenous knowledge and heritage must be the law of the Indigenous people being studied, which defines what constitutes property, identifies who has the right to share knowledge and property, and determines who is to benefit from and who is to be responsible for such sharing. Indigenous peoples' knowledge and heritage are not commodities, nor are they the property of the nation-states and their researchers. Indigenous knowledge and heritage are sacred gifts and responsibilities that must be honoured and held for the benefit of future generations. Unless researchers are aware of and act consistently with the laws of Indigenous peoples, any attempts to learn or to use Indigenous knowledge and heritage are unlawful, illegitimate, and unethical.

Chapter 9

•••

Indigenous Heritage and Eurocentric Intellectual and Cultural Property Rights

Indigenous peoples have the right to practise and revitalize their cultural traditions and customs. This includes the right to maintain, protect and develop the past, present and future manifestations of their cultures, such as archaeological and historical sites, artifacts, designs, ceremonies, technologies and visual and performing arts and literature, as well as the right to the restitution of cultural, intellectual, religious and spiritual property taken without their free and informed consent or in violation of their laws, traditions and customs. — Declaration on the Rights of Indigenous Peoples (1993, art. 12)

It has long been recognized that existing national and international intellectual and cultural property laws are not always compatible with Indigenous peoples' concerns for protecting their knowledge and heritage. In general, the overarching challenge in protecting Indigenous knowledge and heritage is negotiating with the modern concept of property. Most Eurocentric legal thought believes that all thought should be treated as a commodity in the artificial market. In contrast to Eurocentric thought, almost all Indigenous thought asserts that property is a sacred ecological order and manifestations of that order should not be treated as commodities. The role played by property in a sustainable economic order creates a fissure between Eurocentric thought and Indigenous thought.

A quick review of the conceptual development of the property as proprietarian order, on the one hand, and property as market commodity, on the other, illustrates the dialectical path advocates for Indigenous knowledge and heritage must bridge. In the English legal tradition, property was the material foundation for creating and maintaining social order. The central idea was that all land belonged to the Crown. The Crown could determine the proper social order by transferring lands to individuals with certain conditions or in return for services rendered. Property rights were not to satisfy individual preferences or to increase wealth. Estates in land provided the foundation for citizens to increase the well-being of the entire polity.

The modern idea of a fluid society in which individuals readily move, either geographically or, more importantly, in the social hierarchy, was anathema to the proprietarian order, and today it is the language of the marketplace that dominates legal discourse about property. The essence of this discourse is the idea of property as a bundle of rights. The commoditarian concept asserts that property's exclusive purpose is to define in material terms which individuals or corporations are free from Crown coercion or other forms of external interference to pursue their own private agendas and to satisfy their own preferences. Property satisfies individual preferences most effectively through the process of market exchange. The exchange function is so important that in modern society property is often thought to be synonymous with the idea of market commodity.

Modern legal thinkers are so used to thinking of property as a market commodity that it becomes difficult to imagine that property might be intended to benefit anyone other than the individual owner; however, the international substantial development movement has redefined the notion of the public good as ecological order, a notion that is more than familiar to Indigenous thought, and although the language of the market dominates modern legal discourse about property, the vision of property as the foundation of the common good remains viable. The relationship between property as order and property as commodity creates much of the tension and much of the synergy about the issue of protecting Indigenous rights within the Eurocentric legal system.

Culture Versus Nature

European intellectual and cultural property law protects mythical expressions of the individual mind that are distinctive, original, novel, or inventive (depending on the particular action). These rights inhere in individuals or in corporate entities, which are treated as if they were individuals, and are closely related to other forms of personal property rights. These property régimes perceive creativity within an ideology of "high art" or "high technology" predicated on the work of a creator as an emanation of "his" individual personality and solitary labor (the poet in the garret, the artist in the studio, the inventor in the garage or basement). The right of paternity or attribution protects the author's right to have his work attributed to him. Cultural works are treated in a manner similar to a patriarchal father's connection with his children, identifiable as his (in other words, "legitimate") and subject to his control to ensure the protection of his name, honor, and reputation (in the case of rights of integrity). Above all, they protect patriarchal proprietary interests that gain for them economic value in the marketplace. The relations of reproduction associated with intellectual property exist within patriarchal economic systems that are duplicated—"reproduced"—through the laws protecting creative work.

For those who live outside the modern marketplace or who do not perceive creativity, either biological or cultural, in patriarchal economic terms, intellectual and cultural property will always be fundamentally problematic. The idea of individualistic, market-driven legal components creating property rights in the creative interaction of human beings with their world leaves little room for respect for or protection of creation that does not divide creativity into transferable segments capable of having value in economic terms. For Indigenous peoples, this is a disempowering and discriminating bias as their languages do not acknowledge a clear line between biology and culture.

In Eurocentric thought, European man was seen as capable of rising above nature because of his ability to create culture. "Culture" revolved around fairly rigid categories of high art—painting, sculpture, classical music, and so on. Social theorist Pierre Bourdieu (1993) illustrates that culture was dominated by a professional élite of recognized artists, museum and gallery curators, schools of art, critics, academics, and (in the case of Indigenous peoples) anthropologists, archeologists, and ethnographers. Women, Indigenous peoples, children, non-White men, and eventually all non-Europeans, were seen as less than human because they were closer to nature, more driven by biology. In Eurocentric thought, Indigenous peoples' natural affinity with the ecosystems was associated with savagery and their "culture" could never be "high culture"—the domain of artists and connoisseurs (literally from the French "those who know")—but was always "primitive culture."

There was a specific Eurocentric idea about "cultural practice" that influenced and was influenced by the development of the law of intellectual property. It grew out of the political and economic revolutions of the fifteenth century onwards. Eurocentric intellectual and cultural property law is based on the dialectic between nature that has not been "improved" by human agency and nature that has been "improved" by human agency. In the Eurocentric worldview, the human agency used to improve upon nature was often some form of cultural pursuit. In eighteenth-century Eurocentric thought, not only did culture become the act by which European man separated himself from the natural world, but, as literary theorist Terry Eagleton writes, cultural practices and the category of the aesthetic also become detached from social practices:

> The emergence of the aesthetic as a theoretical category is closely bound up with the material process by which cultural production, at an early stage of bourgeois society, becomes "autonomous"—autonomous, that is, of the various social functions which it had traditionally served. Once artefacts become commodities in a market place, they exist for nothing and nobody in particular, and can consequently be rationalized, ideologically speaking, as

> existing entirely and consequently for themselves. It is this notion of autonomy or self-referentiality which the new discourse of aesthetics is centrally concerned to elaborate; and it is clear enough, from a radical political viewpoint, just how disabling any such idea of aesthetic autonomy must be. It is not only, as radical thought has familiarly insisted, that art is thereby conveniently sequestered from all other social practices, to become an isolated enclave within which the dominant social order can find an idealized refuge from its own actual values of competitiveness, exploitation and material possessiveness. It is also, rather more subtly, that the idea of autonomy—of a mode of being which is entirely self-regulating and self-determining—provides the middle class with just the ideological model of subjectivity it requires for its material operations. . . . But there is another reason for the foregrounding of the artefact which aesthetics achieves. What art is now able to offer, in that ideological reading of it known as the aesthetic, is a paradigm of more general social significance—an image of self-referentiality which in an audacious move seizes upon the very functionlessness of artistic practice and transforms it into a vision of the highest good. (1990, 8, 65)

We quote from Eagleton extensively because we believe he has caught the central contradiction that lies at the heart of the meaning of culture and the aesthetic in Eurocentric thought. He emphasizes the artifact, and the individual creator of that artifact, removing the one from any connection with the social dimension from which it comes and reducing the other to a self-referring (or self-promoting) producer, or "author," of meaningless art. The aesthetic, as Eagleton also points out, "is in part spiritual compensation for this degradation; it is just when the artist is becoming debased to a petty commodity producer that he or she will lay claim to transcendent genius" (1990). This is very different from the Indigenous worldview, in which the value of human creativity lies in its relationship to the knowledge and heritage of which it forms part.

The law and the economic structures within which the Eurocentric idea of cultural practice developed were connected to the colonization of Indigenous peoples. Colonization relegated Indigenous cultures and the natural world in which Indigenous peoples lived to the status of commodities that could be taken and owned by non-Indigenous colonizers. The act of colonization was dependent on the notion of appropriation and control through individual agency. For Indigenous peoples, modern intellectual property laws, which are not designed to protect Indigenous knowledge and heritage, can themselves be acts of colonization. This is particularly obvious in the taking of Indigenous knowledge about plants and animals, but, as the special issue of the *University of British Columbia Law Review* "Material Culture in Flux: Law and Policy of Repatriation of Cultural Property" evidences, this is the case in cultural misappropriation as well. Intellectual property lawyer Craig commented:

> Intellectual property law provides the primary mechanism for non-Indigenous governments and corporations to appropriate Indigenous knowledge. . . . [The main international conventions] were developed with virtually no regard for the needs of Indigenous and traditional peoples for the protection of their cultural and intellectual property (usually embodied in communal lifestyles). (1995, 151–52)

From an Indigenous point of view, the continued vitality of Indigenous knowledge and heritage is dependent upon understanding and preserving Indigenous teachings. Indigenous people are seeking the return of cultural heritage held by museums and collectors as one way of reasserting control over how their cultures are depicted. These objects are the physical records of history and the physical manifestations of Indigenous knowledge and heritage; they help define Indigenous identity. Indigenous peoples are also looking for protection against appropriation of their knowledge by others and against inappropriate use of their knowledge by others. All these areas fall within intellectual and cultural property rights.

In Canada, Indigenous knowledge and heritage were transmitted and documented primarily through the oral tradition, but also through dramatic productions, dance performances, wampum belts, birch bark scrolls, totem poles, petroglyphs, and masks. Over the years, these items have been taken from Indigenous peoples by various methods, not all of them legal. The concerns of Indigenous peoples center on the return of and respect for these artifacts (including those that were obtained through legal means), and on the appropriate display and use of cultural items. The Supreme Court of Canada has held that Indigenous customary law is a distinct system of rights dealing with cultural ownership and is the legal equivalent of the English concept of property. As the special rapporteur for the Working Group on Indigenous Populations, Dr. Erica-Irene Daes, has pointed out:

> A song, for example, is not a "commodity", a "good", or a form of "property", but one of the manifestations of an ancient and continuing relationship between a people and their territory. Because it is an expression of a continuing relationship between the particular people and their territory, moreover, it is inconceivable that a song, or any other element of the people's collective identity, could be alienated permanently or completely. (1993, para. 45)

The ownership of Indigenous intellectual and cultural property is governed by a complex *sui generis* system of Indigenous rights. Indigenous artists paint according to strict traditional rules of ownership. They are authorized to paint only certain stories and even though there is room for individual creativity, certain subjects must be portrayed in particular ways. An important distinction between the Indigenous and Eurocentric concepts of ownership is the distribution of rights in Indigenous society. Ownership of certain works may vest in a particular clan, society, or member or members, while the rights to use the work may vest in various other members for various purposes. Dr. Daes goes so far as to suggest that

> Indigenous peoples do not view their heritage in terms of property at all—that is, something which has an owner and is used for the purpose of extracting economic benefits—but in terms of community and individual responsibility. Possessing a song, story or medicinal knowledge carries with it certain responsibilities to show respect to and maintain a reciprocal relationship with the human beings, animals, plants and places with which the song, story or medicine is connected. For Indigenous peoples, heritage is a bundle of relationships rather than a bundle of economic rights. (1993, para. 22)

It is not easy for Eurocentric lawyers and policy makers to reconcile these two very different legal systems: Indigenous customary law, with its group ownership, community involvement, and consensus decision making, and Eurocentric law, with its emphasis on personal rights and negotiations and, particularly, on the concept of an individual artist's intellectual property. As intellectual property lawyer A. Pask noted:

> [Indigenous peoples'] claims can be heard neither in the international régimes governing cultural property, nor in the domestic régimes governing intellectual property. In cultural property law the competing legal values which frame every question are those of national patrimony and the "universal heritage of mankind"; in intellectual property law the interests to be balanced are those of "author" conceived on an individualistic model, and the "public" interest of preserving a common public domain. In all these arenas Indigenous peoples must articulate their interest within frameworks which obliterate the position from which they speak. (1993, 63)

Thus, the present régimes are ill suited for the protection of the intellectual and cultural heritage of Indigenous peoples or any collective rights (McKeough & Stewart 1991, 9–10).

Recovery of Sacred and Ceremonial Objects

In the late 1980s, two events laid the groundwork for a new way of dealing with Indigenous heritage items. These were the UNESCO meetings held in Canada's North and the later repatriation of Inuit art to Canadian northern communities, and the long-term loan to a Canadian art gallery of the Cape Dorset inventory of thirty years of Inuit drawings, prints, and sculptures. Almost 3500 objects of Inuit art collected by the Canadian government were ready for dispersal to other museum collections across Canada. Inuit leaders and elders negotiated with the Government of Canada that although the collection was owned by the government, it could not be sold or given away without the permission of the communities or artists. They further demanded that only under review and selection at the hands of a selection committee with a majority of Inuit could the objects be assigned a new home, wherein the remaining objects could be returned to their communities of origin should they choose.

The justification for these demands lay with the fact that since the government had acquired these objects in the interest of preserving and promoting Inuit culture, it was the Inuit who should have the final decision on where they went. Eventually, three Canadian museums and galleries received portions of the collection, with the remainder going back to the Arctic. This event accentuated the inherent right which Indigenous people ascribe to cultural property regardless of who the material owners may be, in so far as there is a perceived public use in mind for the use of the property and the representation the knowledge. The Inuit of Cape Dorset also decided through their representative cooperative to transfer on long-term loan the bulk of their print works and drawings to a southern Canadian art gallery for the purpose of CD-ROM production, recording, and reproduction in order to preserve their cultural property and heritage in a medium more accessible for public display and use.

Although the Inuit story demonstrated an alternative approach to handling Indigenous heritage, unfortunately it is not representative of the fate of many Indigenous cultural artifacts. The past systematic unlawful "mining" of archeological Indigenous sites for marketable antiquities is now compounded by continuing efforts by tourists, art dealers, and scholars to purchase culturally important objects that are still in use. Poverty and loss of land rights are key factors in this illicit trade, since Indigenous peoples stripped of their ability to subsist by their own means may be reduced to selling their heritage. Indigenous peoples' own customary laws ordinarily forbid the sale of such objects by individuals, but it is difficult and costly to locate and recover objects once they have been taken out of the community. In the face of such cultural appropriation, a number of countries have enacted laws prohibiting exports of Indigenous peoples' heritage, including Australia's *Movable Cultural Property Act* (1986).

In the case of cultural artifacts that have been removed illegally, domestic courts will usually return a stolen object to its owners across international frontiers, applying the laws of the situs of the alleged theft; however, disputes often arise over the interpretation of local laws. In the case of the Parthenon Marbles, for example, the British Museum argued that their removal had been properly authorized by Turkey during the time it had occupied Greece. The same argument was made in a recent litigation over the removal of Byzantine mosaics from a church in the Turkish-occupied portion of Cyprus. A U.S. court, however, concluded that the occupation had not suspended Cypriot law, which recognized the mosaics as the property of the Greek Orthodox Church (see *Autocephalous Greek Orthodox Church of Cyprus v. Goldberg* 1990).

Proof of ownership under traditional or customary laws can be the decisive factor in such cases. A British court rejected an attempt by New Zealand to retrieve some important Maori door panels from London because the claim was based on New Zealand export-control laws rather than on prior ownership by a specific Maori tribe. Because the law of New Zealand was silent as to the ownership rights of Maori cultural property, the New Zealand government was unable to prove good title to the property (see *Attorney-General of New Zealand v. Ortiz* 1982). By contrast, India successfully brought a legal action in the United Kingdom to recover sacred statues of Siva taken illegally from the ruins of Hindu temples. The temples and the god Siva were treated as co-plaintiffs, in accordance with Hindu laws, which was tantamount to recognizing the statues as the property of Hindus as a people (Greenfield 1989).

A case in Bolivia shows that negotiated efforts can work across international borders. The Aymara people of Coroma recently succeeded in arranging for the recovery of *q'epis,* bundles of sacred garments that document the spiritual origins and histories of particular Aymara communities and embody the spirits of their ancestors (Lobo 1991). By tradition, the responsibility for caring for each bundle rotates among families, although their ownership is communal. In the late 1970s, a number of these centuries-old sacred garments disappeared—apparently sold by individuals to North American art dealers. An anthropologist later learned that some of these garments were about to be offered for sale in San Francisco. He alerted the Coroma, who sent representatives to the United States. With support from the Government of Bolivia, they convinced U.S. officials to confiscate the *q'epis* and, in 1989, to impose emergency import restrictions on all Coroma textiles.

In the case of the Coroma textiles, both the United States and Bolivia are parties to the UNESCO conventions on cultural property, Article 191 of the Bolivian constitution forbids the export of cultural property, and the Government of Bolivia supported the efforts of the Coroma people. This was a fortunate, but rare, situation in which there were adequate legal mechanisms in both states, and a spirit of cooperation between the states concerned. It was also fortunate that the people were able to discover where their sacred objects had been taken, and this was by mere accident. The downside is that although the Coroma were able to put a stop to further imports of *q'epis* to the United States by these means, they had to file claims in U.S. courts to prove their ownership and recover possession of individual *q'epis*—a lengthy and costly process.

Wider publication of Indigenous peoples' traditional laws would deprive purchasers of the defense of having no knowledge that objects were improperly acquired. In the case of objects that are well known, or well documented, courts will apply the principle of *caveat emptor.* If the status of objects under local or customary laws is uncertain, however, courts are reluctant to treat the purchaser as a thief.

Unidroit, the International Institute for the Unification of Private Law, has prepared a draft Convention on Stolen or Illegally Exported Cultural Objects (1990). The Unidroit draft opens the courts of each contracting state to claims by the others and requires "compensation" to be paid by the states making claims to innocent purchasers of stolen cultural property. It permits (but does not require) the retroactive application of its provisions. It also prescribes a number of factors to be considered by courts when determining whether to return a particular object. These include the "outstanding cultural importance" of the object to the claiming state, as well as its "use by a living culture" within that state. This last provision is of particular relevance to Indigenous peoples. In some countries, however, Indigenous peoples are not recognized as legal entities capable of owning property collectively or of bringing legal actions in national courts. They may also lack the financial means of pursuing legal actions in other states, forcing them to rely on support from their national governments. The convention came into force in 1995.

In Canada, attempts to introduce new federal or provincial legislation regarding repatriation of cultural property have been futile. The Supreme Court of British Columbia recently refused to grant relief to Indigenous peoples when the province gave a permit to the provincial archeology branch to remove Indigenous burial remains located on residential property development. In 1990, the Canadian government sought to develop a comprehensive policy and legislative framework for archeological property on federal lands. Federal lands include reserve lands and lands in the territories. This framework was intended to operate in addition to existing measures under parks and environmental legislation but introduced amendments to the *Cultural Property*

Export and Import Act (1985), the *Yukon Act* (1985), and the *Northwest Territories Act* (1985).

To the distress of Indigenous peoples of Canada, the Proposed Act Respecting the Protection of the Archaeological Heritage of Canada (1985) appears to be a violation of their treaty and Indigenous rights, and a violation of the fiduciary duties of the Crown regarding Indians. Briefly, the proposed act is problematic for the following reasons. Section 5 states that the ownership of archeological artifacts and specimens is not with First Nations but rather with Her Majesty in Right of Canada. Sections 9, 10, and 11 exclude First Nations governments from having a formal role with respect to the administration of impact assessments, exploration, and the issuance of permits. Sections 20 and 26 exclude First Nations from a formal role in the enforcement and prosecution of offenses under the proposed act, as that act applies to Indian artifacts and specimens and Indian land sites. Section 28 makes no provision for the confidentiality that is entailed by Indian cultural and religious practices. Section 28 makes no reference to First Nations governments playing a formal role in the administration of the export and import of cultural property. No mention is made about the general jurisdiction of First Nations governments over sites found on Indian land or over those Indian cultural sites found off reserves. Although the proposed act did not limit the generality of the concerns of First Nations, it did create another jurisdiction over Aboriginal cultural property rights. This bill was never enacted as law. Similarly, British Columbia's proposed sweeping changes to its heritage legislation allowed for greater Indigenous control and ownership over cultural property, but attempted to vest ownership of Indigenous objects in pre-1858 sites in the Crown. This bill was never enacted as law either.

In the United States comprehensive federal legislation to protect Indigenous cultural property does exist. The *Native American Graves Protection and Repatriation Act* (NAGPRA 1990) defines Indigenous material to which it applies, requires federally funded museums and other agencies to produce inventories of such material in their collections, and gives a right of return based on an elaborate statutory framework. The American Indian Ritual Object Repatriation Foundation is one example of an organization established to educate the public about the importance of returning sacred objects, and to facilitate negotiations for the return of particular objects—especially objects from private collections, which are not covered by NAGPRA. Its founder, Elizabeth Sackler, attracted considerable publicity in 1991 by purchasing sacred Hopi masks at a Sotheby's auction in New York and then returning them to Hopi elders (Sackler et al. 1992).

One frequent issue in repatriation is identifying the appropriate community or religious leader to whom an object should be returned. A Hopi ceremonial shield was discovered by Hopi religious leaders during a visit to the Heard

Museum in Phoenix, Arizona, in 1990. They convinced museum officials that the shield, originally sold by a Hopi man in the 1970s, was an object of ceremonial importance, had been communally owned, and could not have been lawfully sold by an individual. The museum agreed to return the shield, but the Hopi *kiva* to which it had traditionally belonged had, meanwhile, divided into two new sects. This left the Hopi Tribal Council to consult with both groups and reach an agreement on which of them would take custody of the shield. In April 1992, it was agreed that the Coyote Clan of the village of Oraibi would be the new custodian of the shield, and the artifact was returned.

Objects of cultural importance continue to be discovered in museum collections. *The Spirit Sings,* a showcase of Indigenous art that traveled across North America in the mid-1980s, encountered a storm of protest from Indigenous leaders because it displayed objects that had traditional sacred uses. The curatorial team that assembled this exhibition was drawn from the top echelon of Canadian museums. However, the team neglected to undertake a thorough investigation into the legitimacy of acquisition by the museums that purportedly owned the pieces. Furthermore, the team appeared to make little effort to trace the descendants of the families and individuals who had created the original objects to seek their involvement or endorsement. Not only that, but Canadian Indigenous people questioned the morality of presenting sacred objects for public exhibition. For example, the Kahnawake Mohawks resorted to legal means to attempt to prevent the Glenbow Museum in Calgary from displaying a false face mask as part of the exhibition (WFP 1988). *The Spirit Sings* went to the 1988 Calgary Winter Olympics without a balanced partnership with Indigenous peoples, who felt their interests were not adequately represented. The corporate sponsor of the exhibition settled potential suits and damages out of court in an effort to repair the image of the exhibition, but the Olympics were boycotted by a large number of Canadian citizens who were sympathetic to the Indigenous concerns.

Negotiated repatriations of museum collections have been moderately successful. More than ten years ago, chiefs of the Six Nations Iroquois Confederacy discovered that several wampum belts that had been confiscated from their communities in the 1920s by Canadian police were in the collection of the Heye Foundation, a private ethnographic museum in New York City. These objects, made of strung blue-and-white shell beads, are irreplaceable documents of the constitutional and diplomatic history of the Six Nations. After years of negotiations and threats of legal and political actions, the museum agreed to return the belts to Six Nations chiefs in Canada (Fenton 1989). The Mi'kmaw people of eastern Canada have not been so fortunate; a large wampum belt purported to be a recording of a 1610 Mi'kmaw treaty with the Holy See was photographed on display in the Vatican ethnographic museum in the 1960s. The Vatican today denies any knowledge of this object.

Hundreds of equally significant sacred objects from Canada are scattered worldwide. There is no global inventory of dispersed Indigenous cultural property, and objects have been found in museums in nearly every industrialized country.

In 1988, the Assembly of First Nations invited museum curators from Canada and around the world to an Ottawa meeting that resulted in the formation of a joint task to recommend museum guidelines for Indigenous remains and artifacts (Henton 1989b). In 1989, the American Museum of National History rejected an attempt to have the sacred bundle that belonged to Chief Big Bear reclaimed. The museum refused to surrender the bundle, arguing that claims to the bundle could not be determined (Henton 1989a). In the same year, the Canadian Museum of Civilization returned the Starlight bundle, a sacred relic, to the Sarcee people of the Blackfoot Confederacy. It followed the guidelines set out by the International Council of Museums (ICOM) in its 1986 Code of Professional Ethics (Clements 1991).

The Haisla have obtained repatriation of sacred objects from the Stockholm Ethnographic Museum. The return of Kwagiulth potlatch material to the U'Mista Cultural Centre at Alert Bay in British Columbia is another example of negotiated repatriations (Webster 1995). The framework agreement between the Nisga'a people, Canada, and British Columbia provides for the return of cultural material in federal and provincial museums. The material is to be returned on a "cut and choose" basis, whereby the collections will be divided in half and the Nisga'as given the right to either divided collection. All objects are not necessarily of great cultural importance, and many objects, for whatever reason, will continue to be acquired, owned, and displayed by museums. In such instances, Indigenous peoples claim an interest in determining how these objects are interpreted. Museums are a major factor in forming public perceptions of the nature, value, and contemporary vitality of Indigenous cultures. Indigenous peoples and many others rightly believe that museum collections and displays should be used to strengthen respect for their identity and cultures, rather than to justify colonialism, ethnocide, or dispossession.

Indigenous people are not calling for museums to divest themselves of all artifacts. In a report produced jointly by the Assembly of First Nations and the Canadian Museums Association, *Turning the Page* (AFN & CMA 1992), there was general recognition that collections and the museums that care for them can contribute to public education and awareness of the contributions of Aboriginal peoples. Indigenous peoples should define the content of their Indigenous knowledge and cultural heritage. One of the primary tasks of museums and cultural institutions should be documenting this knowledge and conserving it for their communities. Indigenous peoples should also be supported in developing their knowledge for commercial purposes when it is appropriate and they choose to do so. When this knowledge creates benefits for others, policy and legislation should ensure that Indigenous people share those benefits.

Authenticity

Certain forms of Indigenous art are the world's oldest continuous living art tradition. Traditional Indigenous art differs from Eurocentric art in that cultural designs and motifs exhibit a relationship between the pattern and its symbolism and beliefs. It communicates ideas and beliefs or can be "read." This has been described as a kind of "visual literacy." Examples of this are the symbolic literacies of the Mi'kmaq, the birch bark scrolls of the Anishnabi Mitéiwin society, and the rock art of the Algonquian-speaking peoples. Since the spiritual nature of the work is combined with artistic imagery, there is little personal interpretation in these efforts.

Indigenous peoples around the world condemn the expropriation and reproduction of their traditional art and crafts. This issue is a spiritual and psychological threat to authentic practitioners of traditional arts and to Indigenous peoples whose values these arts and crafts express. There is also the problem of economic expropriation when factories overseas mass-produce the items with cheap labor.

Since the 1950s and the marketing of Inuit art by Canadian government–subsidized Arctic cooperatives, every effort has been made to create a legitimacy about Inuit art and its origin. In the 1970s, the Government of Canada encouraged Inuit artists to organize community cooperatives to adopt distinctive trademarks—the "igloo tag" for Inuit products—to ensure their authenticity. The igloo tag has played an important role in the marketing of stenciled prints, which have increased greatly in their popularity and value since the Inuit first experimented with this artistic medium more than twenty years ago. The artists in each cooperative decide annually on a limited number of prints to produce and sell. Only a fixed number of copies are made, and they are marked and numbered. In this way, Inuit artists have avoided the problems of low prices and poor quality associated with mass-production. However, until the 1980s and indeed even past *Masterworks,* the first international exhibition of Inuit art in the 1960s and 1970s, the primary reason for developing and marketing this art was economic—it provided an income to northern peoples whose lives were changing from a subsistence to a wage economy. In the early years, little effort was given over to protecting and ensuring artistic copyright.

By contrast, Navajo and Hopi silversmiths in the United States enjoyed a brief prosperity in the 1970s, until the market was flooded with inexpensive, poor-quality work and imitations. This caused the United States to enact a comprehensive scheme for protecting Indigenous knowledge and heritage.

This scheme can be found in laws protecting Indigenous peoples' rights to ceremonial objects, human remains, the use of traditional religious sites, and the exclusive marketing of artworks and crafts as "Indian" products.

In the United States, the Indian Arts and Crafts Board was established in 1935 to promote and market Indigenous products. In 1990, new federal legislation in the form of the *Indian Arts and Crafts Act* authorized the board to register trademarks for individual artists, as well as for tribes and Indigenous organizations, and made it a crime to sell a product as "Indian" unless it was actually produced by a member of an Indian tribe recognized as such by the U.S. government. Thus, a Native American individual or a Native American group, such as a business owned primarily by Native Americans, can register a trademark just as any other person doing business in the United States can, and can sell their craft work under their trademark. Moreover, the Indian Arts and Crafts Board has a certification mark that is designed to encompass the trademark and that certifies that the article so marked is a genuine Native American craft work (25 U.S.C.A. 305; 25 C.F.R. 301, 304, 307, 308, and 310). Consequently, although there may be no copyright in the articles, the articles are protectable through the use of the trademark and the certification mark.

Additionally, there are civil causes of action (25 U.S.C.A. 305e) and criminal penalties for the misrepresentation of Indian-produced goods (18 U.S.C.A. 1159), and criminal penalties for counterfeiting the Indian Arts and Crafts Board trademark (18 U.S.C.A. 1158). The federal regulations of the U.S. Customs Service provide for the indelible marking of the country of origin on imported Native American-style jewelry to prevent the confusion of imitations with the genuine article (19 C.F.R. 134.43(c-d)). However, tribes and Native Americans still lose profits from the sale of cheap imitations to consumers who perhaps are not aware of the trademark and certification mark, or who do not care whether they purchase authentic articles or imitations. The law has been criticized further for excluding the more than one hundred Indian tribes and groups that currently are not recognized by the government. Artists who are members of these groups can be sentenced to prison for identifying their artworks as "Indian."

The Aboriginal Arts Management Association in Australia is currently developing a labeling scheme to ensure the authenticity of Indigenous products and products that incorporate Indigenous motifs. The association also serves as a central agent for Indigenous artists on matters of copyright, including taking legal action for infringement.

A related issue is the expropriation and ownership of traditional arts. Since the late 1980s, Indigenous peoples and artists have urged that Indigenous representation and heritage rights extend beyond copyright legislation. They have based their claims on inherent definitions of these heritage rights.

Indigenous concerns exist beyond the conventional exhibition and moral rights that state individual artists must by law be involved with the negotiation of these rights. The broader and somewhat deeper position of the Indigenous community concerns the appropriation of knowledge, and hence their heritage, when the artwork is destined for particular public exhibition uses.

Expropriation concerns not only the taking or copying of traditional crafts or items of cultural heritage, but also the taking of oral traditions of a people. This is especially problematic as it relates to crafts that have a sacred and secret character under Indigenous laws. Indigenous people have argued that others should be forbidden from reproducing or disclosing works where this offends their beliefs. Indigenous people are gravely anxious that some segments of their culture are being destroyed, mutilated, or debased by outsiders.

The increasing worldwide popularity of Indigenous peoples' arts and cultures poses a growing challenge to Indigenous peoples' ability to interpret their own cultures, to defend the integrity of their cultures, and, if they wish, to receive compensation from the use and enjoyment of their cultural manifestations by others. The size of the market is suggested by *The Aboriginal Arts and Crafts Industry*, a 1989 report by Australia's Department of Aboriginal Affairs. Retail sales of Australian Aboriginal art alone totaled US$18.5 million in 1988, and involved five thousand Aboriginal artisans. This is a fraction of the total world trade in Indigenous peoples' products.

This trade is dominated by large-scale importers that sell handicrafts in their own chains of retail stores. These importers retail handicrafts at three to seven times the prices they pay to the producers. Indigenous peoples' crafts are also marketed by a small number of non-governmental organizations as a way of supporting Indigenous development. The organizations pay more to the producers, but account for only about 10 percent of all handicraft sales. One reason producer prices remain so low is the ease with which these handicrafts can be copied.

A number of distinctively patterned textiles, such as *ikat* cloth from Sulawesi and Zapotec rugs from Mexico, have obtained large markets in industrialized countries. These items can easily be reproduced at lower cost on machines, however, and when produced in large quantities they quickly lose their novelty and commercial value. For example, a small development project funded in part by the International Labour Organization and by COTESU, the Swiss development agency, has restored traditional weaving among the Jalq'a people of Bolivia and employs several hundred weavers in producing textiles sold in tourist markets within the country. Organizers of the project are reluctant to expand overseas for fear of losing control of the designs to mass-production enterprises (Healy 1992). Legal protection of textile patterns would greatly expand the markets for such Indigenous products and protect them from reproductions.

Inevitably, items depicting traditional arts get into circulation in international and national markets, and Indigenous peoples are not given a fair economic return for sales from which others profit. This raises the issue of ownership of traditional arts. The current intellectual property régimes fail to recognize that Indigenous peoples, rather than individual artists, create and own Indigenous cultural heritage. Copyright in Eurocentric laws, for example, is attributable to each individual person, and is originated by a single person, even in those circumstances where the copyright is jointly owned.

A related issue is access to, or control over, the materials that are traditionally used in producing culturally important objects. For example, traditional basket makers among the Karuk people in California have complained that pollution is destroying the wild grasses they use to weave their baskets. Without access to these plants, their baskets cannot be authentic and lose both their cultural and commercial value. Similarly, the soft red stone that American Indians have long used for making ceremonial pipes comes from a single quarry in Minnesota. U.S. law protects this site, and in principle only Indigenous craftspeople are entitled to use it. Recent consumer interest in Indian pipes, however, has led to the sale of many reproductions.

It has been observed that many art forms viewed as "traditional" are in actuality the result of recent demands for Indigenous artworks by tourists and museums. When large quantities of goods are demanded by Eurocentric consumers, there is a tendency for Indigenous peoples to devise special products that are easier to manufacture than traditional objects and that appeal more to Eurocentric tastes. The carving of soapstone and argillite among the Inuit people of Alaska and Arctic Canada began as an export industry in the 1880s. This fact should not be used to deny the Inuit legal protection, however. Cultures change and develop over time, and new motifs, which are distinctive and represent collective expressions of an Indigenous people, are just as valid as pre-colonial ones.

Communal Rights to Traditional Designs in Modern Artworks

An emerging complication in the protection of intellectual and cultural property is the incorporation of traditional art images and designs into "modern" artworks, by both Indigenous and non-Indigenous artists. Some Indigenous artists complain that their works are only taken seriously if they contain traditional motifs or media such as wood and feathers. Indeed, a group of American Indian artists who largely use Eurocentric media displayed their works at the Palais des Nations in Geneva in 1984 under the title *No Beads—No Trinkets* to make this point. Most works of *individual* Aboriginal artists will be protected under copyright acts, both internationally and nationally, if the artist can show that the work originated from the author and that it was original. Yet, the cultural traditions that lie behind these individual manifestations receive no protection at all and hence are open to abuse. Difficulties arise from the fact that a design is derived from traditional artistic practices dating back possibly millennia. Two important questions form the next discussion: Can such efforts be subject to protection as original work? And who could claim authorship and ownership of such works?

The use of traditional motifs in individual art may be viewed as undermining the integrity of the culture, particularly if these motifs are used by a non-Indigenous artist. There has been widespread commercial exploitation of traditional designs in the international and national markets. These designs have been used, for example, on tea towels, T-shirts, sarongs, table mats, restaurant menus, postcards, souvenirs, wall hangings, posters, fashion items, towels, and carpets. It is against this background of deprivation and dislocation that any examination of the legal protection of communal rights to traditional motifs in modern artworks should take place.

When objects are associated with individual artists, they tend to be accorded greater value and are more easily given legal protection than if they are viewed as communal property. However, Indigenous peoples may view the individual's role in art quite differently. For example, distinctive pottery has long been made and exported by Pueblo women in the United States and by Quichua women in Ecuador. In both cultures, potters' styles fit within recognizable traditional boundaries, but the images these women sculpt or paint are highly individualized. Hence, both group and individual interests need to be considered when protecting these products' artistic merit and commercial value.

The complexity of providing protection for designs is discussed by anthropologist Kenneth Maddock (1988) in connection with Aboriginal Australians' practice of body painting. Some designs are in widespread use, while others have recognized creators and their use is restricted to the initiated men who have purchased the right to wear them. The extent to which a particular motif can be used or reproduced is a matter of local customary law, as well as the history of the particular design and the agreement that was made between its creator and first owner. Maddock concludes that no one general rule can be formulated for all Aboriginal designs. What this demonstrates, moreover, is the need to empower Indigenous peoples themselves, through their own institutions and representatives, to interpret and enforce their own laws relating to the disposition of their heritage. To an extent, Indigenous peoples do not mind the sale and circulation of their traditional designs in modern art unless the works are of a sacred or secret nature. However, there is widespread resentment when Indigenous individuals and groups are not given a fair economic return from the use of their traditions.

The 1989 report of a committee appointed to review the Aboriginal Australian arts and crafts industry (Australia 1989) contains a valuable discussion of these issues. It noted that the sale of artwork does not, in the views of Aboriginal people, terminate the interests of the communities whose traditional motifs have been employed by the artist. The report also stressed that existing copyright laws do not recognize such community rights. *Droit moral* may be invoked to demand correct identification of the creators of particular works, and to protect works from inappropriate or degrading uses, such as the public display of sacred objects, but *droit moral* does not protect the economic interests of the artists or ensure that only authentic, high-quality works are offered for sale. The best means of securing all the rights of Aboriginal people, the committee concluded, was supporting community-controlled cultural institutions and financing local artists' organizations. The report stressed cultural autonomy is integral to the future viability of the industry.

A number of cases involving reproductions of Aboriginal art have successfully been taken to Australian courts by individual artists, as for example in the 1989 case of *Bulun Bulun v. Nejlam Pty. Ltd.* (1989), which involved the unauthorized printing of an Aboriginal painter's works on commercially manufactured T-shirts. Litigation is expensive, however, and government assistance for legal services is inadequate. There has been a tendency to try to settle matters by negotiation, particularly when the dispute is among Aboriginal people themselves—for example, a 1988 case in which the Tiwi Land Council objected to the depiction of Tiwi burial poles in the works of an Aboriginal artist from Sydney. In *Yumbulul v. Reserve Bank of Australia* (1991), an individual Aboriginal artist complained that the national bank had reproduced one of his artworks on ten-dollar bank notes without permission. While the artist himself had signed a document authorizing reproduction, he said that approval was also required, under customary laws, from the elders of the Galpu people, to whom the underlying motif belonged. This case was eventually settled out of court, but the judge commented that the rights of the community, as opposed to those of the individual artist, did not appear to be adequately protected. At least in land disputes, however, Australia's High Court has recognized tribal elders as legal custodians who can launch court actions on behalf of their communities (*Onus v. Alcoa of Australia Ltd.* 1981).

A third case, *Milpurrurru v. Indofurn Pty. Ltd.* (1995), involved the exploitation of Aboriginal artwork without the artists' permission, culminating in substantial reproductions occurring in the form of woven carpets produced in Vietnam and imported into Australia. An action for breach of copyright was filed by three living Aboriginal artists and the Public Trustee, representing five deceased Aboriginal artists. The case centered around section 37 of the *Copyright Act 1968,* which prohibits parallel importation of copyrighted works. Justice Von Doussa, in his judgment of the Federal Court of Australia, awarded additional damages to the Aboriginal artists for culturally based harm following infringement of copyright in their artworks. The judgment reflects the court's willingness to acknowledge the cultural sensibilities of Aboriginal people and protects those sensibilities accordingly, by means of orders for exemplary damages. Moreover, the judgment discusses at length the difficulty of applying the Eurocentric copyright régime to Indigenous peoples.

Nevertheless, Justice Von Doussa did apply the copyright law; however, he made a number of significant concessions to Aboriginal custom, most notably: (1) the observance of an Aboriginal custom not to use the names of deceased Aboriginal artists in the proceedings—they were referred to in the judgment by their skin names only; (2) the award of additional damages under section 115(4) of the *Copyright Act 1968* to reflect culturally based harm; (3) the award of damages as a lump sum to enable Aboriginal clans to take account of the collective ownership of the designs in the allocation of damages amongst the members of the clan; and (4) the award of additional damages for humiliating or insulting behavior with reference to a particular cultural group rather than to the community at large. The court firmly recognized Aboriginal culture and customary law within the usually inflexible boundaries of Eurocentric laws and generally illustrated a sensitive approach to Aboriginal customs and traditions. This judgment gives a clear warning to all concerned that dealings in Aboriginal intellectual property are to be handled with utmost care. Although Aboriginal artists may continue to encounter difficulties framing their claims under the *Copyright Act,* the courts in the future are likely to exhibit a much more sensitive and flexible approach toward the cultural barriers confronted by Australia's Indigenous peoples. Australian intellectual property law professor Kamal Puri argues, "It will be no exaggeration to describe this decision as a 'mini-Mabo' since it has the potential to do for Aboriginal intellectual property rights what *Mabo* has done for Aboriginal land rights" (1995, 303).

The Canadian Museum of Civilization in Ottawa is developing agreements that cover the exhibition of contemporary pieces by Aboriginal artists, the development of commercial products, and the reproduction of older traditional Aboriginal material that is no longer covered by copyright protection.

With the introduction in 1988 of section 3.1.g. of the Canadian *Copyright Act,* which provides artists with the right to exhibit their work publicly or to authorize public exhibitions of their work, the museum buys exhibition rights from the artists or their estates when they purchase an art piece. These exhibition rights are often calculated according the schedule of fees outlined by CARFAC, the Canadian Artists' Representation/le Front des Artistes Canadiens. When the museum commissions a piece and intends to make a reproduction of the work—in the form of a postcard or a poster, for instance—

or develops a range of commercial products with the artist, the artist is paid 5 percent of the gross sale price. In a departure from the widespread use of Aboriginal designs in souvenirs without permission, the museum is developing a range of high-quality utility items such as porcelain, tableware, and upholstery materials in cooperation with renowned Native artists. Creating commercial products of such high quality in partnership with Indigenous artists may increase the value of Indigenous art and designs and decrease the likelihood that such designs will be used without permission.

In another initiative, the museum is in the process of developing and negotiating a memorandum of understanding with the Council of Haida Nations for various rights related to reproductions of traditional Haida materials and designs for which the museum will pay 20 percent of net profits. This development acknowledges the traditional and community rights of the Haida people in their heritage, and recognizes the need to compensate the Haida people for using their heritage. The memorandum does not limit this compensation to the standard duration of copyright protection.

Cultural Appropriation

In 1989, in Toronto, a seminar entitled "Whose Story Is It Anyway?" was organized by Lenore Keeshig-Tobias and Daniel David Moses to discuss the appropriation of Indigenous cultures by non-Indigenous writers, the exclusion of the voices of Indigenous writers from the literary canon, and the different conceptions of property and authorship in Canadian and Native cultures. These and other events brought the issue of cultural appropriation and intellectual property to the pages of the *Globe and Mail* newspaper and to *Maclean's* magazine. During this period two Canadian magazines devoted their front covers to the issue of cultural appropriation. *Fuse Magazine* ran an article by Joane Cardinal-Shubert about the appropriation of Aboriginal visual imagery and a piece by Lee Maracle on appropriation; the summer 1990 issue of *Parallelogramme* featured Loretta Todd's "Notes on Appropriation" (Pask 1993, 59–60).

Aboriginal artists have focused on the right of Aboriginal peoples to determine the appropriateness of the use being made of their cultures and the difficulty of viewing this through the categories of Canadian law. Cardinal-Shubert, for example, raises the problem of expropriation of Aboriginal culture for profit by others (facilitated, of course, by intellectual property law), such as "the alleged pirating and $25 million dollar sale in the Asia Pacific Rim of a traditional design used in hand-knitted Kwakiutl sweaters" (Pask 1993, 60). Loretta Todd's article stressed this connection by linking the issue of cultural appropriation to that of Aboriginal title and decolonization.

Exhibitions

It is generally believed that the intent of an exhibition is to present the artistic style of an artist or artists; however, Indigenous peoples see their artworks as much more than mere objects with messages. They are extensions of Indigenous cultural traditions in every form. Roger Neich of the National Museum of New Zealand (Aoteoroa) has argued that exhibits that focus on artistic style favor particular styles and media, resulting in an "orthodoxy" that can stifle the creative growth of Indigenous cultures (Neich & Nicholson 1995). Many Indigenous artists in the Pacific Northwest Coast of the United States and Canada believe, however, that recent recognition of their works as "high" art, rather than as folk-crafts or curiosities, has helped to revitalize their peoples' traditions and economies.

Indigenous Development International in its paper "Intellectual Property Rights, the Law, and Indigenous Peoples' Art" (1997) argued that Indigenous art exhibitions on the international stage would, therefore—in the best of all worlds—require that the following procedures be adopted. There should be (1) negotiations with individual artists and/or with cooperatives or communities representing artists for exhibition rights; (2) the highest commitment to the presentation of the art piece to protect its "integrity" with no waiving of conventional moral rights; (3) official support or sponsorship from Indigenous nations or peoples; (4) a curatorial or advisory committee with Indigenous representation; (5) a review of all written or promotional material in accordance with Indigenous rights and copyright legislation; (5) representation by Indigenous artists at exhibitions. The paper also noted that at the Cultural Olympiad at the 1996 Atlanta Summer Olympics, in which Inuit and Australian artworks were featured, one or more of these procedures was not followed.

The paper asserted that it is incumbent upon the respective international or national committees and their sponsors to assure themselves first of the moral integrity of the exhibition and its works, presumably with assurance of support from the Indigenous people themselves, and second of the fullest possible execution and assignment of exhibition rights for the purposes of copyright fulfillment. Any exhibition sponsor who sees to it that the eyes of the exhibition are those of the Indigenous perspective honors a much stronger mandate than that of conventional law alone.

Issues in the Performing Arts

Performing arts by Indigenous peoples are often a unique blend of traditional and modern arts. Dance and music are integral parts of Indigenous knowledge and heritage. Indigenous songs are often described in Eurocentric literatures as a mixture of chants, cries, shouts, hums, and other vocalizations.

These songs may invoke the names of spirits and clans, or imitate the sounds of birds and other animals. Many are "message" songs that address ecological and social issues and so help reinforce traditional cultural values. Dancers typically decorate their bodies with natural objects, from ochres to feathers and fur. Performing rights encompass both intellectual and cultural rights.

Performing arts are a powerful means of asserting cultural identity and communicating with others. They act as a mirror that reflects a people's psychic make-up and explains the primeval civilization of a race. They also enable the present generation to appreciate the creative genius of the generations who have gone before. Eurocentric thought categorizes these creative expressions as folklore because they have their source in the life of the people and they evolve continuously. Many see folklore as, in effect, the archeology of the mind. Because folklore is based upon customs and traditions, the works produced by later artists represent a unique continuation of an Indigenous people's time-honored myths and legends (Puri 1995, 297–98).

Modern manifestations of performing arts are also copyright issues. As Indigenous communities seek to strengthen their identities and cultural roots through the arts, many non-Indigenous artists are attempting to use these themes as well. A 1988 roundtable on copyright comprising Aboriginal Australian artists, writers, and actors complained that non-Aboriginals were taking the initiative in utilizing Aboriginal motifs and themes, often resulting in misinterpretations and negative stereotypes. Other problems exist as well. Traditional Balinese dances, like many Indigenous ceremonies, have reportedly been "edited" for tourists, and in the 1970s, a wave of tourist interest in the Toraja people of nearby Sulawesi was accused of transforming traditional Toraja funerals into spiritually empty commercial spectacles. Popular interest in Indigenous cultures has also led to greater incorporation of elements of traditional music and dance into works produced, and in many instances copyrighted, by non-Indigenous performers. The modern powwow circuit in North America provides a model for Indigenous regulation of performing arts, as well as for the problems associated with public display of modern pan-Indian ceremonies.

There is reportedly a growing problem with the unauthorized sale of music recorded in Indigenous communities. Commercial distributors of such recordings generally assume that because traditional songs are old, no royalties need to be paid. Moreover, non-Indigenous performers frequently make modifications to traditional melodies so that they can be copyrighted as "new" or "original" works (Seeger 1991). Amazonian music has become particularly popular in recent years, but Indigenous peoples have rarely received any compensation for this. A commendable exception was the album *Txai* by Milton Nascimento, based on Indigenous Amazonian music, which was sold to raise funds for the promotion of Indigenous rights under an arrangement with

Brazil's Uniao das Nacoes Indigenas. There are also reports of a growing problem with the pirating of the traditional songs of the Mbuti of central Africa. Folk recordings have been appropriated and transformed into commercial recordings with no royalties paid to either the Indigenous artists or their communities.

Indigenous peoples' customary laws regarding rights to music can be complex and differ considerably from national laws. Among the Suya people of Brazil, for instance, both the individual composer and the singer who gives a song its public debut have rights to its use. In addition, songs associated with ceremonies are controlled by clans (Seeger 1991). Among Salish people in the Pacific Northwest region of North America, songs belong to lineages, but in each generation a song may be sung only by a single individual who has been given this right.

The Canadian Native Arts Foundation draws up specific licensing agreements with Indigenous artists to present their artwork on television broadcasts. This benefits the artists and also increases Indigenous peoples' awareness of their performing rights.

Advertising Use of Indigenous Peoples and Arts

The issue of using Indigenous peoples and their arts in advertising overlaps with intellectual property issues. Such use is a misappropriation of personality and culture. Many countries feature Indigenous peoples in advertising designed to attract tourists from overseas. The Indigenous people used in these advertisements have not been consulted or provided with the legal or institutional means to control or reap benefit from increased tourist flows.

A recent example is an advertisement for Air Canada designed by British advertising agent McCann-Erickson that ran in *The European* newspaper's magazine and other U.K.-based publications. Under the headline "Sitting Confortabull" there is a picture of an Indian chief in ceremonial clothing holding a spear sitting behind an overweight White man with a briefcase in an executive-class recliner. The advertisement also shows a teepee and claims "business chiefs get more moccasin room" in first class. National Chief Ovide Mercredi protested to Air Canada and the Canadian Human Rights Commission. He said the advertisement was denigrating, pulled down Indigenous culture, and reinforced the racist stereotype that Indians are lazy and lead lives of leisure. Air Canada extended a complete formal apology, which recognized that the advertisement was both insensitive and inappropriate. They canceled future advertisements.

Many foreign businesses and countries engage in or allow this practice, including Australia, the United States, Indonesia, and most Central American and Andean countries. In Guatemala, the promotion of Mayan culture to tourists and violence against Mayan people exist side by side.

Cultural integrity means that degrading commercial images of Indigenous peoples should be prohibited. There have been a number of recent instances in both the United States and Canada, where Indigenous peoples have successfully protested the use of "Indian" caricatures as mascots or emblems of sports teams with names like "Redskins" or "Warriors." U.S. automobile manufacturers continue to market trucks under the names of Indigenous peoples (for example, "Cherokee"), and Indian symbols continue to be used in selling many other products as well. The right to cultural autonomy and integrity should include the right to respect for one's own name.

Eurocentric lawyers pretend that they can protect Indigenous heritage using laws developed to protect other creative rights under the rubric of intellectual, spiritual, and cultural property rights, but this is a twisted version of equality. Indigenous peoples are victimized by an intellectual and cultural property law system that not only depends on appropriation and control through individual ownership—a concept foreign to Indigenous systems of regulating creativity—but also relies on an ideological structure that relegates Indigenous peoples to a category beneath human ingenuity and creativity, raising serious doubts about the applicability of any Eurocentric law to traditional arts and knowledge. Until changes are made to the existing intellectual and cultural property régime, the taking of the incorporeal property of Indigenous knowledge and heritage without any proper compensation will remain widespread.

Part III

•••

Existing Legal Régimes and Indigenous Knowledge and Heritage

The relevant point is not that the European philosophy of intellectual property is correct, and everyone else in the world is wrong—or vice versa. What the foregoing discussion shows is more basic: that there are many different historical and cultural assumptions about the ownership of ideas. Were it not for trade, international law would be unconcerned with so many different national regimes for intellectual property because each would be strictly a matter of domestic policy. But the fact is that nations do trade, so the difference matters. Fair participation in the global market depends on rules that bind each nation equally, otherwise market distortions will place some nations at a disadvantage. — David Hurlbut, "Fixing the Biodiversity Convention: Toward a Special Protocol for Related Intellectual Property" (1994, 379)

Chapter 10

•••

The International Intellectual and Cultural Property Régime

There can be no doubt that the protection of cultural rights and intellectual property fall within the mandate of the Sub-Commission and the Commission on Human Rights in the light of article 27 of the Universal Declaration of Human Rights, article 15 of the International Covenant on Economic, Social and Cultural Rights and, in the view of the Special Rapporteur, article 17 of the International Covenant on Civil and Political Rights. Accordingly, it is proper for the Sub-Commission to advise the Commission as to how these universally recognized principles of human rights should best be interpreted and applied in particular contexts, such as the context of indigenous peoples. The Sub-Commission would naturally be wise to seek the cooperation of other interested United Nations bodies, as it has in the field of human rights and the environment, but its own judgment is not subordinate to the opinions of expert bodies in other fields. — Dr. Erica-Irene Daes, *Supplementary Report of the Special Rapporteur on the Protection of the Heritage of Indigenous Peoples* (1996b, para. 16)

International law attempts to harmonize the intellectual and cultural property régimes of the various states. Canada is bound by a number of multilateral treaties dealing with human rights, cultural property, and intellectual property. These instruments are only binding at international law, and some are binding as incorporated into Canada's domestic law by federal acts.

At the urging of the Indigenous network, over the last few years several international documents and conferences, such as the UN Conference on Environment and Development, have raised the international profile of issues surrounding "traditional" or "Indigenous" or "local" knowledge. Around the world, there is growing interest in and discussion of the preservation of Indigenous culture, the development of Indigenous economies, and the protection of Indigenous rights. Increasingly, international multilateral treaties and agreements refer to protecting different aspects of Indigenous knowledge and heritage for different purposes. International conferences and bodies are now calling on governments to take account of Indigenous knowledge and heritage in relation to intellectual property rights.

It is important to remember that Eurocentric intellectual and cultural property rights are explicitly protected under international law. Even on the most basic level, Canadian law is derived from English law, which in turn was heavily influenced by the multilateral conventions first drafted in the nineteenth century, mainly the Paris Convention of 1884 and the Berne Convention of 1886 (which covered most of the statutory régimes). In addition, Canadian domestic law must now fulfill the requirements of the 1994 Agreement on Trade-Related Aspects of Intellectual Property (TRIPs), which is administered by the World Trade Organization (WTO) in Geneva. If Canada does not fulfill these requirements, it will risk protests and actions being brought against it within the WTO dispute-resolution fora.

For the sake of brevity and simplicity, we can say for our purposes that international law focuses on the domestic and international recognition of three legal principles: (1) Indigenous peoples' right to exercise control of their traditional territories; (2) Indigenous peoples' right to continue to harvest living resources, within or outside their traditional territories; and (3) Indigenous peoples' right to control and to benefit from the use of their traditional knowledge. These principles have all been affirmed to a greater or lesser extent by recent international instruments. These rights form a subset of the right to self-determination, an overarching right of "all peoples" under the UN Charter. Some states continue to oppose any formal UN action recognizing the application of this important principle to Indigenous peoples (Barsh 1994). It is conceivable, however, that this deadlock will be broken before the end of the UN Decade of the World's Indigenous People (1995–2004).

UN Human Rights Conventions and Covenants

In 1976, the Government of Canada ratified four international human rights conventions that have been interpreted as having special implications for Indigenous knowledge and heritage. The conventions exist in federal jurisdiction and thus cover Indians, land reserved for Indians, and territories. The International Convention on the Elimination of All Forms of Racial Discrimination (1965) forbids any discrimination in the "right to own property alone as well as in association with others" (art. 5(d)). The Committee on the Elimination of Racial Discrimination (CERD), which has a mandate to supervise the convention, has used this clause to challenge state parties' failure to secure collective land rights for Indigenous and tribal peoples (Barsh 1988). For example, at its thirty-fourth session in 1983, CERD requested an explanation of Ottawa's decision to dismiss Mi'kmaw land claims.

The International Covenant on Economic, Social and Cultural Rights and the International Covenant on Civil and Political Rights are the two main legal instruments dealing with human rights in Canada (Hogg 1992, 1377–86). They enshrine the right to self-determination and natural wealth and resources (art. 1); the right to equality before courts and tribunals (art. 14); the right to benefit from the protection of interest resulting from any scientific, literary, and artistic production (art. 15(1)(c)); the right to recognition as a person before the law (art. 16) and the entitlement without discrimination to the equal protection of the law (art. 26); the right to be protected by law for arbitrary or unlawful interference with privacy (art. 17); and the right to cultural, linguistic, and religious freedoms (art. 27).

Canada has adopted the optional protocol to the International Convenant on Civil and Political Rights (1967), which provides that individuals in Canada who claim that any of their human rights have been violated and domestic remedies are not available may petition the UN Commission on Human Rights (Hogg 1992, 1387–88). The decisions of the commission are relevant to the interpretation of the *Canadian Charter of Rights and Freedoms* (Hogg 1992, 822–24). In *Lovelace v. Canada* (1985), an Aboriginal woman was held to have the right of cultural association with her people, despite being married to a non-Indian. This decision caused section 35 of the *Constitution Act, 1982* to be amended to guarantee application equally to male and female persons and an amendment to the *Indian Act*. The *Mikmaw People v. Canada* (1992) case is an on-going case before the Committee for the Rights of Self-Determination under article 1 of this convenant.

Explicitly included in the International Convenant on Civil and Political Rights is the right to self-determination, which is defined as the right of all peoples, "for their own ends, to freely dispose of their natural wealth and resources . . . based upon the principle of mutual benefit." Most Aboriginal peoples in Canada do not regard themselves as the mere "minorities" described within article 27 of the convenant, nevertheless the UN Commission on Human Rights, which supervises the convenant, has ruled that Alberta's leasing of forest lands notwithstanding, the Lubicon Lake Cree land claims settlement in *Ominayak v. Canada* (1990) was a violation of minorities' rights. The commission has even hinted that this provision obliges Canada to devolve some degree of internal self-determination or self-government to Aboriginal peoples. A paraphrase of article 27 appears in article 30 of the UN Convention on the Rights of the Child (1989).

Subsistence harvesting and environmental protection arguably find support in the International Covenant on Economic, Social and Cultural Rights (1967), which recognizes every person's rights to an "adequate standard of living," including "adequate food," and to the "highest attainable standard of physical and mental health" (arts. 11–12). Articles 23 and 24 of the Convention on the Rights of the Child recapitulate these principles in the context of child survival and well-being.

Both article 27(2) of the 1948 UN Universal Declaration of Human Rights and article 15(1) of the International Covenant on Economic, Social and Cultural Rights refer to the right of everyone to "the moral and material interests resulting from any scientific, literary or artistic production of which he is the author." These provisions are aimed at the individual and are crucial to many Indigenous people producing such works.

Article 5(d) of the International Convention on the Elimination of All Forms of Racial Discrimination (1965) prohibits discrimination with respect to the ownership of property, individually or collectively. A government's failure to protect Indigenous peoples' collective rights to their heritage may be discriminatory, if this failure is justified by the argument that Indigenous peoples have a *lesser right* than the state or museums and academic institutions.

In his recent report on the right to own property, the special rapporteur of the Sub-Commission on Prevention of Discrimination and Protection of Minorities, Mr. Luis Valencia Rodriguez, concludes that "the sense of security and dignity gained from being able to own property is an essential prerequisite for the pursuit of happiness and exercise of a variety of other human rights" and is therefore "related to all other human rights and fundamental freedoms" (1993, para. 481). He also draws attention to the growing trend toward international and national recognition of the collective rights of Indigenous peoples to land and other resources as a factor contributing to their economic security and cultural development (paras. 378–96).

UN human-rights mechanisms, such as the Commission on Human Rights, have not thus far been utilized to address questions of protecting the heritage of Indigenous peoples.

The International Intellectual Property Régime

Intellectual property is a familiar legal concept that is exceedingly difficult to define. The principle reason for this difficulty lies in legal history. Intellectual property rights first developed in European law as a mechanism to protect individual and industrial inventions. In British law, each of the established actions developed independently of the others, but all were eventually organized into the concept of intellectual property (literary and artistic endeavors) and industrial property (patents and trade). Another reason for the nebulous qualities of intellectual property is that it is an umbrella term that covers an array of different rights. Problems arise when trying to determine just what comes under the umbrella. No single theory of protection of intellectual property exists. Until the various intellectual property régimes are replaced by some general right, intellectual property will remain an evolving collection of rights whose parts are greater than its sum (McKeough & Stewart 1991, 3–4).

The 1967 Convention Establishing the World Intellectual Property Organization (WIPO) does not define intellectual property. WIPO is one of the sixteen specialized agencies of the United Nations (arts. 57 and 63 of the UN

Charter). Article 2 (viii) of the 1967 convention provides a broad, enumerated list of all matters that might conceivably fall with the concept of intellectual property. The list includes rights related to (1) literary, artistic, and scientific works; (2) performances of performing artists, phonograms, and broadcasts; (3) inventions in all fields of human endeavor; (4) scientific discoveries; (5) industrial designs; (6) trademarks, service marks, and commercial names and designations; (7) protection against unfair competition; and (8) all other rights resulting from intellectual activity in the industrial, scientific, literary, and artistic fields. However, this extended definition excludes rights in trade secrets and know-how. Given the disunity of the emerging rights, structuring the treatment of intellectual property rights is an arbitrary and complex decision. There is no unifying scheme to fill the disturbing gaps in the legal protection of human creativity.

Even if the literature could define intellectual property rights, there are other related transactions and regulations that involve intellectual property rights. These transactions include various plans and agreements between creators and exploiters, such as between authors and publishers or between inventors and manufacturers. They also include issues of licenses and franchises. Other fields of activity and of regulation impinge so strongly on intellectual property rights that they must be considered; for example, international trade with respect to parallel imports of trademarked goods, licensing and requirements related to the transfer of technology in developing countries, competition (antitrust) law, and the full range of potentially anticompetitive effects of intellectual property rights and transactions. Finally, there exists the practical and technical matter of patent and trademark searching.

International intellectual property rights depend significantly on national laws. Despite the existing agreements that attempt to achieve international harmonization of these national régimes; there are significant substantive differences between nations and there is no internationally uniform definition of intellectual property and accruing legal rights.

Copyright of Literary and Artistic Works

The Berne Convention for the Protection of Literary and Artistic Works (1886)

The Berne Convention for the Protection of Literary and Artistic Works, originally adopted in 1886, establishes international standards for harmonizing the copyright laws of state parties. Legal protection can be granted for many forms of creative and literary expression for the author's life plus fifty years or longer.

Article 2(2) of the Berne Convention permits each state party to determine whether a work must be "fixed" in some physical form, such as a written document or photograph, before it can be given copyright protection. The requirement of fixation poses a problem for works of oral literature, poetry, and song, which by their nature are repeated and frequently revised from generation to generation.

Article 6 of the Berne Convention regulates moral rights by providing that, independent of their economic rights and even after their transfer, authors retain the right to claim authorship of their works and to object to any distortions, mutilations, or other modifications of, or other derogatory actions in relation to their works, which would be prejudicial to their honor or reputation. Article 6 of the Rome Revision, 2 June 1928, states:

> (1) Independently of the author's copyright, and even after transfer of the said copyright, the author shall have the right to claim authorship of the work, as well as the right to object to any distortion, mutilation or other modification of the said work which would be prejudicial to his honour or reputation.
>
> (2) The determination of the conditions under which these rights shall be exercised is reserved for the national legislation of the countries of the [Berne] Union. The means of redress for safeguarding these rights shall be regulated by the legislation of the country where protection is claimed.

This article seems to recognize two rights: the right to paternity or attribution and the right to integrity in a work. Moral rights, in their ideal form (for example, in France, where the concept of *droit moral* was born), are perpetual, inalienable, and imprescriptible. Countries of Roman law background have generally incorporated moral rights in their copyright law. Commonly under those laws, moral rights cannot be assigned and after the death of the author, they are exercised by the author's heirs, irrespective of ownership of the economic rights. As noted earlier, Canada has adopted moral rights of a limited nature in its copyright law.

The International Convention for the Protection of Performers, Producers of Phonograms and Broadcasting Organizations (Rome Convention 1961)

Minimum standards for the protection of performers are further elaborated in the International Convention for the Protection of Performers, Producers of Phonograms and Broadcasting Organizations (Rome Convention), adopted in 1961.

The World Intellectual Property Organization (1967)

The World Intellectual Property Organization (WIPO) administers a variety of conventions for the protection of "intellectual property." Some conventions create international mechanisms for the registration and enforcement of property rights; however, most conventions simply establish standards for compatibility and reciprocity of state parties' national legislation. Thus Indigenous peoples generally cannot obtain protection for their heritage directly through WIPO machinery, but WIPO may be used to promote the strengthening of national machinery in the countries concerned.

WIPO undertakes many activities in the areas of copyright law and industrial property that relate to Indigenous peoples, such as its role as the secretariat of the International Convention for the Protection of New Varieties of Plants (UPOV 1961). Many of the issues discussed at this forum were complex and unresolved. In another area of activity, WIPO recommended that the Draft Principles and Guidelines on Protection of Indigenous Heritage not include statements on certain items, such as folklore. WIPO then participated in the UNESCO/WIPO World Forum on the Protection of Expressions of Folklore in 1997 to develop a means of protecting folklore internationally.

Issues Paper Prepared by the Australian Law Reform Commission (1993)

A 1993 issues paper prepared by the Australian Law Reform Commission succinctly explains the difficulties of using existing laws to protect Indigenous peoples' cultural heritage. Traditional motifs are not the sole property of individual artists to sell or withhold freely as they please, but are subject to layers of group rights at the family, community, and tribal levels. Many different individuals may need to be consulted about the disposition of a design or objects that bear it. Copyright laws do not make such fine distinctions, but only recognize a single owner. Furthermore, copyright and other kinds of intellectual-property protection are of limited duration, while Aboriginal peoples regard cultural rights as perpetual. Hence, applying the usual principles of copyright to Aboriginal heritage fundamentally alters the relationship between the artist and the community and does not provide adequate protection.

Patent Protection and Scientific Discoveries

The Paris Convention for the Protection of Industrial Property (1884)

The Paris Convention for the Protection of Industrial Property, which originally came into force in 1884, is aimed at maintaining some minimum uniformity in national laws relating to patents on technology, industrial designs, trademarks, trade names, appellations of origin, and the prevention of unfair competition. There are three limitations on the usefulness of patents for the protection of Indigenous peoples' heritage: (1) patents only apply to "new" knowledge; (2) rights are ordinarily granted to individuals or corporations rather than to cultures or peoples; and (3) the rights granted are of limited duration. Patents are therefore not useful for protecting traditional knowledge, knowledge that people wish to keep confidential, and knowledge that does not meet relatively high standards of inventiveness nor non-obviousness.

The International Convention for the Protection of New Varieties of Plants (1961)

A special legal régime for the protection of plant breeders was launched by the International Convention for the Protection of New Varieties of Plants (UPOV 1961). Canada is one of the member-states that has adopted the convention. It has been amended three times, in 1972, 1978, and 1991. Canada has signed the 1991 amendments to the act, but has not ratified them. This convention presents one model of a *sui generis* system of protection for plant breeders developing new plant varieties. The convention provides exclusive rights to plant breeds for fifteen to twenty years. Until the 1978 amendments, states had to provide either a *sui generis* or patent protection for the same botanical genus or species. Under the 1978 and 1991 amendments, states can provide both forms of protection.

To obtain protection, the applicant must deposit a sample of the plant variety for examination. It must be clearly distinguishable from any plant variety, the existence of which is already a matter of common knowledge. It must also be stable and homogeneous—that is, "it must remain true to its description after repeated reproduction or propagation." There is a presumption of novelty if the variety has never previously been marketed or offered for sale, in which case its distinguishing characteristics may be of either natural or artificial origins. It would, therefore, be possible to obtain protection for traditional cultigens, such as varieties of maize, potatoes, and wild rice, as well as naturally occurring species used for medicine and not previously known by non-Indigenous societies. The major obstacles to obtaining plant breeders' rights are the costs of depositing samples and demonstrating, through repeated propagation trials, that they are stable and homogeneous.

The Budapest Treaty on the International Recognition of the Deposit of Microorganisms for the Purpose of Patent Procedure (1977)

There is an exception to these rules of patentability in the case of the isolation and purification of naturally occurring species of micro-organisms. The Budapest Treaty on the International Recognition of the Deposit of Microorganisms (1977) creates a network of international institutions for the deposit of micro-organisms and for the registration of rights to their commercial use. Indigenous peoples could conceivably use this treaty to assert their rights to strains of yeast and other micro-organisms long used for fermentation. They would need laboratory facilities to isolate and purify these organisms, however.

The Geneva Treaty on the International Recording of Scientific Discoveries (1978)

Indigenous peoples' traditional knowledge of ecosystems includes more than the ability to identify useful species. It includes a wide range of scientific insights into basic processes in ecology and animal behavior. Although scientific discoveries are generally excluded from patent protection, the Geneva Treaty on the International Recording of Scientific Discoveries (1978) offers a mechanism for recognizing the identity of the discoverer. Article 1 of the treaty defines scientific discovery as "the recognition of phenomena, properties or laws of the material universe not hitherto recognized and capable of verification."

Protection of Inventions in the Field of Biotechnology (1987)

"Novelty" is a basic requirement of patentability. A product or process is not ordinarily patentable if it is already known elsewhere in the world. It must also be described in such a way that it can be reproduced. Plants and animals are therefore only patentable if they are created by a process that can be described, controlled, and reproduced, such as genetic engineering. Patenting of species and the biological processes of higher life forms is not permitted under the European Patent Convention (1979) and in some national legal systems, including Canada. In other countries, it is limited to organisms with forms, qualities, or properties that are not already found in nature (WIPO 1987).

The UN Convention on Biological Diversity (1992)

The 1992 UN Convention on Biological Diversity affirms that biological resources are vital to humanity's economic and social development. Its overall objectives are the conservation of biological diversity, the sustainable use of its components, and the fair and equitable sharing of the benefits arising from the utilization of genetic resources. The convention recognizes that biological resources are of more than commercial value to human beings.

The convention has been widely ratified and is in force in Canada. It is being implemented through the Canadian Biodiversity Strategy and the Canadian Conservation Strategy. The convention contains several express references to "Indigenous and local communities," as well as to "local populations" and to "customary uses" of biological resources "in accordance with traditional cultural practices." All these references will be taken to apply to what we define domestically as "the Aboriginal peoples of Canada."

In its preamble, the convention recognizes

> the close and traditional dependence of many Indigenous and local communities embodying traditional lifestyles on biological resources, and the desirability of sharing equitably benefits arising from the use of traditional knowledge, innovations and practices relevant to the conservation of biological diversity and the sustainable use of its components.

This preamble identifies two of the rights of Indigenous peoples: resource use and traditional knowledge. They are addressed separately in paragraphs 10(c) and 8(j) of the convention, respectively. A right to environmental rehabilitation is mentioned in paragraph 10(d) of the convention, which relates logically to the issue of use.

Article 8(a) requires each state party to "[e]stablish a system of protected areas or areas where special measures need to be taken to conserve biological diversity." Indigenous peoples have expressed concern that their territories will be targeted for "protected" status because they are relatively undisturbed and—often due to traditional management practices—enjoy unusually high levels of biodiversity. They do not oppose protection, but they do oppose restrictive management régimes that are imposed upon them without their consent and that interfere with their ability to maintain their own settlements. An example of such interference is where national parks and refuges have been superimposed on the traditional territories of Indigenous peoples, mainly in response to pressure from environmental groups. This concern is addressed, albeit obliquely, by article 10(c) of the convention, which directs state parties to "[p]rotect and encourage customary use of biological resources in accordance with traditional cultural practices that are compatible with conservation or sustainable use requirements." If customary uses of living resources are sustainable, they should not only be respected, but also strengthened. This evokes the rights of Indigenous peoples.

Article 10(d) of the convention directs state parties to "support local populations to develop and implement remedial action in degraded areas where biological diversity has been reduced." This implies that Indigenous peoples and other local communities have the right to some level of financial, as well as administrative, support from the state when they take initiatives to redress environmental degradation. This is the only provision of the convention that clearly assigns some kind of decision-making or priority-setting authority to local communities.

With respect to traditional knowledge, article 8(j) requires that each state party

> [s]ubject to its national legislation, respect, preserve and maintain knowledge, innovations and practices of Indigenous and local communities embodying traditional lifestyles relevant for the conservation and sustainable use of biological diversity and promote their wider application with the approval and involvement of the holders of such knowledge, innovations and practices and encourage the equitable sharing of the benefits arising from the utilization of such knowledge, innovations and practices.

This provision must be read into article 15, which recognizes the sovereignty of each state party over the genetic resources within its territory, while requiring the state parties to "facilitate" access to these resources by other state parties. Two questions arise. A state might try to broker commercial rights to traditional cultigens or to the knowledge of plants used in traditional medicine over objections from the Indigenous people concerned. Alternatively, a state might try to limit the right of Indigenous peoples to license the commercial use of their own medicinal and agricultural knowledge, on their own terms, arguing that they must recognize the state as their sole agent.

The "approval and involvement" clause of article 8(j) means that a state should only "facilitate" access to Indigenous peoples' genetic resources after it has obtained the informed consent of the Indigenous people concerned. It is also clear that states should not approve the study or use of Indigenous peoples' genetic resources without making a provision for the "equitable sharing of the benefits" with the people concerned. It is less clear whether the state can insist on being the sole agent for Indigenous peoples or demand its own share of benefits in the form of super-royalties or taxes on contracts involving traditional Indigenous knowledge or genetic information discovered through the use of this knowledge. Indigenous peoples could presumably exercise their power of approval under article 8(j) to bar access to their genetic resources until the state agrees to allow them to act as their own brokers.

In its decision II/12, the Second Conference of the Parties, held in 1995, requested that the executive secretary explore "the relationship between the objectives of the Convention on Biological Diversity and the TRIPs [Trade-Related Intellectual Property Rights] Agreement" in cooperation with the World Trade Organization and in consultation with "all stakeholders, in particular the private sector and indigenous and local communities." Particular attention should be given to "exploring the relationship between intellectual property rights and the preservation and maintenance of traditional knowledge and practices of indigenous and local communities and the possible role of intellectual property rights in encouraging the equitable sharing of benefits arising from such knowledge and practices."

UN Food and Agriculture Organization and Farmers' Rights

The UN Food and Agriculture Organization (FAO) Intergovernmental Commission on Plant Genetic Resources is concerned with the importance of Indigenous knowledge and practices in agriculture. The basic genetic resources that we use for modern food production were domesticated thousands of years ago; those who develop modern plant varieties draw upon the work and the genetic material in the fields of these farmers. The FAO recently established the International Fund for Plant Genetic Resources in accordance with an agreement recognizing farmers' rights. The International Undertaking on Plant Genetic Resources was adopted in 1983 by the Conference of FAO. The undertaking was a non-binding instrument whose interpretation was only agreed upon ten years after its adoption. In particular, FAO conference resolution 5/89 of 29 November 1989 recognized farmers' rights as rights arising from the "past, present and future contributions of farmers in conserving, improving and making available plant genetic resources, particularly those in the centres of origin/diversity" (FAO 1989).

The conference recognized that there was no mechanism for the implementation of farmers' rights, and in its resolution 3/91 of 25 November 1991, it decided to implement farmers' rights through an international fund for plant genetic resources. Unlike breeders' rights, however, these farmers' rights are not rights of individuals, but the rights of states to benefit from the commercial development of traditional cultigens, such as bananas and rice. When a biotechnology company profits from using genes discovered in traditionally grown varieties of plants, the company is supposed to repay some of this income to the fund, in trust for the countries of origin of the genes. However, there is no mechanism to ensure that farmers or their communities receive any benefit from these payments.

With the entry into force of the 1992 Convention on Biological Diversity, which also recognizes farmers' rights, the Conference of FAO, in resolution 7/93 of 22 November 1993, began the process of revising the International Undertaking on Plant Genetic Resources, in harmony with the convention, including the realization of farmers' rights. The most recent meeting of the Commission on Plant Genetic Resources, held in December 1996, was part of these intergovernmental negotiations at which new proposals were made to strengthen the implementation of farmers' rights. In particular, FAO drew attention to the proposal of the developing countries, which offers a range of protections for Indigenous peoples and ensures full benefits to farmers, Indigenous peoples, and other communities embodying traditional lifestyles.

Technology, "Know-how," and Trade Secrets

Many applications of Indigenous peoples' traditional knowledge to practical problems, such as harvesting fish, manufacturing pottery, or managing forests, might still be patented as "technology." Technology can include any knowledge that is useful, systematic, organized with a view to solving a specific problem, and capable of being communicated in some way to others (see WIPO 1985). The patentability of traditional technology depends on national legislation, however, and many countries may not consider long-held knowledge to be sufficiently novel and inventive to qualify for patent protection.

Although molecules discovered in naturally occurring species cannot be patented as such, a chemical process used to isolate or purify the molecule, or to synthesize it, can be patented as technology. In addition, naturally occurring molecules often provide what biochemists call "leads" or clues for the synthesis of related molecules that have the same valuable characteristics. Thus, although Indigenous peoples may guide biochemists to valuable molecules, only the work done by the biochemists is treated as proprietary.

It is discriminatory to treat the effort involved in isolating a chemical compound in the laboratory as more worthy of legal protection and compensation than the effort involved in centuries of observation and experimentation with naturally occurring species. Furthermore, it is clear that using Indigenous peoples' knowledge to select plants for laboratory analysis significantly reduces the cost of discovering new products. Thus, traditional knowledge has economic value and should not be treated as a "free good."

These problems are not unique to Indigenous peoples; many useful ideas in industry do not qualify for patent protection. These include "know-how" (experience in using a particular technique or device) and trade secrets (such as the formulas used to flavor certain processed foods and beverages). Companies generally protect their know-how and trade secrets by refusing to allow outsiders to visit their factories or speak with their employees, unless they agree to a contract setting out conditions for the use of whatever they learn. Indigenous peoples could also withhold their knowledge except under licensing agreements providing for confidentiality, appropriate use, and economic benefits. For the time being, this appears to be the most effective approach for protecting ecological, medicinal, and spiritual knowledge.

Trademark and Industrial Design Protection

The Paris Convention for the Protection of Industrial Property (1884)

Indigenous peoples' traditional artistic motifs might be brought within existing provisions for the protection of industrial designs defined by the Paris Convention as "the ornamental or aesthetic aspect of a useful article." To be eligible for protection, a design must be "original," however, and in most national legal systems, the duration of protection for industrial designs is less than for copyright—often as little as fifteen years. This can be inadequate for designs of special cultural and spiritual significance, where protecting the integrity of the design may be of greater importance than exploiting its commercial value.

Characteristic motifs that serve to identify an Indigenous people or community might also be protected as collective trademarks. Canada and other states already use special certification marks to identify authentic works by Indigenous peoples. Both are governed by article 7 *bis* of the Paris Convention. Not only designs, but also names or sequences of words can be given trademark protection, so that (for example) clan and tribal names might be included. Unlike copyrights and industrial designs, trademark protection is not limited in duration, but usually requires only registration and continued use. There could be problems under some countries' national laws, however, if a mark or design has already been widely copied by others.

Article 10 *bis* of the Paris Convention forbids unfair competition in trade, which is defined as "acts of such a nature as to create confusion by any means whatsoever with the establishment, the goods, or the industrial or commercial activities of a competitor," as well as "indications or allegations the use of which in the course of trade is liable to mislead the public as to the nature, the manufacturing process, the characteristics, the suitability for their purpose, or the quantity, of the goods." This could be applied to a wide variety of disputes over the authenticity of products employing the designs or folklore of Indigenous peoples. It only applies to products in trade, however, and not to preserving the privacy or integrity of things that Indigenous peoples wish to keep for their own exclusive use.

The Lisbon Agreement for the Protection of Appellations of Origin and Their International Registration (1966)

Although indications of geographical origin cannot be registered as trademarks, they can be used to verify the authenticity of products as provided by the Lisbon Agreement for the Protection of Appellations of Origin and Their International Registration (1966). This provides for the registration of a geographic name "which serves to designate a product originating therein, the quality and characteristics of which are due exclusively or essentially to the geographic environment, including natural and human factors." This registration, in combination with distinctive trademarks, could be used to identify the characteristic products of Indigenous communities.

International Trade and Aid Measures

The Agreement on Trade-Related Intellectual Property (1994)

In 1994, the Final Act Embodying the Results of the Uruguay Round of Multilateral Trade Negotiations created the World Trade Organization (WTO). The Final Act also included the Agreement on Trade-Related Aspects of Intellectual Property (TRIPs), which set new standards for intellectual property rights. These standards are similar to those existing under other international treaties and conventions on intellectual property, which are administered by the World Intellectual Property Organization. What TRIPs does is create new international machinery to enforce these rights through the Council on TRIPs.

Member-states of the WTO may continue to provide "more extensive protection than is required by this Agreement" in national legislation, "provided that such protection does not contravene the provisions of this Agreement" (art. 1.1). Member-states also retain full authority to make laws they "deem necessary" to protect public health and nutrition, and to promote the public interest in sectors of vital importance to their socio-economic and technological development (art. 8). Articles 1 and 8 of the TRIPs agreement permit member-states to give greater protection to the heritage of Indigenous peoples under their national legislation than they are required to give to intellectual property generally—provided that they afford the same special protection to Indigenous peoples who are nationals of other states. Each member-state must accord to the nationals of other members treatment with respect to the protection of intellectual property that is no less favorable than that it accords to its own nationals (art. 3).

The agreement, moreover, fixes certain minimum levels of protection for patents, industrial designs, and other forms of intellectual property. It provides wide coverage of all areas of technology for patent purposes. The agreement obligates state-parties to provide patents for any inventions, whether products or processes, in all fields of technology, provided they are new, involve an inventive step, and are useful. Pharmaceuticals and genetic engineering are included in this coverage, which provides a twenty-year duration of patent rights, a regulated régime of compulsory licensing, and strict enforcement provisions. Industrialized countries have pressed for stringent universal respect for the patents issued to developers of biotechnology. A patent may be refused on the grounds of *ordre public* or morality, terms that are not defined in the agreements. Additionally, a state-party may also exclude patentability for diagnostic, therapeutic, and surgical methods for the treatment of humans or animals.

The agreement enjoins the state-parties to provide effective protection to plant varieties through patents or by an effective *sui generis* system or by any combination thereof. Previously, plant varieties were not protected under the patent law of many countries. Animal varieties, however, are excluded from patentability if they are achieved by biological processes, but the animals and plants developed by micro-organisms as well as by non-biological and micro-biological processes are patentable (art. 27(3)). Article 27 appears to permit member-states, if they so wish, to exclude the traditional ecological and medical knowledge of Indigenous peoples from patentability. Varieties produced by traditional means of breeding and screening will become the subject of patent protection of a new *sui generis* system. Article 39.2 of the TRIPs agreement is broader than the existing concepts of trade secrets and know-how. It is broad enough to cover most of the teachings, ceremonies, songs, dances, and designs that Indigenous peoples consider sacred and confidential and that are currently threatened by commercial exploitation.

Developing countries are required to adopt meaningful and effective plant variety protection systems consonant with their special conditions. Developing countries, farmers' organizations, and grassroots non-governmental organizations opposed this TRIPs agreement, arguing that it will reinforce the ability of transnational corporations to control the medicines and genetically engineered plants they are devising with genetic resources collected in the Southern Hemisphere. Industrialized countries are likewise opposed to any preferences in favor of developing countries with respect to the commercial exploitation of biodiversity. Although the 1992 UN Convention on Biological Diversity calls on all state-parties to contribute proportionally to the costs of conserving highly biodiverse ecosystems in the Southern Hemisphere, several states have made declarations interpreting this very narrowly. The interests of most Indigenous peoples are aligned with developing countries and could be seriously undermined by a GATT (General Agreement on Trade and Tariffs) rule that favors the rights of biotechnology companies over those of the states and peoples who manage biodiverse ecosystems. Developing countries have been urged to adopt a *sui generis* system, such as the International Convention for the Protection of New Varieties of Plants (UPOV 1961), rather than patents.

The WTO Committee on Trade and Environment and its working paper W/8 (WTO 1995) reviewed the TRIPs agreement and its relation to the environment. Paragraphs 77 and 78 of the working paper, which include references to Indigenous peoples and local communities, stated that the TRIPs agreement was not an obstacle to enhancing the protection of Indigenous intellectual property rights. It was also pointed out that subparagraph 3(b) of article 27 of the agreement relating to the protection of plant and animal inventions was due to be reviewed four years after the date of entry into force of the WTO agreement. No concrete proposals have yet been presented.

Since the thrust of the TRIPs agreement was to protect intellectual creations in order to promote technological innovation and technology transfer and dissemination, WTO member-states could resort to existing mechanisms of intellectual property protection in order to cover Indigenous knowledge provided that the provisions of the TRIPs agreement were not contravened. For example, traditional requirements of novelty, inventiveness, and capability of industrial application do not necessarily exclude the patentability of all Indigenous knowledge on the practical use of genetic resources for pharmaceutical purposes.

U.S. Bills

Since 1990 there have been several unsuccessful attempts to enact new U.S. laws that would require respect for the intellectual property of Indigenous peoples. Senate Bill 748, if adopted, would have given priority in U.S. foreign assistance to the protection of Indigenous peoples, including their "proprietorship of the traditional knowledge of plant and animal resources." House Concurrent Resolution 354 would have directed U.S. diplomats to take account of traditional knowledge in the current round of GATT negotiations.

House Bill 1596 would have required that U.S. foreign policy and foreign aid be consistent with the rights of Indigenous peoples. There may be further efforts to tie U.S. aid and trade policy to respect for Indigenous peoples' lands, knowledge, and heritage.

Resolutions of the European Parliament

A 1989 resolution adopted by the European Parliament called upon the European Commission and Council to insert conditions of respect for Indigenous knowledge in overseas-aid agreements. It would be preferable to agree upon universal standards than leave the question of respect for the rights of Indigenous peoples to unilateral economic policies and bilateral negotiations.

UNESCO Machinery for Recovering Cultural Property

UNESCO Declaration of the Principles of International Cultural Co-operation (1966)

The UNESCO (United Nations Educational, Scientific, and Cultural Organization) Declaration on the Principles of International Cultural Co-operation (1966) affirms in article 1 that "[e]ach culture has a dignity and value which must be respected and preserved," and, furthermore, that "[e]very people has the right and duty to develop its culture." This suggests that peoples have collective rights to cultural integrity, including a right to define, interpret, and determine the nature of future changes in their cultures. The central role of traditional forms of cultural transmission and education is stressed in the guidelines set out in the annex to this declaration. The drafters of this declaration believe that safeguarding traditional cultural transmission is the most effective means of ensuring that Indigenous peoples control the further development of their heritage, as well as its interpretation and use by others.

UNESCO Convention on the Means of Prohibiting and Preventing the Illicit Import, Export and Transfer of Ownership of Cultural Property (1970)

The lead agency within the UN system in the field of cultural property and heritage is UNESCO, and the principal instrument in this field is the UNESCO Convention on the Means of Prohibiting and Preventing the Illicit Import, Export and Transfer of Ownership of Cultural Property (1970), which entered into legal force in 1972. In article 1, this convention defines cultural property as

> property which, on religions or secular grounds, is specifically designated by each State as being important for archaeology, prehistory, history, literature, art or science and which belongs to the follow categories:

(a) Rare collections and specimens of fauna, mineral and anatomy, and objects of paleontological interest;
(b) property relating to history, including the history of science and technology and military and social history, to the life of national leaders, thinkers, scientists and artists and to events of national importance;
(c) products of archaeological excavations (including regular and clandestine) or of archaeological discoveries;
(d) elements of artistic or historical monuments or archaeological sites which have been dismembered;
(e) antiquities more than one hundred years old, such as inscriptions, coins and engraved seals;
(f) objects of ethnological interest;
(g) property of artistic interest, such as:
    (i) pictures, paintings and drawings produced entirely by hand on any support and in any material (excluding industrial designs and manufactured articles decorated by hand);
    (ii) original works of statuary art and sculpture in any material;
    (iii) original engravings, prints, and lithographs;
    (iv) original artistic assemblages and montages in any material;
    (v) original artistic assemblages and montages in any material;
(h) rare manuscripts and incunabula, old books, documents and publications of special interest (historical, artistic, scientific, literary, etc.) singly or in collections;
(i) postage, revenue and similar stamps, singly or in collection;
(j) archives, including sound, photographic and cinematographic archives;
(k) articles of furniture more than one hundred years old and musical instruments.

UNESCO is moving to protect the heritage of Indigenous peoples. It has established an intersectoral task force to deal with matters concerning Indigenous peoples, coordinated by Mme. Lourdes Arizpe, the UNESCO assistant director-general for culture. In 1966, UNESCO brought the Final Report of the Principles and Guidelines for the Protection of the Heritage of Indigenous Peoples to the attention of the Ninth Session of the Intergovernmental Committee for the Promotion of the Return of Cultural Property to its Countries of Origin or Its Restitution in Case of Illicit Appropriation. UNESCO is proposing that it would be the appropriate body to undertake the "comprehensive annual report" described in paragraph 55 of the principles and guidelines. Paragraph 55 provides: "The United Nations should publish a comprehensive annual report, based upon information from all available sources, including indigenous peoples themselves, on the problems experienced and solutions adopted in the protection of indigenous peoples' heritage in all countries."

UNESCO suggests that this report could be contained in a special chapter of its planned biennial reports on the state of culture.

In 1978, Canada acceded to the convention and its vast definition of cultural property. The enactment of the federal *Cultural Property Export and Import Act* (1985) is intended to be consistent with this convention.

The convention provides two main mechanisms for the protection of culturally important objects. A state-party can request other state-parties to impose emergency import controls on an object or class of objects. A state-party can also request the return of illegally exported objects under certain conditions, at the expense of the state-party making the request.

The convention has several shortcomings. Requests must be made by states, both states involved in a dispute must be parties to the convention, and the removal of the object must have occurred after the convention came into force in both states—necessarily after 1972. Most of the largest art-importing states, such as France, Germany, the United Kingdom, and Japan, are not parties to the convention, and Indigenous peoples lost much of their cultural property before 1972.

UNESCO Convention on Protection of the World's Cultural and Natural Heritage (1972)

In 1976, Canada ratified the 1972 UNESCO Convention on Protection of the World's Cultural and Natural Heritage. Anthony Island in the Queen Charlotte Islands is an ancient Haida village that has been declared to be an UNESCO World Heritage Site according to this convention.

OAS Convention on the Protection of the Archeological and Artistic Heritage of the American Nations (Convention of San Salvador 1976)

The OAS (Organization of American States) Convention on the Protection of the Archeological and Artistic Heritage of the American Nations (Convention of San Salvador 1976) takes the same approach and has the same shortcomings as the UNESCO conventions.

UNESCO Intergovernmental Committee for Promoting the Return of Cultural Property to Its Country of Origin (1978)

In 1978, UNESCO established the Intergovernmental Committee for Promoting the Return of Cultural Property to Its Country of Origin with a mandate to undertake good offices and mediation at the request of states. The committee can also organize projects with such organizations as the International Council of Museums and UNESCO national committees to conduct inventories of cultural property. Thus far, Indigenous peoples have not been able to participate in the work of the committee. Moreover, the committee has avoided disputes between states and their constituent peoples; for example, it declined to take up Scotland's claim to the Stone of Scone because it was an internal affair of the United Kingdom. State ownership can conflict with the interests of Indigenous peoples. When the Afo-A-Kom statue was returned to Cameroon in 1974, a dispute arose between state authorities and the Kom people over custody. It was eventually agreed to return the statue to its traditional site in Kom territory rather than to the national capital. The Government of Australia has returned Aboriginal materials repatriated from other countries to their Aboriginal owners, but in many other countries, repatriated objects are kept by the state and not returned to the peoples who produced them.

Protection of Folklore

Folklore is the knowledge of the people. The legal position on folklore has been an important issue in international copyright debate for more than two decades. Only a few of the copyright laws in force contain specific provisions on folklore. Puri (1995) states that the position across Europe and other Western countries is that expressions of folklore are generally considered to belong in the public domain. In most of these countries, traditional art and traditional societies are not living entities and thus are considered part of the public domain. As soon as works cease to be protected by copyright, they fall into the public domain and from that moment form part of the common heritage of humankind, without anyone exercising any further monopoly over them. Thenceforth, the use of such works is free. Reproduction, performance, translation, or adaptation of works in the public domain can be made without anyone's consent. However, the copyright laws in these countries give protection to collections or compilations of works of folk art.

The various parties asserting claims to folklore include primarily arrangers and collectors. They, along with their collecting societies, have recently been involved in conflicts with those who maintain that folklore (that is to say, folk songs, folk music, and so on) is strictly in the public domain and that no private property rights exist therein. It should be noted that the compiler is given protection only so far as the writing, selection, or arrangement of the works of folk art reflects the characteristics of an individual and independent creation (Puri 1995, 330). International law has thus to take a role in protecting Indigenous folklore. The Australian Working Party, which prepared a comprehensive report entitled *Intellectual Property Aspects of Folklore Protection* (1981), defined Aboriginal folklore as "the body of traditions, observances, customs and beliefs of Aboriginals as expressed in Aboriginal music, dance, craft, sculpture, painting, theatre and literature." Thus, folklore consists of verbal expressions, musical expressions, performing arts expressions, and tangible expressions.

The Tunisian Literary and Artistic Property Act (1966)

In 1963, WIPO and UNESCO, under the initiative of the African countries, organized the first international meeting on the legal problems associated with folklore. The *Tunisian Literary and Artistic Property Act* introduced national protection for folklore and works inspired by folklore. Article 6 provided that folklore constituted a part of the national heritage, and that its exploitation with gainful intent by persons other than those representing public national organizations required authorization from the Department of Cultural Affairs. The act also provided that copyright in works that had been inspired by folklore (that is to say, works composed with the aid of elements borrowed from the cultural heritage of Tunisia and perpetuated by tradition) could not be assigned without the consent of the ministry.

Amendments to the Berne Convention (1971)

The Berne Convention was amended in 1971 to enable state-parties to designate "competent authorities" to control the licensing, use, and protection of national folklore. WIPO interprets this as including, in each state, "traditional manifestations of their culture that are the expression of their national identity" (Protection of Expressions of Folklore 1971). However, Indigenous peoples would certainly object to state management of their folklore as a part of national patrimony, with royalties being paid to the state instead of to their own communities. Each state could, consistent with the Berne Convention, delegate responsibilities for the definition, protection, and licensing of folklore to Indigenous peoples themselves, but so far as could be determined, no state has yet done so. Indeed, only a small number of states, among them Bolivia and Chile, have thus far adopted national folklore laws at all.

The Tunis Model Copyright Law and Protection of Folklore (1976)

The 1976 Tunis Model Copyright Law and Protection of Folklore for Developing Countries recognized the need for economic recompense and the need to protect a cultural legacy that is an essential part of the community. The committee of governmental experts was convinced that folklore could fit within the copyright mold. The model law provided for protection of economic and moral rights in folklore without limitation in time. The model law also provided for rights in folklore to be exercised by a "competent authority" and not by Indigenous owners. The competent authority would grant authorizations for any use of folklore made with gainful intent and outside the traditional context. The model law also placed particular emphasis on the fact that "[c]opies of national folklore made abroad, and copies of translations, adaptations, arrangements, or other transformations of works of national folklore made abroad, without the authorization of the competent authority, shall be neither imported nor distributed" in the national territory (s. 6(3)). Three special features of the model law deserve special mention: (i) protection of folklore for an indefinite period; (ii) exemption of folklore works from the requirement of fixation; and (iii) introduction of the concept of moral rights to prevent the destruction and desecration of folklore works.

Section 17 of the model law introduced the concept of *domaine public payant* by providing:

> The user shall pay to the competent authority . . . percent of the receipts produced by the use of works in the public domain or their adaptation, including works of national folklore. The sums collected shall be used for the following purposes: (i) to promote institutions for the benefit of authors and of performers such as societies of authors, cooperatives, guilds, etc., and (ii) to protect and disseminate national folklore.

According to this doctrine, a work that has fallen into the public domain may be used without restriction, subject to the payment calculated as a percentage of the receipts produced by the use of the work or its adaptations. *Domaine public payant* essentially envisages a revenue-raising scheme under which the users of works of folklore pay a percentage of the income they receive from the use of the works or their adaptations, to a competent authority.

Model Provision for National Laws on the Protection of Expressions of Folklore Against Illicit Exploitation and Other Prejudicial Actions (1982)

In 1982, WIPO drafted its Model Provisions for National Laws on the Protection of Expressions of Folklore Against Illicit Exploitation and Other Prejudicial Actions. In the 1985 the Model Provisions were adopted, establishing a *sui generis* protection mechanism for the expression of folklore lying outside copyright laws for the works of folklore (UNESCO & WIPO 1985, 5.) It protects against the unauthorized use of expressions of folklore, the misrepresentation of the source of expressions of folklore, the wilful distortion of folklore in a way prejudicial to the interests of the relevant community, and it includes a provision for international extension of protection based on reciprocity. This protection includes the tangible expressions of culture such as pottery, costumes, jewelry, and basketry. Fixation is not required. The model law forbids any use with "gainful intent and outside its traditional or customary context without authorization by a competent authority or the community itself," as well as any kind of publication or use that either fails to identify the ethnic origins of folklore or distorts its contents. Some African states have adopted legislation based on the WIPO model.

In 1984, UNESCO and WIPO produced a Draft Treaty for the Protection of Expressions of Folklore Against Illicit Exploitation and Other Prejudicial

Actions. It is not yet in force. Both UNESCO-WIPO models provide for a competent authority to regulate the use of works or expressions of folklore but leave the designation of this authority up to individual national governments on the grounds that the ownership of folklore may be regulated in different ways in different countries. These models provide for respect for Indigenous folklore; however, they do not incorporate Indigenous peoples into the national decision-making processes, and they accept wide ministerial discretion over important Indigenous issues.

In 1989 the General Conference of UNESCO meeting adopted a recommendation on the importance of intangible heritage in enabling each people to assert its cultural identity and in enabling humankind as a whole to maintain its cultural diversity (UNESCO 1989). The recommendation provides the framework for identifying and preserving this form of heritage. It also alerts the public to the problems involved in preserving these heritages through education and access to cultures. It recognizes the importance of protecting the traditional culture and folklore of minorities, and it identifies complex legal problems, including the concept of "intellectual property." It also raises issues of protecting communicators, collectors, and the material collected. Lastly, it describes the best means of disseminating traditional culture and it encourages the continuing creation of this form of heritage, which is not just more vulnerable but more "alive" than others. Since 1995, using the recommendation as a working tool, UNESCO has been checking around the world, region by region, on the progress being made in safeguarding intangible heritage. It is currently attempting to organize an international conference to bring all these regional surveys together into a global report.

In 1997, UNESCO and WIPO sponsored the World Forum on the Protection of Expressions of Folklore in Phuket, Thailand, which was attended by 180 participants from fifty countries. The participants noted the lack of an international standard for the protection of folklore and also the inadequacy of the copyright régime to confer such protection and the need to strike a balance between the interests of the communities owning the folklore and the users of the expressions of folklore. The resulting Phuket Plan of Action provides for the establishment of a committee of experts, in cooperation with UNESCO, to look into the conservation and protection of folklore, the holding of regional consultative fora, and the drafting of a new international agreement on the *sui generis* protection of folklore by the Committee of Experts (see note in *Industrial Property and Copyright 1997,* 213–14).

Special International Instruments Concerned with Indigenous Peoples

Within the last decade, an enormous amount of energy has been spent drafting international standards for protecting Indigenous peoples. This has illustrated the unique place of Indigenous peoples in international law. These special international instruments attempt to apply preemptive principles to the context of Indigenous peoples and their rights.

International Labour Organization Convention on Indigenous and Tribal Peoples in Independent Countries (1989)

The International Labour Organization Convention on Indigenous and Tribal Peoples in Independent Countries provides the strongest statements on Indigenous rights. Convention No. 169 refers to the protection of the whole institutional system of Indigenous land-tenure law and management, and requires Indigenous peoples' consent to the protective régime. No government voted against the adoption of Convention No. 169 when it was presented to the Seventy-sixth International Labour Conference in 1989. The convention came into force in international law in 1991, but the process of ratification has just begun. Canada has not ratified this instrument, but Mexico has, making it a potential NAFTA (North American Free Trade Agreement) concern. Other state-parties are Bolivia, Colombia, Costa Rica, Paraguay, Peru, and Norway. Agenda 21 in 1992 appealed for wider ratification of the convention (see paras. 26.2 and 26.4(a)).

Article 4 is the heart of Convention No. 169:

> 1. Special measures shall be adopted as appropriate for safeguarding the persons, institutions, property, labour, cultures and environment of the peoples concerned.
> 2. Such special measures shall not be contrary to the freely-expressed wishes of the peoples concerned.

In addition, "the integrity of the values, practices and institutions of these peoples shall be respected." They "shall have the right to retain their own customs and institutions" and the right "to control, to the extent possible, their own economic, social and cultural development" (arts. 5, 7, and 8).

State-parties are directed to "respect the special importance for the cultures and spiritual values of the peoples concerned of their relationship with [their] lands or territories" (art. 13). While these provisions do not refer explicitly to cultural or intellectual property, they appear to be broad enough to require measures to protect all the heritage, as defined here, of the peoples concerned, and to require respect for Indigenous peoples' own laws and institutions respecting their heritage. State-parties are also bound to respect "the integrity of the values, practices and institutions of these peoples" (art. 5); to provide them with "means for the full development of [their] own institutions and initiatives" (art. 6); to consult with them "in good faith and . . . with the objective of achieving agreement or consent" whenever any action is considered which may affect them directly (art. 6); and to allow them "to exercise control, to the extent possible, over their own economic, social and cultural development" (art. 7).

With particular respect to resource use, state parties recognize "the rights of ownership and possession of the peoples concerned over the lands which they traditionally occupy," as well as their right to continue to use the resources on lands which they may not occupy, but "to which they have traditionally had access for their subsistence and traditional activities" (art. 14). Natural-resource rights include "management and conservation," and the maintenance of traditional land-tenure systems (arts. 15 and 17). Moreover, "[t]raditional activities of the peoples concerned, such as hunting, fishing, trapping and gathering, shall be recognized as important factors in the maintenance of their cultures and in their economic self-reliance and development" (art. 23).

The UN Sub-Commission on Prevention of Discrimination and Protection of Minorities (1991)

The UN Sub-Commission on Prevention of Discrimination and Protection of Minorities emphasized, in its resolution 1991/32 of 29 August 1991, that the international trafficking in Indigenous peoples' cultural property "undermines the ability of Indigenous peoples to pursue their own political, economic, social, religious and cultural development in conditions of freedom and dignity." This applies with equal urgency to all aspects of Indigenous peoples' heritage. Further erosion of Indigenous peoples' knowledge will not only be destructive of these peoples' self-determination and development, but will also undermine the development of the countries in which they live. For many developing countries, Indigenous peoples' knowledge may hold the key to achieving sustainable national development, without greater dependence on imported capital, materials, and technologies. Protecting the heritage of Indigenous peoples will require urgent and effective international action due to the growth of biotechnology industries, the continuing destruction of Indigenous peoples' lands in many parts of the world, and the popularity of Indigenous peoples' art and cultures for tourism and export.

Principle 22 of the Rio Declaration on Environment and Development (1992)

Indigenous peoples were an integral part of the world mobilization of grassroots movements leading up to the Earth Summit held in Rio de Janeiro, Brazil, in 1992. They were heaped with praise for their ecological wisdom, for their respect for natural processes, and for their sanity in the face of crass consumerism.

The Rio Declaration on Environment and Development, Principle 22, affirms that "Indigenous peoples and their communities and other local communities have a vital role in environmental management and development because of their knowledge and traditional practices. States should recognize and duly support their identity, culture and interests and enable their effective participation in the achievement of sustainable development." This emphasis on the "vital" importance of Indigenous peoples' traditional knowledge of the ecosystems in which they live provides strong support for national and international measures to protect the heritage of these peoples.

The UN Technical Conference on Practical Experience in the Realization of Sustainable and Environmentally Sound Self-Development of Indigenous Peoples (1992)

Indigenous peoples have been particularly vulnerable to the loss of their heritage as distinct peoples. Usually viewed as "backward" by governments, they have been the targets of aggressive policies of cultural assimilation. Their arts and knowledge were frequently not regarded as world treasures and were simply destroyed in the course of colonization. Their bodies were often valued more highly than their cultures and were collected by museums. Tourism, a growing consumer demand for "primitive" art, and the development of biotechnology threaten Indigenous peoples' ability to protect what remains of their heritage.

The UN Technical Conference on Practical Experience in the Realization of Sustainable and Environmentally Sound Self-Development of Indigenous Peoples, convened at Santiago, Chile, 18–22 May 1992, recommended that "the United Nations system, with the consent of Indigenous peoples, take measures for the effective protection of property rights (including the intellectual property rights) of Indigenous peoples. These include, *inter alia,* cultural property, genetic resources, biotechnology and biodiversity" (rec. 10). The experts also stressed the importance of strengthening Indigenous peoples' own institutions, and of exchanges of information among institutions and peoples worldwide. The instruments adopted by the 1992 UN Conference on Environment and Development have reinforced these recommendations.

Agenda 21 of the UN Conference on Environment and Development (1992)

In 1992, 174 states attending the UN Conference on Environment and Development in Rio de Janeiro, Brazil, adopted Agenda 21 without a vote. The agenda was subsequently endorsed by the UN General Assembly, also without a vote, in its resolution 47/190 of 22 December 1992. Agenda 21 is not a legally binding convention, but a statement of policy by the international community. The consistency and virtual unanimity of the intergovernmental support for Agenda 21 provides a sound basis for arguing that it has achieved, or is very close to achieving, the status of customary international law. Its customary-law status is continually being reinforced by its role as the basic operating program for the UN Commission on Sustainable Development.

Agenda 21 includes a separate chapter on programs for Indigenous peoples, as well as references to Indigenous peoples in its chapters on biodiversity and biotechnology, deforestation, living marine resources, and freshwater resources. Paragraph 26 of the agenda is devoted entirely to the "role of Indigenous people" and calls upon states, *inter alia,* to "adopt or strengthen appropriate policies and/or legal instruments that will protect Indigenous intellectual and cultural property and the right to preserve customary and administrative systems and practices" (para. 26.4(b)).

With respect to the issue of resource use, the most relevant provisions of Agenda 21 are found in paragraph 26.3, which calls on governments to take measures "in full partnership with Indigenous people and their communities." These measures include

- Recognition that the lands of Indigenous people and their communities should be protected from activities that are environmentally unsound or that the Indigenous people concerned consider to be socially and culturally inappropriate;
- Recognition that traditional and direct dependence on renewable resources and ecosystems, including sustainable harvesting, continues to be essential to the cultural, economic and physical well-being of Indigenous people and their communities.

In the same spirit, paragraphs 17.80–17.83 call on governments to take account of the "special needs and interests" of Indigenous peoples in the management of fisheries, including their "nutritional and other development needs," as well as protecting "their right to subsistence" in international fishing treaties. Likewise, paragraph 11.12(e) calls for the adoption of national forest-management policies that "support the identity, culture and the rights of Indigenous people," including their right to "adequate levels of livelihood and well-being."

Agenda 21 foresees the need for direct participation in decision making and management to ensure that the rights of Indigenous peoples are truly respected. Paragraph 26.6(a) directs governments to

> [d]evelop or strengthen national arrangements to consult with Indigenous people and their communities with a view to reflecting their needs and incorporating their values and traditional and other knowledge and practices in national policies and programmes.

With respect to traditional knowledge, paragraph 15.4(g) of Agenda 21 urges governments to

> [r]ecognize and foster the traditional methods and the knowledge of Indigenous people and their communities, emphasizing the particular role of women, relevant to the conservation of biological diversity and the sustainable use of biological resources, and ensure the opportunity for the participation of those groups in the economic and commercial benefit derived from the use of such traditional methods and knowledge.

This directive is repeated, in nearly the same terms, in the paragraph of Agenda 21 on biotechnology (para. 16.39(a)) and marine living resources (para. 17.82(c)).

In summary, then, Agenda 21 recognizes Indigenous peoples' rights (1) to be "protected" from environmental degradation and interferences with their "sustainable harvesting" of living resources; (2) to share in the benefits of any traditional knowledge they choose to share with others; and (3) to have their values, needs, and management practices incorporated into national policies and programs, through processes of direct consultations and "partnership." These principles were reaffirmed at the International Conference on Population and Development held in Cairo in 1994. Paragraph 6.27 of the program of action adopted by the conference also refers to the rights of land ownership and environmental restoration.

Governments should respect the cultures of Indigenous peoples. They should enable Indigenous peoples to have tenure and to manage their lands. They should also protect and restore the natural resources and ecosystems on which Indigenous communities depend for their survival and well-being and, in consultation with Indigenous peoples, take these resources and ecosystems into account in the formulation of national population and development policies.

The Montreal-based Secretariat of the Convention on Biological Diversity was undertaking relevant work in the field of Indigenous heritage. Complementary activities also fell within the UN Environment Programme's (UNEP) mandate, and implementation of the convention at the national level, as called for in article 6 of the convention, is facilitated by UNEP.

Canada should also take particular account of the recommendations made by the Intergovernmental Working Group on Forests. An initiative of the Malaysian and Canadian governments, the working group met twice in 1994, at Kuala Lumpur and Ottawa, with representatives of thirty-one states as well as intergovernmental and non-governmental organizations. The final report (Canadian Forest Service 1995) concluded that sustainable forestry includes

> giving an appropriate return to local communities, including Indigenous people, for the use of their knowledge of the special properties of plants and animals, for example, by recognising intellectual property rights.

The participants also concluded that traditional use and management of forests contributes to biodiversity, and they recommended the establishment of "national and global networks of forests managed for multiple uses by communities and Indigenous people for community survival."

Agenda 21 encourages governments and international institutions to cooperate with Indigenous peoples in "recognizing and fostering the traditional methods and knowledge" of these peoples and applying this knowledge to managing resources (paras. 15.4(g), 16.7(b), 16.39(a), 17.75(b), and 17.82(c)). These provisions, adopted by a consensus of all member-states, offer strong support for devising new international measures for the protection of Indigenous peoples' heritage, in partnership with these peoples themselves.

In the 1992 Rio Declaration on Environment and Development, the UN Conference on Environment and Development stressed the "vital role" that Indigenous peoples may play in achieving sustainable development "because of their knowledge and traditional practices" (Agenda 21, vol. 1, annex I, principle 22). The conference also called on governments and intergovernmental organizations, "in full partnership with Indigenous peoples," to take measures to recognize traditional forms of knowledge and enhance capacity-building for Indigenous communities based on the adaptation and exchange of traditional knowledge (Agenda 21, vol. III, para. 26.3). It is our view that these conclusions and recommendations not only apply to Indigenous knowledge that is narrowly biological, botanical, or ecological but—in view of the special relationship that exists between Indigenous peoples and their territories—to all aspects of Indigenous peoples' heritage and knowledge.

Maatatua Declaration on Cultural and Intellectual Property Rights of Indigenous Peoples (1993)

Indigenous peoples have also consulted with each other on an international level to discuss the protection of their folklore. The First International Conference on the Cultural and Intellectual Property Rights of Indigenous Peoples, held in Aotearoa, New Zealand in 1993, produced the Maatatua Declaration on Cultural and Intellectual Property Rights of Indigenous Peoples (reprinted in Posey & Dutfield 1996, 205–08), which emphasized the right of Indigenous peoples to self-determination and their status as "exclusive owners of their cultural and intellectual property." Included among the key recommendations to Indigenous peoples were that they should define for themselves their own intellectual and cultural property; that they should develop a code of ethics that external users must observe when recording their traditional and customary knowledge in visual, audio, or written form; and that they should develop and maintain their traditional practices and sanctions for the protection, preservation, and revitalization of their traditional intellectual and cultural properties.

The declaration called for the establishment of an appropriate body with appropriate mechanisms to preserve and monitor the commercialism or otherwise of Indigenous cultural properties in the public domain; to generally advise and encourage Indigenous peoples to take steps to protect their cultural heritage; to allow a mandatory consultative process with respect to any new legislation affecting Indigenous peoples' cultural and intellectual property rights; and to establish international Indigenous information centers and networks. States and national and international agencies are asked (1) to recognize that Indigenous peoples are the guardians of their customary knowledge and have the right to protect and control the dissemination of that knowledge; (2) to note that existing protection mechanisms are insufficient for the protection of Indigenous peoples' cultural and intellectual property rights; (3) to accept that the cultural and intellectual property rights of Indigenous peoples are vested with those who created them; (4) to develop, in full cooperation with Indigenous peoples, an additional cultural and intellectual property rights régime incorporating the following: collective as well as individual ownership and origin, retroactive coverage of historical as well as contemporary works, protection against debasement of culturally significant items in a cooperative rather than competitive framework, a principle that the first beneficiaries are to be the direct descendants of the traditional guardians of that knowledge, and a multi-generational coverage span.

Chapter 11

•••

The Canadian Constitutional Régime

The existing aboriginal and treaty rights of the aboriginal peoples of Canada are hereby recognized and affirmed. — Constitution Act, 1982 (pt. II, s. 35(1))

The Indigenous peoples of Canada have been working on protecting Aboriginal and treaty rights in the Constitution of Canada. The imperial Crown sought to deal with most Aboriginal nations by prerogative treaties, while the delegation of political authority or responsible government over the immigrants and refugees was constructed by acts of the imperial or U.K. parliament. Since the Aboriginal peoples' existing legal order and treaties were excluded from this constitutional state building, in the constitutional reform process Aboriginal peoples have struggled to articulate and protect their constitutional rights. They have also sought to merge the original treaty federalism with provincial federalism. Additionally, Aboriginal people have sought constitutional protection of their Indigenous knowledge, languages, and heritage from European languages and worldviews. The textual symbol for these pre-existing rights in the Canadian constitution has become "Aboriginal rights."

Indigenous claims were framed by a variety of linguistic and contextual solitudes. The first solitude was having a need to protect and revitalize Indigenous consciousness and its order, but having no powerful audience. The second solitude was struggling to frame our Indigenous vision into English constitutional clauses. From 1978 to 1980 we struggled to have our voice about Aboriginal and treaty rights heard by federal and provincial officials. During the process of being heard, another solitude arose. While we were translating among multiple Indigenous languages to discover the right English words, the solitude of doubt arose. Doubt arose in the context of becoming more suspicious of every nuance of English grammar and the meanings of words and purposes. This was a hollow time of second-guessing decisions, of forging compromises, and of wondering about cloudy future translations in the penumbra of legal interpretation. Yet, our efforts were successful.

Canadian constitutional reforms were viewed as another transcultural dialogue and treaty. It was a dialogue about uniformity and diversity, justice and injustice, and our exclusion from and the terms of our inclusion into the Constitution of Canada. Aboriginal demands were constrained by the traditions and languages of the colonialists. Both the traditions and the languages distorted and misdescribed our aspirations. Our existing "Aboriginal and treaty rights" were affirmed in the *Constitution Act, 1982*. We then sought to chart our future against historical demands that we assimilate into British or French cultural norms, and against the outright rejection of our normative values and cultures. We argued that the existing language in the *Charter of Rights and Freedoms* imposed a dominant Eurocentric culture on us, and we asked if the personal rights in the *Charter* were culturally neutral or ethnocentric. As a result, our constitutional rights were protected from the personal rights régime of the *Charter*. However, the process of translating these constitutional rights into the diverse Aboriginal languages, and our attempts to make them fit within the Indigenous worldview remain difficult. This process became a deep deliberation. We will recount the Mi'kmaw experience, in which we and many other interpreters participated.

The Mi'kmaw elders and interpreters pondered the problems of the *Constitution Act, 1982* for three years before they made their decision. They pondered the proper words to describe the section entitled "Rights of the Aboriginal Peoples of Canada." They decided on the concept of the Aboriginal or Indian way or style or *L'nuwey*. Then they translated section 35 that provided "[t]he existing Aboriginal and treaty rights of the Aboriginal peoples of Canada are hereby recognized and affirmed" as "how the Treaties speak" or *Anku'kamkewel Telklusikl*. In contrast, the *Canadian Charter of Rights and Freedoms* was simply translated as "the English way or style" or *Aklasie'wey*. The general non-delegation clause in the *Charter*, section 25, which created a protective interpretive zone for existing Aboriginal or treaty rights from the personal right construct, became translated as "that force which holds us together" or *Mawnuksikw*.

Instead of implementing our existing constitutional rights after 1982, however, the First Ministers attempted to force Aboriginal peoples into confusion about the meaning of these simple constitutional clauses. What do Aboriginal rights mean? What is the scope of treaty rights? Using its various contextual mysteries, the Eurocentric wordworld created a context of doubt around these questions. This increased hesitation in Aboriginal leaders and language speakers. Countless years of trans-worldview dialogue further confused the various Aboriginal linguistic communities.

This discussion was compounded by the tension and solitude of waiting for the federal and provincial governments to adjust to a new constitutional order that limited their authority and power. Seeking to communicate old wisdoms and visions, Aboriginal leaders and thinkers were forced into new rounds of constitutional discussions. These discussions were not about implementing our existing Aboriginal and treaty rights, but about creating "self-government." We knew about the need for and the dignity of self-control and the concept of self-determination, but the concept of "self-government" was a Eurocentric construct, an imposed and inanimate idea. It was not similar to an Aboriginal and treaty rights clause; it was an introduction into Eurocentric imaginality surrounding power and government. All we had to do was imagine how we were going to govern our communities and limit the regulation of our lives by the federal and provincial governments. Similar to the way in which Karl Marx had envisioned Communism and other thinkers had come up with theories of democratic government, we could create our own imaginary form of society. However, we had to create it in English or French, so that our neighbors could understand it.

In 1992, Aboriginal people participated in the multilateral meetings on the constitution. This was another visit to the restless solitudes of the structure and content of British constitutional thought and the realm of legal languages. By now, some Aboriginal people were aware of the exquisite solitude of constitutional words and the illusion of benign translatability. We began to extend our existing protective interpretive zone to Aboriginal governments and treaties. In the 1993 Charlottetown Accord, the clause "The Aboriginal peoples of Canada have the inherent right to self-government within Canada" was a linguistic paradox in the constitutional wordworld. The inherent right puzzled Eurocentric lawyers and scholars, while Aboriginal people were concerned about the meaning of "self-government within Canada." Eventually the Mi'kmaw elders translated the clause into "what we are connected with, what makes us" or *Wetapesikw*. This translation is a return to the Aboriginal worldview governing the implicate order.

In the meantime, the Eurocentric mind at the negotiating table demanded a definition of the word "self-government." This was strange predicament. "Self-government" was the concept the First Ministers had introduced. They wanted us to have delegated self-government, a grant of authority from them. We insisted that our right to control ourselves and our people was not a delegated right. It was a fundamental source of our language and culture. Both Aboriginal languages and cultures emanated from this internal source. It was an inherent right that was recognized and ascertainable by our ancient agreements with the keepers of environmental forces, with other Aboriginal peoples, and with the imperial Crown.

After trying to translate the term into different Aboriginal languages, the Aboriginal participants in the constitutional process responded by saying that definitions were inconsistent with their worldviews. Nevertheless, to help the other participants in the constitutional process understand Aboriginal desires, Aboriginal participants agreed to place the inherent right to self-government in an Aboriginal context. The First Ministers agreed upon the resulting contextual clause. In the Charlottetown Consensus Report, the contextual clause stated:

> [T]he exercise of the right referred to in subsection (1) [inherent right to self-government] includes the legislative authority of governments of the Aboriginal peoples (i) to safeguard and develop their languages, cultures, economies, identities, institutions and traditions; and (ii) to develop, maintain and strengthen their relationship with their lands, seas, waters, resources and environment; so as to determine and control their development as peoples, according to their own values and priorities and ensure the integrity of their societies. (McRoberts & Monahan 1993, 348)

The contextual clause of self-government was translated as the "Aboriginal or Indian vision" or *L'nuwey*. This clause reflected an Algonquian worldview instead of a Eurocentric worldview. One part of the contextual worldview protected Aboriginal languages that define cultures, identities, and traditions, as well as institutions and economies; the other part protected Aboriginal peoples' relationship with the environment. Together these inherent rights' contexts sought to protect the development and integrity of Aboriginal peoples, and their values and priorities.

The most difficult translation process was understanding the justiciability clause. The justiciability clause created a five-year delay in enforcing the inherent right of self-government. After a long time, the Mi'kmaw elders translated this as the "disappearing, reappearing ink-rights" or *Keskateskewey.*

These few examples show the fundamental problem of benign translation of the English language and worldview into the Algonquian language and the Mi'kmaw worldview. There are many others.

Interpreting the Constitution of Canada

The Constitution of Canada is a fragmented series of documents surrounded by unwritten Aboriginal and English conventions. In *Reference re Secession of Quebec* (1998), Chief Justice Lamer of the Supreme Court stated that the constitution is more than a written text. It embraces the entire global system of rules and principles that govern the exercise of constitutional authority. He rejected any superficial or fragmented reading of selected provisions of the written constitutional enactment. Instead, he stated that lawyers and courts must make a more profound investigation of the underlying principles animating the whole of the constitution. These animating principles include federalism, democracy, constitutional supremacy, the rule of law, and respect for minorities. Those principles must inform the overall appreciation of the constitutional rights and obligations (see para. 32). In the context of protecting Indigenous rights, these principles affirm the international principles governing Indigenous rights and the principles of Aboriginal and treaty rights for the Aboriginal peoples of Canada.

A holistic constitutional interpretation requires reconciliation of the original constitutional documents with the recent reforms protecting Aboriginal and treaty rights. The original form of constitutional federalism divides legislative jurisdiction over the control of personal property and cultural properties between the federal and provincial governments. The federal government has legislative jurisdiction over federal property, patents of inventions and discovery, copyrights, Indians and lands reserved for Indians, shipping, navigation, and the regulation of trade and commerce. Under this delegated authority from the Crown, the federal government has enacted legislation that directly and indirectly affects archeological and cultural property of national importance. Similarly, the provinces possess jurisdiction over provincial Crown lands, property, and civil rights within provincial boundaries. They have enacted provincial parks and heritage conservation régimes.

Since Confederation, the Crown has made efforts to extend the principles of federalism, democracy, constitutional supremacy, and the rule of law to those unjustly excluded from participation in Canada's political system. In the last constitutional reform, section 35 of the *Constitution Act, 1982* affirmed the Aboriginal and treaty rights of Aboriginal peoples. This extended constitutional protection and the rule of law to Aboriginal and treaty rights. Aboriginal rights are derived from Indigenous knowledge and heritage, while treaty rights were forged in the prerogative power in foreign jurisdiction reconciliation as part of the Constitution of Canada. This constitutional amendment links Indigenous knowledge and heritage and the old prerogative régime protecting treaty rights with the parliamentary régime or responsible government in Canada. These new constitutional rights create limitations on federal and provincial governments and enacted laws and regulations.

Section 91 (22, 23) of the Constitution Act, 1867

In the growth of early copyrights and trademarks and through the 1623 Statutes of Monopolies, the British parliament laid the structure for intellectual property rights. The act limited the prerogative powers of the Crown to grant monopolies to trade by granting inventors monopoly rights over their inventions. The provision that the "first and true inventor" of a new invention had exclusive rights to that process for fourteen years was an exception to the Crown's power to grant monopolies. The statutes form the basis of most patent law in the English common-law countries, such as Canada. They support the idea of monopolies on non-tangible goods (that is to say, ideas), which can be treated as property because they promote economic efficiency. Granting monopolies over certain ideas stimulates further innovation because there is an economic return on inventing something new. The monopolies to intellectual property existed for a limited time and were transferable.

These intellectual property principles were delegated to the federal government in the *Constitution Act, 1867*, by section 91(22), "Patents of Inventions and Discovery," and (23), "Copyrights." This legislative power is limited to those established actions familiar in mid-nineteenth century. These sections provide for federal power over copyright, patents, designs, plant breeders' rights, and trademarks. The fundamental criterion for protection is that the knowledge be novel or original, useful, and distinctive. Each category defines the criteria differently and provides different protection in terms of duration, degree of inclusion, and use of property. An open question remains about federal power over trade secrets or economic torts and the newer régimes of rights.

Section 91(24) of the Constitution Act, 1867

Exclusive jurisdiction over "Indians, and Lands reserved for the Indians" is allocated to Canada's parliament by section 91(24) of the *Constitution Act, 1867.* This has long been interpreted as applying to Inuit as well as "Indians." In *Delgamuukw v. British Columbia* (1997), the Supreme Court of Canada held that section 91(24) of the *Constitution Act, 1867* gives the federal government exclusive jurisdiction to make laws in relation to Aboriginal tenure and rights in lands reserved for Indians. No constitutional authority exists for provincial jurisdiction to make laws concerning lands reserved for Indians.

The scope of the federal authority as stated in *Delgamuukw* is a shared jurisdiction with Aboriginal peoples under section 35 of the *Constitution Act, 1982*. The federal government has to justify any laws or regulations that interfere with the existing tenure or rights of Aboriginal peoples, and provide fair compensation for any infringing law or regulation. Reading both constitutional sections together, the court ruled that the federal government has a constitutional fiduciary responsibility to "safeguard one of the most central of native interests—their interest in their lands" from provincial interference (para. 181).

The provincial governments may exercise some regulatory authority over Indians under a lawful delegation of the federal power; however, such federal delegation cannot infringe on Aboriginal or treaty rights under section 35 of the *Constitution Act, 1982*. In cases where a court has found a justified infringement on these constitutional rights, the court has required fair compensation to the Aboriginal peoples.

Section 35 of the Constitution Act, 1982

The supremacy of parliament has been restricted by section 35(1) of the *Constitution Act, 1982,* which declares: "The existing aboriginal and treaty rights of the Aboriginal peoples of Canada are hereby recognized and affirmed." Section 35 refers to two distinct categories of rights: rights of "Aboriginal" origin and rights derived from specific treaties. These rights became entrenched, constitutionally, if they still "existed" on the date the *Constitution Act, 1982* came into force.

Constitutional respect for these rights was a condition of Canadian independence from London. In *R. v. Secretary of State for Foreign and Commonwealth Affairs ex parte Indian Association of Alberta* (1982), Lord Denning concluded that the United Kingdom's responsibilities to its one-time Aboriginal allies and treaty partners had been delegated to Canada. He also found that section 35 "does all that can be done to protect the rights and freedoms of the Aboriginal peoples of Canada" by making them part of the constitution "so that they cannot be diminished or reduced." No parliament should do anything to lessen the worth of these guarantees. They should be honored by the Crown in respect of Canada "so long as the sun rises and the river flows." That promise must never be broken. The nature and content of the rights were thus secured, and the extent to which parliament may continue to regulate their exercise has been the subject of considerable controversy between Aboriginal peoples and the federal and provincial governments.

The Supreme Court of Canada has articulated a complex definition of Aboriginal rights. Before 1982, Aboriginal rights were seen as parts of the common law that could be overridden by federal or provincial legislation; however, as constitutional rights they are part of a coexisting constitutional régime that is the supreme law of Canada (*R. v. Sparrow* 1990; *R. v. Badger* 1996; and Hogg 1992, 53–59).

Aboriginal rights are being defined by the judiciary in relation to other constitutional laws on a case-by-case basis. In *R. v. Sparrow* (1990), the Supreme Court of Canada defined the content and nature of an Aboriginal right as a constitutional right. The unanimous court held that Aboriginal rights are those activities that are "an integral part" of an Aboriginal group's "distinctive culture" (402). The court emphasized that in applying this integral test, it is crucial that courts and decision makers "be sensitive to the Aboriginal perspective itself on the meaning of the rights at stake" (402). In applying the "integral to a distinctive culture" test to the facts in *Sparrow,* the court looked to practices, customs, and traditions as evidence of the existence of the right in Aboriginal culture (402). Also as an interpretative tool in defining these constitutional rights, the court stressed that "[t]his approach is consistent with ensuring that an Aboriginal right should not be defined by incorporating the ways in which it has been regulated in the past" (401). Moreover, reviewing courts must avoid a "frozen rights" approach to constitutional rights by insisting that Aboriginal rights be interpreted in a way that does not "freeze" them in the forms in which they were exercised prior to contact with Europeans. The court added: "[T]he phrase 'existing Aboriginal rights' must be interpreted flexibly so as to permit their evolution over time" (397).

Chief Justice Lamer, writing for the majority in *R. v. Van der Peet* (1996), articulated the constitutional context in which Aboriginal rights must be considered. *Van der Peet* involved an Indian woman selling fish to others under the alleged right. Lamer pointed out that Aboriginal rights are a special species of rights in the Constitution of Canada because, unlike the general *Charter* rights, Aboriginal rights do not apply to all citizens. For example, Lamer noted that all Canadians, including Aboriginal Canadians, could make a claim under the equality guarantee of the *Charter;* however, he pointed out, Canadians cannot make a claim to an Aboriginal right under section 35(1) of the *Constitution Act, 1982*. In fact, under section 25 of the *Charter*, no *Charter* rights can be said to abrogate or derogate from Aboriginal rights. In that respect, Lamer noted, there is a "necessary specificity" to Aboriginal rights: one has a claim to an Aboriginal right only by virtue of being an Aboriginal person under section 35.

Lamer articulated two crucial factors underlying the special constitutional status of Aboriginal rights. The first factor is self-evident fact. It requires judicial respect for the fact that Aboriginal societies lived on the land before the arrival of Europeans:

> [W]hen Europeans arrived in North America, Aboriginal peoples were already here, living in communities on the land, and participating in distinctive cultures, as they had done for centuries. It is this fact, and this fact above all others, which separates Aboriginal peoples from all other peoples from all other minority groups in Canadian society and which mandates their special legal, and now constitutional status. (para. 30)

The second factor involves the continuing importance of reconciling the Aboriginal rights existing before European arrival with the Crown's subsequent assertion of sovereignty (397).

Against these two contexts, Lamer refined the judicially created definition of Aboriginal rights in the Constitution of Canada by developing a two-step test. First, a reviewing court must determine the precise nature of the right claimed. Second, it must determine that "an activity [is] an element of a practice, custom or tradition integral to the distinctive culture of the Aboriginal group claiming the right" (310). This test is "directed at identifying the crucial elements of those pre-existing distinctive societies" (310). Indeed, the test focuses the reviewing court's attention on identifying the practices, traditions, and customs central to an Aboriginal society before contact with Europeans. These practices, traditions, or customs are seen as Aboriginal rights.

With respect to Aboriginal rights, the Supreme Court, in *R. v. Sparrow* (1990), concluded: "[T]he test of extinguishment . . . is that the Sovereign's intention must be clear and plain if it is to extinguish an Aboriginal right" (1098–99). In the case of traditional fisheries and land in British Columbia, no federal or provincial action prior to 1982 evinced "a clear and plain intention" to reduce Aboriginal peoples to an equal legal footing with non-Aboriginal Canadians. Aboriginal fisheries had been regulated, to some extent, but the underlying historical right was never explicitly abolished, and therefore still "existed" in the sense of section 35:

> The nature of s. 35(1) itself suggests that it be construed in a purposive way. When the purposes of the affirmation of Aboriginal rights are considered, it is clear that a generous, liberal interpretation of the words in the constitutional provision is demanded. . . . The relationship between the Government and Aboriginals is trust-like, rather than adversarial, and contemporary recognition and affirmation of Aboriginal rights must be defined in light of this historic relationship. (1106–8)

The Supreme Court in *Delgamuukw v. British Columbia* (1997) was clear that as long as Aboriginal peoples maintain their Indigenous relationship to their land, Aboriginal tenure continues under the section 35. It is part of their Aboriginal rights. However, the court drew a clear distinction between Aboriginal tenure and Aboriginal rights. Aboriginal rights exist independent of Aboriginal tenure and have a distinct test (*R. v. Van der Peet* 1996).

All governments and third parties must recognize and respect Aboriginal tenure or title and rights. The Supreme Court in *Delgamuukw* summarized the three components of this Aboriginal title:

> First, aboriginal title encompasses the right to exclusive use and occupation of land; second, aboriginal title encompasses the right to chose to what uses land can be put, subject to the ultimate limitation that those uses cannot destroy the ability of the land to sustain future generations of aboriginal peoples; and third, the lands held pursuant to aboriginal title have an inescapable economic component. (para. 166)

More importantly, the court stated that neither the federal nor the provincial government has a right to extinguish Aboriginal tenure.

Similar to all rights in the Constitution of Canada, Aboriginal tenure has limits. *Delgamuukw v. British Columbia* (1997) articulated these limitations. Aboriginal people cannot use the land in a way that destroys their relationship to land (para. 166) or is irreconcilable with the nature of their attachment, the sustainable development standard (para. 111). This is consistent with the ecologically based tenure of most Indigenous peoples.

In certain situations, the court has held that the federal government may regulate events within Aboriginal tenure and rights. Such regulations or infringements under section 35 of the *Constitution Act, 1982*, the court said in

Delgamuukw v. British Columbia (1997), must be justified by a valid legislative objective that is compelling and substantial (para. 161) and consistent with the special fiduciary relations between the Crown and Aboriginal peoples (para. 162).

In *R. v. Sparrow* (1990), the objective of conservation and resource management was accepted within federal jurisdiction as a valid legislative objective as long as it was consistent with the Crown fulfilling its fiduciary obligations to Aboriginal peoples. The Supreme Court stated:

> We find that the words "recognition and affirmation" incorporate the fiduciary relationship referred to earlier and so import some restraint on the exercise of sovereign power. Rights that are recognized and affirmed are not absolute. . . . [F]ederal power must be reconciled with federal duty and the best way to achieve that reconciliation is to demand the justification of any government regulation that infringes upon or denies Aboriginal rights. (1109)

The Supreme Court elaborated a three-step test for justification, once the existence of an "Aboriginal right" has been proved and the Aboriginal party has demonstrated interference by government. Government must prove (1) that the regulation is "reasonable," (2) that it does not impose an "undue hardship" on Aboriginal people, and (3) that it does not prevent them from exercising their rights "by their preferred means." The justices were not exhaustive in their discussion of justification, but they recognized conservation of resources as a "reasonable" regulation while rejecting public safety as a reasonable regulation of Aboriginal rights.

Even if a reasonable ground for regulation exists, however, there must be an analysis of alternatives. For example, could the same objectives be achieved by means that are less restrictive of the Aboriginal rights? The Supreme Court emphasized that "the honour of the Crown is at stake in dealings with Aboriginal peoples." In conflicts involving Aboriginal and Canadian people, the "special trust relationship and the responsibility of the government vis-a-vis Aboriginals must be the first consideration." *Sparrow* did not offer much guidance for determining the contents of "Aboriginal rights," although the justices did note that section 35 "must be interpreted flexibly," so as to permit "evolution" of its coverage—for example, fishing with new kinds of fishing gear. Thus, the court held that existing Aboriginal rights can be "affirmed in a contemporary form rather than in their primeval simplicity and vigour" (1092).

The Supreme Court has affirmed in *Sparrow* that the constitutional rights of Aboriginal peoples will be enforced like any other constitutional rights. They are "unalterable by the normal legislative process and unsuffering of laws inconsistent with it." The judiciary has a duty "to ensure that the constitutional law prevails. This position is fundamental to creating the foundations to create a just and fair land tenure system. Where changes are necessary, they should be made. The law and the legal system must be made relevant by constitutionally reconciling and linking Aboriginal tenure with the tenure of common law.

The Supreme Court of Canada, in *R. v. Badger* (1996), has ruled that the extent of parliament's power to continue to regulate the exercise of treaty rights is similar to the *Sparrow* test (Henderson 1997). In the case of *R. v. Simon* (1986), however, the court ruled that "Indian treaties should be given a fair, large, and liberal construction in favour of the Indians" and stated that the court would "demand strict proof of the fact of extinguishment in each case where the issue arises." In *R. v. Sioui* (1990), moreover, the court characterized Indian treaties as "sacred" in law (1063). The court stated: "[I]t is impossible to avoid the conclusion that a treaty cannot be extinguished without the consent of the Indians concerned" (1061).

Section 25 of the Canadian Charter of Rights and Freedoms

Section 25 of the *Charter* provides special protection for Aboriginal rights from those rights located in the immigrants' creative imagination. It states that the *Charter* does not affect Aboriginal rights and freedoms:

> The guarantee in this Charter of certain rights and freedoms shall not be construed so as to abrogate or derogate from any Aboriginal, treaty or other rights or freedoms that pertain to the Aboriginal peoples of Canada.

Section 25 expressly protects any rights or freedoms that have been recognized by the *Royal Proclamation* of October 7, 1763, and any rights or freedoms that now exist by way of land claims agreements or may be so acquired. On May 30, 1992, at the Multilateral Meeting on the Constitution, the federal and provincial governments and the Aboriginal peoples agreed to amend section 25 to provide for "any right or freedom to the exercise or protection of their languages, cultures or traditions." The amendment was not implemented, but the agreement continues as a convention in the Constitution of Canada.

Interpreting courts cannot interpret any individual freedoms in the *Charter* as limiting Aboriginal rights. Neither section 25 nor the rest of the *Charter* lists these uniquely protected rights of Aboriginal peoples. Instead, section 25 is an analytical placeholder and protector for the "existing Aboriginal and treaty rights of the Aboriginal peoples of Canada" found in section 35 of the *Constitution Act, 1982*. These Aboriginal and treaty rights are sequestered from the control by reasonable limits prescribed by democratic law in the *Charter*. They are part of the supreme law of Canada.

Sections 25 and 35 of the *Canadian Charter of Rights and Freedoms* are complementary, and they locate a constitutional home for Aboriginal rights.

They affirm and protect Aboriginal rights as fundamental rights in the conscience of the nation. On the one hand, section 25 defines Aboriginal rights as an integral and legitimate part of the new constitutional order in Canada and explicitly protects these rights from the Eurocentric personal rights guarantees. On the other hand, section 35 protects these fundamental rights from the secular representative régimes of the immigrants, who create legislation either in popular assemblies or in parliament and who appoint judges to the courts. Aboriginal rights are found in the ancient base of the worldviews, languages, customary teachings, knowledge, and practices of Aboriginal peoples. These rights are not found in Eurocentric religions or artificial laws based on rules from above or in popular legislation or in majority intolerance.

Thus, in postcolonial Canada, the Constitution of Canada explicitly protects Indigenous knowledge from the secular and religious rights and freedoms of individuals and from the laws of their elected governments. Under the rule of law, these sections settle public policy debate around these issues and create a legal shield around Aboriginal rights. At the center of these constitutional rights is the ability of Aboriginal peoples to define their own contexts or ideas of existence, of meaning, and of spirituality surrounding the mystery of human life and to control their own thoughts and identity. Often this megaright is talked about as a right to ecological and cognitive integrity from Eurocentric thought.

Indigenous Knowledge and Heritage as an Aboriginal Right

Within the context of the Constitution of Canada, Indigenous knowledge and heritage is an existing Aboriginal right. The "promise" of protecting Aboriginal rights, as it was termed by the Supreme Court in *R. v. Sparrow* (1990, 1083), recognized not only the ancient occupation of land by Aboriginal peoples, but their contribution to the building of Canada and the special commitments made to them by successive governments (see *Reference re Secession of Quebec* 1998, para. 82). The protection of these rights, so recently and arduously achieved, reflects an important underlying constitutional value. Aboriginal peoples look to the Constitution of Canada for the protection of their knowledge, ecological relationships, and linguistic and heritage rights.

Existing Aboriginal rights create new constitutional contexts for the interpretation of governmental responsibility for protecting Indigenous knowledge and heritage in Canada. In fact, the court, in *R. v. Van der Peet* (1996), requires that these rights arise before contact with Europeans and be integral to a distinctive Indigenous order. The Supreme Court acknowledged that these cultural rights arise within the system of beliefs, social practices, and ceremonies of the Aboriginal peoples. They are traced back to their ancestral

Indigenous order and their relationship with the ecology. Indigenous ecological order and legal systems are *sui generis* to the Canadian order, but are protected by Canadian constitutional law and the rule of law. The constitutional law of Canada provides constitutional protection to repatriation claims for cultural property, as well as to modern manifestations of Indigenous knowledge and heritage. The court's approach suggests that Aboriginal rights are to be defined by the Indigenous traditions of the Aboriginal peoples in Canada as perceived by them and as supported by evidence. The term "*sui generis*" categorizes this approach: these rights are found in Aboriginality rather than in Eurocentric traditions and rights deriving from the European Enlightenment.

For the Aboriginal peoples of Canada, Aboriginal rights perform several vital functions. These constitutional rights are a bond that strengthens cohesiveness and identity and raises the quality of life. No systematic collection of Aboriginal customary laws in Canada exists, nor has anyone prepared any manuals or handbooks compiling all aspects of Aboriginal law covering Indigenous knowledge and heritage. Despite this lack of written laws, there is a collection of material in social science literature on Aboriginal traditions and ways of life and on the spiritual relations between these traditions and the land, including detailed studies of kinship, religion, and family structures. Although most of these writings are contaminated by Eurocentric bias, once they are decontaminated they may be helpful in understanding the nature and scope of Indigenous knowledge and heritage.

Also, the Supreme Court's analysis of Aboriginal rights in *R. v. Sparrow* (1990) emphasized that any interpretations of Aboriginal cultures must be "sensitive to and [have] respect for the rights of Aboriginal peoples on behalf of the government, courts and indeed all Canadians" (1119). Little doubt exists that language, systems of ecological and spiritual beliefs and knowledge, and ceremonies are an integral and distinctive part of Indigenous knowledge and heritage.

Aboriginal peoples throughout Canada maintain that they continue to enjoy Aboriginal or treaty rights to harvest all the resources they traditionally utilized, by the most efficient available methods, throughout their traditional Aboriginal territories, and under their own systems of management. These activities are characterized as traditional ecological knowledge in international law. They also assert the right to continue to enjoy access and privacy in relation to sacred sites, and the right to retain total control of their traditional knowledge and to dispose of it as they choose. Since parliament has never expressly extinguished any of these Indigenous knowledge and heritage systems, any exercise of federal regulatory power that infringes on these rights must, at a minimum, meet the justification test in *Sparrow* and the *Delgamuukw* test of fair compensation. In *Delgamuukw v. British Columbia*

(1997), the court stated in its justified infringement test that

> [i]n keeping with the duty of honour and good faith on the Crown, fair compensation will ordinarily be required when aboriginal title is infringed. The amount of compensation payable will vary with the nature of the particular aboriginal title affected and with the nature and severity of the infringement and the extent to which aboriginal interests were accommodated. (para. 169)

This affirms the existing principle that the Crown cannot expropriate a property interest or right without compensation and applies this principle to external regulation of Aboriginal tenure and rights.

The court has suggested that past compensation is appropriate for federal and provincial regulation of Aboriginal tenure (*Delgamuukw* 1997, para. 145). Justice La Forest stated that Aboriginal tenure is a compensable right that can be traced back to the *Royal Proclamation, 1763* (para. 203). Also Justice Macfarlane, for the majority of the B.C. Court of Appeal, held that compensatory damages from the province may be the appropriate remedy for pre-1982 regulatory infringements of Aboriginal title (1993, 537). These issues revolve around past land grants and licenses by the Crown to third parties.

The Supreme Court of Canada, in its *Sparrow* decision, has refused to freeze Aboriginal rights to any particular point in history; instead, they have adopted a flexible interpretation of Aboriginal rights that allows for their exercise in a contemporary manner (1093). The court held that the traditional law or custom of Aboriginal rights was not frozen at the moment of the arrival of Europeans in Canada, and subsequent developments, variations, or manifestations of these rights do not extinguish the traditional customs or laws or make them less effective in Canadian law. Aboriginal people use different aspects of their cultural property laws to reflect the past and to make improvements for their future. Their cultural traditions give them a chance for creative self-expression through music, song, dance, speech, and many other avenues. Such cultural manifestations create invisible bonds among individuals and groups, and forge social and spiritual contacts with their ancestors.

Additionally, support for Aboriginal rights over federal and provincial law can be derived from the doctrine of implied repeal under section 52(1) of the *Constitution Act, 1982*. This doctrine states that when the courts determine that there are two inconsistent or conflicting statutes, the later in time is deemed to impliedly repeal the earlier to the extent of the inconsistency. Since section 35 is the later in time to federal and provincial legislative authority, it repeals impliedly any inconsistent federal and provincial legislative powers.

In 1997, in *Union of Nova Scotia Indians v. Canada*, the union and five Indian bands of Cape Breton applied for a judicial review of the decisions of the minister of fisheries and the minister of the environment to accept an environmental screening report on dredging the sea bottom to deepen the channel in Bras d'Or Lakes. The environmental screening report was made under the Canadian *Environmental Assessment Act.* Justice Mackay of the Federal Court of Canada held that the failure of federal ministers to consider the effect of the project on the Aboriginal rights of the Mi'kmaq constituted a failure to act with fairness. The failure to address their Aboriginal rights and interest in the assessment process was an error in law and a breach of the constitutional fiduciary duty owed to the Mi'kmaq. The ministers' decision to approve the report was set aside for reconsideration. This case began the challenges to federal environmental assessment using Aboriginal rights under section 35 of the *Constitution Act, 1982*.

Aboriginal rights protect the knowledge and heritage of the Aboriginal peoples of Canada. This is the highest protection possible in Canadian law. As the next chapter will demonstrate, both federal and provincial legislation and regulatory régimes must become consistent with Aboriginal knowledge and heritage, especially in the area of cultural and intellectual property law. At present, these régimes and their legislation are not consistent with the constitutional rights of Aboriginal peoples.

Chapter 12

•••

The Canadian Legislative Régime

The Constitution of Canada is the supreme law of Canada, and any law that is inconsistent with the provisions of the Constitution is, to the extent of the inconsistency, of no force or effect. — Constitution Act, 1982 (pt. VII, s. 52(1))

In contrast with Canada's achievements in international law and constitutional reform, the federal and provincial governments and the administrative régimes have ignored Aboriginal and treaty rights. These régimes have engaged in creative avoidance of Indigenous knowledge and heritage, and they have not responded to Canadian constitutional reform in any significant way. Thus, Canadian legislators have not passed any new legislation to protect, preserve, or enhance the rights of Indigenous peoples to their knowledge and heritage. One reason for this passivity is the underepresentation of Aboriginal interests in the federal parliament (Henderson 1994; Macklem 1997).

Many types of intellectual and cultural property are created and protected by a variety of federal and provincial laws. Under the new Constitution of Canada, these laws have to be consistent with existing Aboriginal and treaty rights. The attempt to protect Indigenous knowledge and heritage in Canada is just beginning. Already Aboriginal and treaty rights are creating challenges for the existing régime when it comes to protecting Indigenous ideas, information, and inventions as private property for a specific time.

The Canadian legal system prevents others from copying, selling, or importing a product without authorization. Although these laws are sufficient to protect individual rights or the rights of corporations when considered as individuals, they are inadequate to protect Indigenous knowledge and heritage. Scholars who have reviewed the Canadian system assert it discriminates against the constitutional rights of Aboriginal peoples. There are compelling interests in protecting Indigenous knowledge and heritage as Aboriginal rights and in eliminating these discriminatory régimes in Canada.

At present Eurocentric cultural and intellectual property régimes govern Indigenous communities. Although these régimes are effective in limited cases, they do not serve the unique relationship that Indigenous peoples have with their ecological orders, heritage, and knowledge. Indigenous thought and languages, artistic works, traditional designs, and oral traditions are not simply viewed as commodities owned by individuals. These gifts are not valued for the economic benefits they may yield; they are valued as integral parts of the Indigenous order.

Most legal commentators and the UN special rapporteur for the Working Group on Indigenous Populations (Daes 1993, para. 32) have concluded that the current legal system of intellectual property, based on the assumption that intellectual property is a transferable commodity, is "not only inadequate for the protection of Indigenous people's heritage but inherently unsuitable." These commentators argue for a reform of intellectual and cultural property régimes to protect Indigenous peoples. These legal reforms must recognize the close and continuing links Indigenous peoples have to their ecosystems, their languages, and their heritage. Such recognition is vital to a fair legal order. Indigenous peoples cannot survive or exercise their fundamental human rights as distinct nations, societies, and peoples without the ability to conserve, revive, develop, and teach the wisdom they have inherited from their ancestors (Daes 1993, para. 1.3).

Federal Cultural Property Law

Archeological Artifacts

The federal government has not asserted a comprehensive legislated claim to ownership of cultural property located on federal lands, that is to say, on federal properties, lands reserved to Indians, and territorial lands. The policy of the federal government in Federal Archaeological Heritage Protection and Management is to assert ownership to archeological resources on federal Crown land (Canada 1988, 57–59). Federal law that protects Aboriginal artifacts is complicated and several statutes must be consulted. There is a wide array of justifications for an Aboriginal and a treaty right to ownership and jurisdiction over Indian archeological artifacts. The legal footings are premised on the fact that such artifacts arose from linguistic, cultural, and religious practices that were in existence for millennia prior to the European occupation. The legal justification for Aboriginal ownership, jurisdiction, and sovereignty over Indian archeological artifacts at or removed from archeological sites stems from section 35 of the *Constitution Act, 1982*, the Crown's fiduciary duty to protect status Indians, international law governing the protection of minority cultures, federal policies with respect to Aboriginal peoples' jurisdiction, and rights and principles of interpretation of laws affecting Indians.

Indian Act (1985)

Ownership of Aboriginal cultural property on reserve lands is governed by the *Indian Act* (1985). The Crown does not claim ownership of personal property located on lands reserved for Indians. Section 2(1) of the *Indian Act* defines reserve lands as tracts of land, "the legal title to which is vested in Her Majesty, that [has] been set apart by Her Majesty for the use and benefit of a band." Certain limited protections for Indian artifacts found on reserves is contained in the *Indian Act*. Section 91 of the act protects Indian grave houses, carved grave poles, totem poles, carved house posts, pictographs, and petroglyphs. Section 91 provides:

> 91. (1) No person may, without the written consent of the Minister, acquire title to any of the following property situated on a reserve, namely:
> (a) an Indian grave house;
> (b) a carved grave pole;
> (c) a totem pole;
> (d) a carved house post; or
> (e) a rock embellished with paintings or carvings.
> (2) Subsection (1) does not apply to chattels referred to therein that are manufactured for sale by Indians.
> (3) No person shall remove, take away, mutilate, disfigure, deface or destroy any chattel referred to in subsection (1) without the written consent of the Minister.
> (4) A person who violates this section is guilty of an offence and liable on summary conviction to a fine not exceeding two hundred dollars or to imprisonment for a term not exceeding three months.

Section 92 prevents trade for profit with an Indian for goods or chattels:

> 92. (1) No person who is
> (a) an officer or employee in the Department;
> (b) a missionary engaged in mission work among Indians; or
> (c) a school teacher on a reserve;
> shall, without a licence from the Minister or his duly authorized representative, trade for profit with an Indian or sell to him directly or indirectly goods or chattels, but no such licence shall be issued to a full-time officer or employee in the Department.
> (2) The Minister or his duly authorized representative may at any time cancel a licence issued under this section.
> (3) A person who contravenes subsection (1) is guilty of an offence and liable on summary conviction to a fine not exceeding five hundred dollars.
> (4) Without prejudice to subsection (3), an officer or employee in the Department who contravenes subsection (1) may be dismissed from office.

Section 93 prevents the removal of materials from reserves:

93. A person who, without the written permission of the Minister or his duly authorized representative,
   (a) removes or permits anyone to remove from a reserve
      (i) minerals, stone, sand, gravel, clay or soil, or
      (ii) trees, saplings, shrubs, underbrush, timber, cordwood or hay, or
   (b) has in his possession anything removed from a reserve contrary to this section, is guilty of an offence and liable on summary conviction to a fine not exceeding five hundred dollars or to imprisonment for a term not exceeding three months, or to both.

Cultural Property Export and Import Act (1985)

Pursuant to Canada's assent to the 1970 UNESCO Convention on the Means of Prohibiting and Preventing the Illicit Import, Export and Transfer of Ownership of Cultural Property, the federal government enacted the *Cultural Property Export and Import Act* (1985). This act's stated purpose is to preserve the natural heritage in Canada and is designed to protect movable cultural property. This act provides some protection for Aboriginal art and artifacts. The definition of cultural property is broad enough to include Aboriginal archeological property and objects of artistic and scientific interest worth $2000. By including certain articles on the Canadian Cultural Property Export Control List, the federal government can prevent the objects from leaving Canada:

4. (1) The Governor in Council, on the recommendation of the Minister made after consultation with the Secretary of State for External Affairs, may by order establish a Canadian Cultural Property Export Control List.

(2) Subject to subsection (3), the Governor in Council may include in the Control List, regardless of their places of origin, any objects or classes of objects hereinafter described in this subsection, the export of which the Governor in Council deems it necessary to control in order to preserve the national heritage in Canada;
   (a) objects of any value that are of archaeological, prehistorical, historical, artistic or scientific interest and that have been recovered from the soil of Canada, the territorial sea of Canada or the inland or other internal waters of Canada;
   (b) objects that were made by, or objects referred to in paragraph (d) that relate to, the Aboriginal peoples of Canada and that have a fair market value in Canada of more than five hundred dollars;
   (c) objects of decorative art, hereinafter described in this paragraph, that were made in the territory that is now Canada and are more than one hundred years old:

(i) glassware, ceramics, textiles, woodenware and works in base metals that have a fair market value in Canada of more than five hundred dollars; and

(ii) furniture, sculptured works in wood, works in precious metals and other objects of decorative art that have a fair market value in Canada of more than two thousand dollars;

(d) books, records, documents, photographic positives and negatives, sound recordings, and collections of any of those objects that have a fair market value in Canada of more than five hundred dollars;

(e) drawings, engravings, original prints and water-colours that have a fair market value in Canada of more than one thousand dollars; and

(f) any other objects that have a fair market value in Canada of more than three thousand dollars.

(3) No object shall be included in the Control List if that object is less than fifty years old or was made by a natural person who is still living.

(4) For the purposes of this Act, an object within a class of objects included in the Control List is deemed to be an object included in the Control List.

Historic Sites and Monuments Act (Canada) (1985)

Canada has the power under the *Historic Sites and Monuments Act* (1985) to enter into agreements for the protection of archeological sites that have been recognized as nationally significant by the Historic Sites and Monuments Board of Canada. The minister of the environment is not bound to accept board recommendations or to act upon them. An inventory of archeological resources in historic sites is kept by the federal government on a departmental or project basis. No systematic mechanism for excavation permits has been developed.

National Parks Act (1985)

Archeological resources in national parks and national historic parks are protected by the Canadian Parks Service under the *National Parks Act* (1985) and its regulations. The Canadian Parks Service also conducts inventories of archeological resources in national parks and historic sites and may issue permits to archeologists. General protection is offered to cultural property in national and historic parks through the trespass provisions of the act, found in section 30. However, archeological sites and historic lands, including Indian lands, can be expropriated, purchased, or otherwise acquired for the purposes of establishing a park. Property in Aboriginal burial grounds, petroglyph sites, and archeological sites has been vested in the federal Crown in the designation of Port au Choix National Historical Park in Newfoundland, Fortress Louisburg in Nova Scotia, Kejimkujik National Park in Nova Scotia, and

Kouchibougac National Park in British Columbia.

Territorial Lands Act (1985)

Land-use regulations under the *Territorial Lands Act* (1985) prohibit the use without a permit of land within thirty meters of a known or suspected archeological site. The regulations also require that the authorities must be notified if archeological resources are accidentally discovered. The *Yukon Act* (1985) and the *Northwest Territories Act* (1985) govern the issuance of permits to archeologists. The regulations are administered by the territorial governments.

National Museums Act (1985)

The *National Museums Act* (1985) makes provision for the curation and conservation of collections of artifacts. The Canadian Museum of Civilization acts as the repository of collections generated by its research activities and other archeological activities within federal jurisdiction.

Environmental Assessment and Review Process

The federal Environmental Assessment and Review Process provides some protection for archeological resources within federal jurisdictions. These guidelines do not require that threats to archeological resources be considered.

Yukon Comprehensive Land Claims Umbrella Final Agreement (1990)

The Yukon Comprehensive Land Claims Umbrella Final Agreement (1990) provides for cooperation with the First Nations in the management of heritage resources. The agreement provides for protection of First Nations' resources, giving them a priority over other Yukon heritage resources, and provides for preparation of an inventory of ethnographic resources. It also provides for the protection, care, and custody of the resources, and reasonable access to artifacts. The agreement provides for a management scheme consistent with these principles and calls for the formation of a Yukon heritage board composed of First Nations and government members. The board will recommend heritage resource policy; designate heritage parks, sites, landmarks, and watercourses; manage documentary resources; and consult with affected Yukon First Nations before naming geographical areas. First Nations' approval is required for access to burial sites and First Nations will be consulted about proper treatment of these sites. The government also agrees in principle to assist in the repatriation of resources originating from the Yukon.

Nunavut Settlement Agreement in Principle Between Inuit of the Nunavut Settlement Area and Her Majesty in Right of Canada (1990)

Articles 36 and 37 of the Nunavut Settlement Agreement provide for Aboriginal participation in future heritage resource management, as well as federal assistance in the repatriation of heritage resources. The parties did not agree on the issue of title to heritage resources; this was left to the final negotiations. Article 36 concerns archeology, while article 37 concerns ethnographic objects and archival materials. Section 36 states:

> The archaeological record of the Inuit of Nunavut is a record of Inuit use and occupancy of lands and resources through time. The evidence associated with their use and occupancy represents a cultural, historical, and ethnographic heritage of Inuit society, and as such, Government recognizes that Inuit have a special relationship with such evidence which shall be expressed in terms of special rights and responsibilities.

Article 29 of the failed Dene/Métis Comprehensive Land Claim Agreement in Principle (1988) had similar provisions.

Federal Intellectual Property Law

Intellectual property has been described as "all those things which emanate from the exercise of the human brain" or more specifically "rights which are enjoyed in the produce of the mind" (Phillips 1994, 1). Within the English common-law tradition, intellectual property consists of a set of property rights protected because of their commercial value. These property rights are mainly creatures of statute and, unlike other forms of property, are limited by the terms of their individual statutory régimes. Copyright, for example, cannot exist at common law.

William Cornish has stated bluntly: "Intellectual property protects applications of ideas and information that are of commercial value" (1989, 5). It is absolutely clear that the current system of intellectual property is designed to enhance and protect the commercial value of such things as ideas, information, expression, and inventions. All such creations are treated as commodities to which property rights adhere. The only exception is moral rights, which are protected under sections 14.1, 14.2, 28.1, and 28.2 of the *Copyright Act*. According to David Vaver (1997), even these non-commercial rights have a significant commercial impact in identifying the author and maintaining the integrity of works.

The major intellectual property statutory régimes in Canada are copyright, industrial designs, patents, plant breeders' rights, trademarks, economic torts (passing off), misappropriation of personality, and confidentiality as trade secrets.

Copyright Act (1985)

The Canadian *Copyright Act* protects literary, dramatic, musical, and artistic works, as well as films, sound recordings, computer programs, and (to some extent) broadcasts. Since the eighteenth-century case of *Donaldson v. Beckett* (1774), no preexisting or parallel body of copyright-type law exists at English common law. This is codified in Canadian law as section 63 of the *Copyright Act*.

Copyright is essentially an individual right protecting expression. *Preston v. 20th Century Fox Canada Ltd. et al.* (1990) established that copyright does not protect ideas or the content of expression. The term of duration of copyright for literary, dramatic, musical, and artistic works is the author's life (not the owner's) plus fifty years from the year of death of the author (s. 6). Where the author is deemed to be the first owner of copyright, no assignment of copyright (otherwise than by will) will vest rights in the assignee or grantee beyond twenty-five years after the death of the author, other than assignment of copyright in a collective work or a license to publish the work as part of a collective work. Reversionary interests devolve on the author's legal representatives as part of his or her estate. Any agreement to the contrary will be void (see ss. 14(1) and (2)).

For photographs, films, and sound recordings, the term is fifty years from the year of the making of the work (ss. 10(1), 11, and 11.1). Copyright arises automatically, although registration may be useful for evidentiary purposes and is commonly done in Canada (ss. 53–58). The first owner of a work is deemed to be the author, although ownership may be assigned or, as in the case of work done during the course of employment, pass automatically to the employer (s. 13). The person who commissions an engraving, photograph, or portrait will also be deemed to be the first owner (s. 13(2)). There are also special limitations on ownership in the case of journalists (s. 13(3)).

Copyright may be assigned, in whole or in part, or it may be licensed, in whole or in part, leading to the possibility that there will be many different owners or licensees of different aspects of a work. Once an author assigns her or his copyright, however, s/he loses all control over the work. There is a very low level of originality required in securing copyright protection. The only legal requirement seems to be a minimal level of skill and effort going into the work such that it has not been copied from a previous work (see in particular *University of London Press Ltd. v. University Tutorial Press Ltd.* 1916 and *Ladbroke (Football) Ltd. v. William Hill (Football) Ltd.* 1964).

Moral Rights

Moral rights were added to Canadian legislation in 1988 mainly to meet the requirements of the Berne Convention, article 6 *bis,* which requires that such rights be protected. Moral rights are (1) the right of integrity and (2) the right of paternity or attribution. The first right allows an author to protect a work from distortion, mutilation, modification, use in an inappropriate context, or (possibly) destruction where these acts are done "to the prejudice of the honour or reputation of the author" (*Copyright Act*, s. 28.2(1)).

Section 28.2(1) states:

> 28.2 (1) Nature of right of integrity—The author's right to the integrity of a work is infringed only if the work is, to the prejudice of the honour or reputation of the author,
> (a) distorted, mutilated or otherwise modified; or
> (b) used in association with a product, service, cause or institution.
> (2) Where prejudice deemed—In the case of a painting, sculpture or engraving, the prejudice referred to in subsection (1) shall be deemed to have occurred as a result of any distortion, mutilation or other modification of the work.
> (3) When work not distorted, etc.—For the purposes of this section,
> (a) a change in the location of a work, the physical means by which a work is exposed or the physical structure containing a work, or
> (b) steps taken in good faith to restore or preserve a work shall not, by that act alone, constitute a distortion, mutilation or other modification of the work.

Destruction is not specifically mentioned, and since the list is exhaustive, it might be argued that destruction is not included (a curious result, but in line with authorities from other jurisdictions). It may also be argued that destruction is a form of mutilation or modification and therefore falls under the act. The right is narrowly defined, and in particular changes in location, physical means of exposing a work, and good-faith attempts to preserve a work are not breaches of this right.

In an Indigenous context this may mean that inappropriate presentation of a work of art, even though contrary to the spirit of the work under Aboriginal law, may not be covered. Likewise this is an individual right, similar to all copyright, and acts or omissions that are contrary to the moral rights of a group or community would not be recognized.

The only Canadian decision on the right of integrity is *Snow v. Eaton Centre Ltd.* (1982). In this case, the artist had created a sculpture in which sixty white geese were displayed hanging under the glass atrium of the Eaton's Centre in downtown Toronto. The sculpture is meant to convey the image of a flock of geese flying against the backdrop of sky. For the 1982 Christmas shopping season, the centre's decorating staff tied ribbons around the necks of the geese. The plaintiff, "an artist of international reputation," took the view "that the work as presently displayed is prejudicial to his honour and reputation" under the old section 12(7) of the act (prior to the 1988 amendments) (105). The court agreed that the plaintiff's subjective judgment on this point was reasonable, that indeed "his naturalistic composition has been made to look ridiculous by the addition of ribbons and . . . [that] it is not unlike dangling earrings from the Venus de Milo" (105). The court awarded him an injunction requiring the "[r]ibbons to be removed by Monday, December 6, 1982 at 9:00 a.m." (106). The matter went no further, and the moral right of integrity has not been further litigated in Canada.

Section 14.1 of the *Copyright Act* also defines a second type of moral right, which allows an author to insist that his or her name be attached to a work, or that a pseudonym be used, or that he or she remain anonymous. Again this is an individual right and does not allow a group or community to insist on attribution of a work to them. Moral rights cannot be assigned, but they may be waived in whole or in part. The existence of a waiver has generated some criticism, in that waiver of rights would almost always be demanded, and many individual artists are not in sufficiently effective bargaining positions to object (see Vaver 1997). This is especially so of employees, who lose copyrights automatically in any event (see *Copyright Act*, s. 13(2), and Vaver 1997). It is not clear whether this waiver must be in writing. Moral rights exist for the same period of time as the copyright in a work under section 14.2, and may be inherited by the author's heirs.

Performers' Rights

The *Copyright Act* has been expanded to include performers' rights. There is major new legislation being drafted now, to be tabled soon, which will also effect performers' rights and the recording industry. (See also *Status of the Artist Act* 1992, and two Quebec acts on the status of artists: *Loi sur le Statut Professionnel et les Conditions d'Engagement des Artistes de la Scène, du Disque et du Cinema* (1997) and *Loi sur le Statut Professionnel des Artistes des Arts Visuels, des Métiers d'Art et de la Littérature et sur leurs Contrats avec les Diffuseurs* (1998).)

The Industrial Design Act (1985)

The *Industrial Design Act* (1985) protects the visual appearance of mass-produced articles. A "design" is defined in section 2 of the act as "features of shape, configuration, pattern or ornament and any combination of those features that, in a finished article, appeal to and are judged solely by the eye." Section 10(1) provides for the period of protection as ten years from the date of registration. There is no protection without registration, unlike copyright, which arises automatically.

The Patent Act (1985)

The *Patent Act* (1985), the Patent Cooperation Treaty Regulations, and the Patented Medicines Regulations cover the protection of inventions, which are defined in section 2 as "any new and useful art, process, machine, manufacture or composition of matter, or any new and useful improvement in any art, process, machine, manufacture or composition of matter." No invention will be protected until it has first gone through an extensive examination process to determine whether it is both novel and inventive (sometimes called non-obviousness, s. 35), resulting in the grant of a patent by the Patent Office (s. 42). Section 44 provides that a patent lasts for twenty years from the date of the filing of the application (which may be two or three years prior to the grant of the patent).

A crucial element in the application for, and granting of, a patent for an invention is the description of the invention contained in the specification, and the claim or claims of monopoly attached to the specification. Section 34 states:

> 34. (1) Specification.—An applicant shall in the specification of his invention
> (a) correctly and fully describe the invention and its operation or use as contemplated by the inventor;
> (b) set out clearly the various steps in a process, or the method of constructing, making, compounding or using a machine, manufacture or composition of matter, in such full, clear, concise and exact terms as to enable any person skilled in the art or science to which it appertains, or with which it is most closely connected, to make, construct, compound or use it;
> (c) in the case of a machine, explain the principle thereof and the best mode in which he has contemplated the application of that principle; and
> (d) in the case of a process, explain the necessary sequence, if any, of the various steps, so as to distinguish the invention from other inventions.
>
> (2) Claims to be stated distinctly.—The specification referred to in subsection (1) shall end with a claim or claims stating distinctly and in explicit terms the things or combinations that the applicant regards as new and in which he claims an exclusive property or privilege.

The examination process for patentability presents fairly high hurdles over which an inventor, or the owner of rights in an invention, must jump. Priority of the claim is crucial, meaning that any application filed, patent granted, or invention published prior to the date on which an inventor applies for a patent will mean, for the most part, that the invention will not be granted a patent on the grounds that it is not novel. In addition, an invention must be useful, have some commercial or manufacturing purpose, and involve an inventive step on the prior art (sometimes described as non-obviousness). The invention must also not be a discovery or a mere principle of nature (s. 26(3)).

These hurdles have proven to be particularly difficult in the patenting of biotechnological inventions involving the genetic manipulation of cells, cell lines, and other microbiological or genetic material. In *Re Application of Abitibi Co.* (1982), the Canadian Patent Appeal Board held that "all micro-organisms, yeasts, molds, fungi, bacteria, actinomycetes, unicellular algae, cell lines, viruses or protozoa" were potentially patentable life forms. However, the first attempt at patenting a new multicellular plant life form in Canada failed on the ground that it did not fulfill the requirements of the definition of an invention under the *Patent Act*, section 2 (*Re Application for Patent of Pioneer Hi-Bred Ltd.* 1986; *Pioneer Hi-Bred Ltd. v. Canada (Commissioner of Patents)* 1987 and 1989; see also Marusky 1990).

The United States has taken the lead in the patenting of life forms, beginning with *Diamond v. Chakrabarty* (1980), in which the U.S. Supreme Court held that a human-made form of bacteria designed to break down oil in crude oil spills could be patented. In *Ex parte Hibberd* (1985), a complex multicellular plant was patented and finally, in *Re Allen* (1987), an animal. In 1988 the U.S. Patent and Trademark Office granted a patent to a genetically altered mouse developed by scientists at Harvard University.

Since then there have been several patents granted to plants and animals. Even human-derived, human-altered cell lines have been patented in the United States In *Moore v. Regents of University of California* (1990), the California Court of Appeal was willing to grant control over the human body to the patient, by recognizing a property right in the human body. The California Supreme Court reversed this decision, in part, by refusing to recognize a right of property or ownership in human body parts. Federal law had already granted patent rights to genetically altered cell lines derived from the cells of the patient in this case. They were, however, judged to be substantially different from those taken from his body and, therefore, no longer claimable by him. The interesting result seems to be that a human being has no right of property in her or his own body, including cellular material, but that human cell tissue may be used to create artificially altered cells, which may be owned under the terms of patent law, but not by the patient from whom they were originally taken. The patent in this case involved "a single cell suspension of the [cancerous] cell-line and various proteins produced from it." The case did hold that the patient should at least have given consent to the use of his bodily material before it was taken (for extended discussions, see Crespi 1995; Churchill 1994; and Gollin 1993, 159).

For the time being, under the Canadian rules set out in the *Manual of Patent Office Practice,* this issue has been resolved. Section 12.03.01(a) reads: "Subject matter for the process of producing a new genetic strain or variety of plant or animal, or the product thereof, is not patentable. This exclusion does not include a micro-biological process or product thereof." The Federal Court of Appeal in *Pioneer Hi-Bred*, however, had difficulties with the reproducibility of the invention of a new plant form, required under the act (s. 34(1)(b)).

Canada does not presently grant patents for living things, other than micro-organisms. Thus Canada has yet to follow the lead of other countries (particularly the United States) in protecting either the process or the result of genetic manipulation of higher life forms, including humans. But the recognition of these rights in Canada would appear to be only a matter of time.

The Plant Breeders' Rights Act (1990)

In the case of the creation of new plant life forms, some of these hurdles have, however, been overcome in Canada, under separate patent-like protection with the *Plant Breeders' Rights Act* (1990), which covers the protection of new varieties of invented plants. Under this act, a plant variety is defined in the act as "any cultivar, clone, breeding line or hybrid of a prescribed category of plant that can be cultivated." Propagating material is defined in section 2 as "any reproductive or vegetative material for propagation, whether by sexual or other means, of a plant variety, and includes seeds for sowing and any whole plant or part thereof that may be used for propagation." A plant variety is deemed to be new under section 4(2) of the act if it

(a) is, by reason of one or more identifiable characteristics, clearly distinguishable from all varieties the existence of which is a matter of common knowledge at the effective date of application for the grant of the plant breeders' rights respecting that plant variety;
(b) is stable in its essential characteristics in that after repeated reproduction or propagation or, where the applicant has defined a particular cycle of reproduction or multiplication, at the end of each cycle, remains true to its description; and
(c) is, having regard to the particular features of its sexual reproduction or vegetative propagation, a sufficiently homogeneous variety.

A "sufficiently homogeneous variety" is described in section 4(3) of the act as "that, in the event of its sexual reproduction or vegetative propagation in substantial quantity, any variations in characteristics of plants so reproduced or propagated are predictable, capable of being described and commercially acceptable." Under section 5(1) of the act, these rights include the selling of propagating material (such as seeds) in Canada, making repeated use of the propagating material to make another plant variety, and authorizing such acts. Section 6(1) provides that plant breeders' rights last for eighteen years from the day the certificate of registration is issued. As with patents more generally, annual fees must be paid.

Researchers and plant breeders would prefer to be able to obtain protection under the *Patent Act*, rather than plant breeders' rights legislation in Canada and elsewhere. Under section 19(2) of the *Plant Breeders' Rights Act,* many grants of rights include protective directions mandating the owner

> not to sell during the subsistence thereof propagating material of the plant variety unless the sale is made in good faith for purposes of scientific research, is part of a transaction involving the sale of the plant breeders' rights or consists of the sale of propagating material for the purpose of accumulating stock for subsequent resale to that person.

In addition, in section 32(2)(a) of the act, the rights may be granted subject to a compulsory license in which the commissioner will endeavor to ensure that "the plant variety is made available to the public at reasonable prices, is widely distributed and is maintained in quality." Finally, under section 30(1), a holder of plant breeders' rights must

> ensure that the holder is in a position, through the period of registration of the holder as such, to furnish the Commissioner at the Commissioner's request with such propagating material of that variety as is capable of so reproducing it that its identifiable characteristics correspond with those taken into account for the purpose of granting those rights; and . . . provide the Commissioner at the Commissioner's request with such facilities, free of charge, and with such information as the Commissioner deems necessary in order to be satisfied that the holder is causing the propagating material to be maintained.

Patent holders do not normally have such restrictions or continuing monitoring of their inventions imposed on them once the grant of patent has been sealed.

Plant breeders' rights are not generally designed to cover material that has been genetically manipulated through some biotechnological process, such as cell mutation or gene splitting, although there is nothing in the act that limits protection to plants that have been developed only through selective breeding. "Naturally" developed plant varieties are still the most common form of alteration of species of plants and animals. But the major push now is to provide legal protection for cell lines and processes of genetic manipulation that bypass the long, labor-intensive development of plant and animal species by humans through the old process of selective breeding. There is also considerable judicial controversy over the possibility of patenting altered cell lines taken from human beings. Arguments are made that biogenetic engineering is not substantially different from older techniques of species' alteration for human purposes, and there is some force to these arguments.

The Trade Marks Act (1985)

Both patents and plant breeders' rights are limited in time (twenty years and eighteen years respectively). Where the initial intellectual property protection runs out, owners of rights, in particular, in valuable medicines, chemicals, plant varieties, or other material derived from any source may continue their market advantage through the judicious use of distinctive signs and symbols under the *Trade Marks Act* (1985) and Regulations. Trademarks, of course, can be used in contexts far beyond what may initially be protectable by patents or other forms of intellectual property. Nevertheless, many pharmaceutical companies have continued their monopoly over certain products indirectly through the advantage created by a well-known brand name, or by a proliferation of brand names all designating the same product or similar products. A trademark may not be descriptive of any product, so there is nothing to prevent a single product from being designated by a range of different names. Trademarks and designations may be protected under statute, or through the common law action of passing off (see below). Section 2 of the act protects distinctive signs and symbols used to designate the origin of goods or services in a commercial context:

> (a) a mark that is used by a person for the purpose of distinguishing or so as to distinguish wares or services manufactured, sold, leased, hired, or performed by him from those manufactured, sold, leased, hired, or performed by others;
> (b) a certification mark;
> (c) a distinguishing guise; or
> (d) a proposed trade-mark.

A "certification mark" is defined as

> a mark that is used for the purpose of distinguishing or so as to distinguish wares or services that are of a defined standard with respect to
> (a) the character or quality of the wares or services;
> (b) the working conditions under which wares have been produced or the services performed;
> (c) the class of persons by whom the wares have been produced or the services performed; or
> (d) the area within which the wares have been produced or the services performed, from wares or services that are not of that defined standard.

A "distinguishing guise" is defined as

(a) a shaping of wares or their containers, or
(b) a mode of wrapping or packaging wares the appearance of which is used by a person for the purpose of distinguishing or so as to distinguish wares or services manufactured, sold, leased, hired or performed by him from those manufactured, sold, leased, hired or performed by others.

Also under section 2, trademarks to be registered must be "used by a person for the purpose of distinguishing . . . wares or services manufactured, sold, leased, hired or performed by him from . . . others." Alternatively under sections 30(e) and 40(2), a proposed trademark must be intended to be used in the course of trade so as to distinguish the goods or services of the owner or of a licensee of the mark. The Registrar of Trade Marks may require evidence of use of the trademark from the registered owner, and if this evidence is not forthcoming, or if the trademark has not been used in the two-year period prior to the request, the mark may be expunged or amended to reflect the lack of use (s. 45). Under section 57(1), the Federal Court of Canada also has exclusive original jurisdiction "on the application of the Registrar or of any person interested, to order that any entry in the register be struck out or amended on the ground that at the date of the application the entry as it appears on the register does not accurately express or define the existing rights of the person appearing to be the registered owner of the mark."

Under section 18(1), the registration of any mark is invalid if (a) the trademark was not registerable at the date of registration, (b) the mark is no longer distinctive, or (c) the mark has been abandoned. Under section 10, if any mark has "by ordinary and *bona fide* commercial usage become recognized in Canada as designating the kind, quality, quantity, destination, value, place of origin or date of production of any wares or services," it may not be adopted or used as a mark. Trademarks must be distinctive of the particular goods or services manufactured or supplied by the owner or licensee of the mark to which it is attached. If a mark becomes generic or used as a general description of any goods or services of the same kind, it has lost its distinctiveness. Section 9 lists a range of prohibited marks.

Federal Common Law

"Passing off" in Economic Tort Law

Economic tort law of "passing off" involves protecting business reputation or goodwill. This tort has expanded considerably in recent years to cover distinctive commercial marketing strategies such as get-up, packaging, advertising campaigns, and slogans. It heavily overlaps with trademarks, which provide statutory protection for some forms of property that may also be protected by passing off. A derivative area that has generated much interest lately is the protection of geographical derivations or names, such as Champagne wine (see in particular *Erven Warnink Besloten Vennootschap v. J. Townsend & Songs (Hull) Ltd.* 1979; *Hogan v. Koala Dundee Pty. Ltd.* 1988; and *Seiko Time Canada Ltd. v. Consumers Distributing Co. Ltd.* 1980).

Proprietary interests in marks, signs, symbols, names, or business get-up associated with a commercial interest can only be maintained if the mark or sign is distinctive or is capable of becoming so (what is called acquiring a "secondary meaning"). This is true for both passing off and trademarks. If anything, the standard for passing off is higher in that business reputation or goodwill (the proprietary interest that is being protected) means the sign, mark, or get-up must have already acquired a meaningfully distinctive reputation in the eyes of the consuming public such that they recognize it as attached to the owners' goods or services.

For example, in *J.B. Williams Co. v. H. Bronnley & Co.* (1909), it was asked:

> What is it necessary for a trader who is a plaintiff in a passing-off action to establish? It seems to me that in the first place he must, in order to succeed, establish that he has selected a peculiar—a novel—design as a distinguishing feature of his goods, and that his goods are known in the market, and have acquired a reputation in the market, by reason of that distinguishing feature, and that unless he establishes that, the very foundation of his case fails. (771; also see, Stewart 1993)

This is still an expression of the law in relation to passing off in Canada (see *Oxford Pendaflex Canada Ltd. v. Korr Marketing Ltd.* 1982; *Parke, Davis & Co. v. Empire Laboratories Ltd.* 1964; and *Ciba-Geigy Canada Ltd. v. Apotex Inc.* 1992).

Misappropriation of Personality

Misappropriation of personality may also be called rights of publicity. These rights are closely related to rights of privacy and a form of passing off called character merchandising. This group of rights protects celebrities and well-known human personalities, and (in the case of character merchandising) fictional characters from misappropriation of their images, distinctive styles, even voices by others. Recent cases have dealt with sports personalities, Elvis Presley, Bela Lugosi (as Dracula), news readers, Elizabeth Taylor, and other film and television stars (see *Krouse v. Chrysler Canada Ltd.* 1973; *Carson v. Here's Johnny Portable Toilets, Inc.* 1983; *Hogan and Others v. Pacific Dunlop Ltd.* 1988).

Confidentiality or Trade Secrets

Confidentiality or trade secrets protects information that is divulged under terms of secrecy or confidence. It is unclear whether this area falls under the common law, or whether it is more accurately described as a matter of equity or fiduciary duty. Many types of information, know-how, marketing strategies, recipes and formulas, commercial as well as non-commercial information between married couples, doctor/patient information, priest/penitent information, lawyer/client information, information between friends and business associates, and government information can be protected here. There has been a lot of case law on the rights of employees in using or taking away with them information gained during the course of their employment (see in particular *Saltman Engineering Co. v. Campbell Engineering Co.* 1948; *Seager v. Copydex Ltd.* 1967; *Coco v. A.N. Clark (Engineers) Ltd.* 1969; *International Corona Resources Ltd. v. LAC Minerals Ltd.* 1989; and *Pharand Ski Corp. v. Alberta* 1991).

An invention or process may not qualify for a patent because it does not satisfy the requirements for patentability. Yet, the invention may still have great utility and commercial value. In that situation, an inventor can seek protection in trade secrets law. Even if an invention is patentable, the inventor may choose to treat the invention as a trade secret in order to prevent disclosure to others and to retain control over her or his invention for as long as she or he can keep it a secret, rather than for just the patent period.

Trade secrets may be protected under tort law or contract law. The misappropriation of trade secrets or the breach of a confidential relationship without a contract is a matter of tort law or equity; an action may be brought for breach of contract providing for the confidentiality of trade secrets disclosed by one party to another; and there are criminal sanctions for the misappropriation of trade secrets. The main features of trade secrets laws in general are the maintenance of confidentiality and the encouragement of invention and competition through the prevention of unfair trade practices and unfair competition.

Confidentiality is the key to trade secrets; obviously, once the information is revealed, there is no trade secret and the value of the intellectual property has been nullified. The trade secret must be information, including a formula, pattern, compilation, program, device, method, technique, or process, that derives independent economic value, actual or potential, from not being generally known to and not readily ascertainable through ordinary and legitimate means by other persons. The owner of the trade secret must take reasonable efforts to preserve secrecy by restricting access to the information only to others with a need to know, such as employees engaged in making a product, and/or by contracting for the confidentiality of any information shared with these others.

Miscellaneous Common Law Principles

Since existing federal legislation does not make a comprehensive claim to ownership of any cultural or intellectual resources, and protective measures are scattered throughout various legislation, common-law principles currently govern the determination of title issue in relation to cultural resources on or under federal and provincial jurisdictions. In 1973, the Supreme Court held in *Calder v. British Columbia* that Aboriginal title is protected by the common law. In 1983, the Supreme Court established that the common laws of Canada falling within the jurisdiction of federal parliament are paramount to provincial law (*Bisaillon v. Keable* 1983, 340). In 1989, the Supreme Court stated that Aboriginal rights have become an integral part of unwritten federal common law operating in the Constitution of Canada (e.g., Wilson, J. in *Roberts v. Canada* 1989, 340). These judicial decisions create greater autonomy for Aboriginal and treaty rights, and directly conflict with incorporation of provincial law by reference in section 88 of the *Indian Act*. Additionally, in regulating any conflict between the federal and provincial legislative jurisdictions, the courts have held that where there are conflicting or inconsistent laws, it is the federal law that prevails.

The Supreme Court of Canada has also addressed the concept of Aboriginal real property and its relationship to the English land system and common law. In 1984, in *R. v. Guerin* (at 358), the Supreme Court asserted that the Crown had a legal duty to First Nations in relation to their Aboriginal lands, which the majority called a fiduciary duty. The Supreme Court decided that Aboriginal land title is *sui generis* and is protected by section 35 of the *Constitution Act, 1982* (*Guerin* 1984, 382; *Delgamuukw* 1997). The court stated that Aboriginal title is a "pre-existing legal right not created by Royal Proclamation, . . . or by any other executive or legislative provision" (*Guerin,* 336). Canadian courts have affirmed the difficulty of placing Aboriginal tenure under the British schema of land tenure. In *Canadian Pacific Ltd. v. Paul* (1988, 678), the Supreme Court stated: "The inescapable conclusion from the Court's analysis of Indian title up to this point is that the Indian interest in land is truly *sui generis*. It is more than the right to enjoyment and occupancy, although, as Dickson J. pointed out in *Guerin*, it is difficult to describe what more in traditional [English] property terminology."

In *Delgamuukw v. British Columbia* (1993), Justice Macfarlane, for the British Columbia Court of Appeal, stated that "[t]he courts have identified Aboriginal rights as *sui generis*. Their unique nature has made them difficult, if not impossible, to describe in traditional property law terminology" (23). Justice Hutcheon stated that Aboriginal rights to land are of such a nature as to compete on an equal footing with proprietary interests (262–64).

To understand the new *sui generis* interest of Aboriginal rights, however, the courts and their legal analysis will have to understand bi-cognitive contexts and interrelated Aboriginal worldviews. In other words, they will have to overcome their Eurocentric biases and prejudices and see the deep structure or "big picture." A similar analysis may be applied to Indigenous knowledge and heritage as Aboriginal rights. Any description of Indigenous knowledge is a unique legal interest in Canada and independent from other intangible or intellectual property systems.

With the creation of a constitutional category of Aboriginal rights in the Constitution of Canada, the courts have placed clear limitations on federal and provincial legislatures. As of 1982, the courts can no longer maintain that Aboriginal rights exist at the pleasure of the Crown. Canadian common law is developing in regard to the question of ownership of objects of art, religion, and technology created by the ancestors of an Aboriginal civilization. Such objects may fall within the constitutional category of Aboriginal rights, within the *sui generis* interest or ownership of a band or individual Indian, or within the ordinary principles of property law, including such things as inheritance, trust, and sale. But even when the case is not clear, First Nations governments and Aboriginal individuals may wish to assert ownership of cultural artifacts because of their importance to the Aboriginal peoples concerned. For example, when cultural objects are discovered by archeologists, ownership may be in doubt if the objects are found on Crown or private land. The law in these cases is based almost exclusively in statutes, some of which are reviewed above.

In the case of human remains, it is common for a great deal of respect to be shown to the wishes of local bands, even when the identity of the deceased is unknown. In some provinces, heritage legislation gives the nearest band council a say in the disposition of such remains. Apart from a statute, however, there is little protection for such human remains. The matter has been the subject of little litigation, so the common law in this area has not developed.

Provincial Law

All provinces have addressed the need to protect archeological resources located on public provincial lands and private lands under the broad category of historical resources. Most provinces provide for designation of historical resources, reporting of funds, government ownership of archeological resources, control of excavations on public and private lands through a permit system, archeological impact assessments, stop orders, and penalties for noncompliance. Of course, this view is not compatible with any continuing rights of *sui generis* interest or ownership in Aboriginal nations to which the artifacts once belonged. The question has never been litigated, either in treaty areas or in non-treaty areas.

The Quebec *Cultural Property Act* (1972) is the most striking example of such legislation. It prohibits export from the province of any recognized or classified cultural property without permission of the minister of cultural affairs. Under articles 20 and 22, if the recognized cultural property is more than fifty years old, the government may acquire it by preemption. Article 1(a) defines cultural property as a work of art, a historic property, a historic monument or site, or any archeological property or site. Archeological property is any movable or immovable property indicating prehistoric or historic human occupation, which could well cover those cultural objects not included under the heading "works of art."

Similarly, Saskatchewan has the *Heritage Property Act* (1979–80); Alberta has the *Historical Resources Act* (1980); and British Columbia has the *Heritage Conservation Act* (1979). Under the *First Peoples' Heritage, Language and Culture Act* (1996), British Columbia has enacted legislation to establish a funding agency intended to "preserve and enhance" Aboriginal culture.

Most provincial heritage acts and cemeteries acts are vague on the protection of Aboriginal burial grounds and skeletal remains. The exceptions are the Saskatchewan *Heritage Property Act* and the Prince Edward Island *Ancient Burial Grounds Act* (1988). In a case decided under the *Heritage Property Act,* the Saskatchewan Court of Queen's Bench granted an injunction to prevent the excavation of an Indian burial site on private land so as to give the local band council an opportunity to investigate and relocate the remains (*Touchwood File Hills Qu'Appelle District Council Inc. v. Davis* 1987). In Prince Edward Island's *Ancient Burial Grounds Act*, the burial grounds are vested in the Crown, with protective and administrative duties given to the minister.

Provincial parks legislation enables the provincial government to designate provincial lands as parks or historic sites and to secure privately owned areas of historical interest. These include parks such as St. Victors Petroglyphs Historic Park in Saskatchewan, Head Smashed in Buffalo Jump in Alberta, and the Nanaimo Petroglyph Park in British Columbia. Objects on these lands are presumed to be owned by the province.

Alberta also has a *Foreign Cultural Property Immunity Act* (1980), which applies to cultural property that is ordinarily kept in a foreign country but is brought into the province under an agreement between an owner or custodian and the provincial government or institution for the purpose of temporary exhibition, display, or research. Cultural property is defined in section 1 to include products of archeological excavations or discoveries, elements of artistic or historical monuments, or dismantled archeological sites, and objects of artistic or ethnological interest.

Our review of the Canadian legislative régime of intellectual and cultural property shows that it ignores the constitutional rights of Aboriginal peoples of Canada and their Aboriginal knowledge, heritages, and rights. The existing statutory and regulatory fines are insignificant and inadequate to prevent the misappropriation of these properties and resources by interested parties. A comprehensive reform of the Canadian legislative régime is necessary. We will now turn our attention to the needed reforms.

Part IV

The Need for Legal and Policy Reforms to Protect Indigenous Knowledge and Heritage

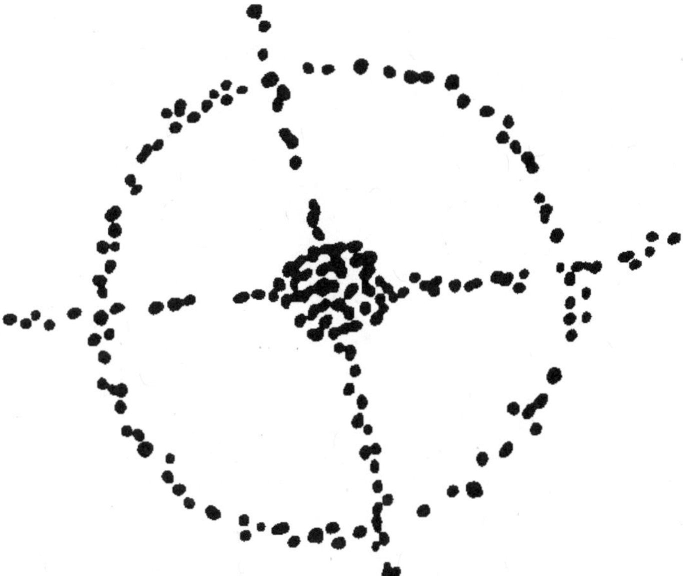

[T]he racism against Indigenous peoples is not based on biological characteristics but cultural and political ones. [It is] a new form of racism, when a modern society sets itself up as a standard. . . . [R]acism in the guise of state theories of cultural, rather than biological, superiority results in rejecting the legitimacy or viability of Indigenous peoples' own values and institutions.
— UN Seminar on Indigenous Peoples and States (in Barsh 1989, 601–02)

Chapter 13

•••

Rethinking Intellectual and Cultural Property

> *An emerging issue in the debates about the rights of indigenous peoples has concerned whether their traditional knowledge might be entitled to protection under the national and international system of intellectual property law. That possibility seems doubtful, however. . . . And the requirements of U.S. patent law that an invention be novel, useful, non-obvious, and not be a product of nature appear to be insuperable obstacles to any domestic protection for such knowledge.* — Congress Research Service, *Report to Congress on Biotechnology, Indigenous Peoples, and Intellectual Property Rights* (1993, i)

The question of whether the Indigenous knowledge might be entitled to protection as a form of intellectual property has only recently arisen and for that reason the issue remains both complex and uncertain, but it appears doubtful that much protection exists under the existing national and international system of laws. Indigenous knowledge does not appear to meet the requirements of Canadian patent law that inventions be novel, useful, non-obvious, and not be a product of nature. Copyright law and trade secrets law might afford some protection, but it seems doubtful that those protections would be of much economic benefit. The human rights of Indigenous peoples have not yet been fully defined, and discussions of their rights have just begun to address the issue of intellectual property rights.

Eurocentric intellectual property law centers on the question of who has the rights to exploit particular creations of the human mind. What Eurocentric intellectual property law purports to do is to create a balance between the desirability of protecting rights in ideas and information for the purpose of fostering their development and rewarding producers and entrepreneurs, and the societal requirements of obtaining cheap and ready access to such ideas and information. This balance extends across the field of different legal systems.

The question is how much intangible interest can be regarded as property. Property itself has been classified as land and things. Sir William Blackstone (1762–69, 2:17) defined intangible interests as "things," even though they existed only in "contemplation." This created the idea of imaginary property as a commodity. Tangible possession of land and resources gave way to intangible and speculative interest based on nothing more than the promises, hopes, and expectations of the mercantile order. Today the property as commodity concept is so dominant that most property writers assert that the English law of property is not concerned with land as a material resource but only with incorporeal rights, such as private rights in things and intellectual and cultural property (see Cheshire 1976; Lawson 1965, 16). As the utilitarian Jeremy Bentham complained in *Introduction to Principles of Moral and Legislation:*

> In almost every case in which the law does anything for a man's benefit or advantage, men are apt to speak of it, on some occasion or other, as conferring on him a sort of property. . . . The expedient then has been to create, as it were, on every occasion, an ideal being and to assign to a man this ideal being for the object of his property; and these sort of objects to which men of science . . . came . . . to give the name of "incorporeal." (1789, 211)

Until recently, it was considered unlikely that intellectual property rights could pertain to the collective, transhistorical qualities and assets of Indigenous cultures, even though these Indigenous interests in the ecology are no more incorporeal than Eurocentric rights in the marketplace. However, Posey and Dutfield (1996) illustrate that the traditional lifestyles, knowledge, and biogenetic resources of Indigenous, traditional, and local peoples have been deemed by governments, corporations, and others to be of some commercial value, and therefore, to be property that might be bought and sold and regulated by international law. This may protect Indigenous knowledge and heritage, but it does so by turning them into commodities. This creates an uneasy remedy. Perhaps Eurocentric intellectual rights could protect Indigenous knowledge and heritage as proprietarian rights instead? This suggestion requires us to look at the structure of the existing intellectual rights régimes.

Copyright

Shelly Wright, a noted intellectual rights law professor, has reported on the limitations of Eurocentric intellectual rights (1994). She demonstrates that the ideological underpinnings of intellectual property are resolutely patriarchal and replicate a Eurocentric model of creativity and proprietorship. Copyright, in particular, prevents the proliferation of illegitimate copies of a work by creating a patriarchal relationship between the author and his creation. This relationship emphasizes the importance of being able to identify the particular author responsible for creating a work, and gives to him the absolute right to control and exploit the work for economic gain. Even though anonymous, pseudonymous, and joint authors are protected in all copyright régimes—including the moral right to remain anonymous or to be known only by a pseudonym (*Copyright Act,* ss. 6.1, 6.2, and 14.1(1))—such protection is nevertheless limited and problematic. Within both copyright and moral rights, the assumption is that anonymity or the use of a pseudonym is the choice of a particular individual and not because a work's origin is unknown. In order to enjoy copyright or moral rights, all works (except films or sound recordings) must be authored by an individual human being (see ss. 5(1) and 11). Even in the case of neighboring rights, such as in films or sound recordings, the "maker" must still be identifiable as a body corporate, if not an individual. Where works are created through communal, rather than individual or joint individual, endeavor, copyright and moral rights will likely not apply at all.

Copyright is completely alienable by the author to another, usually a publisher or art dealer, for economic exploitation. The relationship between author and creation is seen as a lineal one of cause and effect and can be demonstrated by a family likeness or by substantial similarity between the work and subsequent reproductions. If the reproductions are copies made without the consent of the copyright owner, they will be infringements of copyright. Where the similarity is close enough, the reproductions will be assumed to be copies of the original work without the necessity of proving actual conscious copying or actual access, so long as the copier had some opportunities of access to the work. For example, in *Francis Day & Hunter v. Bron* (1963), the court held that

> (i) In order to constitute reproduction within the meaning of the Act, there must be (a) a sufficient degree of objective similarity between the two works, and (b) some causal connection between the plaintiffs' and the defendants' work. (ii) It is quite irrelevant to inquire whether the defendant was or was not consciously aware of such causal connection. (iii) Where there is a substantial degree of objective similarity, this of itself will afford *prima facie* evidence to show that there is a causal connection between the plaintiffs' and the defendants' work; at least, it is a circumstance from which the inference may be drawn. (iv) The fact that the defendant denies that he consciously copied affords some evidence to rebut the inference of causal connection arising from the objective similarity, but is in no way conclusive. (22)

This imposes a very high burden or presumption of copying on the defendant, where the works in question are "objectively similar." The paternalistic right of exploitation and control is characterized by the fundamental need to identify the source of works for the purpose of establishing property rights. Within copyright, this is what "originality" means: the origin of the work. This drive bears a striking ideological resemblance to laws of marriage, the control of female reproduction to ensure the legitimacy of children, the control of inheritance, and property rights in land and chattels. It also bears a striking resemblance to the colonial legal struggles to identify, control, and appropriate Indigenous lands, resources, and knowledge.

This paternal authorial connection is also seen as an alienable right in which the relational nature of the reproductive or familial ties are ignored in favor of authoritarian control for economic purposes. This paternal construction is also similar to the bourgeois family, an arrangement in which all rights originally belonged to the husband and father to exploit as he saw fit. It has only been since reforms to the law in relation to marriage and matrimonial property that this heavily patriarchal picture has been somewhat modified. This patriarchal basis for the relationship between author and work is even more clearly expressed in the paternalistic and individualistic moral rights of "paternity" and integrity. These deep structural similarities in the legal system are central to most commentators' call for legal reform.

Intellectual property law tends to be described and to describe itself in a schizophrenic way. On the one hand, by superficially describing itself as providing protection for authors, makers, designers, and others, it would seem to have a very libertarian, individualist ethic—as if all creators operated in the domain of "high art" or "high technology." On the other hand, intellectual property law provides the legal means for allowing, in theory, the orderly operation of the marketplace in which culture and technology are bought and sold. It also, especially in the commercial areas of passing off, trademarks, and trade practices, takes cognizance of the consumer and of material civilization. Material civilization becomes largely, though not wholly, a culture of consumption—of the commodification of culture. Intellectual property performs a crucial role in the protection of commodities; technology and culture need not be high.

The identification of intellectual property with invention and creation distracts our attention away from the commodification of culture that is the real basis for intellectual property. Indigenous knowledge and heritage tend to be seen as existing within the area of material or everyday culture. Since this layer has been largely taken over by the consumption of commodity items, it is in exploitation that Indigenous knowledge becomes "visible" to the non-Indigenous world. Thus biogenetic material becomes part of the "common heritage of mankind" that can be appropriated by anyone. Because ownership is difficult to establish, consumption becomes unfettered or uncontrolled. Indigenous culture may be exploited through forms of "tourist art," or it may be removed into the higher sphere of museums, which are controlled by experts such as archivists and archeologists. The paradigm within which intellectual property functions has no space for forms of cultural production that are not capable of being commodified or stratified into "high" and "low." The marketplace is not the appropriate place for creation to be shared, but it is the only place in which intellectual property can operate.

Moral Rights

Similar tensions exist between copyright and moral rights and protection of personality. Common law jurisdictions emphasize economic rights, whereas civil jurisdictions also include (at least within copyright) the notion of moral rights, or the rights of authors to protect the attribution and integrity of their work. Both of these rights are included in Canadian law. These stresses go to the core of Eurocentric liberal social theory and law. The bourgeois ideology of the lonely artist, unconnected to his social or cultural context, creating "great works" is clearly at the heart of moral rights, and is closely related to the protection of celebrity or personality rights more generally, and ultimately intellectual property rights as a whole.

Moral rights are not usually seen as property rights, but Vaver (1988) makes it clear that their effective enforcement is closely tied to the economic value of an individual artist's work. They are clearly not communal rights, although if there is more than one author, they may each share copyright and presumably moral rights as joint authors under section 9(1) of the *Copyright Act.* The individualistic nature of the rights suggests that they work most effectively within the prevailing theoretical model of free and equal individuals exchanging work for valuable consideration, although in practice most moral rights are waived and unlikely to be protected through litigation. In fact, moral rights raise difficult issues associated with the underlying basis of copyright law, in that they attempt to bring into a system designed to protect economic rights, rights more closely associated with psychological theories of the subject author as a self-actualizing individual capable of exercising control and of owning aspects of creative cultural life to the exclusion of those less gifted.

Jeff Berg has suggested that the personality-based individual rights boundaries for existing moral rights do not adequately explain the community or social value that these rights might represent. As he has explained:

> To bring the idea of culture into the theory of moral rights requires reexamining its premise that the source of creative work is in the "inviolable personality." The right of personality describes creative activity in terms of an entirely private expression of the self in the material object. . . . The expressionist theory leaves the source, the motivation, and the structure of "creativity" in the realm of subjectivity, consistent with the abstract freedom of choice of the free subject in liberal social theory. (1991, 341)

This perspective operates very well within the commodity-exchange paradigm of the social interaction of modern society—where value is accorded within the marketplace through commercial transactions between equal and free individuals—that affects all aspects of intellectual property law. Berg suggests that the theory of "gift exchange" or "vision" prevalent in many Indigenous or non-European cultures offers a better explanation for the power that moral rights can have as a means of supporting the communication of art as "an exchange of communally accessible and valuable meaning, i.e., as symbolic exchange." Basing his analysis on that of political economist C.A. Gregory (1982) and mythologist and writer Lewis Hyde (1979–83), Berg says:

> Conceived as gift, art has an unrealized visionary and restorative potential. Appreciating it requires a shift in our conception of creativity, from evaluation of its transitory commercial worth to its status as a perennial cultural bond. As with "women's work", the unquantifiable but foundational importance of the contribution of artists must come at the expense of quantifying creativity in terms of "equal pay for work of equal value." (1991, 367)

Personality or Publicity Rights

The newly emerging right of protection of personality or publicity rights bears a striking resemblance to moral rights. Within the common law right of protection of personality, the two *Crocodile Dundee* cases from Australia illustrate the process of protecting the personality. These cases involve the creation and protection of a character (Mick "Crocodile" Dundee as played by Paul Hogan in two films) that draws largely on Australian outback culture and that owes much of its authenticity to its incorporation of Indigenous themes and motifs. The Indigenous connection is made quite explicit, at least in the first film. Although neither of these two cases directly addresses the problem of intellectual and cultural borrowings, particularly from an Indigenous source, they both involve interesting questions about who should benefit from the creation and appropriation of particular images.

What is buried beneath these cases and the whole Australian bush culture from which Paul Hogan was drawing his characterization is the misappropriation of Indigenous knowledge, ways of life, attachment to country, and personality. More problematic is the ascribing of the misappropriation to a particular form of colonial male culture—the culture of the bush, of "mateship," and of male mastery of a harsh natural world, which includes Indigenous people. These colonial misappropriations are an intertextual subtheme that raised some interesting issues as they were replicated when the Crocodile

Dundee image was awarded protection from further appropriation by the Australian courts.

As with moral rights, personality rights or character merchandising are perceived as individualistic rights adhering to a particular person. They are in fact quintessentially personal, "privatizing" the publicity rights of known celebrities or well-known fictional characters. But as intellectual property professor Rosemary Coombe has said:

> Who authors the celebrity? Where does identity receive its authorization? . . . [T]he law constructs and maintains fixed, stable identities authorized by the celebrity subject. . . . In determining whether to grant a property right in a celebrity's persona, we might consider the traditional liberal justification in support of private property. The idea that people are entitled to the fruits of their own labor, and that property rights in one's body and its labor entail property rights in the products of that labor, derives from John Locke and is persuasive as a point of departure. . . . Publicity rights are justified on the basis of the celebrity's authorship—her investment of time, effort, skill and money in the development of the image. [But h]ow much of a star's celebrity and its value is due to the individual's own efforts and investments? . . .
>
> Star images must be made, and, like other cultural products, their creation occurs in social contexts and draws upon other resources, institutions, and technologies. . . . Even if we only consider the production and dissemination of the star image, and see its value as solely the result of human labor, this value cannot be entirely attributed to the efforts of a single author. Moreover, . . . the star image is authored by its consumers as well as its producers; the audience makes the celebrity image the unique phenomenon that it is. (1992, 365–69)

Or, as Marilyn Monroe said just before her death: "I want to say that the people—if I am a star—the people made me a star, no studio, no person, but the people did" (370).

In addition, the creation of a persona or character is also a function of previously existing characters, and the social and cultural milieu out of which such images are drawn. In the case of characters, images, personae, or other commercial signs taken from Indigenous peoples, this theory of individual creation tends to crystallize the images into the property of a single non-Indigenous individual. Crocodile Dundee's character and its legal protection, therefore, continue the myth of White male "mastery" through misappropriation, colonization, and lack of adequate acknowledgment of the multiple sources from which the image is derived.

The "multiplicity of meanings" that Coombe talks about extends to the range of meanings that this kind of taking has for Indigenous peoples, and for the societies that sanction and rest on this taking. Paul "Crocodile Dundee" Hogan successfully created, marketed, and legally protected an image in which European male stereotypes of the Australian colonial experience are grafted onto caricatures of traditional Indigenous lifestyles and knowledge. He then sold this image through the ironic contrast with modern Australian and American society. Both the Indigenous sources for this persona or character (it borders on a cartoon) and the reality of pioneer experiences for real individuals, male and female, are lampooned and degraded. The opportunity to enrich the cultural environment through the "gift" of creative expression is lost through commercial exploitation and a legal régime that rewards the individual proprietor at the expense of the various communities touched by his caricature.

Protection of personality or rights of publicity are in fact closely related to moral rights, as is indicated in the only case in Canada on this issue. In *Snow v. Eaton Centre Ltd.* (1982), the personal right of the artist to protect his reputation or persona as an artist was given paramountcy over the commercial interests of the Eaton's Centre to decorate their premises, including any attached artworks, as they saw fit. The vision of the artist in creating a particular image, a sculpture called *Flight Stop,* remains inviolate, and the various social and cultural antecedents for his work, and its use and position in its subsequent social setting, become irrelevant.

The geese may contain a multiplicity of meanings, including a clearly commercial meaning in that they are a prominent part of a setting devoted to commercial retail sale, but these meanings fade into insignificance beside the paramount interest of the artist to protect his own personality and character as they are represented in this work. This is so even though property rights in the sculpture had passed to the new owner, the Eaton's Centre. Under this judicial decision, moral rights can be seen as a type of residual property right remaining with the artist (unless he or she is forced to waive this right, as is generally the case under the new legislation) that protects his or her own personality or character contained in the work. The work becomes like the celebrity image or persona—a commodity severable from the creator but nevertheless still valuable as an expression of his or her individual effort. This value is retained only if the creator can maintain control over the use and dissemination of the image or work.

Patents, Trademarks, and Passing Off

The requirement of attachment combined with transferability, value, and control is even more important in the law of trademarks and passing off. The view of creativity as an ideology of "high art" or "high technology" ignores the reality of much actual creation, which is usually neither "high" nor individual. Most creativity is mundane and designed for commercial purposes. Technology is usually either simple or utilitarian (indeed it must be *useful* in order to be protected by patent law) or, even where it is complex, the work is done by teams of researchers working for large corporations, government-sponsored research institutes, or universities.

Bowrey (1994) argues that artistic creation inevitably borrows from the past, usually consciously so, and in the work of many postmodern artists, previously existing works are deliberately used in situations that are manifestly intended to violate existing ideologies of the solitary, subjective genius of modern art, and as a consequence, usually violate the law of copyright. Vaver (1997) argues that in the case of trademarks, passing off, and protection of personality rights, it is abundantly clear that intellectual property rights protect commercial interests. One result of this commercial purpose is the commodification of creativity and its appropriation through ownership by corporate producers and marketers of modern culture. What we as a community share as cultural artifacts are in fact commodities owned and controlled by others. Coombe (1991), for example, asks: "Who authorizes Thumper?" This question could well be rephrased to say simply: "Who owns Thumper?" or at least Thumper's mother in the Disney film *Bambi.* The artistic imagery and familiar saying "If you can't say anything nice, don't say anything at all" of one of modern society's most cherished childhood memories is owned and controlled by Walt Disney Studios (Lawrence 1989, 51).

In relation to biogenetic engineering, protectable under some patent jurisdictions and through plant breeders' rights, there are considerable concerns about the rapidity with which biotechnology may be used to alter existing plant and animal characteristics, and the accompanying commodification and commercialization of the processes and results of cellular and genetic manipulation. This is usually accompanied by the degradation and reduction in biodiversity of previously "natural" areas, which are often inhabited and cared for by Indigenous peoples. Hitherto, with the limited exception of plant breeders' rights, selective breeding and alteration of species could not be protected by intellectual property laws. The extension of patents to include this new method of biological production has resulted in extensive "bio-prospecting" in many countries. In developing countries, in particular, the interests of local farmers, Indigenous peoples, or even nation-states are being ignored in favor of mainly Western corporate interests in pharmaceutical, chemical, and agricultural research, which may lead to property rights in favor of these interests to the exclusion of the originators of biological material. It is feared that the biological diversity and environmental sustainability of many habitats, particularly tropical rainforests, may be at risk.

The Commodification of Culture

The bringing together of Indigenous knowledge and scientific knowledge has benefited Eurocentric knowledge, but not Indigenous peoples. Since 1990 the Fetzer Institute in Kalamazoo, Michigan, has been funding dialogues between Indigenous elders and leaders in Eurocentric scientific communities to discuss the issue of respect for the integrity of Indigenous scientific knowledge. These dialogues have created new insights into the relationship between these knowledge systems.

In summary, intellectual property developed in Europe as a result of the autonomization and commodification of culture from the fifteenth century onwards. It also worked to create and maintain this commodification. The various legal régimes that we call intellectual property attached exclusive property rights to this autonomous culture to enhance its commodification—culture could then be bought and sold in the marketplace. Production of culture was and is controlled (but not completely) by the sphere of corporate capitalism with its ideology of freedom and individualism, whereas material or everyday life has become a culture of consumption. Intellectual property regulates the middle layer of the marketplace, bringing production and consumption together within a financial or commercial relationship.

On its face, intellectual property appears to be value neutral. However, it strongly mirrors the individualistic capitalism that developed in the eighteenth and nineteenth centuries in Europe and that is now largely driven by the demands of twentieth-century corporate capitalism. As a result, intellectual property protects only some kinds of culture, technology, communication, information, and ideas. It has proven an awkward and inadequate tool for the protection of culture, communication, and technology that fall outside its ideological underpinnings. This is especially so of material cultures such as ethnic or folk art, women's culture, some types of conventional or utilitarian technology, and traditional knowledge. It also has problems dealing with forms of knowledge in the area of high art or high technology, such as computer software and biotechnology. The major push for amendment of the law comes from the top, so that areas such as computer technology or biogenetic engineering are receiving a lot of attention, and the law is gradually being altered to accommodate these forms of knowledge. Culture and knowledge on the "bottom"—where Indigenous knowledge is so often situated—tend to be ignored.

Chapter 14

•••

Current International Reforms

Conscious that, in various situations, indigenous people are unable to enjoy their inalienable human rights and fundamental freedoms, determined to do everything possible to promote the enjoyment of the human rights and fundamental freedoms of indigenous people, and bearing in mind that international standards must be developed on the basis of the diverse situations and aspirations of the world's indigenous people. . . .

Affirming its recognition of the value and diversity of the cultures and forms of social organization of indigenous people, and that the development of indigenous people within their countries will contribute to the socio-economic, cultural and environmental advancement of all the countries of the world. — Commission on Human Rights, Resolution 1997/32

Because of the diversity of the legal systems on the planet, the international legal order has been seeking legal reforms to international trade. As a minor part of these reforms, the United Nations is attempting to isolate legal remedies to protect Indigenous knowledge. Specifically the Commission on Human Rights has stated it is important that the relevant agencies, intergovernmental organizations, non-governmental organizations, businesses, media, academics, and nations-states make an effort to harmonize activities that relate to the protection of the heritage of Indigenous people. There is broad agreement that the existing legal frameworks for the protection of Indigenous knowledge and heritage are discriminatory and inadequate. International lawyers agree some form of *sui generis* special protection is necessary to encourage Indigenous people to share their knowledge and expertise with the international community; however, they disagree on issues of benefit-sharing between governments and Indigenous peoples. As well, there is disagreement about the extent to which Indigenous communities are entitled to apply their own customary laws to disputes over the disposition of their heritage and knowledge.

UN Economic and Social Council's Mandate on the Principles and Guidelines for the Protection of the Heritage of Indigenous Peoples

In its resolution 1990/25 of 31 August 1990, the Sub-Commission on Prevention of Discrimination and Protection of Minorities entrusted to Dr. Erica-Irene Daes the task of preparing a working paper on the ownership and control of the cultural property of Indigenous peoples (Daes 1991). This paper was submitted to the Working Group on Indigenous Populations at its ninth session. After considering the conclusions and recommendations contained in the working paper, the sub-commission, in its resolution 1991/32 of 29 August 1991, decided to entrust Dr. Daes with the further task of preparing, for submission at its forty-fifth session in 1993, a study of measures that should be taken by the international community to strengthen respect for the cultural property of Indigenous peoples. At the same session, the sub-commission, in its resolution 1991/31 of 29 August 1991, requested that the secretary-general of the United Nations prepare a concise note on the extent to which Indigenous peoples can utilize existing international standards and mechanisms to protect their intellectual property, drawing attention to any gaps or obstacles and to possible measures for addressing them (Daes 1991).

At its forty-fourth session in 1992, the sub-commission welcomed the concise note of the secretary-general on intellectual property and concluded in its resolution 1992/35 of 27 August 1992 that "there is a relationship, in the laws or philosophies of Indigenous peoples, between cultural property and intellectual property, and that the protection of both is essential to the Indigenous peoples' cultural and economic survival and development." The sub-commission recommended that Dr. Daes include a consideration of this relationship in her report and changed the title of this study accordingly.

The Economic and Social Council, in its decision of 20 July 1992, approved the appointment of Dr. Daes as special rapporteur. It requested that Dr. Daes prepare a study on the protection of the cultural and intellectual property of Indigenous peoples (Daes 1993), taking into account information made available to her by Indigenous peoples and relevant international standards. Indigenous peoples commented on the report during the eleventh session of the Working Group on Indigenous Populations (Daes 1993, paras. 163–76), and in the light of these comments, the working group recommended that further work on this topic be undertaken.

In preparing her report, the special rapporteur took into account the relationship between this study and the following: (1) the relevant activities of intergovernmental bodies, in particular the planned completion of the Draft Declaration on the Rights of Indigenous Peoples by the working group; (2) the anticipated implementation, by the new UN Commission on Sustained Development, of the provisions of Agenda 21 (1992) relating to Indigenous peoples; and (3) the ongoing work by the Inter-American Commission on Human Rights on a possible Inter-American Legal Instrument on the Rights of Indigenous Peoples.

On 26 August 1993, the Sub-Commission on Prevention of Discrimination and Protection of Minorities endorsed the conclusions and recommendations contained in the study of the special rapporteur (Resolution 1993/44).

Also they requested that the special rapporteur expand her study with a view to elaborating draft principles and guidelines for the protection of the heritage of Indigenous peoples, and that she submit a preliminary report containing such principles and guidelines at its forty-sixth session. The Commission on Human Rights endorsed the mandate for an expanded study in its decision 1994/105 of 4 March 1994.

In elaborating the principles and guidelines, the special rapporteur relied extensively on various declarations of the Indigenous peoples, such as the Kari-Oca Declaration of the World Conference of Indigenous Peoples on Territory, Environment and Development (1992) and the Mataatua Declaration of the First International Conference on Cultural and Intellectual Property Rights of Indigenous Peoples (1993). Their own conception of the nature of their heritage and their own ideas for ensuring the protection of their heritage are central to the "new partnership" with Indigenous peoples symbolized by the International Year of the World's Indigenous People in 1993.

The special rapporteur underscored the fact, emphasized by the Mataatua Declaration, that Indigenous peoples have repeatedly expressed their willingness to share their useful knowledge with all humanity, provided their fundamental rights to define and control this knowledge are protected by the international community. Greater protection of the Indigenous peoples' control over their own heritage, in the opinion of the special rapporteur, would not decrease the sharing of traditional cultural knowledge, arts, and sciences with other peoples. On the contrary, Indigenous peoples indicated that their willingness to share, teach, and interpret their knowledge and heritage would increase.

In developing the principles and guidelines, the special rapporteur found it useful to bear in mind that the heritage of an Indigenous people is not merely a collection of objects, stories, and ceremonies, but a complete knowledge system with its own concepts of epistemology, philosophy, and scientific and logical validity. The diverse elements of an Indigenous people's heritage can only be fully learned or understood by means of the pedagogy traditionally employed by these peoples themselves, including apprenticeship, ceremonies, and practice. Simply recording words or images fails to capture the whole context and meaning of songs, rituals, arts, or scientific and medical wisdom. This underscores the central role of Indigenous languages, through which each people's heritage has traditionally been recorded and transmitted from generation to generation.

The special rapporteur also considered it fundamental to recognize and renew the central and indispensable role of land as the classroom in which the heritage of each Indigenous people has traditionally been taught. Heritage is learned through a lifetime of personal experience traveling through and conducting ceremonies on the land. Much or all of an Indigenous people's traditional territory must therefore remain accessible to and under the control of the people themselves, so that they can continue to teach, develop, and renew their knowledge systems fully by their own means of cultural transmission. Indeed, ceremonies and traditional artistic works are regarded as means of renewing human relationships with the land, even as "deeds" to the territory, so that they can never be detached geographically and used elsewhere without completely losing their meaning.

The special rapporteur especially noted that this relationship is not merely with the physical aspects of the land, but is also conceived of as direct and personal kinship with each of the species of animals and plants that co-exist with people in the same territory. Biological, zoological, and botanical knowledge is not simply a matter of learning the names, habits, and uses of species, but of carefully maintaining and periodically renewing ancient social and ceremonial relationships with each species. An Indigenous person does not only harvest medicinal plants, for instance, but visits them, prays with them, and, through ceremonies, helps them. For this reason, Indigenous peoples do not believe that their knowledge of ecology and the uses of plants and animals, rituals, or medicine can ever be alienated completely. Like human family relationships, these forms of knowledge are permanent and collective. They can be shared, however, under the right circumstances, with properly initiated persons.

The special rapporteur recommended that the sub-commission request that the secretary-general submit the principles and guidelines to Indigenous peoples' organizations, governments, specialized agencies, and non-governmental organizations for their comments. On the basis of these comments and those of the sub-commission, the special rapporteur was to be entrusted with presenting her final report to the sub-commission at its forty-seventh session in 1995. If the sub-commission then adopted the principles and guidelines, this would be the first formal step toward committing the United Nations to the protection of Indigenous peoples' heritage. The principles and guidelines would then be transmitted to the General Assembly, through the Commission on Human Rights and the Economic and Social Council.

The Principles and Guidelines for the Protection of the Heritage of Indigenous Peoples (1995) defined "heritage" as traditional knowledge and provided for the protection of the transmission of Indigenous heritage (paras. 14–18), and the recovery and restitution of Indigenous heritage (paras. 19–24). They also regulated the activities of researchers and scholarly institutions (paras. 32–38), business and industry (paras. 40–45), and artists, writers, and performers (paras. 46–48) concerning Indigenous heritage.

In her report, the special rapporteur respectfully recommended that the principles and guidelines be considered by the sub-commission as a matter of the highest priority, with the aim of transmitting them to the Commission on

Human Rights at its fifty-second session (Daes 1995, para. 31). The special rapporteur hoped that it would be possible for the General Assembly to adopt a declaration of principles and guidelines on the heritage of Indigenous peoples in 1996. She urged that the declaration should constitute a strong message about the commitment of the United Nations to the goals and objectives of the Decade of Indigenous Peoples (Daes 1995, para. 32).

The special rapporteur further recommended implementing the mandates for interregional technical exchanges and communication networks among Indigenous peoples (Daes 1995, 34), and convening a UN technical meeting to propose mainly practical modalities for the cooperation of relevant UN bodies and specialized agencies in protecting the heritage of Indigenous peoples. The participants were to include representatives of governments, relevant UN bodies such as the United Nations Environment Programme, the specialized agencies, in particular the International Labour Organization and UNESCO, as well as the largest feasible number of representative organizations of Indigenous peoples actively involved in the protection of heritage (Daes 1995, para. 33). The special rapporteur argued that such initiatives were urgently required to further the global recognition of the value and diversity of the world's Indigenous cultures and forms of social organization. Additionally such urgent initiatives were required "to bring the erosion of these irreplaceable cultures to a speedy end" (Daes 1995, para. 33).

In 1997, the Report of the Technical Meeting on the Protection of the Heritage of Indigenous Peoples stressed that the heritage of Indigenous cultures should not be destroyed (para. 32). The meeting also recognized that the Final Report and the Draft Principles and Guidelines on the Protection of the Heritage of Indigenous Peoples drawn up by the special rapporteur were valuable (para. 29). The meeting recommended that the Commission on Human Rights should take action on the principles and guidelines submitted to it by the sub-commission (para. 34). It also recommended that the special rapporteur should be invited before the commission to present and analyze the draft principles and guidelines (para. 35).

Additionally, the meeting concluded that it was important that the relevant agencies and bodies of the UN system coordinate and harmonize their efforts to protect the heritage of the world's Indigenous peoples (para. 27). It was recommended that the special rapporteur should continue her work collecting information about Indigenous heritage from Indigenous peoples (para. 28) and from national, regional, and international organizations, and that she should submit this information annually to the sub-commission and the commission (para. 32). The meeting suggested that the study of a number of contemporary problems relating to Indigenous heritage should continue (para. 37). In particular, the meeting recommended that the study of the relationship between the concepts of "heritage of humankind" and "national sovereignty" should be analyzed and duly considered (para. 37). Delegates also recommended the adoption of additional means and measures for more effective protection of Indigenous heritage (para. 32), as well as the extension of cooperation and assistance to the special rapporteur (para. 33). Furthermore, it recommended the special rapporteur should be entrusted to elaborate the draft mandate and scope of a trust fund to be established by the General Assembly of the United Nations to act, *inter alia*, as a global agent for the recovery of compensation for Indigenous heritage (para. 35).

In 1997, the Sub-Commission on Prevention of Discrimination and Protection of Minorities, in its resolution 1997/13, requested that the UN high commissioner for human rights convene a seminar on the Draft Principles and Guidelines for the Protection of the Heritage of Indigenous Peoples. In resolution 1997/112, the Commission on Human Rights approved decision 1997/287 of the Economic and Social Council, which recommended that Dr. Erica-Irene Daes be entrusted with a continuing mandate concerning the heritage of Indigenous people, with the purpose of facilitating cooperation and coordination and of promoting the full participation of Indigenous people in those efforts. Additionally, the commission requested that the secretary-general provide the special rapporteur with all the assistance necessary to accomplish her work.

In February-March 2000, the seminar on the Draft Principles and Guidelines for the Protection of the Heritage of Indigenous Peoples convened with Indigenous experts and representatives from intergovernmental and non-governmental organizations to consider the draft. The final revisions to the draft and the report of the seminar prepared by Dr. Erica-Irene Daes will be submitted to the Sub-Commission on the Promotion and Protection of Human Rights (formerly the Sub-Commission on the Prevention of Discrimination and Protection of Minorities) for its consideration. If the Draft Principles and Guidelines are accepted, they will then be presented to the Commission on Human Rights for consideration at its general assembly.

United Nations Decade of the World's Indigenous Peoples (1995–2004)

On 21 December 1993, the UN General Assembly, in resolution 48/163, proclaimed 1995–2004 to be the Decade of the World's Indigenous People. When developing activities for this decade, governments should encourage practical workshops involving professional, academic, and scientific experts and Indigenous peoples, as recommended by the Working Group on Indigenous Populations (E/CN.4/Sub. 2/1993/29, para. 225), and the study of the special rapporteur (Daes 1993, para. 181). Such workshops should increase awareness of and respect for Indigenous peoples' heritage among researchers, scholars, legislators, educators, and representatives of governments, business, and industry, and develop model national legislation.

In 1997, the Commission on Human Rights, in resolution 1997/32, requested that the high commissioner for human rights consider organizing a workshop for research and higher education institutions focusing on Indigenous issues in education in consultation with Indigenous people and in collaboration with UNESCO and other relevant UN bodies. The aim of the workshop would be to improve the exchange of information between such institutions and to encourage future cooperation. The commission also recommended that the high commissioner for human rights, when developing programs within the framework of the International Decade of the World's Indigenous People and the UN Decade for Human Rights Education, give due regard to the development of human rights training for Indigenous people.

Draft Declaration on the Rights of Indigenous Peoples (1994)

The Draft Declaration on the Rights of Indigenous Peoples, which is currently being reviewed by an *ad hoc* working group of the UN Commission on Human Rights, is a comprehensive interpretation of how UN human rights covenants apply to Indigenous peoples. If it is adopted, the declaration will establish policy for the UN system and might evolve into customary international law. The articles in the declaration set minimum standards for the survival, dignity, and well-being of Indigenous peoples (art. 42).

The declaration provides that Indigenous peoples have the right to maintain and strengthen their distinct political, economic, social, and cultural characteristics (art. 4), and a right not to be subjected to ethnocide, cultural genocide, or assimilation (arts. 6–7). Part III of the declaration is concerned with culture, religion, and linguistic identity (arts. 12–29); it addresses in general terms the heritage of Indigenous peoples. Articles 12 to 14 provide:

12. Indigenous peoples have the right to practice and revitalize their cultural traditions and customs. This includes the right to maintain, protect and develop the past, present and future manifestations of their cultures, such as archeological and historical sites, artifacts, designs, ceremonies, technologies and visual and performing arts and literature, as well as the right to the restitution of cultural, intellectual, religious and spiritual property taken without their free and informed consent or in violation of their laws, traditions and customs.
13. Indigenous peoples have the right to manifest, practice, develop and teach their spiritual and religious traditions, customs and ceremonies; the right to maintain, protect, and have access in privacy to their religious

and cultural sites; the right to the use and control of ceremonial objects; and the right to the repatriation of human remains.

States shall take effective measures, in conjunction with the Indigenous peoples concerned, to ensure that Indigenous sacred places, including burial sites, be preserved, respected and protected.

14. Indigenous peoples have the right to revitalize, use, develop and transmit to future generations their histories, languages, oral traditions, philosophies, writing systems and literatures, and to designate and retain their own names for communities, places and persons.

States shall take effective measures, especially whenever any right of Indigenous peoples may be affected, to ensure this right and also to ensure that they can understand and be understood in political, legal and administrative proceedings, where necessary through the provision of interpretation or by other appropriate means.

Articles 24, 28, and 29 also provide protection of Indigenous knowledge:

24. Indigenous peoples have the right to their traditional medicines and health practices, including the right to the protection of vital medicinal plants, animals and minerals.

They also have the right to access, without any discrimination, to all medical institutions, health services and medical care. . . .

28. Indigenous peoples have the right to the conservation, restoration and protection of the total environment and the productive capacity of their lands, territories and resources, as well as to the assistance for this purpose from States and through international cooperation. . . .

States shall also take effective measures to ensure, as needed, that programmes for monitoring, maintaining and restoring the health of Indigenous peoples, as developed and implemented by the peoples affected by such materials, are duly implemented.

29. Indigenous peoples are entitled to the recognition of the full ownership, control and protection of their cultural and intellectual property.

They have the right to special measures to control, develop and protect their sciences, technologies and cultural manifestations, including human and other genetic resources, seeds, medicines, knowledge of the properties of fauna and flora, oral traditions, literatures, designs and visual and performing arts.

These articles reflect general principles that have already been adopted in a number of recent conventions for the protection of the environment. The fundamental right of Indigenous peoples to the protection and enjoyment of their heritage has already been given international recognition in the existing human rights convenants, and in conventions on the environment that make express references to Indigenous communities.

Protecting Traditional Ecological Knowledge

The 1992 UN Conference on Environment and Development recognized the need for development projects to protect the traditional ecological knowledge and conservation practices of Indigenous peoples. This need has now been generally addressed in several major conventions on the protection of the global environment. There exists a strong basis in international conventional law for concrete measures at the international, regional, and national levels to protect the heritage of Indigenous peoples, in particular the economic, social, cultural, and spiritual relationships that exist between Indigenous peoples and their ancestral territories and resources.

The Convention on Biological Diversity was opened for signature at the UN Conference on Environment and Development on 5 June 1992 and entered into force on 29 December 1993. The convention has thus far been ratified by 134 states. Implementation is entrusted to the executive secretary of the convention, under the direction of the Conference of the Parties. The executive secretary is serviced by the UN Environment Programme (UNEP), which has established a special office in Montreal for this purpose. Articles 8(j) and 10(c) of the convention provide for respect, protection, preservation, and maintenance of Indigenous knowledge, innovation, and practices.

The UN Convention to Combat Desertification in Those Countries Experiencing Serious Drought and/or Desertification, Particularly in Africa was opened for signature on 14 and 15 October 1994. In terms that are similar to article 8(j) of the Convention on Biological Diversity, article 17.1(c) of the convention requires state parties to respect, protect, and utilize traditional and local knowledge and conservation practices. In particular, article 18.2 of the Convention on Desertification commits state parties to compile information on traditional knowledge and practices with the participation of local populations; to promote the integration of traditional knowledge with modern technologies; and to ensure that local populations benefit directly and equitably from any dissemination or commercial development of their knowledge.

The Commission on Sustainable Development was established, *inter alia,* to monitor global progress in the implementation of the principles and program of action adopted by the UN Conference on Environment and Development. In its decision 1995/226, the Economic and Social Council approved the establishment of an open-ended, *ad hoc* Intergovernmental Panel on Forests (IPF), under the supervision of the Commission on Sustainable Development, to pursue a consensus on the conservation and sustainable development of forests. At its first session, held from 11 to 15 September 1995, IPF adopted element 1.3 of its program:

> Consistent with the terms of the Convention on Biological Diversity, encourage countries to consider ways and means for the effective protection and use of traditional forest-related knowledge, innovations and practices of forest-dwellers, Indigenous people and local communities, as well as fair and equitable sharing of benefits arising from such knowledge, innovations and practices.

In its decision II/9, the Second Conference of the Parties to the Convention on Biological Diversity requested that the executive secretary of the convention "provide advice and information pertaining to the relationship between Indigenous and local communities and forests" to IPF. The executive secretary issued a progress report in January 1996 entitled "Indigenous and Local Communities and Forests," which in paragraph 12 underscores the emergence of scientific evidence that, *inter alia:*

> (a) The language, culture and knowledge of Indigenous and local communities are disappearing at alarming rates;
> (b) Many presumed "natural" ecosystems or "wilderness" areas are in fact "human or cultural landscapes" resulting from millennial interactions with forest-dwellers;
> (c) Traditional knowledge is complex, sophisticated, and critically relevant to understanding how to conserve forest ecosystems and to use them sustainably. (IPF 1996a)

The progress report of the executive secretary concluded that the protection and utilization of traditional knowledge would depend on the support given to Indigenous peoples to document, evaluate, and utilize their own systems of knowledge (para. 15). It also concluded that recognition of the "rights" of Indigenous people to their traditional knowledge "would enable commitments made by countries under human rights conventions, covenants and agreements to be harmonized at the national level with international commitments on environment, development, and trade" (para. 14).

This report was considered at the second session of IPF, held from 11 to 22 March 1996 in Geneva, together with a background report prepared at the request of IPF by the secretary-general of the United Nations. IPF decided to pursue a substantive discussion of

> [w]ays and means to ensure effective protection of Indigenous rights and payment of royalties on intellectual property rights in the context of national legislation, and to ensure the fair and equitable sharing of benefits, involving

> local communities and forest dwellers, including ways to determine clearly which individuals belonged to which group. (IPF 1996b)

The progress report of the executive secretary of the Convention on Biological Diversity report was considered at the third meeting of the parties to the convention in 1996.

The Commission on Genetic Resources for Food and Agriculture of the UN Food and Agriculture Organization (FAO) is engaged in drafting a global plan of action and an international undertaking regarding the conservation and utilization of plant genetic diversity. The second extraordinary session of the commission (1996) discussed the role of Indigenous peoples and communities in the *in situ* conservation of plant genetic diversity. The legal counsel for FAO advised the commission to harmonize the draft of its global plan with the relevant provisions of the Convention on Biological Diversity. Also in 1996, the role of Indigenous peoples in conserving genetic resources was discussed at the Fourth International Technical Conference on Plant Genetic Resources in Leipzig, Germany.

A special international convention focusing on property rights in Indigenous knowledge might also be negotiated under the auspices of WIPO, the UN Environmental Programme, or the UN Working Group on Indigenous Peoples. The convention could create a uniform standard for property rights in Indigenous knowledge. Alternatively, the convention could create standard procedures for negotiating with Indigenous peoples for the right to use their knowledge and create procedures for reimbursing them.

Another possibility is that a subsidiary agreement to the Convention on Biological Diversity could be negotiated requiring that the government of a country that has genetic resources and receives technology or royalties from a developed country for access to its genetic resources must pass on some of the benefits to the relevant Indigenous peoples. Article 2 of the convention considers “genetic resources” as a commodity or raw material used in the processes of biotechnology. Canada has not formulated any law and has very little policy dealing with genetic resources. Canadian policy briefly mentions the rights of Indigenous peoples but does not address the specific issue of requiring reimbursement to Indigenous peoples for their traditional knowledge or otherwise requiring protection of that knowledge. The convention requires only that the country itself be compensated.

Chapter 15

•••

Enhancing Indigenous Knowledge and Heritage in National Law

National laws should guarantee that Indigenous peoples can obtain prompt, effective and affordable judicial or administrative action to prevent, punish and obtain full restitution and compensation for the acquisition, documentation or use of their heritage without proper authorization of the traditional owners. — Principles and Guidelines for the Protection of the Heritage of Indigenous Peoples (1995, art. 25)

The Principles and Guidelines for the Protection of the Heritage of Indigenous Peoples define the proper role of national legislation and governments:

25. National laws should guarantee that Indigenous peoples can obtain prompt, effective and affordable judicial or administrative action to prevent, punish and obtain full restitution and compensation for the acquisition, documentation or use of their heritage without proper authorization of the traditional owners.
26. National laws should deny to any person or corporation the right to obtain patent, copyright, or other legal protection for any element of Indigenous peoples' heritage without adequate documentation of the free and informed consent of the traditional owners to an arrangement for the sharing of ownership, control and benefits.
27. National laws should ensure the labeling and correct attribution of Indigenous peoples' artistic, literary and cultural works whenever they are offered for public display or sale. Attribution should be in the form of a trademark or an appellation of origin, authorized by the peoples or communities concerned.
28. National laws for the protection of Indigenous peoples' heritage should be adopted following consultations with the peoples concerned, in particular the traditional owners and teachers of religious, sacred and spiritual knowledge, and wherever possible, should have the consent of the peoples concerned.
29. National laws should ensure that the use of traditional languages in education, arts and the mass media is respected and, to the extent possible, promoted and strengthened.

30. Governments should provide Indigenous communities with financial and institutional support for the control of local education, through community-managed programmes, and with use of traditional pedagogy and languages.
31. Governments should take immediate steps, in cooperation with the Indigenous peoples concerned, to identify sacred and ceremonial sites, including burial sites, and protect them from unauthorized entry or use.

We affirm these principles. However, there is more to discuss.

National Protection Strategies

The assertion that Indigenous knowledge and heritage should merit legal reconciliation and protection can be viewed in different ways. One view stresses the rights of Indigenous peoples who are unwillingly enmeshed in nation-states and emphasizes the use of intellectual property as a means to express ethnic autonomy and to redress exploitation. Another view stresses the merits of local knowledge and emphasizes the use of intellectual property régimes to provide incentives for all people to experiment with and protect biological resources. The common ground between these views is that constitutional or legal rights should be extended to Indigenous knowledge. Three approaches to compensating Indigenous knowledge can also be distilled: (1) international and national agencies can extend enriched rights to Indigenous peoples; (2) Indigenous peoples can attempt to utilize existing intellectual property law; and (3) Indigenous peoples can assert rights under their *sui generis* or unique legal systems.

Several proposals have been made in the literature. One possibility is a convention or other agreement between Indigenous peoples and the government or private contracts with companies. A second possibility is the establishment of a *sui generis* régime focusing on property rights under national law. Such a régime could create standard procedures for negotiating with Indigenous peoples for the right to use their knowledge and uniform standards for reimbursing them. A variation of this *sui generis* régime is to create a central authority that would collect royalties and profits derived from the use of Indigenous knowledge and disburse them equitably among all Indigenous peoples of the nation-state. A third possibility is that a subsidiary agreement to international conventions could be negotiated that would require the government of a country that has genetic resources and receives benefits, technology, or royalties from another country to pass some of the benefits to the relevant Indigenous peoples.

In Canada, there have been widespread calls for reform. Recently, two Canadian researchers (Pask 1993; Coombe 1993) adopted a similar position to that of the UN special rapporteur (Daes 1993): they recognized the imperative of giving Indigenous peoples control over their own heritage. But as of yet Canadian governments have avoided those calls. What emerges from the detailed work of both these writers is that there is a fundamental need to recognize Indigenous peoples' own laws and customs regarding culture, and that it is both inefficient and inappropriate to simply place facets of cultural and intellectual heritage into the existing Western legal framework. As Coombe acknowledges: "First Nations peoples strive to assert that the relationship that stories, images, motifs and designs have to their communities cannot be subsumed under our traditional European categories of art and culture and the possessive individualism that informs them" (1993, 284).

While the protection of Indigenous knowledge in the United States is more advanced than in Canada, there exists no comprehensive scheme to cover all aspects of Indigenous heritage in that country either. The existence of the *Native American Graves Protection and Repatriation Act* (NAGPRA 1990) affirms "that the sacred culture of Native Americans and Hawaiians is a vital living heritage which is a crucial ingredient in the on-going lifeway of the United States." Developments in academic writings have also progressed in the United States, to the extent that a proposed Model Tribal Act to Protect Cultural Heritage has been drafted (Strickland & Supernaw 1993).

Fair and Equitable Sharing of Benefits

Generosity and reciprocity are core values of Indigenous cultures. If Indigenous communities are empowered to maintain and develop their own forests and forest-related knowledge, they will undoubtedly share a large part of their ecological and medical science with other Indigenous and non-Indigenous peoples. The decision as to what may properly be shared, the means by which it may be shared, and the recompense, if any, that may justly be demanded must be left to each Indigenous people and to the actual holders of the kinds of knowledge concerned (individuals, families, clans, "societies," or communities). External rules limiting Indigenous peoples' share of the benefits of their own heritage and knowledge will be counterproductive, as they will simply result in communities refusing to reveal what they know—or, as social scientists and anthropologists have gradually realized to their chagrin—under duress, Indigenous people will disseminate incomplete or distorted information.

Assuming that Indigenous people are eventually accorded the freedom to share knowledge on their own terms, the extent to which they receive fair and equitable benefits in practice will depend on three factors: (1) the degree to which they are fully informed about the potential commercial value of their knowledge and about the legal consequences of any agreements they may make with outsiders; (2) the extent to which they possess the institutional capacity, at the community level, to engage in effective negotiations, as well as the financial resources, juridical standing, and expertise to take legal action when necessary to enforce their rights: and (3) the extent to which effective and affordable legal remedies exist.

The first two factors—information and institutional capacity—can be addressed through programs of national cooperation, as described above. In particular, we believe that the Indigenous peoples of Canada will be responsive to the development of global networks for the direct sharing of expertise among Indigenous communities because they anticipate cultural understanding and respect from other Indigenous peoples.

The third factor—effective legal remedies—poses a more difficult challenge. In some countries, Indigenous communities do not enjoy legal "standing" under domestic private law. They cannot institute legal proceedings in their collective capacity or on behalf of their constituent families, clans, or individual members. In most national legal systems, moreover, Indigenous knowledge is not recognized as "property" that can be defended or recovered by a private legal proceeding. Indigenous knowledge also falls outside the definitions of intellectual property in the Paris and Berne Conventions. Hence, if Canada or some state parties enact special domestic measures to give their Indigenous peoples additional legal protection, other state parties may not be bound to enforce these measures—a serious weakness in light of the transnational character of the enterprises that would be most likely to seek to exploit traditional knowledge for its commercial, biomedical, and genetic applications.

We believe there is a need, then, for the government to adopt an authoritative declaration to the effect that Indigenous peoples are the true owners of their ecological knowledge and that disputes over rights to the acquisition and commercial application of this knowledge must be resolved in accordance with the laws of the peoples concerned.

The Importance of Indigenous Use and Management of Ecosystems

There are at least three main reasons why the continued use and management of ecosystems by Indigenous peoples is important for conserving Indigenous knowledge and biological diversity: (1) Indigenous peoples tend to use, and therefore to value and protect, a much larger variety of species than their non-Indigenous neighbors; (2) Indigenous peoples tend to make modifications to their environments with the aim of *increasing* the diversity of ecological niches and associated species; and (3) the traditional knowledge of Indigenous peoples is not only particularly rich in local ecological detail and predictive power, but continues to be updated and supplemented as long as the people are able to use the ecosystems and study their behavior.

Indigenous peoples' traditional economic systems have relatively low impacts on biological diversity. They tend to be "eclectic," harvesting a small amount of every useful species, which has little or no effect on intraspecific population dynamics or interspecific niche competition. Hunting peoples, for example, may harvest a hundred different species of birds, mammals, and invertebrates. Even the Blackfoot of the Great Plains of North America, who were characterized as bison hunters by European settlers, relied heavily on many other prey species, such as elk, deer, wild sheep and goats, antelope, rabbits, ducks, and geese, especially in the winter and spring. Of course, the environment places limits on the breadth of Indigenous peoples' diet: in the Arctic, there are far fewer prey animals available to hunters than in temperate forests. In any event, dietary breadth is limited by what is available rather than by social choices.

Similarly, horticulturists plant highly diversified gardens with many varieties of each food species. The gathering of medicinal plants is also a highly eclectic undertaking as healers utilize every plant community. By comparison, settlers and commercial producers target a small number of marketable species for harvesting and modify the ecosystem radically in order to boost the output of these few species. In Blackfoot territory, for example, settlers targeted the largest prey mammal—the bison—and exterminated it within twenty years. Then they replaced the entire community of feral herbivores with cattle and replanted the prairies with two species of European forage grasses. On the Pacific coast of Canada, settlers targeted seven species of salmonids for commercial harvesting, in a region where the Indigenous economy had utilized virtually all species of fish and shellfish. Settlement began in the 1850s; salmonids required artificial enhancement (in the form of hatcheries) for their survival by the 1890s. Other marine species utilized moderately by Indigenous peoples have since been targeted commercially, one after another, and have become threatened: halibut, anchovies, sturgeon, dogfish (a small shark), and rockfish.

Furthermore, Indigenous peoples try to increase the biological diversity of the territories in which they live as a strategy for increasing the variety of resources at their disposal and, in particular, for reducing the risk associated with fluctuations in the abundance of particular species. Since each species is subject to different limitations and its abundance varies, to some extent, in response to different factors, an increase in the variety of niches and species not only stabilizes the average total biomass of the system—obviously, one of the principal conservational justifications for preserving biodiversity—but also tends to stabilize the harvestable output of food and materials.

As a result, the territories in which Indigenous peoples live are shaped environments with biodiversity as a priority goal, notwithstanding the fact that the modifications may be subtle and can be confused with the natural evolution of the landscape. For example, Indigenous peoples typically burn "yards and corridors" in forests to create islands of regrowth and increased edge effects. Berries and medicinal herbs are particularly abundant in early successional stages of forest recovery from fire. Islands and edges also attract large mammals. Periodic firing also prevents the forest as a whole from becoming oligarchic. Firing was also practiced on the North American prairies to produce forage with a high nitrogen content for large mammals such as bison; indeed, the northern Great Plains would have been more savanna-like in the absence of this practice. Settlers assumed that the parklike architecture of North American temperate forests and the relative treelessness of the north-central plains were natural phenomena. Interestingly, however, there is evidence that many highly diverse, open-textured temperate forests filled in and became oligarchic in the 1700s and 1800s, after settlers displaced Indigenous hunters and horticulturists. It is important to bear in mind that horticulturists are usually also hunters (or fishers). Gardens attract wildlife, and most horticultural societies engage in a great deal of "garden hunting." They also leave large tracts of forest uncultivated, and these areas serve as refuges to conserve animal populations. On the prairies, settlers not only stopped the annual firing of grassland patches but through aggressive plowing and draining destroyed the natural patchwork of ponds and marshes that once maintained a rich diversity of birds and small mammal species throughout the region.

Indigenous knowledge of ecosystems is taught, learned, and updated on the land through direct personal observation. Removing the people from the land or preventing them from carrying out traditional subsistence practices breaks the generation-to-generation cycle of individual experiences and empirical study. Once dispossessed of their direct interaction with the ecosystem, Indigenous peoples lose the means of transmitting their old knowledge effectively, and also lose the means of acquiring new knowledge. The quality of models and data passed along to succeeding generations through words alone degenerates. Basic concepts may survive, but they lose their concrete meanings. What remains is as abstract as Western theories of ecological dynamics. To continue to serve as an empirical resource that can add substantially to Western science, traditional knowledge must be maintained as an integral part of traditional lifestyles.

Present Status of Ecologically Related Knowledge

In North America, ecologically related knowledge is in imminent danger of being lost—despite the fact that the governments of Canada and the United States have taken important steps over the past twenty years to resolve land claims, to increase Indigenous communities' control of forest management on their remaining lands, and to consult with Indigenous peoples on the management of public lands. There are three principal reasons for the continuing erosion of Indigenous knowledge: (1) Indigenous languages are not being fully maintained; (2) Indigenous children are spending much less time engaged in traditional activities on the land; and (3) Indigenous communities are increasingly relying on university-trained technicians for guidance in managing forests.

Indigenous knowledge is taught through a combination of practical experience, observation, and dialogue. By the 1920s, most North American Indigenous children were taken from their communities by public authorities and placed in special schools, where they were forbidden to speak their mother tongues. By the 1960s, most children were able to attend public schools closer to their homes, although most instruction continued to be in English or French. To this day, a majority of Indigenous children are instructed in English or French, although a growing number of schools in Indigenous communities offer special classes to maintain or restore elementary fluency in Indigenous languages. At the same time, television has become a major factor in the lives and learning of Indigenous children, and (with the exception of Alaska and northern Canada) North American television programming is in European languages. As a result, there has been a marked decline in the proportion of Indigenous children who speak Indigenous languages. Canadian Indigenous communities have witnessed a decline of more than 50 percent in the use of Indigenous languages since the 1960s. Moreover, those children who continue to speak Indigenous languages tend to use a pidgin in combination with English or French and never learn the full technical and conceptual vocabulary of their elders. It is common to hear young people say: "My grandfather uses big words that I don't understand." Unfortunately, those "big words" include the scientific terms needed to discuss ecology.

It is increasingly uncommon for Indigenous children to spend time in the bush with their older kinfolk engaged in such traditional activities as hunting, fishing, foraging, or gathering medicinal plant materials. In many communities, of course, there is simply nowhere to conduct these activities, due to settlement, environmental degradation, or the taking of land by public authorities. Restrictions on harvesting wildlife and plants imposed on Indigenous peoples on conservational grounds also limit the opportunities of today's children to experience ecosystems firsthand. Even where the opportunity to engage in these activities remains, however, fewer children participate than just a generation ago. School schedules conflict with the time required for engaging in subsistence activities and an increasing number of children, influenced by television, conceive of traditional activities as primitive, dirty, unnecessary hardships that are associated with poverty and isolation. They want to be modern and have the material wealth they imagine White children enjoy. They may even feel ashamed of spending time with elders who are illiterate, who speak little or no English, and who work in the forest rather than at an office.

Ironically, as Indigenous children learn less of their own languages and spend less time in traditional activities, Indigenous communities are increasingly turning to the universities for technical skills in forestry and other fields of ecosystem management. University training programs in forestry and ecology do not incorporate Indigenous knowledge or management practices in their curricula; indeed, most forestry programs continue to promote "maximum wood production" as a management goal. Indigenous youth who pursue university training in forestry are inculcated with a scientific and social-policy perspective that is largely incompatible with their own communities' knowledge systems and that discourages them from later seeking knowledge from their elders. As a result, highly abstract Western concepts of forest dynamics are displacing richly detailed, locally specific knowledge stored within Indigenous communities.

Effective Protection of Knowledge and Practices

Traditional lifestyles are sustainable and are compatible with the preservation of biodiversity as long as the peoples concerned are not stressed by the reduction of their land area, intrusions by settlers, or environmental degradation of the ecosystems upon which they depend for their subsistence. Indigenous peoples' traditional ecological management practices ordinarily leave a large "margin for error" in seasonal forecasts of the abundance of wildlife and plants, choosing to err on the side of underestimating harvestable surpluses as a way of minimizing the risk of compromising long-term food supplies. Hunting, logging, and clearing by settlers can quickly exhaust this margin for error, forcing Indigenous peoples to overharvest resources in order to survive. The maintenance of traditional lifestyles depends entirely on the protection of Indigenous peoples' rights to their territories and, where displacement has already occurred, the return or control of lands to Indigenous communities so that they have a sufficient land base to regain sustainable self-sufficiency.

With respect to Indigenous knowledge, we stress the necessity of recognizing and respecting, in both national legislation and international law, the principle that any acquisition, publication, scientific use, or commercial application of Indigenous knowledge must be in accordance with the customary laws of the peoples concerned, as determined by them. This principle has been endorsed by the special rapporteur of the Sub-Commission on Prevention of Discrimination and Protection of Minorities, Dr. Erica-Irene Daes, in her study and recommended guidelines for the protection of Indigenous peoples' heritage (Daes 1995, especially at paras. 4–9). The special rapporteur has also recommended that the UN system assist Indigenous peoples financially and technically so that they can build the local capacity to monitor and collaborate with any research by outsiders on their own terms, as well as conduct their own research into the ecologies where they live. In her view (and ours), the most effective means of preventing the unjust exploitation of Indigenous peoples' knowledge is to ensure that the people have information, training, and institutional structures of their own to evaluate external research proposals, to negotiate collaborative agreements with outside researchers, and, if necessary, to take private legal action to prevent the licensing or sale of knowledge that is not properly acquired from them.

Similarly, the UN Conference on Environment and Development, in paragraph 26.2 (a)(vii) of Agenda 21, encourages governments to collaborate with Indigenous peoples and the United Nations in capacity building and in the formation of networks for the exchange of traditional technical expertise. UN studies and reports, and transnational investments and operations on the lands of Indigenous peoples have echoed this recommendation (see Report of the Centre on Transnational Corporations, UN 1994, 13; Report of the United Nations Technical Conference on Practice Experience in the Realization of Sustainable and Environmentally Sound Self-Development of Indigenous Peoples, UN 1992, p. 18 para. 22; and Report of a Consultation between Representatives of Indigenous Peoples and International Development, Human Rights and Other Agencies, UN 1993, p. 5, paras. 20–22). Additionally, this recommendation has been affirmed by recent resolutions of the General Assembly (GA res. 46/128, annex para. C(e); GA res. 49/214, para. 7). The coordinated implementation of these recommendations should be given priority by Canada in its federal statute on the Convention on Biological Diversity.

Chapter 16

•••

Canadian Policy Considerations

The Government of Canada indicated that it supported in principle the efforts of the Special Rapporteur to develop ways of strengthening respect for the heritage of indigenous people. They could include the use of education to help preserve, protect and promote the languages, cultures and heritage of indigenous people, and the use of distinctive labels or marks to ensure the authenticity of indigenous artistic and literary works. The Government of Canada emphasized the importance of consulting with indigenous communities, scholars, scientists, business and industry before adopting any specific national measures. Priority should be given to examining ways of using existing national laws more effectively. — Dr. Erica-Irene Daes, *Supplementary Report on the Protection of the Heritage of Indigenous Peoples* (1996b, para. 10)

In Canada Indigenous knowledge and heritage are protected as constitutional rights under the concept of Aboriginal rights. This should give them special protection as vested rights held by Aboriginal peoples. Existing Indigenous knowledge and heritage are viewed as *sui generis* and as such are independent of and pre-exist federal and provincial legislation. No extinguishment of these rights has been acknowledged by the Supreme Court of Canada. The rights can be regulated for fair compensation, if the Crown can establish a valid substantial and compelling legislative objective, such as conservation of resources, and if the Crown can demonstrate that the legislative objective is consistent with the fiduciary obligation of the Crown and with the honor of the Crown toward Aboriginal peoples.

These principles suggest that federal and provincial governments have a constitutional obligation to protect Indigenous knowledge within their respective jurisdictions, especially as part of heritage conservation régimes and intellectual property régimes. Since existing federal legislation does not explicitly place the ownership of cultural property or intellectual knowledge in the federal Crown, it will be difficult to argue that there has been a statutory expropriation of these Aboriginal rights. Moreover, because the courts have established the rule of interpretation that ambiguous phraseology in statutes regarding Aboriginal rights shall be interpreted in favor of the Indians, it is difficult to argue that these rights can be statutorily expropriated.

On the basis of equality between Aboriginal rights and other heritage protection in federal and provincial law under the both section 15 (modern rights) and section 25 (Aboriginal rights) of the *Charter of Rights and Freedom*, one might reasonably argue that the federal government has an affirmative fiduciary obligation to assist in the development of a legislative scheme that protects the cultural and intellectual property of the Aboriginal peoples. Using these sections of the *Charter,* Aboriginal peoples could argue for equal treatment of their *sui generis* cultural and intellectual property rights before and under the law, as well as for the right to equal protection and benefit. Given the complexity and cultural sensitivity of these issues, it is essential for governments to work in cooperation with Aboriginal peoples to establish policies, principles, and guidelines for the protection of the entire heritage of Aboriginal peoples in Canada. For such a complex problem, it is impossible to prescribe any strategy that will work unilaterally.

To protect Indigenous knowledge and heritage in the national legal system, the federal government should exercise its fiduciary obligation under section 35(1) of the *Constitution Act, 1982*. The courts have recognized that existing Aboriginal and treaty rights create positive rights as well as negative rights (Macklem 1997). The positive rights require the government to provide protection for those elements integral to Indigenous knowledge and heritage. With the representatives of Aboriginal peoples who hold these Aboriginal and treaty rights, the federal government should seek to provide new legislation to protect Indigenous knowledge and heritage. Alternatively, they should provide new treaties or agreements that incorporate the protection and enhancement of Indigenous knowledge and heritage. Finally, if the federal government is unwilling to act, the Aboriginal peoples of Canada should implement laws under their Aboriginal and treaty rights to protect and enhance their knowledge and heritage.

The Government of Canada has not emphasized its constitutional obligations in discussions relating to the protection of Indigenous knowledge and heritage in Canada. It has emphasized the importance of consulting with Indigenous communities, scholars, scientists, businesses, and industries before adopting any specific national measures. It has also asserted that priority should be given to examining ways of using existing national laws more effectively. Such broad consultation was carried out by the Royal Commission of Aboriginal Peoples and the results are contained in its report (RCAP 1996b).

Report of the Royal Commission on Aboriginal Peoples

Since the discovery of the American continent, there have been few defining intellectual reviews of the legitimacy of the colonial treatment of its Indigenous peoples. In the sixteenth century, the Castilian Crown created a series of juntas to discuss proper relations with the Aboriginal nations in the colonies, including the famous debates in 1551 between Bartolomé De Las Casas and Juan Ginés de Sepúlveda. These debates on the nature of the Indians were generated by the Spanish universities, and eventually, the juntas rejected the conquest of American Indians and affirmed Indian republics. In the 1630s, at the beginning of the British plantations in North America, John Cotton and Roger Williams of the Massachusetts Bay Colony engaged in a famous debate about the legitimacy of the English rights in Aboriginal lands. This debate limited the applicability and validity of the *terra nullius* argument, affirmed Aboriginal *imperium* and *dominum*, and created the idea of prerogative treaty and land purchases. Another defining study for policy reform was the British Parliamentary Committee's *Report of the Select Committee of the House of Commons on Aborigines, 1837,* which surveyed the problems of Aborigines within British colonial policy. In 1977, the United States issued a report from the American Indian Policy Review Commission, and in 1987, the United Nations published Mr. José Martínez Cobo's massive *Study of the Problems of Discrimination Against Indigenous Populations.*

The 1996 *Report of the Royal Commission on Aboriginal Peoples* (RCAP 1996b) is a defining moment in the life of Canada. It continues the tradition of the grand studies of Indigenous peoples for policy reform. The Royal Commission was appointed by the federal government to help prevent violent solutions to Aboriginal issues. In the commission's words, it was established to "restore justice to the relationship between Aboriginal and non-Aboriginal people in Canada and to propose practical solutions to stubborn problems." This report is unique, since it is a cooperative effort between leading Canadian and Aboriginal academics, governments, and politicians.

The Royal Commission issued its report to Canadian governments in November 1996. The commission took five volumes (about four thousand pages) to explain what was needed to restore justice to the relationship between Aboriginal people and Canadians. To propose practical solutions to stubborn problems took over four hundred recommendations (some 110 pages). In summary, the report called for an equitable and fair relationship among federal, provincial, and First Nations governments, and explained that such a relationship would require the investment of technical support.

Central to the commission's report is that after the imperial treaty process, Canadian governments created a relationship with Aboriginal peoples based on "false premises" (RCAP 1996b, 2:1). These false premises were particularly virulent strains of the epidemic of empire that contaminated and still contaminate Canadian policy frameworks. They are known, among others, as colonialism, ethnocentrism, racism, and sexism. These false assumptions contaminated the legal and policy contexts of the *Indian Act* and residential schools (1:247). As a consequence, Aboriginal peoples were removed from their homelands, their nationhood was suppressed, their governments were undermined, and their identity and cultures were destroyed. Canadian governments attempted to replace Aboriginal cultures, spirituality, and identities with Eurocentric models of personality. For the most part, the social experiment has been a failure, leaving Aboriginal peoples lost between two worldviews and struggling with perpetual self-doubt. The commission concluded that the "legacy of our colonial history bears heavily upon Aboriginal people in the form of culture stress. It also distorts the perception of non-Aboriginal people, sustaining false assumptions and a readiness to relegate Aboriginal people to the margins of Canadian society" (3:586).

The commission recommended a new direction in Canadian policy. Policy reform would encompass cultural issues of language, spirituality, child care, and traditional ways of life, and social issues of poverty, health, housing, and family violence. The commission also pointed out that critical changes were required if the educational system was to serve as a vehicle for cultural and economic renewal. The report asserted governments must take measures to support and enhance cultural identity and to improve service delivery systems, especially in the areas of health and social well-being, education, and culture. The report affirmed that the culture and identity of Aboriginal peoples are matters of vital concern to their life and health. The commission recommended that culture and identity should be the core of Aboriginal jurisdiction in any implementation of the inherent right of Aboriginal self-government (2.33(11); 2.35) and recommended that, through negotiations with Canadian governments, Aboriginal nations should foster cultural autonomy (2.4.2). The report also affirmed the Aboriginal view of their traditional culture: It is a way of life shaped by intimate relationships with the land; reinforced by a worldview attributing life and spirit to all elements of the biosphere; and expressed in ethically ordered behaviors in social, economic, and political spheres.

The commission reported that Aboriginal people should define the content of their Indigenous knowledge and cultural heritage. Culture, in the report's view, is dynamic; it is grounded in ethics and values that provide a practical guide and a moral compass, enabling people to adapt to changing circumstances. It described how contemporary Aboriginal peoples reach into their traditions for wisdom and strength to cope with the diverse responsibilities of modern environments. It discussed how the traditional wisdom at the core of Aboriginal culture often transcends time and circumstance, but the way it is applied differs from one situation to another. It also affirmed the role of kinship—that is, the extended network of kin and community—to demonstrate how traditional teachings are applied in everyday life. The commission recommended a renewed partnership based on the principles of mutual recognition, mutual respect, sharing, and mutual responsibility. These principles form the ethical basis for a new partnership to break the existing despair.

The report recommended that federal, provincial, and territorial governments collaborate with Aboriginal organizations and communities to prepare a comprehensive inventory of historical and sacred sites, involving elders as expert advisers (3.6.1). It urged these governments to review legislation affecting sacred and historical sites to ensure that Aboriginal organizations and communities have access to urgent remedies to prevent or arrest damage to significant heritage sites, whether they be threatened by human actions or by natural processes (3.6.2). The report also recommended that, in collaboration with Aboriginal organizations, Canadian governments review legislation affecting historical and sacred sites and the conservation and display of cultural artifacts to ensure that (1) Aboriginal interests are recognized in designing, protecting, developing, and managing sites significant to Aboriginal culture and heritage and in conserving, repatriating, and displaying Aboriginal cultural artifacts; (2) Aboriginal people are fully involved in planning and managing heritage activities relevant to their cultures; and (3) Aboriginal people share the economic benefits that may accrue from appropriate development of relevant heritage sites and display of cultural artifacts (3.6.3).

The report recommended that museums and cultural institutions adopt ethical guidelines to govern all aspects of collection, disposition, display, and interpretation of artifacts related to Aboriginal culture and heritage, including the following: (1) involving Aboriginal people in drafting, endorsing, and implementing the guidelines; (2) creating inventories of relevant holdings and making such inventories freely accessible to Aboriginal people; (3) cataloguing and designating the appropriate use and display of relevant holdings; (4) repatriating, on request, objects that are sacred or integral to the history and continuity of particular nations and communities; (5) returning human remains to the families, communities, or nations of origin, on request, or in consultation with Aboriginal advisers on appropriate disposition, where remains cannot be associated with a particular nation; and (6) ensuring that Aboriginal people and communities have effective access to cultural education and training opportunities available through museums and cultural institutions (3.6.5).

The commission also recommended that Aboriginal, federal, provincial, and territorial governments, in collaboration with Aboriginal elders, artists, educators, and youth, develop and implement joint strategies to ensure that Aboriginal people have (1) effective access to cultural and heritage education; (2) resources to develop facilities for the display of cultural artifacts; and (3) the means to participate in exchanges and joint undertakings with museums and cultural institutions (3.6.5). It also recommended that Aboriginal, federal, provincial, and territorial governments include heritage research, conservation, and presentation in the list of skills identified as priorities in building the capacity to implement self-government (3.6.6).

The commission recommended that the federal government, in collaboration with Aboriginal people, review its legislation on the protection of intellectual property to ensure that Aboriginal interests and perspectives, in particular collective interests, are adequately protected (3.6.7).

The commission recommended that federal, provincial, and territorial governments recognize promptly that determining Aboriginal language status and its use is a core power in Aboriginal self-government (3.6.8). It recommended these governments affirm and support Aboriginal nations and their communities in using and promoting their languages and in declaring them official languages within their nations, territories, and communities where they choose to do so (3.6.8).

The commission also recommended that each Aboriginal nation in the process of nation building, capacity building, and negotiating and implementing self-government consult with its constituent communities to establish priorities and policies with respect to Aboriginal language conservation, revitalization, and documentation. Included within these priorities and policies are (1) assessing the current state of Aboriginal language use and vitality; (2) determining priorities of communities for language conservation, revitalization, and documentation; (3) consulting on the most effective means of implementing priorities; (4) facilitating initiatives to support Aboriginal language use in families and the broader community; (5) incorporating Aboriginal languages in education policies and programs; (6) enhancing cooperation among nations and communities of the same language group to promote research, curriculum development, and language elaboration; (7) using Aboriginal language in public forums and Aboriginal government business; and (8) declaring the relevant Aboriginal language to be the official language on that nation's territory (3.6.9).

The commission recommended that the federal government make a commitment to endow an Aboriginal Languages Foundation for the purpose of supporting Aboriginal initiatives in the conservation, revitalization, and documentation of Aboriginal languages, the foundation to be capitalized by an annual federal grant of $10 million for five years, beginning in 1997. The foundation would be eligible to receive charitable contributions, to be matched by the federal government in a ratio of two dollars for each dollar contributed. The foundation would be established to support language initiatives undertaken or endorsed by Aboriginal nations and their communities. It would be developed by a federally funded planning body, with a majority of First Nations, Inuit, and Métis representatives, and it would have a two-year mandate. Its operations would be directed by a board with a majority of First Nations, Inuit, and Métis members (3.6.10).

The commission recommended that the Government of Canada explicitly recognize the special status of Aboriginal-language broadcasting in federal legislation (3.6.11). Specifically, it recommended that in regions with significant Aboriginal population concentrations, the Canadian Radio-television and Telecommunications Commission include in license conditions for public and commercial broadcasters requirements for fair representation and distribution of Aboriginal programming, including Aboriginal-language requirements (3.6.12). Another recommendation required public and private media outlets to address the need for training and better representation of Aboriginal peoples in public communication (3.6.13–18).

The commission recommended that governments cooperate to establish and fund an Aboriginal Arts Council, with a minimum twenty-year lifespan and an annual budget equivalent to 5 percent of the Canada Council budget, to foster the revitalization and development of Aboriginal arts and literature (3.6.19). It urged governments, public agencies, and private organizations that provide support for the visual and performing arts to review all aspects of their programs to ensure that criteria for grants and awards are relevant to Aboriginal arts and artists; and to ensure Aboriginal people and perspectives are adequately represented on decision-making bodies, juries, advisory committees, and staff. This review should be undertaken in cooperation with Aboriginal artists and performers (3.6.20). Furthermore, the report urged governments, in cooperation with Aboriginal artists, writers, and performers, to support and promote the revitalization and development of Aboriginal literary, visual, and performing arts by (1) supporting training programs in schools, cultural institutions, and professional associations; (2) ensuring the participation of Aboriginal students in professional studies in the arts; and (3) accommodating requirements for the appropriate display and performance of Aboriginal arts in the design of public facilities in Aboriginal communities and the community at large (3.6.21).

Operational Principles

Seven basic principles should be considered in reviewing Canadian laws and policies to protect, preserve, and enhance Indigenous knowledge and heritage; many of them inform the Royal Commission's report and recommendations.

1. *Partnership.* The national review and reform process should be undertaken in formal partnership with Aboriginal peoples, particularly through field hearings at the community level, national-level seminars with Aboriginal cultural and scientific leaders, and the secondment of Aboriginal institutions and expertise.
2. *Self-government.* The reforms should be consistent with and as far as

possible reinforce the long-standing federal policy of promoting Aboriginal self-government. This means determining the feasibility of designating Aboriginal entities as the proper authorities for specific tasks and responsibilities.

3. *Fiduciary responsibility.* Traditional Indigenous knowledge is arguably a reserved "Aboriginal right" under section 35 of the *Constitution Act, 1982.* If so, it is also a matter to which federal fiduciary duties of protection attach, together with (among other things) lands and funds. The possibility that proposed federal action might adversely affect such rights should always be carefully considered.
4. *Locality of knowledge.* Traditional forms of knowledge and the responsibilities that attach to them vary among Aboriginal societies; hence national laws and policies must be flexible enough to accommodate local variations and local self-definition. Local Aboriginal authorities must ultimately answer the question "whose right to what."
5. *Groundedness of knowledge.* Traditional knowledge is generally grounded in specific uses of particular ecosystems. It is inseparable from landforms, environmental quality, survival of particular species, and subsistence activities. Knowledge is taught, learned, tested, and expanded through traveling and using a specific territory. Modifying the landscape, biodiversity, or human ecology jeopardizes knowledge. This connection of knowledge with the continuity of human ecology is reflected in UNESCO's conception of "biosphere," and in articles 8 and 10 of the UN Convention on Biological Diversity.
6. *Individuality of knowledge.* Each particular kind of knowledge has traditional "owners," usually individuals who are related by kinship to the previous owners and who have undergone tests to demonstrate their eligibility to acquire and their responsibility to use the knowledge. Customs of eligibility and proper procedure vary greatly among Aboriginal societies and must be respected if knowledge is to be transmitted fully.
7. *Knowledge and national heritage.* Although knowledge is local and individual, it has the potential to contribute to the heritage and well-being of all people in Canada. Preserving the value of this asset not only depends on conserving human ecology and respecting customary laws within Canada, but it ensures that Canada's international trade and intellectual property rights commitments are compatible with domestic heritage protection.

Canadian Reforms

Consistent with the recommendations of the *Report of the Royal Commission on Aboriginal Peoples*, Canadian governments, in collaboration with Aboriginal nations and their representatives, should undertake domestic legislative measures and program initiatives to protect, preserve, and enhance Indigenous knowledge and heritage in Canada. The reforms we recommend, all of which build on Canada's existing legislative framework, would bring Canadian law and policy to the forefront of Indigenous knowledge and heritage protection internationally.

Together, Canadian and Aboriginal governments should implement the Aboriginal Language Foundation to protect and develop the Aboriginal languages that control the knowledge of Aboriginal peoples. Languages contain not only intellectual and cultural knowledge, but also procedures for maintaining and renewing this knowledge. The preservation and enhancement of Aboriginal languages could be acknowledged formally as a constitutional Aboriginal right and as an element of the inherent right to self-government.

Indian and Northern Affairs Canada (INAC), in cooperation with Aboriginal nations, could facilitate the devolution of the minister's heritage conservation authority under section 91 of the *Indian Act,* through, among other things, special programs of financial and technical assistance. Conservation and enhancement of knowledge and cultural heritage could be acknowledged formally as an element of the inherent right to self-government.

In partnership with Aboriginal nations, INAC could ensure, through its participation in the negotiation of unresolved land claims, that heritage conservation is expressly and thoroughly addressed in final settlement agreements. This is the current trend. Final agreements should include, at a minimum, the identification of significant ecosystems and important cultural sites, and should assign responsibility for conserving them as an intrinsic part of the parties' legal obligations.

The INAC partnership with Aboriginal nations could also engage Parks Canada and Heritage Canada in a review, in collaboration with Aboriginal communities, of the significant cultural values and traditional uses of existing parks and heritage sites, with a view to assuring their protection through co-management agreements. The partnership could also develop a program to assist Aboriginal organizations and communities with the identification and documentation of important sites and resource uses, which could be added to the national parks and heritage site system. The partnership could consider proposing legislation based on the Australian model, which authorized the minister to designate special Aboriginal heritage sites at the request of Aboriginal people.

The partnership could collaborate with Aboriginal educational institutions to make an inventory of culturally significant materials in museums, both within Canada and abroad, and to make this information available to Aboriginal communities. A program of financial, technical, and legal assistance could be established to assist communities in repatriating significant materials, in providing facilities for the conservation of these materials under community control, and in making shared-custody arrangements with museums. Canadian museums and teaching institutions could be encouraged to repeat the UN draft guidelines on museum holdings as a condition of federal financial support.

The partnership could consider proposing new legislation to authorize the minister, or a special Aboriginal commission, to designate individuals as masters of traditional knowledge or arts upon the recommendation of Aboriginal communities. The main aim of this designation would be to validate the national importance of these individuals and to increase the interest of young people in learning their skills. Financial stipends should ordinarily not be involved. Japan's designation of individuals as "living cultural treasures" could be taken as a model.

The partnership could consider proposing new legislation authorizing the minister, or a special Aboriginal commission, to designate particular traditional resource-use sites as living laboratories to be conserved, under local Aboriginal management, for the study of Aboriginal ecology and resource management, and for maintaining the associated systems of ceremonies and knowledge. This would build on the original objectives of UNESCO's Man and the Biosphere Program and might be undertaken in cooperation with the UN Environmental Programme's Secretariat of the Convention on Biological Diversity and the World Heritage Office of UNESCO.

The partnership could consider programs of financial and technical cooperation with Aboriginal communities and institutions for this purpose. It could engage with the Federal Environmental Review Agency to facilitate anticipatory mapping of Crown lands for heritage sites and cultural sensitivities.

The partnership could engage Environment Canada and Aboriginal educational and scientific institutions in developing a protocol for assessing the impact of proposed activities on Aboriginal heritage and knowledge, a routine requirement of the Federal Environmental Review Agency. At a minimum, this protocol could aim at ensuring the compatibility of any proposed activities with articles 8 and 10 of the Convention on Biological Diversity.

In accordance with the Convention on Biological Diversity, the partnership could take immediate steps to ensure that the Department of Fisheries and Oceans, the Canadian Wildlife Service, the Canadian Forest Service, and, as far as possible through intergovernmental agreements, relevant provincial forest and wildlife agencies (1) minimize the impact of conservation measures on traditional Aboriginal uses of resources; (2) promote and help finance the widest possible use of comanagement agreements with Aboriginal communities; and (3) tender ecological research on species utilized by Aboriginal peoples to Aboriginal institutions.

The partnership could consider, in collaboration with Aboriginal organizations and communities, draft legislation that would extend special protection to Aboriginal heritage and knowledge, through registration with a special national commission or trustee, based on the model of the WIPO Model Provisions for National Laws on the Protection and Expression of Folklore. Special legislation would be needed to overcome limitations in the *Copyright Act* ("originality"), the *Patent Act* ("inventiveness," "novelty"), and the *Seeds Act*, respecting protectability, the duration of the protection, and the holder of the rights. Compatibility of the special legislation with NAFTA and GATT requires careful attention. The WIPO model provisions have a foundation in the Berne Convention, which was amended in 1971 to permit registration of "folklore" to a trustee designated by national law. Other restrictions, such as expiry of the protection after a term of years, still apply. Under subsequent trade liberalization treaties, however, cross-boundary differences in scope and duration of protection may be challenged as restrictive in effect.

The partnership could consider developing measures, in collaboration with Aboriginal organizations and communities, to establish a comprehensive and effective program of trademark protection for Aboriginal products and services, building upon Canada's previous experience with arts and crafts designations. Aboriginal governments, trade associations, arts organizations, and scientific institutions could be given authority to create and register unique trade names and trademarks that could be deposited in a special national registry. Also, the partnership could consider a program to heighten public awareness of these trademarks in Canada and abroad, and to provide financial, technical, and legal assistance to Aboriginal people and organizations to pursue infringements.

The partnership could recommend amendments to the *Cultural Property Export and Import Act* for the purposes of (1) restricting the export of any moveable cultural property that an Aboriginal community or Aboriginal traditional owners request be protected, regardless of monetary value, and (2) directing the minister to recover cultural property, on behalf of the traditional Aboriginal owners, within Canada as well as abroad, including the use of administrative procedures in UNESCO.

The partnership could develop legislation, in collaboration with Aboriginal organizations and communities, authorizing the federal courts to hear civil actions brought by traditional Aboriginal owners for (1) recovering culturally significant objects, (2) protecting the privacy of holders of traditional Aboriginal knowledge, and (3) ensuring confidentiality where traditional knowledge has been conditionally shared or licensed. The customary laws of the Aboriginal peoples concerned should be made dispositive in any dispute over ownership or authorized use.

Programs of federal funding for Aboriginal primary and secondary education should give the highest priority to the restoration and maintenance of Aboriginal languages, not only through special language training courses but also through instruction presented in Aboriginal languages. Equal fluency, rather than English or French dominance, could be an explicit policy, and greater efforts could be made to support educational institutions that develop and publish Aboriginal-language instructional materials. Federal funding for Aboriginal higher education could target the establishment and strengthening of centers for research on traditional knowledge and its applications, and the training of younger Aboriginal scholars in this field. Highest priority should be given to colleges and institutes chartered or operated by Aboriginal communities and to university-based programs that are directly accountable to Aboriginal peoples. A "center of excellence" could be identified in each of the principal biogeographic regions of Canada in the spirit of UN General Assembly resolutions 49–214 and 50/176 (on the International Decade of the World's Indigenous People).

The partnership could engage the National Science and Engineering Research Council and the Social Sciences and Humanities Research Council in the development of strategic initiatives to support capacity building and research in the field of traditional knowledge, targeting institutes chartered or operated by Aboriginal communities and university-based programs that are directly accountable to Aboriginal peoples. Funding councils should be urged to bring their ethical research standards into conformity with the UN Draft Principles and Guidelines.

International Reforms

The Department of Foreign Affairs and International Trade (DFAIT) and Aboriginal peoples of Canada, in a cooperative partnership, could engage to ensure the speedy consideration, adoption, and implementation of the UN Draft Principles and Guidelines on the Heritage of Indigenous Peoples. This partnership could also promote international support for adoption of the relevant provisions of the UN Draft Declaration on the Rights of Indigenous Peoples and the Draft Inter-American Declaration on the Rights of Indigenous Peoples.

The Government of Canada has indicated that it supported in principle the Draft Principles and Guidelines for the Protection of the Heritage of Indigenous Peoples. The partnership could expand the principles to include the use of education to help preserve, protect, and promote the languages, cultures, and heritage of Indigenous peoples, and the use of distinctive labels or marks to ensure the authenticity of Indigenous artistic and literary works. However, the Government of Canada should reconsider its attempt to strike a balance between its desire to protect the interests of Indigenous peoples and artistic freedom, and its concern that allowing Indigenous peoples to revoke their consent to the use of their heritage, or to reassert rights to elements of their heritage that have already passed into widespread public use, could have an adverse impact on science, medicine, and art. These financial concerns should not be allowed to impede reform to the discriminatory law under which Indigenous people have to struggle.

In conjunction with Aboriginal organizations, DFAIT, in partnership with Aboriginal nations, should play a larger role in preparing Canada's annual reports to the Commission on Sustainable Development and in ensuring that each report contains an explicit audit of measures taken thus far to implement Canada's obligations to Aboriginal peoples under Agenda 21 (in particular, chap. 26). The DFAIT-Aboriginal partnership should also consider the establishment of a program to increase the participation of Aboriginal people in the work of the commission, including as non-governmental representatives and as Aboriginal experts seconded to the commission's New York office and to the UN Food and Agriculture Organization (FAO).

Consistent with Canada's initiative of placing traditional knowledge on the agenda of this new policy body, Aboriginal peoples should play a leading technical role in the panel's deliberations. In collaboration with the Canadian Forest Service, DFAIT and the Aboriginal peoples of Canada could facilitate the organizing of an Aboriginal working group on traditional knowledge for the purpose of preparing and submitting independent scientific reports to the panel. The National Aboriginal Forestry Association recently raised the possibility of establishing such a technical group.

An intergovernmental task force with the Aboriginal peoples of Canada could be created to promote reform. Such a task force could promote the creation of a special unit of Indigenous experts within the Secretariat for the Convention on Biological Diversity, which was recently relocated to Montreal and, in cooperation with DFAIT and in partnership with Aboriginal nations, encourage other state parties to contribute voluntarily to the additional cost of such a technical and scientific body. INAC, in partnership with Aboriginal nations, could also consider creating a special dedicated fellowship fund to encourage Aboriginal scholars and science students to engage in research or training as residents of the secretariat's Montreal office.

The task force could encourage the convening of parliamentary hearings on the desirability of ratifying the ILO Convention and collaborate with the ILO Ottawa liaison office and Aboriginal educational institutions to raise public awareness of the convention and understanding of ILO provisions, especially within Aboriginal communities. Whether or not the convention is ultimately ratified, the review exercise should help build political support for domestic legislative action on the issues with which the convention is concerned.

Canada continues to play a large and positive role in UNESCO, the lead

UN agency in scientific and cultural affairs, and could influence UNESCO's commitment to making its existing programs more accessible to Indigenous peoples. This could include assistance in conserving sites of cultural or ecological importance through the World Heritage Center and Man and Biosphere Programme; recovering cultural material through the mediation of the Committee on Moveable Cultural Property; and developing information-sharing links between Indigenous peoples in different regions through UNESCO's Chairs in Communications (ORBIQUAM), which has a site at the University of Quebec-Montreal.

As a first step, DFAIT could facilitate an exchange of proposals from Aboriginal organizations, Aboriginal educational institutions, and the Canadian committee for UNESCO. DFAIT should also consider the possibility of helping organize broadly representative delegations of Aboriginal educators, cultural authorities, and scientists to the next UNESCO General Assembly to help explore these ideas with other countries and UNESCO officials.

Many Canadian Aboriginal organizations and institutions are interested in participating more actively in exchanges of expertise with Indigenous communities abroad. For instance, in Canada both the International Development Research Centre (IDRC) and the Canadian International Development Agency (CIDA) work with Indigenous communities abroad. Funded by parliament, IDRC focuses on helping scientists and communities in developing countries do research to find solutions to their social, economic, and environmental problems. CIDA is a Canadian government body responsible for administering most of Canada's Official Development Assistance Program. IDRC's mandate is research production and application while strengthening research capacity in the Southern Hemisphere; CIDA's role is to provide funds for practical solutions to development (IDRC 1999). Both IDRC and CIDA should be encouraged to make greater use of Aboriginal expertise at all levels; to facilitate direct contacts between Aboriginal institutions in Canada; and to set aside special funding (1) for the establishment of technical networks linking individual experts, communities, and institutions on areas such as ecology and traditional medicine, (2) for the secondment of Aboriginal experts to CIDA and IDRC projects that involve Indigenous peoples, and (3) for the recruitment of Aboriginal college and university students as trainees to participate in CIDA- or IDRC-supported projects.

DFAIT, in partnership with Aboriginal nations, should also consider engaging CIDA, IDRC, and relevant Aboriginal institutions in devising procedures to ensure that CIDA projects, and other international development-assistance programs to which Canadians contribute financially, respect the rights of Indigenous peoples and, in particular, take into account the UN's Draft Principles and Guidelines for the Protection of the Heritage of Indigenous Peoples.

Canada is an active party to a growing web of wildlife management treaties, which increasingly affect the ability of Aboriginal peoples to maintain their traditional uses of living resources. These include regional arrangements on such resources as migratory birds, polar bears, Arctic caribou, salmon, halibut, and fur-bearing animals; and global arrangements such as the Convention on International Trade in Endangered Species (CITES 1995), the Convention on the Rights of the Sea (1998), and the Agreement on Highly Migratory and Straddling Fish Stocks (1995). Aboriginal peoples have an interest in the equitable application of these treaties and in the negotiation of the terms of new conservation measures. They can also make significant scientific contributions to these arrangements.

As a first step, DFAIT should consider cooperating with Aboriginal educational institutions and with Aboriginal studies departments in the universities to produce a clear guidebook for Aboriginal communities, surveying Canada's treaty commitments in the field of wildlife conservation treaties and their relationship to domestic conservation measures. This guidebook should be followed by publication of an annual review of the status of implementation of Canada's obligations and the conflicts that have arisen with Aboriginal resource uses. Aboriginal expertise should be routinely included in Canada's delegation to conferences for the negotiation and adjustment of wildlife treaties, and the DFAIT-Aboriginal partnership should consider designating at least one Aboriginal institution to serve as a center for gathering data from Aboriginal communities and for coordinating Aboriginal expertise that may bear on Canada's wildlife treaties.

Many Aboriginal as well as non-Aboriginal groups have raised concerns about the impact of NAFTA on Canada's cultural heritage. The anticipated expansion of NAFTA membership to Latin America will mean a significant growth of Canadian trade with other countries that have important Indigenous heritages. This will increase trade in Indigenous peoples' cultures, products, arts, and knowledge, and undoubtedly also lead to trade disputes regarding the protection of Indigenous heritage and intellectual property. Heritage and intellectual property rights will be targets of legal challenges, and there will be international pressure to harmonize these rights across national boundaries.

DFAIT should consider collaborating with Aboriginal organizations and Aboriginal legal experts to bring these issues to the attention of Canadian trade officials, to ensure that they are taken into account in ongoing NAFTA negotiations, and to develop the relevant expertise required for the negotiations. The DFAIT-Aboriginal partnership should also consider facilitating technical meetings between Indigenous legal and cultural affairs experts of present and anticipated NAFTA member countries to seek a common base of understanding of what measures could be taken to mitigate any adverse effects of trade liberalization. One possible solution would be the negotiation of a side agreement, like the NAFTA side agreement on the environment, to protect Indigenous heritage.

Complementary measures should be considered in relation to global trade liberalization, administered by the new World Trade Organization (WTO) at Geneva. The new WTO rules on TRIPs (Trade-Related Intellectual Property Rights) will ordinarily supersede any inconsistent provisions of past treaties on intellectual property rights to which Canada is a party, such as the Berne and Paris Conventions. Hence future diplomatic efforts to defend Canada's domestic protection of Aboriginal peoples' cultural and knowledge will need to focus on WTO rather than WIPO. The tendency of WTO will be to disallow high national standards of protection, the opposite of WIPO's objectives. Aboriginal participation in Canadian diplomacy at the WTO will therefore become essential, lest Canada's domestic initiatives to protect Aboriginal rights risk being struck down as barriers to trade.

Part V

•••

Conclusion

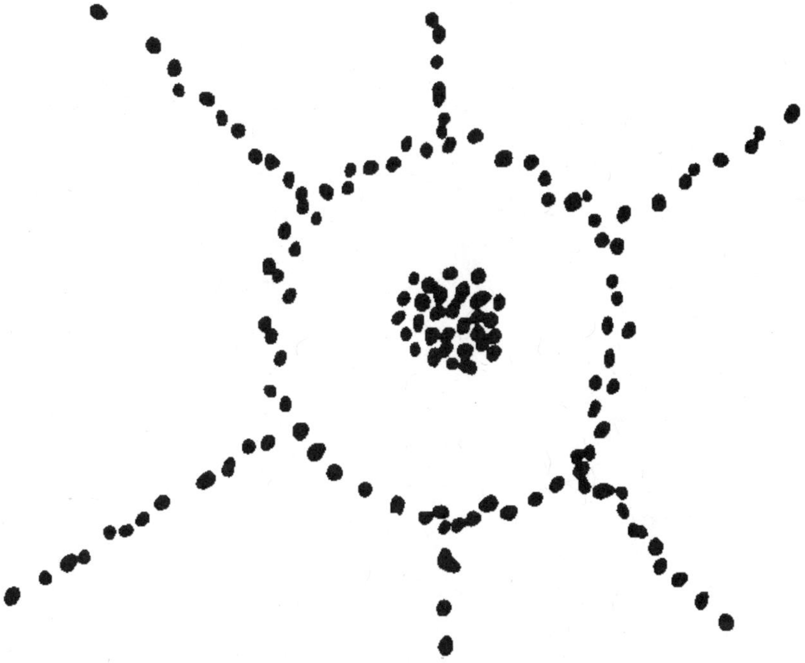

[O]ne of the purposes of the United Nations, as set forth in the Charter, is the achievement of international cooperation in solving international problems of an economic, social, cultural or humanitarian character and in promoting and encouraging respect for human rights and fundamental freedoms for all without distinction as to race, sex, language or religion. — Commission on Human Rights, Resolution 1997/32

•••

Conclusion

The land is everything to me.
The land is part of my language, part of the way I perceive the world.
The water, the trees, the smell of pine, the smell of autumn, the smell of wet leaves in the springs.
It is all part of my imagination, part of my dreams.
— Gerald Vizenor, Anishinaki poet and writer (1993, 35)

The land remains part of the language, imagination, and dreams of most traditional Indigenous peoples. All known life exists in a thin layer wrapped around the globe between the earth's molten core and the hostile environment of space. Although life extends from the deep trenches of the oceans to the highest mountain peaks, in proportion to the earth, this realm is no thicker than the shine on a billiard ball (Lean & Hinrichsen 1994, 4). Already more than sixbillion humans exist on the land realm. The surfaces of the land realm constitute only 30 percent of the water planet; yet, half the land realm is hard to live upon. One-third of the land realm is arid or semi-arid, 11 percent is under permanent ice cover, and 10 percent is tundra. Only 11 percent of the land is good for farming, and almost all of this is already in use. Most of the remaining one-third of the land is seen as too poor, too thin, or too wet to be of value to agriculture (Lean & Hinrichsen 1994, 4).

Of the sixbillion humans, nearly one-quarter of the earth's Indigenous peoples are unable to meet their basic needs for food, housing, and clothing. By 2100, the world's population is expected to double, and this growth fuels both the destruction of the environment and human destitution. The World Commission on Environment and Development—the Brundtland Commission—found that rising poverty in poor countries and increasing pollution in rich ones are both unsustainable developments (WCED 1987). These factors create tension on existing farm lands and demand a new perspective of the landscape.

The modern contexts of Eurocentrism are seriously endangering Indigenous knowledge and heritage. Rapid economic development guided by Eurocentric theories has subordinated the strategy of sustainable development. Eurocentric laws have denied equal protection of the law to Indigenous knowledge and heritage. Transforming any of the entrenched Eurocentric contexts will be difficult; yet such a transformation is a prerequisite to obtaining respect for Indigenous worldviews. The challenge of protecting Indigenous knowledge and heritage requires the transformation of all these interdependent areas. This is a huge undertaking that will require concerted, comprehensive effort. It will require many generations working together with persistence. It will take vision, trust, and tolerance, which can be manifested by skilled diplomacy, strategic agreements, and deliberate commitments by all parties. Creating these transformations and respecting Indigenous knowledge and heritage is an intimidating task but a necessary goal for the end of colonialism and for the construction of postcolonial global and national orders.

Indigenous peoples' search for belonging and for respect for their knowledge and heritage is a broad and essential project, both internationally and nationally. It involves acknowledgment and recognition by governments, corporations, and individuals that Indigenous peoples are peoples within the meaning of the UN human rights covenants. It involves acknowledgment that Indigenous peoples have the right to have their knowledge, heritage, and identity protected, preserved, and enhanced. Because of the powerlessness and marginalization of Indigenous peoples, the search is complicated.

Protecting intellectual property rights for Indigenous peoples is a growing global problem. Over the last decade, an astonishing interest has been generated in the existing knowledge of Indigenous peoples. All peoples need a new awareness of Indigenous peoples if the Eurocentric biases that have been strengthening in the last five hundred years are to be overcome. As we have tried to demonstrate, these biases have fundamentally flawed the response of the educational and legal systems to Indigenous knowledge and heritage. It is difficult for most Eurocentric thinkers to glimpse the possibilities of an enlarged awareness of Indigenous thought. It requires them to think beyond their teachings and their artificially constructed frameworks. Yet, daily Indigenous peoples are forced to make this cognitive leap to physically survive, typically on about a dollar a day.

Survival for Indigenous peoples is more than a question of physical existence, however. It is an issue of protecting, preserving, and enhancing Indigenous worldviews, knowledge systems, languages, and environments. It is a matter of sustaining spiritual links with ecosystems and communities. Unfortunately, these ecosystems and communities are often critically endangered. The awareness that the demise of Indigenous populations and the loss of their languages is causing the demise of Indigenous knowledge and the loss of biological diversity has not stopped the rush on Indigenous knowledge systems by outsiders. These outsiders have not attempted to prevent the extermination of Indigenous peoples or their ecosystems; instead they have intensified their efforts to access, to know, and to assert control over this endangered knowledge and these endangered resources. This is such a tragic response.

The emerging dialogue about Indigenous knowledge is about shattering paradigms and contexts. As the indivisible nature of Indigenous knowledge is understood, the issues associated with protecting its vital, living, dynamic forces are confronted. Indigenous knowledge defies and challenges modern classifications of intellectual, cultural, and spiritual rights. A new consciousness is required. New consciousnesses are not unknown in Eurocentric thought. Every age has had a knowledge system consistent with the ruling social process of the time. Each age's empowering conceptions—its capacity to conceive—have been both liberated and bounded by its context, which saturates most educated minds. Often one forgets that these shared judgments are human artifacts. Each age has had to nullify its explanations of the world when they have been demonstrated to be wrong or have become inadequate. Often, these shared judgments are transformed when external events change the fundamental assumptions on which they are based. This evaluative process in Eurocentric thought is often obscured by the idea of continual progress. However, to move from one error to another is not progress; it is merely change.

Human consciousness needs a new version of humanity that respects Indigenous knowledge and heritage. Tinkering with the existing legal and knowledge system is necessary, but tinkering will not resolve the global and systemic discrimination against Indigenous knowledge and heritage. Both internationally and nationally, *sui generis* legal régimes to protect, preserve, and enhance Indigenous knowledge and heritage must be established.

Humanity must be liberated from the limitations of Eurocentric thought and law. Eurocentric thought and law must recognize their historical discrimination against Indigenous peoples. They must recognize that Indigenous peoples are aware that the discrimination against Indigenous knowledge and heritage is remediable. Eurocentric thought must recognize that Indigenous peoples are aware that existing legal systems are failing to remedy the situation because Eurocentric laws protect Eurocentric interests.

The older Eurocentric debates on the philosophy, economics, and jurisprudence of what knowledge or which ideas can be treated as property are being exposed as a source of discrimination against Indigenous knowledge and heritage. These current debates over protecting, preserving, and enhancing Indigenous knowledge and heritage are showing the deeply rooted ethnocentric criteria of intellectual and cultural property that are discriminatory against Indigenous knowledge. The principal reason for this continued discrimination is the resistance of Eurocentric nations and societies to developing neutral laws for a multicultural society. Multicultural societies must have laws that respect different worldviews. There are compelling interests in eliminating this discrimination across international markets and within nations.

The protection of Indigenous knowledge and heritage represents the protection and preservation of Aboriginal humanity. Such protection is not about preserving dead or dying cultures. It is about the commercial exploitation and appropriation of living consciousnesses and cultural orders. It is an issue of privacy and commerce. The use of Indigenous knowledge for private or public profits by others under existing laws is a central issue. Other surrounding issues present numerous ethical and legal questions. Indigenous knowledge and heritage must be approached with respect and sensitivity.

Internationally, a convention protecting Indigenous knowledge and heritage with an appropriate enforcement agency is required. A declaration will not be sufficient to effect change. Nationally, such a convention must be implemented or a similar convention and law with the Indigenous peoples could be enacted. However, these laws must be interrelated with Eurocentric legal régimes and seen as equal, coexisting side by side, protecting all humanity and its products based on their heritage.

All peoples must have equal dignity and essential worth. Their languages, heritages, and knowledge must be equally respected by public institutions and by all peoples. Their ecological order and intellectual integrity must be respected by the market economies. Equality and respect require cooperative frameworks, efforts, and innovations to protect Indigenous intellectual, cultural, and trade policies. Indigenous peoples must be actively involved in the development of any new convention or laws. They need representatives to discuss how to move toward developing these legal régimes. Their participation will develop new sensitivities to what is sacred, to what is capable of being shared, and to what is fair compensation for the sharing of information among diverse peoples. Community-based partnerships are also needed to resolve the nature of fair compensation and the ethics of research. Public education is needed to develop an understanding of the new régimes and frameworks.

The issues associated with protecting Indigenous knowledge are deeply concerned with the structural inability of Eurocentric law to give Indigenous peoples control of their humanity, heritage, and communities. The absence of protection of the humanity of Indigenous peoples in international and Canadian law is disturbing. As Indigenous peoples, we have had more than our share of adversity and tragedy because of the denial of the manifestation of our humanity. International and national law should embrace and celebrate the world's cultural and intellectual diversity for the richness and depth this diversity brings to life on earth.

Acronyms

ACUNS—Association of Canadian Universities for Northern Studies
AFN—Assembly of First Nations
CARFAC—Canadian Artists' Representation/le Front des Artistes Canadiens
CERD—Committee on the Elimination of Racial Discrimination
CIDA—Canadian International Development Agency
CITES—Convention on International Trade in Endangered Species
CMA—Canadian Museums Association
DFAIT—Department of Foreign Affairs and International Trade, Canada
FAO—Food and Agriculture Organization
FBPM—Fundacao Brasiliera de Plantas Medicinais
FEARO—Federal Environmental Review Agency
FMCA—Fonds Mondials pour le sauvegarde des Cultures Autochthones
G&M—*Globe & Mail*
GATT—General Agreement on Trade and Tariffs
IARC—International Agricultural Research Center
ICOM—International Council of Museums
IDRC—International Development Research Centre
INAC—Indian and Northern Affairs Canada
ILO—International Labour Organization
INBio—Instituto Nacional de Biodiversidad
IPF—Intergovernmental Panel on Forests
NAFTA—North American Free Trade Agreement
NAGPRA—Native Graves Protection and Repatriation
NCI—National Cancer Institute
NIH—National Institutes of Health
OAS—Organization of American States
RAFI—Rural Advancement Foundation International
RCAP—Royal Commission on Aboriginal Peoples
SAA—Society for Applied Anthropology
SEB—Society for Economic Botany
SIIT—Saskatchewan Indian Institute of Technologies
SSHRC—Social Sciences and Humanities Research Council
TEK—Traditional Ecological Knowledge
TRIPs—Trade-Related Aspects of Intellectual Property Rights
UN—United Nations
UNCTAD—United Nations Conference on Trade and Development
UNCSP—United Nations Commission on Sustainable Development
UNDP—United Nations Development Programme
UNEP—United Nations Environment Programme
UNESCO—United Nations Educational, Scientific and Cultural Organization
UNTS—United Nations Treaty Series
UPOV—International Convention for the Protection of New Varieties of Plants
USFATF—United States Federal Agencies Task Force
WCED—World Commission on Environment and Development

WFP—*Winnipeg Free Press*
WIPO—World Intellectual Property Organization
WTO—World Trade Organization

•••

References

Abram, David. 1996. *The Spell of the Sensuous: Perception and Language in a More-Than-Human World.* New York: Pantheon Books.

ACUNS. 1982, reprinted 1988. *Ethical Principles for the Conduct of Research in the North.* Ottawa: ACUNS.

AFN. 1988. *Tradition and Education: Towards a Vision of our Future*. Ottawa: AFN.

———. 1990. *Towards Linguistic Justice for First Nations.* Ottawa: AFN.

———. 1992. *Rebirth of First Nations Languages*. Ottawa: AFN.

AFN & CMA. 1992. *Turning the Page: Forging New Partnerships Between Museums and First Peoples*. Task Force Report on Museums and First Peoples. Ottawa: AFN and CMA.

Ahenakew, Freda, & Shirley Fredeen, eds. 1987. *Our Languages, Our Survival.* Saskatoon, Sask.: Saskatchewan Indian Languages Institute.

Albers-Schonberg, Georg. 1984. "The Continuing Importance of Natural Products for Medicine." Paper presented at the 2nd Princess Chulabhorn Science Congress, 2–6 November, Bangkok.

Alexander, Gregory. 1998. *Commodity and Property in American Legal Thought, 1776-1970.* Chicago: University of Chicago Press.

American Indian Policy Review Commission. 1977. *Final Report.* 10 vols. Washington, D.C.: U.S. Government Printing Office.

Amin, S. 1988. *Eurocentrism.* New York: Monthly Review Press.

Anaya, S. James. 1991. "Indigenous Rights Norms in Contemporary International Law." *Arizona Journal of International and Comparative Law* 8: 1–39.

Anyinam, Charles. 1995. "Ecology and Ethnomedicine: Exploring Links Between Current Environmental Crisis and Indigenous Medical Practices." *Social Science and Medicine* 40(3): 321–29.

Apple, M.W., & L.K. Christian-Smith, eds. 1991. *The Politics of the Textbook*. New York: Routledge.

Atran, S. 1990. *Cognitive Foundations of Natural History*. Cambridge: Cambridge University Press.

Attridge, I., ed. 1996. *Biodiversity Law and Policy in Canada: Review and Recommendations.* Electronic publication. Toronto: Canadian Institute on Environmental Law and Policy.

Augustine, S. 1997. "Traditional Aboriginal Knowledge and Science Versus Occidental Science." Unpublished manuscript prepared for the Biodiversity Convention Office of Environment Canada.

Australia. 1981. Intellectual Property Aspects of Folklore Protection.

Australia, Department of Aboriginal Affairs. 1989. *The Aboriginal Arts and Crafts Industry Report.*

Australian Law Reform Commission. 1993. *Issues Paper*.

Ayoungman, Vivian, & Elizabeth Brandt. 1989. "Language Renewal and Language

Maintenance: A Practical Guide." *Canadian Journal of Native Education* 16(2): 42–77.

Balick, Michael. 1984. "Palms, People, and Progress." *Horizons* 3(4): 32–37.

———. 1990. "Ethnobotany and the Identification of Therapeutic Agents From the Rainforest." Pp. 22–39 in *Bioactive Compounds From Plants,* ed. D.J. Chadwick & J. Marsh. New York: John Wiley and Sons.

Barfield, Owen. 1957. *Saving of Appearances: A Study in Idolatry.* New York: Harcourt, Brace, Jovanovich.

Barsh, Russell. 1982. "The Economics of a Traditional Coastal Indian Salmon Fishery." *Human Organization* 41(2): 171–76.

———. 1988 "The Ethnic Factor in Security and Development: Perceptions of United Nations Human-Rights Bodies." *Acts Sociologica* 31(4): 333–41.

———. 1989. "United Nations Seminar on Indigenous Peoples and States." *American Journal of International Law* 83(3): 599.

———. 1994. "Indigenous Peoples in the 1990s: From Object to Subject of International Law." *Harvard Human Rights Journal* 7: 33–86.

———. 1999. "Socially Responsible Investigating and The World's People." Paper delivered to Calvert Group meeting at Banff.

Battiste, Marie. 1984. "An Historical Investigation of the Cultural and Cognitive Consequences of Micmac Literacy." An unpublished doctoral dissertation. Stanford: Stanford University.

———. 1986. "Micmac Literacy and Cognitive Assimilation." Pp 23–44 in *Indian Education in Canada: The Legacy,* vol 1., ed. J. Barman, Y. Hébert, & D. McCaskill. Vancouver: University of British Columbia Press.

———. 1996. "Maintaining Aboriginal Language, Culture, and Identity in Modern Society." CD ROM. *Seven Generations: An Information Legacy of the Royal Commission on Aboriginal Peoples.* Hull, P.Q.: Canada Communications.

———, ed. 2000. *Reclaiming Indigenous Voice and Vision.* Vancouver: University of British Columbia Press.

Bell, Catherine. 1992a. "Aboriginal Claims to Cultural Property in Canada: A Comparative Legal Analysis of the Repatriation Debate." *American Indian Law Review* 17: 457–521.

———. 1992b. "Reflections on a New Relationship: Comments on the Task Force Guidelines for Repatriations." Paper Presented at Canadian Museums Association, Legal Affairs and Management Symposium.

Bell, Martin. 1979. "The Exploitation of Indigenous Knowledge: Whose Use of What and for What?" *IDS Bulletin* 10(2): 44–51.

Bentham, J. [1789] 1970. *Introduction to Principles of Moral and Legislation,* ed. J.H. Burns & H.L.A. Hart. London: Athlone Press.

Berg, Jeff. 1991. "Moral Rights: A Legal, Historical and Anthropological Reappraisal." *Intellectual Property Journal* 6: 341.

Blackstone, Sir William. 1770. *Commentaries on the Laws of England.* Oxford: Clarendon Press.

Blaut, J.M. 1993. *The Colonizer's Model of the World: Geographical Diffusionism and Eurocentric History.* New York: Guilford Press.

Biggar, H.P. 1922–38. *The Works of Samuel de Champlain,* reprinted, translated, and annotated by six Canadian scholars under the general editorship of H.P. Biggar. Toronto: The Champlain Society.

Bjorkquist, S. 1999. *The Regulation of Agriculture Biotechnology in Canada.* Electronic publication. Toronto: Canadian Institute on Environmental Law and Policy.

Bohm, David. 1980. *Wholeness and the Implicate Order*. London: Routledge and Kegan Paul.

Bohm, David, & F. David Peat. 1987. *Science, Order, and Creativity.* New York: Bantam Books.

Bourdieu, Pierre. 1993. *The Field of Cultural Production: Essays on Art and Literature,* edited and introduced by Randal Johnson. New York: Columbia University Press.

Bowrey, Kathy. 1994. "Copyright, The Paternity of Artistic Works, and the Challenge Posed by Postmodern Artists." *Intellectual Property Journal* 8: 285–317.

Brody, H. 1981. *Maps and Dreams: Indians and the British Columbia Frontier.* Vancouver: Douglas &McIntyre.

Brown, Joseph E. 1964. *The Spiritual Legacy of the American Indian.* Lebanon, Penn.: Pendle Hill.

Cajete, Gregory. 1986. "Science: A Native American Perspective: A Culturally Based Science Education Curriculum." Unpublished doctoral dissertation, International College, Los Angeles.

———. 1995. *Look to the Mountain: An Ecology of Indigenous Education*. Durango, Colo.: Kivaki Press.

———. 1999. *Ignite the Sparkle: An Indigenous Science Model.* Skyland, N.C.: Kivaki Press.

———. 2000a. "Indigenous Knowledge: The Pueblo Metaphor of Indigenous Education." Pp. 181–91 in *Reclaiming Indigenous Voice and Vision,* ed. Marie Battiste. Vancouver: University of British Columbia Press.

———. 2000b. *Native Science: Natural Law of Interdependence.* Santa Fe, N.Mex.: Clearlight.

Canada. 1988. *Federal Archaeological Heritage Protection and Management: A Discussion Paper.* Ottawa: Department of Communications.

———. 1995. Federal-Provincial-Territorial Working Group, *Canadian Biodiversity Strategy: Canada's Response to the Convention on Biological Diversity.* Ottawa: Minister of Supply and Services.

———. 1996. *Environmental Assessment in Canada: Frameworks, Procedures & Attributes of Effectiveness,* Ottawa, March.

Canadian Forest Service. 1995. *International Dialogue on Forests: Approaches, Opportunities and Options for Action*. Ottawa: Minister of Supply and Services.

Caporale, Lynn. 1992. The Merck/INBio Agreement: "A Pharmaceutical Company Perspective." Paper presented at the Rainforest Alliance symposium on Tropical Forest Medical Resources and the Conservation of Biodiversity, January. New York: Rockefeller University.

Cardinal-Shubert, Joane. 1989. "In the Red: Money, Appropriation and Native Imagery." *Fuse Magazine* 13(fall): 20.

Capotorti, P. Special Rapporteur. 1991. *Study on the Rights of Persons Belonging to Ethnic, Religious and Linguistic Minorities.* UN Publication No. E.91.XIV.2. Geneva: United Nations.

Champagne, D. 1994. *The Native North American Almanac.* Detroit: Gale Research.

Chapin, Mac. 1991. "How the Kuna Keep the Scientists in Line." *Cultural Survival Quarterly* 15(3)(summer): 17.

Chatwin, B. 1993. *Songlines.* New York: Viking.

Cheshire, G.C., & E.H. Burn. 1976. *Cheshire's Modern Law of Real Property.* 12th ed. London: Butterworths.

Churchill, Jane. 1994. "Patenting Humanity: The Development of Property Rights in the Human Body and the Subsequent Evolution of Patentability of Living Things." *Intellectual Property Journal* 8: 249.

Cleary, Linda, & Thomas Peacock. 1998. *Collected Wisdom: American Indian Education.* Boston: Allyn and Bacon.

Clements, Rececca. 1991. "Misconceptions of Culture: Native Peoples and Cultural Property Under Canadian Law." *University of Toronto Faculty of Law Review* 49(winter): 1–26.

Clifford, James. 1983. "On Ethnographic Authority." *Representations* 2: 118–46.

Clifford James, & George E. Marcus, eds. 1986. *Writing Culture: The Poetics and Politics of Ethnography.* Berkeley: University of California Press.

Cobo, J. Martínez. 1986/87. *Study of the Problem of Discrimination Against Indigenous Populations.* E/CN.4/Sub.2/1986/7 and Add.1-4. UN Publication No. E.86.XIV.3. Geneva: United Nations.

Coetzee, J.M. 1980. *Waiting for the Barbarians*. New York: Penguin.

Cole, Michael, John Gay, & Joseph Glick. 1971. *The Cultural Context of Learning and Thinking.* New York: Basic Books.

Comaroff, Jean. 1985. *Body of Power, Spirit of Resistance: The Culture and History of a South African People.* Chicago: University of Chicago Press.

Congress Research Service. 1993. Report to Congress on Biotechnology, Indigenous Peoples, and Intellectual Property Rights.

Coombe, Rosemary J. 1991. "Objects of Property and Subjects of Politics: Intellectual Property Laws and Democratic Dialogue." *Texas Law Review* 69: 1853–80.

———. 1992. "Authorizing the Celebrity: Publicity Rights, Postmodern Politics, and Unauthorized Genders." *Cardozo Arts & Entertainment* 10: 365.

———. 1993. "The Properties of Culture and the Politics of Possessing Identity: Native Claims in the Cultural Appropriation Controversy." *Canadian Journal of Law and Jurisprudence* 6: 249.

Cornish, W.R. 1989. *Intellectual Property: Patents, Copyright, Trade Marks and Allied Rights.* 2nd ed. London: Sweet & Maxwell.

Craig. 1995. In *University of British Columbia Law Review,* special edition, "Material Culture in Flux: Law and Policy of Repatriation of Culture Property."

Crespi, Stephen. 1995. "Biotechnology Patenting: The Wicked Animal Must Defend Itself." *E.I.P.R.* 9: 431.

Crewdson, R. 1984. "Cultural Property—A Fourth Estate." *Law Society Gazette* 18: 126.

Cultural Survival Quarterly. 1991. "Intellectual Property Rights: The Politics of Ownership." *Cultural Survival Quarterly* 15(3): 3

Daes, Erica-Irene. 1991. (Special Rapporteur of the Working Group on Indigenous Populations). *Working Paper*. E/CN.4/Sub. 21/1991/34.

———. 1993. *Study on the Protection of the Cultural and Intellectual Property Rights of Indigenous Peoples.* E/CN.4/Sub. 21/1993/28. Sub-Commission on Prevention of Discrimination and Protection of Minorities, Commission on Human Rights, UNESCO.

———. 1994. *Preliminary Report of the Special Rapporteur: Protection of the Heritage of Indigenous Peoples.* E/CN.4/Sub.2/1994/31. Sub-Commission on Prevention of Discrimination and Protection of Minorities, Commission on Human Rights, UNESCO.

———. 1995. *Final Report of the Special Rapporteur: Protection of the Heritage of Indigenous Peoples.* E/CN.4/Sub.2/1995/26. Sub-Commission on Prevention of Discrimination and Protection of Minorities, Commission on Human Rights, UNESCO.

———. 1996a. (Chairman-Rapporteur of the Working Group on Indigenous Populations). *On the Concept of Indigenous People.* E/CN.4/Sub.2/AC.4/1996/2. Sub-Commission on Prevention of Discrimination and Protection of Minorities, Commission on Human Rights, UNESCO.

———. 1996b. *Supplementary Report on the Protection of the Heritage of Indigenous Peoples.*

Deloria, Vine Jr. 1973. *God Is Red.* New York: Grosset & Dunlap.

Dickason, Olive. 1992. *Canada's First Nations.* Edmonton: University of Alberta Press.

Dooling, D.M., & P. J. Smith eds. 1989. *I Become Part of It.* New York: HarperCollins.

Du Bois, W.E.B. 1969 [1903]. *The Souls of Black Folk.* New York: New American Library.

Duran, Eduardo, & Bonnie Duran. 1995. *Native American Postcolonial Psychology.* New York: State University Press.

Dussel, E. 1988. "Was America Discovered or Invaded?" *Concillium* 200.

Eagleton, Terry. 1990. *The Ideology of the Aesthetic.* Oxford: Basil Blackwell.

Eide, A. 1993. "In Search of Constructive Alternatives to Secession." In *Modern Law of Self-Determination,* ed. C. Tomuschat. Dordrecht: Martinus Nijhoff.

Emery, Allan R., et al. 1997. "Guidelines for Environmental Assessments and Traditional Knowledge." Unpublished. Ottawa: Centre for Traditional Knowledge.

FAO . 1983. International Undertaking on Plant Genetic Resources.

———. 1989. Report of the Intergovernmental Commission on Plant Genetic Resources, Rome.

Fenton, William N. 1989. "Return of Eleven Wampum Belts to the Six Nations Iroquois Confederacy on Grand River Canada." *Ethnohistory* 36(4): 392–410.

Findeisen, Christina, & Sarah Laird. 1991. "Natural Products Research and the Potential Role of the Pharmaceutical Industry in Tropical Forest Conservation." A report prepared by the Periwinkle Project of the Rainforest Alliance. New York: Rockefeller University.

Findlay, L.M. In press. *Always Indigenize! The Radical Humanities in Post Colonial Universities.* Ariel.

Fitzpatrick, P., ed. 1991. *Dangerous Supplements: Resistance and Renewal in Jurisprudence.* London: Pluto.

Fox, Richard, ed. 1991. *Recapturing Anthropology: Working in the Present.* Santa Fe, N.Mex.: School of American Research Press.

Fredeen, S. 1988. A Foundation for a Cree Immersion Education. Unpublished master's thesis, University of Saskatchewan, Saskatoon.

Freeman, Milton M.R. 1993. "The International Whaling Commission, Small-type

Whaling and Coming to Terms With Subsistence." *Human Organization* 52(3): 243–51.
Freire, Paulo. 1973. *Pedagogy of the Oppressed.* New York: Seabury Press.
G&M. 1989. "Native Remains to be Returned by Smithsonian." 12 September, A11.
Glavin, T. 1989. "RCMP Seek Missing Heritage Stone." *Vancouver Sun*, 22 September. B1, B4.
Gollin, Michael A. 1993. "An Intellectual Property Rights Framework for Biodiversity Prospecting." Pp. 159–97 in *Biodiversity Prospecting*, ed. Walter Reid et al. Washington, D.C.: World Resources Institute and others.
Goodwin, Richard N. 1974. *The American Condition*. New York: Doubleday.
Greenberg, J.H. 1987. *Languages in the Americas*. Stanford: Stanford University Press.
Greenfield, Jeannette. 1989. *The Return of Cultural Treasures*. New York: Cambridge University Press.
Gregory, C.A. 1982. *Gifts and Commodities*. London: Academic Press.
Grenier, Louise. 1998. *Working With Indigenous Knowledge: A Guide for Researchers*. Ottawa: International Development Research Centre.
Hanke, Lewis. 1959. *Aristotle and the American Indians.* Chicago: Henry Regnery.
Hannum, Hurst. 1990. *Autonomy, Sovereignty and Self-Determination: The Accommodation of Conflicting Rights.* Philadephia: University of Pennsylvania Press.
Healy, Kevin. 1992. "Ethnodevelopment Among the Jalq'a of Bolivia." *Grassroots Development* 16(2): 22–34.
Hegel, Georg Wilhelm Friedrich. [1806] 1910. *The Phenomenology of Mind.* Trans. J.B. Baillie. London: S. Sonnenschein & New York: Macmillan.
Henderson, James. Y. 1994. "Empowering Treaty Federalism." *Saskatchewan Law Review* 58(2): 242.
———. 1995. "Mi'kmaw Tenure in Atlantic Canada." *Dalhouise Law Journal* 18(2): 196.
———. 1997. *The Mi'kmaw Concordat.* Halifax: Fernwood Press.
Henton, D. 1989a. "Fight Continues for Sacred Bundle for Chief Big Bear." *Toronto Star,* 17 April, A11.
———. 1989b. "Outrage: Native Challenge Study of Sacred Bones." *Toronto Star,* 26 August, A14.
Hessel, P. 1993. *The Algonkin Nation: The Algonkins of the Ottawa Valley.* Arnprior, Ont.: Kichesippi Books.
Hill, N.S., Jr., ed. 1994. *Words of Power: Voices from Indian America.* Golden, Colo.: Fulcrum.
Hobbes, Thomas. [1651] 1968. *Leviathan; or the Matter, Form, and Power of a Commonwealth, Ecclesiastical and Civil,* ed. C.B. McPherson. Baltimore: Penguin.
Hobsbawn, Eric. 1996. *The Age of Extremes.* New York: Vintage Books.
Hogan, Linda. 1995. *Dwellings: A Spiritual History of the Living World*. New York: W.W. Norton.
———. 1998. *Power*. New York: W.W. Norton.
Hogg, Peter W. 1992. *Constitutional Law of Canada.* 3rd ed. Toronto: Carswell.
hooks, bell. 1988. *Talking Back: Thinking Feminist, Thinking Black.* Toronto: Between the Lines.
______. 1997. *Cultural Criticism and Transformation Video*. London: University of West Minister.
House of Commons. 1990. Standing Committee on Aboriginal Affairs.

Hughes, J.D. 1983. *American Indian Ecology.* El Paso, Tex.: Western Press, University of Texas.

Hultkrantz, Åke. 1981. "The Problem of Christian Influence on Northern Algonkian Eschatology." In *Belief and Worship in Native North America*. Syracuse: Syracuse University Press.

Hume, M. 1989. "These Graves Were Robbed under Guise of Science." *Vancouver Sun*, 22 September, B5.

Hurlbut, David. 1994. " Fixing the Biodiversity Convention: Toward a Special Protocol for Related Intellectual Property." *Natural Resource Journal* 34: 379–409.

Hutchinson, A.C. 1984. "From Cultural Construction to Historical Deconstruction." *Yale Law Journal* 94: 209.

Hyde, Lewis. 1979–1983. *The Gift: Imagination and the Erotic Life of Property*. New York: Vintage.

ICOM. 1971. *Code of Ethics*.

IDRC. 1995. *Annual Report 1998/99*. Ottawa: IDRC.

Indigenous Development International. 1997. "Intellectual Property Rights, the Law, and Indigenous Peoples' Art."

Inglis, Stephanie. In process. "Degrees of Commitment to Truth: A Study of Modality in Mi'kmaq." Unpublished Ph.D. thesis, Memorial University of Newfoundland, St. John's.

Inuit Circumpolar Conference. 1991. Principles and Elements for a Comprehensive Arctic Policy, Alaska, Greenland, Canada; Council for International Organizations of Medical Sciences. International Guidelines for Ethical Review of Epidemiological Studies. Geneva: WHO.

Jaine, Linda, ed. 1993. *Residential Schools: The Stolen Years*. Saskatoon, Sask.: University of Saskatchewan Extension Press.

Janke, Terri. 1998. *Our Culture, Our Future: Report on Australian Indigenous Cultural and Intellectual Property Rights*. Sydney, Australia: Australian Institute of Aboriginal and Torres Strait Islander Studies. Also at http://www.icip.lawnet.com.au.

John Paul II. 1998. *To Build Peace, Respect Minorities: World Day of Peace Statement*, December 8. In *Origins* 18: 466.

Johnson, M. 1992. "Belcher Islands Reindeer Mangement Project." In *Lore: Capturing Traditional Environmental Knowledge*. Ottawa: Dene Cultural Institute/IDRC.

Johnston, Basil H. 1988. *Indian School Days*. Toronto: Key Porter.

Kagedan, Barbara Laine. 1996. "The Biodiversity Convention, Intellectual Property Rights, and Ownership of Genetic Resources: International Developments." Paper prepared for Intellectual Property Policy Directorate, Industry Canada, January.

Kawagley, A. Oscar. 1993. *A Yupiaq World View. A Pathway to Ecology and Spirit.* Prospect Heights, Ill.: Waveland Press.

King, Steven R. 1992. "Pharmaceutical Discovery. Ethnobotany, Tropical Forest and Reciprocity: Integrating Knowledge, Conservation, and Sustainable Development." In *Sustaining Harvest and Marketing of Rain Forest Products,* ed. M.J. Plotkin & L. Famolare. Washington, D.C.: Island Press.

Knockwood, Isabelle. 1992. *Out of the Depths: The Experience of Mi'kmaw Culture at the Indan Residential School at Shubenacadie, Nova Scotia*. Lockeport, N.S.: Roseway.

Larson, F.H. 1965. *Introduction to the Law of Property*. Oxford: Clarendon Press.
Lawrence, John Shelton. 1989. "Donald Duck v. Chilean Socialism: A Fair Use Exchange." P. 51 in *Fair Use and Free Inquiry: Copyright Law and the New Media,* John Shelton Lawrence & Bernard Timberg. 2d ed. New Jersey: Ablex.
Lean, G., & Don Hinrichsen. 1994. *WWF as the Environment.* Santa Barbara, Calif.: ABC-Clio.
Lennox C., & I. Wildeboer. 1998. *Action Guide. A Human Rights Resource Manual for Secondary Schoools*. Ottawa: United Nations Association in Canada.
Levinas, Emmanuel. 1969. *Totality and Infinity: An Essay on Exteriority.* Trans. Alphonso Lingis. Pittsburgh, Penn.: Duquesne University Press.
Levy-Bruhl, L. 1966. *How Natives Think.* Trans. Lilian A. Clare. New York: Washington Square Press.
Linden, E. 1991. "Lost Tribes, Lost Knowledge." *Time,* 23 September, 46–56.
Lipka, Jerry. 1990. "Integrating Cultural Form and Content in One Yup'ik Eskimo Classroom: A Case Study." *Canadian Journal of Native Education* 17(2): 18–32.
Little Bear, L. 1994. "What's Einstein Got to Do With It?" Pp. 69–76 in *Continuing Poundmaker & Riel's Quest: Presentations Made at a Conference on Aboriginal Peoples and Justice,* ed. R. Gosse, J.Y. Henderson, & R. Carter. Saskatoon, Sask.: Purich.
______. "Jagged Worldviews Colliding." Pp. 77–85 in *Reclaiming Indigenous Voice and Vision,* ed. Marie Battiste. Vancouver: University of British Columbia Press.
Lobo, Susan. 1991. "The Fabric of Life: Repatriating the Sacred Coroma Textiles." *Cultural Survival Quarterly* (Summer): 40–46.
Lyotard, J.F. 1987. *Anaylses et Réfléctions sur Montesquieu, De l'Esprit des Lois, La Nature et La Loi.* Paris: Edition Marketing.
Macklem, Patrick. 1997. "Aboriginal Rights and State Obligations." *Alberta Law Review* 36: 97.
MacNutt, F.A. 1909. *Bartholomew De Las Casas: His Life, His Apostolate, and his Writings*. New York and London: G.P. Putnam's Sons.
Maddock, Kenneth. 1988. "Copyright and Traditional Designs—An Aboriginal Dilemma." *Aboriginal Law Bulletin* 2 34(10): 8–9.
Maffi, Luisa. 1966. Unpublished position paper for the interdisciplinary working conference "Endangered Languages, Endangered Knowledge, and Endangered Environments."
Maracle, Lee. 1989. "Native Myths: Trickster Alive and Crowing." *Fuse Magazine* (Fall): 13–29.
Marcus, George, & M. Fisher. 1986. *Anthropology as Cultural Critique: An Experimental Moment in Human Sciences.* Chicago: University of Chicago Press.
Marusky, Randy. 1990. "The Patentability of New Plant Life Form in Canada." *Canadian Business Law Journal* 16: 333–40.
Maryuama, Magorah, & Arthur M. Harkins. 1978. *Cultures of the Future.* The Hague, Netherlands: Mouton.
Maybury-Lewis, David. 1992. *Millennium: Tribal Wisdom and the Modern World.* London: Viking Penguin.
McKeough, J., & Andrew Stewart. 1991. *Intellectual Property in Australia.* Sydney, Australia: Butterworths.
McRoberts, K., & P. Monahan. 1993. *The Charlottetown Accord, The Referendum*

and The Future of Canada. Toronto: University of Toronto Press.

Medical Research Council of Canada. 1987. *Guidelines on Research Involving Human Subjects*. Ottawa: Medical Research Council of Canada.

Memmi, Albert. 1963. *The Colonizer and the Colonized.* Boston: Beacon Press.

______. 1969. *Dominated Man: Notes Toward a Portrait.* Boston: Beacon Press.

Merleau-Ponty, Maurice. 1962. *Phenomenology of Perception.* Trans. Colin Smith. London: Routledge and Kegan Paul.

Milloy, John, S. 1999. *A National Crime: The Canadian Government and the Residential School System, 1879-1986*. Winnipeg: University of Manitoba Press.

Minnick, E. 1990. *Transforming Knowledge*. Philadelphia, Penn.: Temple University Press.

Momaday, N. Scott. 1993. : "The Legacy of First Nations, The Prophesies of Turtle Island." Speech at Cry of the Earth, 22 November, United Nations, New York.

Morre, Henrietta. 1988. *Feminism and Anthropology.* Cambridge: Cambridge University Press.

Nascimento, Milton. 1979. *Txai*. Album. Sony Brazil.

NCI. 1992. *The Letter of Intent and Material Transfer Agreement.*

Neich, R., & B. Nicholson. 1995. In *Gauguin and Maori Art,* Bronwen Nicholson et al. Birkenhead, Auckland, N.Z.: Godwit.

Neumann, F.L. 1957. "Types of Natural Law." Pp. 69–91 in *The Democratic and the Authoritarian State: Essays in Political and Legal Theory,* ed. H. Marcuse. Glencoe: Free Press.

Nicholson, Bronwen, et al. 1995. *Gauguin and Maori Art.* Birkenhead, Auckland, N.Z.: Godwit.

NIH. 1992. National Science Foundation and U.S. Agency for International Development. "International Cooperative Biodiversity Groups," RFA No. TW-92-01 (12 June 1992).

Noël. Lise. 1994. *Intolerance, A General Survey.* Trans. A. Bennet. Montreal & Kingston: McGill-Queen's University Press.

OAS. 1997. Proposed American Declaration on the Rights of Indigenous Peoples, Inter-American Commission on Human Rights, (OAS) Doc. OEA/Ser/L/VI.II.95 Doc. 6.

O'Meara, Sylvia, & Douglas A. West, ed. 1996. *From Our Eyes: Learning From Indigenous Peoples.* Toronto: Garamond.

Otto, R. 1957. *The Ideal of Holy: An Inquiry into the Non-Rational Factor in the Idea of Divine and Its Relation to the Rational.* 2d ed., trans. J.W. Harvey. London: Oxford University Press.

Pask, A. 1993. "Cultural Appropriation and the Law: An Analysis of the Legal Regimes Concerning Culture." *Intellectual Property Journal* 8: 57–86.

Peat, David. 1994. *Lighting the Seventh Fire: The Spiritual Ways, Healing and Science of the Native American.* New York: Carol.

Peccei, Aurelio. 1979. *The Human Quality*. Oxford, N.Y.: Pergamon.

Phillips, J. 1994. *Butterworths Intellectual Property Law Handbook.* London: Butterworths.

Phillips, Susan. 1972. "Participant Structures and Communicative Competence: Warm Springs Children in Community and Classroom." In *Functions of Language in the Classroom,* ed. C.B. Cazden, V.P. John, & D. Hymes. New York: Teachers College Press.

Poovery, Mary. 1988. *Uneven Developments: The Ideological Work of Gender in Mid-Victorian England.* Chicago: University of Chicago Press.

———. 1995. *Making a Social Body: British Cultural Formation, 1830–1864.* Chicago: University of Chicago Press.

Posey, Darrel A., & Graham Dutfield. 1996. *Beyond Intellectual Property: Toward Traditional Resource Rights for Indigenous Peoples and Local Communities.* Ottawa: IDRC.

Powers, W.K. 1987. "The Plains." In *Native American Religions: North America,* ed. I.E. Sullivan. New York: Macmillan.

Puri, Kamal. 1995. "Cultural Ownership and Intellectual Property Rights Post-Mabo: Putting Ideas into Action." *Intellectual Property Journal* 91(12): 293–347.

RAFI. 1990. *Lifelore: Toward a Third World Trade Union for Biological Intellectual Property.* July. Manitoba, Canada.

Rahner, K. 1979. "Towards a Fundamental Interpretation of Vatican II." *Theological Studies* 40: 717.

RCAP. 1994a. *Ethical Guidelines for Research.* Ottawa.

———. 1994b. *Toward Reconciliation: Overview of Fourth Round.* Ottawa: Canada Communication Group.

———. 1996b. *Bridging the Cultural Divide. A Report on Aboriginal Peoples and Criminal Justice In Canada.* Ottawa: Canada Communication Group.

———. 1996b. *Report of the Royal Commission of Aboriginal Peoples,* 5 vols. Ottawa: Canada Communication Group.

Reddy, M.A., ed. 1993. *Statistical Record of Native North Americans.* Detroit, Mich.: Gale Research.

Roberts M., & P.R. Wills. 1998. "Understanding Maori Epistemology." Pp. 43–47 in *Tribal Epistemologies,* ed. H. Wantischer. Brookfield: Ashgate.

Robertson, Robert E. 1990. "The Right to Food—Canada's Broken Covenant." Pp. 185–216 in *1989-1990 Canadian Human Rights Year Book.*

Rodriguez, Louis Valencia. 1993. (Special Rapporteur). E/CN.4/1993/15.

Rosaldo, Renato. 1989. *Culture and Truth: The Remaking of Social Analysis.* Boston: Beacon Press.

Rose, Carol. 1994. *Property and Persuasion: Essays on the History, Theory and Rhetoric of Ownership.* Bolder, Colo.: Westview.

SAA. 1991. "Proposal for Ethics Consideration Aspects of Intellectual Property Rights." Drafted by Tom Greaves of Bucknell University.

Sackler, Elizabeth, Martin Sullivan, & Richard Hill. 1992. "Three Voices for Repatriation." *Museum News* (September/October 1992), 58–61.

Said, Edward. 1992. *Culture and Imperialism.* Cambridge, Mass.: Harvard University Press.

Saskatchewan Indigenous Languages Committee. 1991. *Socio-linguistic Survey of Indigenous Languages in Saskatchewan: On the Critical List.* Saskatoon, Sask.: Saskatchewan Indigenous Languages Committee.

SEB. 1991. "Professional Ethics in Economic Botany: A Preliminary Draft of Guidelines." Drafted by Christine Padoch and Brian Boom of The New York Botanical Garden.

Seeger, Anthony. 1991. "Singing Other Peoples' Songs." *Cultural Survival Quarterly* (Summer 1991): 36–39.

Shaman Pharmaceuticals. 1992. Supply and Royalty Commitments to Countries and/ or Institutes Supplying Raw Plant Material to Shaman Pharmaceuticals.

SIIT. 1992. *Literature Review: Aboriginal Mother Tongue Issues*. Saskatoon, Sask.: Multiculturalism and Citizenship Canada.

Smith, Gavin. 1989. *Livelihood and Resistance: A Study of Peasants and the Politics of Land In Peru.* Berkeley: University of California Press.

Smith, Graham. 1997. "The Development of Kaupapa Maori Theory and Praxis." A Ph.D. dissertation. University of Auckland, New Zealand.

———. 2000. "Protecting and Respecting Indigenous Knowledge." Pp. 209–24 in *Reclaiming Indigenous Voice and Vision*, ed. Marie Battiste. Vancouver: University of British Columbia Press.

Smith, Linda Tuhiwai. 1999. *Decolonizing Methodologies: Research and Indigenous Peoples*. London: Zed Books.

Smith, N.V. 1984. *Uneven Development: Nature, Capital, and the Production of Space.* New York: Blackwell.

Snow, Chief John. 1977. *The Mountains Are Our Sacred Places.* Toronto: Samuel Stevens.

Spender, Dale. 1980. *Man Made Languages*. London: Routledge and Kegan Paul.

SSHRC. 1977. *Ethics: Guidelines for Research with Human Subjects.* Ottawa.

———. 1998. Policy Statement of Ethical Conduct in Research on Human Subjects. Ottawa.

Standing Committee on Aboriginal Affairs. 1990. *Aboriginal Literacy and Empowerment: You Took My Talk.* Fourth Report. Ottawa: Queens Printer.

Stogre, Michael. 1992. *That the World May Believe.* Sherbrooke, P.Q.: Editions Paulines.

Strickland, R., & K. Supernaw 1993. "Back to the Future: A Proposed Model Tribal Act to Protect Native Cultural Rights." *American Indian Law Review* 46: 161–201.

Suzuki, David. 1997. *The Sacred Balance: Rediscovering Our Place in Nature.* Vancouver: Greystone Books, Douglas & McIntyre.

Tarnopolsky, W., & W.F. Pentney. 1982. *Discrimination and the Law.* Toronto: Carswell, looseleaf.

Tri-Council Policy Statement. 1998. *Ethical Conduct for Research Involving Humans.* Ottawa.

Turpel, Mary Ellen. 1989–1990. "Aboriginal Peoples and the Canadian Charter: Interpretive Monopolies, Cultural Differences." Pp. 3–45 in *Canadian Human Rights Yearbook.*

Ulin, Robert. 1991. "Critical Anthropology Twenty Years Later: Modernism and Postmodernism." *Anthropology: Critique of Anthropology* 11(1): 81–132.

UN. 1989. Report of the United Nations Seminar on the Effects of Racism and Racial Discrimination on the Social and Economic Relations between Indigenous Peoples and States. UN Commission on Human Rights, 45th Sess., UN Doc. E/CN.4/ 1989/22.

———. 1992. Draft Document on the Rights of Indigenous Peoples. Report of the Working Group on Indigenous Populations on Its Tenth Session. UN Commission on Human Rights, E/CN4/ Sub.21/1992/93, Annex I: 44–52.

———. 1992. Record of the United Nations Conference on Environment and Development. Rio de Janeiro, 3–4 June, vol. I, res. 1, annex II. UN Publication, Sales No. E.93.I.8.

———. 1992. Report of the United Nations Technical Conference on Practical Experience in the Realization of Sustainable and Environmentally Sound Self-Development of Indigenous Peoples. E/CN.4/Sub. 2/1992/31.

———. 1993. Report of a Consultation between Representatives of Indigenous Peoples and International Development, Human Rights and Other Agencies. E/CN.4/1993/AC. 4/TM. 3/1.

———. 1993. Report of the United Nations Conference on Environment and Development. S/CONF.151/REV.1 (vol. I).

———. 1994. Draft Declaration on the Rights of Indigenous Peoples before the Working Group of Government. E/CN.4/Sub.2/1994/2/Add. 1.

———. 1994. International Conference on Population and Development. Cairo. A/CONF.171/13, para. 6.27.

———. 1994. Report of the Centre on Transnational Corporations. E/CN.4/Sub. 2/1994/40.

———. 1997. Report of the Technical Meeting on the Protection of the Heritage of Indigenous Peoples.

UNDP. 1994. *Conserving Indigenous Knowledge: Integrating Two Systems of Innovation; An Independent Study by the Rural Advancement Foundation International.* New York: UNDP.

UNESCO. 1945. *Conference for the Establishment of the United Nations Educational, Scientific, and Cultural Organization*, ECO/CONF./29. 16 November.

———. 1970. *Cultural Rights as Human Rights.* Paris: UNESCO.

———. 1989. Recommendation on the Safeguarding of Traditional Culture and Folklore. Adopted by the General Conference at its twenty-fifth session. Paris, 15 November.

———. 1999. *Modern Science and Other Systems of Knowledge.*

UNESCO-WIPO. 1984. Draft Treaty for the Protection of Expressions of Folklore Against Illicit Exploitation or Other Prejudicial Actions. Geneva, Switzerland.

———. 1985. Model Provisions for National Laws on the Protection of Expressions of Folklore Against Illicit Exploitation and Other Prejudicial Actions. Geneva, Swizerland.

———. 1976. Tunis Model Law on Copyright Law for Developing Countries and Protection of Folklore Committee of Experts, Feb/ March, Tunis.

Unger, Roberto Mangabeira. 1976. *Law in Modern Society.* New York: Free Press.

———. 1984. *Passion: An Essay on Personality.* New York: Free Press.

———. 1987. *Social Theory: Its Situation and Its Task: A Critical Introduction to Politics, A Work in Constructive Social Theory.* Cambridge: Cambridge University Press.

UNIDROIT Draft Convention on Stolen or Illegally Exported Cultural Objects. 1990. Unidroit study LXX, Doc. 19.

U.S. National Park Service. 1990. *Keepers of the Treasures: Protecting Historical Properties and Cultural Traditions on Indian Lands.*

USFATF. 1979. *American Indian Religious Freedom Act Report* Washington, D.C.: U.S. Department of Interior.

Valeria, Alia, ed. 1992. Round Table on Aboriginal Peoples and Humanities Scholarship. Charolettetown: University of Prince Edward Island.

Vaver, David. 1987. "Author's Moral Rights-Reform Proposal for Canada: Charter or

Barter of Rights for Creators." *Osgoode Hall Law Journal* 25(winter): 749–86.
———. 1988. "Author's Moral Rights and the Copyright Law Review Committee's Report: W(h)ither Such Rights?" *Monash University Law Review* 14(December): 284–97.
———. 1990. "Intellectual Property Today: Of Myths and Paradoxes." *Canadian Bar Review* 69: 98–128.
———. 1997. *Intellectual Property Law: Copyright, Patents, and Trademarks.* Concord, Ont.: Irwin Law.
Vecsey, Christopher, ed. 1991. *Handbook of American Indian Religious Freedom.*
Vecsey, C., & Robert W. Venables, eds. 1980. *American Indian Environments: Ecological Issues in Americas Indian History.* Syracuse, N.Y.: Syracuse University Press.
Vizenor, Gerald. 1993. "Poem 3." In *Native Peoples* 6(3): 17.
Voegelin, C.F. 1977. *Classification and Index of the World's Languages*. New York: Elsevier.
Von Maltzahn, K.E. 1994. *Nature as Landscape. Dwelling and Understanding.* Montreal & Kingston: McGill-Queen's University Press.
Wax, Murray L., R.H. Wax, & R.V. Dumont, Jr. 1964. "Formal Education in an American Indian Community." *Social Problems* 11(suppl.): 95–96.
WCED. 1987. *Our Common Future.* Oxford: Oxford University Press.
Weatherford, Jack. 1988. *Indian Givers: How the Indians of the Americas Transformed the World.* New York: Fawcett.
Weber, Max. 1966, 1954. *Wirtschaft und Gesellschaft: English Selections.* Edited with introduction and annotations by Max Rheinstein; translation from Max Weber, *Wirtschaft und Geselleschaft,* 2nd ed. (1925) by Edward Shil and Max Rheinstein. Cambridge: Harvard University Press.
Webster, G. Crammer. 1995. In *University of British Columbia Law Review,* special edition, "The Potlach Collection Repatriation," 137.
Wells, Kathryn. 1996. "The Cosmic Irony of Intellectual Property." *Culture and Policy: A Journal of the Australian Key Centre of Cultural and Media Policy* 7(3): 45.
Wenzel, George W. 1991. *Animal Rights, Human Rights: Economy and Ideology in the Canadian Arctic.* London: E. Finter.
WFP. 1988. "Sacred Mohawk Mask to be Displayed at Museum, Judge Rules." 29 January, 12.
Whorf, Benjamin. 1956. *Language, Thought and Reality,* ed. J. Carroll. Cambridge: M.I.T. Press.
Wilbert, W., & G. Haiek. 1991. "Phytochemical Screening of a Warao Pharmacopoeia Employed to Treat Gastrointestinal Disorders." *Journal of Ethnopharmacology* 34(1): 7–11.
WIPO (World Intellectual Property Organization). 1985. *The Elements of Industrial Property.* WIPO Doc. WIPO/IP/AR/85/7.
———. 1997. *Industrial Property and Copyright: Monthly Review of World Intellectual Property Organization*, No. 6 June 1997: 213–14.
Wolf, Eric R. 1969. *Peasant Wars of the Twentieth Century.* New York: Harper.
Wolfson, H. 1968. *Philo.* 2 vols. Cambridge: Harvard University Press.
Wright, Shelley. 1994. "A Feminist Exploration of the Legal Protection of Act." *Ca-*

nadian Journal of Women and the Law 7: 59–96.
WTO. 1995. Committee on Trade and Environment. Working Paper W/8.
Young, Iris. 1990. *Justice and the Politics of Difference.* Princeton: Princeton University Press

•••

Acts, Regulations, and Guidelines

Aboriginal and Torres Strait Islander Heritage (Interim Protection) Act, 1984, No. 79 (Australia).

Act Respecting the Protection of the Archaeological Heritage of Canada. 1988. Proposed act in *Federal Archaeological Heritage Protection and Management: A Discussion Paper.* Ottawa: Department of Communications.

Agenda 21. 1992. UN Conference on Environment and Development, annex 2, c. 26, UN Doc. A/CONF.1511 261, rev. l (vol. 1).

Agreement for the Implementation of the Provisions of the United Nations Convention on the Law of the Sea of 10 December 1982, Relating to the Conservation and Management of Straddling Fish Stocks and Highly Migratory Fish Stocks. 1995. UN Doc. A/CONF. 164/37 8 September.

Agreement on Trade-Related Aspects of Intellectual Property (TRIPs). 1994. Final Act of the Uruguay Round of Multilateral Trade Negotiations. WTO, Geneva.

American Indian Religious Freedom Act, 1981, 42 U.S.C. (supp. V).

Ancient Burial Grounds Act. R.S.P.E.I. 1988, c. A-11 (Prince Edward Island).

Berne Convention for the Protection of Literary and Artistic Works. 1886. (Revised at Paris 1896; completed Berne 1914; last amended 1979.) C.L.T.W. Multilateral Conventions, Item H-1, 1 Basic Documents on International Economic Law [B.D. I.E.L.] 711, WIPO Publication 287(e) [Paris Act].

Budapest Treaty on the International Recognition of the Deposit of Microorganisms for the Purpose of Patent Procedure. 1977. Budapest, 28 April. 17 I.L.M. 285, I.P.L.T. Multilaterial Treaties, Text 2-004, WIPO Publication 277(e).

Canadian Charter of Rights and Freedoms, Schedule B to the *Canada Act* 1982 (U.K.) 1982, c. 11.

Canadian Convervation Strategy. 1991. Ottawa: Minister of Supply and Services Canada.

Cemeteries Act, R.S.O. 1927, c. 317 (Ontario).

Charter of the United Nations. 1945. Can. T.S. 1945 No. 7, 26 June.

Constitution Act 1867 (U.K.), 30 & 31 Vict. c. 3 (formerly the *British North America Act, 1867*).

Constitution Act, 1982, Schedule B to the *Canada Act 1982* (U.K.), c. 11.

Convention Establishing the World Intellectual Property Organization (WIPO). Signed Stockholm, 14 July 1967 and as amended 28 September 1979. WIPO Publication 250(e).

Convention on Biological Diversity. 1992. UNTS No. 30619. U.N.E.P., 5 June.

Convention to Combat Desertification in Those Countries Experiencing Serious Drought and/or Desertification, Particularly in Africa. 1994. UNTS No. 33480 ICCP/COP[3]/20/Add.1.

Convention on International Trade in Endangered Species (CITES). 1995. UNTS No. 14537.
Convention on the Rights of the Child. 1989. UNTS No. 27531. UN Doc. A/RES/44/25.
Convention on the Rights of the Sea. 1998. UNTS No. 31363.
Copyright Act, 1968. Statutes of the Commonwealth of Australia, Act No. 63 of 1968 as amended. Consolidated as in force on 8 October 1999 (includes amendments up to Act No. 105 of 1999).
Copyright Act, R.S.C. 1985, c.C-42, as amended (Canada).
Covenant of the League of Nations. 1919.
Cultural Property Act, S.Q. 1972, c. 119 (Quebec).
Cultural Property Export and Import Act, R.S.C. 1985, c. C-51 (Canada).
Declaration on Environment and Development, 1992. Agenda 21, c. 17, Part III (17.97-17-137), C.R.S.R. 97-588 ENR (U.N.C.E.D.).
Declaration on Principles of International Law Concerning Friendly Relations and Cooperation Among States in Accordance With the Charter of the United Nation. 1970. UN G.A. RES. 2625 (XXV) 25 UN GAOR. Supp. No. 28121 (adopted by consensus).
Declaration on the Rights of Indigenous Peoples as Agreed Upon by the Members of the Working Group on Indigenous Peoples and the Human Rights Experts. 1993. E/CN.4/Sub. 21/1993.
Dene/Métis Comprehensive Land Claim Agreement in Principle. 1988. Ottawa: Department of Indian and Northern Affairs.
Environmental Assessment Act, R.S.O. 1990, c. E.18 (Ontario).
European Patent Convention (EPC). 1973. As amended by the act revising Article 63 EPC of 17 December 1991 and by the decisions of the Administrative Council of the European Patent Organisation of 21 December 1978, 13 December 1994, 20 October 1995, 5 December 1996, and 10 December 1998.
Final Act Embodying the Results of the Uruguay Round of Multilateral Trade Negotiations. 1994. WTO, Geneva.
First Peoples' Heritage, Language and Culture Act, R.S.B.C. 1996, c. 147 (British Columbia).
Foreign Cultural Property Immunity Act, R.S.A. 1980, c. F-12.5 (Alberta).
Geneva Treaty on the International Recording of Scientific Discoveries. 1978. Geneva I.P.L.T. Multilateral Treaties, Text 1-003.
Heritage Conservation Act, R.S.B.C. 1979, c. 165 (British Columbia).
Heritage Property Act, S.S. 1979–80, c. H-2.2 (Saskatchewan).
Historic Sites and Monuments Act, R.S.C. 1985, c. H-4 (Canada).
Historical Resources Act, R.S.A. 1980, c. H-8 (Alberta).
Indian Act, R.S.C. 1985, c. I-5 (Canada).
Indian Arts and Crafts Act, 1990, 25 U.S.C. 305 (U.S.A.).
Industrial Design Act, R.S.C 1985, c.I-9 as amended (Canada).
International Convenant on Civil and Political Rights. 1967. UNTS No. 14668; G.A. Res. 2200, 21 UN GAOR Supp. No. 16, UN Doc. A/6316 at 52.
International Covenant on Economic, Social and Cultural Rights. 1967. UNTS No. 14531; G.A. Res. 2200, 21 UN GAOR Supp. No. 16, UN Doc. A/6316 at 49.
International Convention for the Protection of New Varieties of Plants (UPOV). 1961.

Paris, 2 December, 815 UNTS 89 (original text). Geneva I.P.L.T. Multilateral Treaties, Text 1-004 [UPOV Convention].

International Convention for the Protection of Performers, Producers of Phonograms, and Broadcasting Organizations. 1961. Rome, 26 October, 496 UNTS No. 43, WIPO Publication 328 (E) [Rome Convention].

International Convention on the Elimination of All Forms of Racial Discrimination. 1965. UNTS No. 9464; G.A. Res. 2106A (XX), 20 UN GAOR Supp. No. 14, UN Doc. A/6014 (1965) 47.

International Labour Organization Convention on Indigenous and Tribal Peoples in Independent Countries. 1989. No. 169, 28 I.L.M. 1382.

Kari-Oca Declaration of the World Conference of Indigenous Peoples on Territory, Environment and Development. 1992. Kari-Oca, Brazil, 15–30 May.

Lisbon Agreement for the Protection of Appellations of Origin and Their International Registration. 1966. As revised at Stockholm, 14 July 1967. UNTS No. 13171, WIPO Publication 264(e).

Literary and Artistic Property Act, 1994, Republic of Tunisia, Law No. 12 replaced by Law. No. 36.

Loi sur le Statut Professionnel des Artistes des Arts Visuels, des Métiers d'Art et de la Littérature et sur leurs Contrats avec les Diffuseurs, L.R.Q. 1998, c. S-32.01 as amended (Quebec).

Loi sur le Statut Professionnel et les Conditions d'Engagement des Artistes de la Scène, du Disque et du Cinema, L.R.Q. 1997, c. S-32 as amended (Quebec).

Mataatua Declaration on Cultural and Intellectual Property Rights of Indigenous Peoples. 1993. First International Conference on the Cultural and Intellectual Property Rights of Indigenous Peoples, 12–18 June, Whakatane, Aotearoa.

Narwhal Protection Regulations, C.R.C., c. 820 (Canada).

National Museum of the American Indian Act, 1991 20 U.S.C. 80q (U.S.A.).

National Museums Act, R.S.C. 1985, c. N-13 [now *Museums Act,* R.S.C. 1985, c. M-13-4] (Canada).

National Parks Act, R.S.C. 1985, c. N-14 (Canada).

Native American Graves Protection and Repatriation Act. 1990. Pub. L. 101-601, 104 Stat. 3048 (codified as amended at 25 U.S.C.S. §§ 3001-30013 [NAGPRA] (U.S.A.).

Native American Language Act, P.L. 101–477, section 102(9)(1990) (U.S.A.).

Native Title Act, 1993 (Cth) (Australia).

Northwest Territories Act, R.S.C. 1985, c. N-27 (Canada).

Nunavut Settlement Agreement in Principle Between Inuit of the Nunavut Settlement Area and Her Majesty in Right of Canada. 1990. Ottawa: Department of Indian Affairs and Northern Development.

Organization of American States (OAS) Convention on the Protection of the Archeological and Artistic Heritage of the American Nations. 1976. OAS, 16 June, 15 I.L.M. 1350 [Convention of San Salvador].

Paris Convention for the Protection of Industrial Property. 1884. Paris, March 20, 1883, 161 C.T.S. 409, Treaty Series (U.S.) T.S. 379.

Patent Act, R.S.C. 1985, c. P-4 as amended (Canada).

Patent Cooperation Treaty (PCT) Regulations, 1995 W.I.P.O.

Patented Medicines Regulations, SOR/93-133 & 134, SOR/94-688, SOR/96-423.
Plant Breeders' Rights Act, S.C. 1990, c. 20 as amended (Canada).
Principles and Guidelines for the Protection of the Heritage of Indigenous Peoples. 1990-1995 E/CN.4/Sub.2/1995/26 and E/CN.4/Sub. 2/1995/31.
Protection of Expressions of Folklore. 1971. WIPO Doc. GIC/UK/CNR/VI/12.
Protection of Inventions in the Field of Biotechnology. WIPO/IP/ND/87/2.
Protection of Moveable Cultural Heritage Act, 1986. Statutes of the Commonwealth of Australia, Act No. 11 of 1986 as amended. Consolidated as in force on 16 August 1999 (includes amendments up to Act No. 101 of 1999).
Royal Proclamation of 1763, R.S.C. 1985, Appendix II, No. 1.
Seeds Act, R.S.C. 1985, c. S-8 (Canada).
Status of the Artist Act, S.C. 1992, c. 33 (Canada).
Statutes of Monopolies, 1623 21 Jac. 1, c. 3.
Territorial Lands Act, R.S.C. 1985, c. T-4 (Canada).
Trade Marks Act, RSC 1985, c. T-13 as amended and Regulations (Canada).
UN Univeral Copyright Convention. 1971. UNTS No. 13444, Paris.
UN Universal Declaration of Human Rights. 1948. G.A. res. 217A (III), UN Doc A/ 810 at 71.
UNESCO Convention on the Means of Prohibiting and Preventing the Illicit Import, Export and Transfer of Ownership of Cultural Property. 1970. Adopted by the General Conference of UNESCO at its sixteenth session, Paris, 14 November, 823 I.N.T.S. 231.
UNESCO Convention on Protection of the World's Cultural and Natural Heritage. 1972. Adopted by the General Conference of UNESCO on 16 November, T.I.A.S. 8226 [Heritage Convention].
UNESCO Declaration of the Principles of International Cultural Co-operation. 1966. UNESCO Doc. 14C/Res.
Yukon Act, R.S.C. 1985, c. Y-2.
Yukon Comprehensive Land Claims Umbrella Final Agreement. 1990. Ottawa: Department of Indian Affairs and Northern Development.

•••

Legal Cases

Attorney-General of New Zealand v. Ortiz, [1982] 1 Q.B. 347, [1982] 3 W.L.R. 571, [1983] 3 W.L.R. 809.
Autocephalous Greek Orthodox Church of Cyprus v. Goldberg, (1990) 917 F.2d 278, 717 F. Supp. 1374.
Badoni v. Higginson, (1980) 638 F. 2d. 172 (10th Cir. U.S.A.).
Bisaillon v. Keable, [1983] 2 S.C.R. 333 (Supreme Court of Canada, hereinafter S.C.C.).
Bulun Bulun v. Nejlam Pty. Ltd., (1989) NTG 3 (Federal Court, Australia).
Calder v. Attorney General of British Columbia, [1973] S.C.R. 313, 7 C.N.L.C. 91 (S.C.C.).
Canadian Pacific Ltd. v. Paul, [1989] 1 C.N.L.R. 47, [1988] 2 S.C.R. 654 (S.C.C.).
Carson v. Here's Johnny Portable Toilets, Inc., (1983) 698 F.2d 831 (6th Cir. U.S.A.).
Charrier v. Bell, 496 So. 2d 601 (La. Ct. App. 1986), cert. denied, 498 So. 2d 753 (La. 1986).

Ciba-Geigy Canada Ltd. v. Apotex Inc., [1992] 3 S.C.R.120 (S.C.C.).
Coco v. A.N. Clark (Engineers) Ltd., [1969] R.P.C.41 (Chancery Division, England).
Delgamuukw v. British Columbia, [1998] 1 C.N.L.R. 14 (S.C.C.), reversing in part (1993) 10 D.L.R. (4th) 470, [1993] 5 C.N.L.R. 1. (Macfarlane J. A.) (Hutcheon J.A.), varying in part [1991] 5 C.N.L.R. 1; [1991] 3 W.W.R. 97.
Diamond v. Chakrabarty, (1980) 477 U.S. 303.
Donaldson v. Beckett, (1774) 2 Bro. P.C. 129.
Erven Warnink Besloten Vennootschap v. J. Townsend & Songs (Hull) Ltd., [1979] 3 W.L.R. 68 (House of Lords, England).
Ex parte Hibberd, 227 U.S. Patents Quarterly (BNA) 443 (PTO Bd. App. & Int. 1985).
Fools Crow v. Gullet, (1982) 541 F. Supp. 785 (D.S.D. U.S.A.).
Foster v. Mountford, (1976) 29 F.L.R. 233.
Francis Day & Hunter v. Bron, (1963) Ch. 587, (1963) 2 All E.R. 16 (Court of Appeal, England).
Hogan v. Koala Dundee Pty. Ltd., (1988) 12 I.P.R. 508 (Federal Court, Australia).
Hogan and Others v. Pacific Dunlop Ltd., (1988) 12 I.P.R. 225 (Federal Court, Australia).
International Corona Resources Ltd. v. LAC Minerals Ltd., [1989] 2 S.C.R. 574 (S.C.C.).
J.B. Williams Co. v. H. Bronnley & Co., (1909) 26 R.P.C.765.
Jack and Charlie v. The Queen, [1986] 1 W.W.R. 21 (S.C.C.).
Krouse v. Chrysler Canada Ltd., (1973) 40 D.L.R.(3d) 15 (Court of Appeal, Ontario).
Ladbroke (Football) Ltd. v. William Hill (Football) Ltd., (1964) 1 W.L.R. 273 (House of Lords, England).
Lovelace v. Canada, 1 United Nations, Human Rights Committee - Selected Decision under the Optional Protocol (1985) at 83.
Lyng v. Northwest Indian Cemetery Protective Association, (1988) 485 U.S. 439 (United States Supreme Court).
Mabo v. Queensland, [1992] 5 C.N.L.R. 1, [1992] 66 A.L.R.J. 408, 175 C.L.R. 1 (High Court, Australia).
MacMillan Bloedel Ltd. v. Mullein, [1984] 61 B.C.L.R. 145.
Mahe et al. v. The Queen in Right of Alberta, [1990] 1 S.C.R. 342 (S.C.C.).
McCrady v. Ontario, Ont. Gen. Div., Kuriski J., Doc. No. 1867, October 1, 1991 (unreported). Doc. No. Thunder Bay 1867-90, October 26, 1992 (unreported); [1993] 61 O.A.C. 286 (Div. Ct.).
Míkmaw People v. Canada, (1992) Report of the Human Rights Committee, UN Doc. A/47/40. UN GAOR, 47th Sess., Supp. No. 40 at 213.
Milpurrurru v. Idofurn Pty. Ltd., (1995) 30 I.P.R. 209.
Mitchell v. Peguis Indian Band, [1990] 3 CNLR 46, [1990] 2 S.C.R. 85 (S.C.C.).
Moore v. Regents of University of California, 215 Cal. App. ed at 715, 249 Cal. Rptr. 494 (Cal. App. 2 Dist. 1988), aff'd in part, rev'd in part, 51 Cal. 3d 120, 793 P. 2d 479, (1990) 271 Cal. Rptr. 146.
Nanoose Indian Band et al. v. The Queen and Intrawest Corporation et al., (1995) 57 B.C.A.C. 117, 94 W.A.C. 117 (Court of Appeal, British Columbia).
Ominiyak (Lubicon Lake Band) v. Canada, 1990 Report of the Human Rights Committee, UN Doc. A/45/40., vol. II, para. 32.1, at 27; UN GAOR 45th Sess., Supp. No. 40.

Onus v. Alcoa of Australia Ltd., (1981) 149 C.L.R. 27.

Oxford Pendaflex Canada Ltd. v. Korr Marketing Ltd., [1982] S.C.R. 494 (S.C.C.).

Parke, Davis & Co. v. Empire Laboratories Ltd., [1964] S.C.R. 351 (S.C.C.).

Pharand Ski Corp. v. Alberta, (1991) 7 C.C.L.T. 225 (Court of Queen's Bench, Alberta).

Pioneer Hi-Bred Ltd. v. Canada (Commissioner of Patents), (1986) 11 C.P.R. (3d) 311, (1987) 14 C.P.R. (3d) 491, (1987) 3 F.C. 8, (1989) 60 D.L.R. (4th) 223, [1989] 1 S.C.R. 1623 (S.C.C).

Preston v. 20th Century Fox Canada Ltd. et al. (1990) 33 C.P.R. (3d) 242 (Federal Court Trial Division, Canada).

R. v. Badger, [1996] 2 C.N.L.R. 77, [1996] 1 S.C.R. 771 (S.C.C.).

R. v. Guerin, [1985] 1 C.N.L.R. 120, [1984] 2 S.C.R. 335 (S.C.C.).

R. v. Secretary of State for Foreign and Commonwealth Affairs exparte Indian Association of Alberta, [1982] 3 C.N.L.R. 195, (1982) 2 W.L.R. 641 (House of Lords, England).

R. v. Simon, [1986] 1 C.N.L.R. 153, [1985] 2 S.C.R. 387 (S.C.C.).

R. v. Sioui, [1990] 3 C.N.L.R. 127, [1990] 1 S.C.R. 1025 (S.C.C.).

R. v. Sparrow, [1990] 3 C.N.L.R. 160, [1990] 1 S.C.R. 1075, 70 D.L.R. (4th) 385 (S.C.C.).

R. v. Syliboy, [1929] 1 D.L.R. 307 (Nova Scotia County Court).

R. v. Van der Peet, [1996] 2 S.C.R. 507, [1996] 4 C.N.L.R. 177 (S.C.C.).

Re Allen, 2 U.S. Patents Quarterly 2d (BNA) 1425 (PTO Bd. app. & Int. 1987).

Re Application of Abitibi Co. (1982) 62 C.P.R.(2d) 81.

Reference re Secession of Quebec, [1998] 2 S.C.R. 217, 161 D.L.R. (4th) 385 (S.C.C.).

Roberts v. Canada, [1989] 1 S.C.R. 322, [1989] 2 C.N.L.R. 146 (S.C.C.).

Saltman Engineering Co. v. Campbell Engineering Co., (1948) 65 P.C. 203 (Court of Appeal, England).

Seager v. Copydex Ltd., [1967] 2 All E.R. 415 (Court of Appeal, England).

Seiko *Time Canada Ltd. v. Consumers Distributing Co. Ltd.* (1980) 29 O.R. (2d) 221; rev'd in part 1 C.P.R.(3d) 1 (S.C.C.).

Sequoyah v. Tennessee Valley Authority, (1980) 620 F. 2d 1159 (6th Cir. U.S.A.).

Snow v. Eaton Centre Ltd., (1982) 70 C.P.R. (2nd) 105 (High Court, Ontario).

Touchwood File Hills Qu'Appelle District Council Inc. v. Davis, [1987] 1 C.N.L.R. 180 (Court of Queen's Bench, Saskatchewan).

Union of Nova Scotia Indians v. Canada, (1997) 4 C.N.L.R. 280 (Federal Court Trial Division, Canada).

University of London Press Ltd. v. University Tutorial Press Ltd., (1916) 2 Ch. 601.

Wilson v. Block, (1983) 709 F. 2d. 735 (D.C. Cir. U.S.A.).

Yumbulul v. Reserve Bank of Australia, (1991) 2 I.P.R. 481.

•••

Index